Babe Ruth
and the Creation
of the Celebrity Athlete

Babe Ruth
and the Creation
of the Celebrity Athlete

THOMAS BARTHEL

McFarland & Company, Inc., Publishers

Jefferson, North Carolina

LIBRARY OF CONGRESS CATALOGUING-IN-PUBLICATION DATA

Names: Barthel, Thomas, 1941– author.
Title: Babe Ruth and the creation of the celebrity athlete / Thomas Barthel.
Description: Jefferson, North Carolina : McFarland & Company, Inc.,
Publishers, 2018 | Includes bibliographical references and index.
Identifiers: LCCN 2018024088 | ISBN 9781476665320 (softcover : acid free paper) ∞
Subjects: LCSH: Ruth, Babe, 1895–1948. | Baseball players—United
States—Biography. | Baseball players—United States—Social
conditions—20th century. | Mass media and sports—United
States—History—20th century. | Endorsements in advertising—United
States—History—20th century.
Classification: LCC GV865.R8 .B37 2018 | DDC 796.357092 [B] —dc23
LC record available at https://lccn.loc.gov/2018024088

BRITISH LIBRARY CATALOGUING DATA ARE AVAILABLE

ISBN (print) 978-1-4766-6532-0
ISBN (ebook) 978-1-4766-2662-8

Front cover: Photograph of Babe Ruth taken outside the White House
in Washington, D.C., December 7, 1921 (Library of Congress)

Printed in the United States of America

*McFarland & Company, Inc., Publishers
Box 611, Jefferson, North Carolina 28640
www.mcfarlandpub.com*

This book has been written,
as almost all of my others have,
to make my son,
Michael Barthel, proud

Table of Contents

Author's Note
and Acknowledgments

This book's research, like my six other books, is the result of my work alone. There were no other researchers. Interviews were neither sought nor conducted. (Any living Yankees player would have been more than 100 years old during my research.)

I especially thank, first, Michael Barthel for his good advice on certain chapters of this book as well as his many offers to contribute even more. Bill Jenkinson generously contributed data about barnstorming games. His kindness will be remembered.

Hamilton College has continued to support my work by granting me status as a Scholar In Residence.

The Kirkland Town Library, Clinton, NY, especially Ruth Cosgrove, has helped me with every one of my books.

Let us not forget Eliot Asinof, F. C. Lane, Marshall Smelser and Marvin Miller, those who saw the truth behind and beneath the nonsense and lies.

As usual, any searching for information and data about baseball must use the good offices of both Baseball-Almanac.com and Baseball-reference.com. The research library at the National Baseball Hall of Fame has continued its welcoming and helpful attitude.

Listed below are those persons and organizations that helped to make my book. Many of them are local historians who may not know how much their quiet work is appreciated. Some did not even tell me their names, just their e-mail addresses. For any I have omitted through error, please forgive my clumsiness.

To these, and more, thank you: Allen County Museum, Lima, OH; Rachel Arnold; Shirley Ayres, executive director, Bradley Beach, NJ, Chamber of Commerce; Charlie Bevis; Bruce Blake, for information on South Dakota; Marc Blau; T. Scott Brandon; Richard Brown, librarian, *Rutland (VT) Herald*; Brown County Historical Society, New Ulm, MN; Patrick Carpentier; Clem Comly; Mark A. Cruciani; Kendel Joy Darragh, University of Michigan Library; Deadwood Chamber of Commerce and the Adams Museum, Deadwood, SD; Riva Dean, for information on Spokane, WA; Dennis Dillon, for information on Reading, PA, in 1928; David Eskenazi; Clare Ellis, Sacramento Room librarian, Sacramento, CA; Evelyn Ellis, Lindenhurst, NY, village historian; Andrea Faling; Cappy Gagnon; Patrick Gallagher; Lauren Miranda Gilbert, for help with San Jose, CA; Gary Goldberg; Steve Gross, Greenwood Lake historian; Bob Harris; Michael Haupert; Howard W. Henry; Eileen Huff, local historian for Drumright, OK; Bill Jenkinson; David A. Jones; Kansas Historical Society; Mark Kober; John Kovach, for South Bend help; Randy Krzmarzick; P. Leighton; R. J. Lesch, for information on Des Moines, IA; Long Beach

Public Library reference staff; Lynn, MA, Historical Society; McClelland Library, Pueblo, CO; Tom McDade; David McDonald; Norm McNeil; David Mook, reference librarian, Sioux City Public Library; John P. Maranto; Minnehaha County Historical Society, Sioux Falls, SD; Jack Morris, for information on East Coventry, PA; Nebraska State Historical Society; D. Earl Newsom, for information on Drumright, OK; Joe Niese; Oklahoma Historical Society; Pops O'Maxfield; Old Village Hall Museum, Lindenhurst, NY; Kevin Paczkowski; Armand Peterson; David Rain; Michael Runge; Shirley Ryan; Santa Barbara Historical Society; Mark Schubin; Bill Secrest, Jr., local history librarian, Fresno County Public Library; Shanaman Sports Museum, Tacoma, WA; John Shiffert; Sioux City Public Library Reference Desk staff; E. H. L. Smith; SSmith2084; Jim Sweetman; Tom Taber; Bob Tholkes; Stew Thornley; Bob Timmermann, for information on Washington Park in 1919; Dennis Vanlanger; Mayor Jesse Woodring, Sunbury, PA; and Bill Young.

Preface

By 2016, more than 100 years after Babe Ruth began his professional career, if we sensibly ignore the biographies in movie form, we are compelled to understand George Herman "Babe" Ruth as a vulgar man with a balancing vitality. The print biographies say that we ought to know him as someone with a natural candor. We should admire how far he could hit a baseball with a bat and how free of most restrictions he made himself. In his time, his narrative was written as that of a person who was a large child and a hero to children. Ruth's funeral was presided over by one Roman Catholic Cardinal, 44 priests and 12 altar boys, a ceremony somehow deemed fitting. These books, graceful or not, mostly awestruck, wished us to understand Ruth as larger than life, and therefore as beyond the ordinary. That narrative has rarely been challenged.

Yet we now live in a time so far away from Ruth's that it has become seemingly impossible to discover information about many of the people who told Ruth's tales in his own time. We cannot look up their biographies or know their feelings about the work they did. One baseball writer who spent every day for a while with Ruth, Sidney Whipple, cannot even be found in the research library dedicated to baseball at the Hall of Fame in Cooperstown, for example.

There is no reason why books about baseball people must repeat the tired language of sports writing. The hyperbole of the diction, the search for explosive verbs, and the fawning on both the game of baseball and its players feel untruthful and incomplete, as if the choice of words was hiding or ignoring something. The heavy and constant use of superlatives props up sport because it has proved to be essentially like any other form of entertainment. This book will try its best to eschew sportswriter jargon. This book will not call George Herman Ruth merely the name "Babe."

This book is not interested in what Ruth ate, nor his fondness for whorehouses. Very few things he is supposed to have said were his own words, since those words often sound far too literary for him. Ruth was an entertainer, a vaudevillian in fact, and like others in that trade, he had his speeches carefully crafted and well-rehearsed and could repeat those remarks over and over in towns all across the country, either on stage or at the hundreds of banquets he attended. Why not? No one was keeping track, no one recorded them, and most of his audiences at lunches just wanted to be able to say they had been in the same room with one of the first American celebrities.

The ubiquity of celebrities was, to a great extent, established by Babe Ruth, and then virtually forgotten for four decades. True, the famous held a spotlight and were given passing notice, but they were understood to be trivial figures until the word "superstar" came into common usage in the 1970s. But "Ruth, with the aid of ghostwriters and an astute agent, learned how to turn himself into an immensely marketable product."[1] This was accomplished even though, as even a book for children acknowledges, "he could be loud, obnoxious and abrasive."[2] This book looks at the transformation, a makeover that gloried in lies, reasoning that "Whether it actually happened or not … it is now part of the great Babe Ruth legend."[3]

One of the curious parts of the great Babe Ruth legend is the extent to which rational people will go. Ruth was given such a place of importance by the media, via his agent, that he was assigned credit for any good, or bad, thing that happened in baseball. Too much home run hitting and not enough of the so-called "small" game? The fault was Ruth's. The sport's fans cynical outlook toward baseball caused by the Black Sox scandal? Washed clean by Babe Ruth. Attendance at major league games that had not kept pace with population growth for many years but increased once Ruth starting hitting baseballs over the fences? Ruth did that, so all say. While it is true that attendance rose when the Yankees came to town and at their home field, attendance at games in the National League did not expand as much as in the American. Attendance at non–Ruth games, for example, in many American League parks did not make not great leaps forward. Yet Ruth is given the credit. *Post Hoc*—after Ruth—*ergo propter hoc*—therefore he caused everything to grow and become beautiful.

For the most part, this book is not concerned with guessing at the source of Ruth's behavior. The book does not choose to accept the memories of kindly old men, nor does it particularly care about stories of gluttony, adultery or physical prowess. Although Ruth lived in the world, he ignored most parts of it that did not affect him personally. But they did affect him nevertheless, because people were busy around him, aiding him—Christy Walsh, sportswriters—and attitudes were in place which boosted him—ideas about masculinity, about celebrity. Technology too raised him up through the spread of radio and the movies, and advances in newspapers. If the world outside of his own pleasures held little interest for him, they entered into his life anyway. Those parts will be examined in interchapters.

Babe Ruth Incorporated would not have been possible without technological advances in radio, in advertising, in printing—the massing of media—in the use of the telephone as well as in the growth and influence of newspapers and the automobile. Impossible as well would be the ability of Ruth to function in his world—now long dead—a world of fraternal societies, of luxurious travel thanks to Pullman cars, and of an optimistic America then congratulating itself on winning The Great War and, for a decade, feeling certain of the wealth that awaited them from Wall Street. And then there was that super metropolis: New York City.

Ruth's biographers, both in books and in movies, have decided either to downplay or ignore the businessman and paid entertainer aspect of Ruth's life. It is clear that the player, the businessman, spent much of his time involved with both commerce and show business. Nevertheless, those two aspects are mostly ignored, and the mark of the disinterest in the money aspect of Ruth's career is the almost complete silence about his business partner of 14 years—Christy Walsh—in narratives on Ruth's life.

This book, by using more than 600 sources, shows Ruth to be someone intent on making money for himself and for almost everyone he came into contact with, in the largest cities and in towns small and large, for businessmen large and small. This book began in the Library of Congress microfilm room, where small-town and medium-sized newspapers were studied. There is a reason why this book concentrates as much as pos-

Babe (second from left) with fellow barnstormers in Oil City, Pennsylvania, October 1923.

sible on primary sources. So many times over the years, stories have been told either with attribution, with false attribution, or, in the cases of many of Ruth's hedonistic stories, with claims to have been directly witnessed by many different teammates in many different years, or even no year at all.

Additional recent scholarship, partly through the celebrations connected with Ruth's birth centennial, have included a special issue of *The Sporting News* as well as a conference at Hofstra University. These and much more have revealed the enormous sweep and extent of Ruth's commercial influence and how much of a pioneer he was in the marketing of sports celebrities. Then too, ledgers of the New York Yankees from the Ruth years had been donated to the Baseball Hall of Fame and were analyzed by scholars.

Virtually ignored were the many years Ruth went out on the road after the season. No matter how much money he made and adulation he received, for almost 75 percent of his professional life, Ruth headed for villages and small cities from coast to coast. Ruth made tens of thousands of dollars by barnstorming, by going directly to the public literally from Portland, Maine, to San Diego, and barnstorming even in Drumright, Oklahoma, in Oil City, Pennsylvania, and in Sleepy Eye, Minnesota. It made no difference to Ruth, as in Tarkio, Missouri, if the town's population was listed at 1,500. If the local businessmen offered him enough money, if people would turn out to see him play, he would step off the train in their towns.

Lost among the Babe Ruth books, lost among the myths, legends and falsehoods, the plain, though ignored, fact remains that Ruth was a wage earner, an employee. He worked for a smaller corporation, a team, and a larger corporation, Organized Baseball, a phrase now capitalized. And from his first year as a professional, he became known as an eager consumer of whatever his appetites lusted after. Therefore, money had to come to him to pay for his pleasures, and this book concentrates not only on how he made money for himself but also on how he made money for so many others.

So this book sees Ruth as a capitalist, as a baseball player who knew he was an entertainer and a businessman. He found ways to attract money to himself and to accept cash from the many businesses who eagerly employed him in order to generate profits for themselves and paydays for him. After all, of all the plaques in the gallery at the Baseball Hall of Fame, those plaques that establish the main achievements (numbers mostly), the writer of the plaque for George Herman "Babe" Ruth decided to list as his primary achievement "Greatest Drawing Card in History of Baseball."

(Note: Unless otherwise indicated, the source for barnstorming games is always the local newspaper.)

Introduction

In no field of American endeavor is invention more rampant than in baseball, whose whole history is a lie from beginning to end, from its creation myth to its rosy models of commerce, community, and fair play. The game's epic feats and revered figures, its pieties about racial harmony and bleacher democracy, its artful blurring of sport and business—all of it is bunk, tossed up with a wink and a nudge.[1]

With rare exception, books on Ruth's life have treated the player with reverences of many varieties: his strength, his sexual potency, his stamina, his willingness to spend time with children, his likeability. Most books have articulated their admiration of Ruth by dwelling on his rise from poverty, and identifying him as the man who saved the game of baseball.

He was also a man about whom tall tales might be told over and over without any true source being credited, yet still accepted as absolute truth. Out of the many, here are two:

1. After Ruth left a St. Louis whorehouse, he would always stop off next door at a bakery at about five in the morning and gulp down a dozen freshly baked donuts.[2]

2. "While in St. Louis he rented an entire brothel for a night and, one by one, partook of every lady there. The morning after this vigorous workout, he ate an 18 egg omelet."[3]

How do such stories grow? Joe Dugan, a teammate, is quoted this way: "He ate a hat once. He did. A straw hat. Took a bite out of it and ate it."[4] A writer wishing to emphasize Ruth's zaniness and appetite might select for his piece—"he ate a hat"—and so Ruth ate the hat and not a piece of the hat. So the warped story became just one more colorful tale.

This hat story came from a man at age 76. Many studies such as the one cited report that "as they age, adults experience less negative emotion … and become less likely to remember negative than positive emotional materials."[5]

In an unscientific way, many of us were taught simply not to speak ill of the dead. But more to the point, first, how reliable is Dugan's eyewitness testimony? In a much more demanding way to test the validity of the Dugan stories, the finest worker in the field of eyewitness testimony and memory, Elizabeth Loftus, "has spent most of her life steadily amassing a clear and brilliant body of work showing that memory is amazingly fragile and inventive. Her studies on more than 20,000 subjects are classics demonstrating that eyewitness testimony is often unreliable, that false memories can be triggered in up to 25 percent of individuals. As Loftus explains, "just because someone says something confidently doesn't mean it's true."[6]

Second, still unknown are the questions and their phrasing that were asked of Ruth's teammate. Were the questions posed in such a way so as to elicit a certain kind of answer? If you asked Dugan, "How generous a guy was Ruth?" the questioner presupposed Ruth was generous and did not give Dugan the opportunity to answer whether Ruth was generous or not. Or the questioner knew that writing about good guys, lively and colorful guys, leads to the sale of your work. Ruth, in the popular opinion after years of an adoring press, was a fine fellow.

The first five biographies of Ruth were all published within a year of 1974, once publishers became alert in late 1973 to the fact that Henry Aaron was about the break Ruth's record for career home runs. Robert Creamer's *New York Times* obituary admitted that "Mr. Creamer began the book in 1969 and rushed to finish it." The market could not wait.

His biographers—print, film, web—tell many colorful stories without attribution, and their favorite tales always concern Ruth's appetites: hunger for food, for drink, for sex. The reality that Ruth had most of the attributes of a glutton are supposedly excused by the tales that his gluttony rarely hurt his performance on the baseball field. In the golden hues of fond memory, and good copy, no matter what he did to his body, he didn't simply perform, he excelled. In these stories, the more he drank and ate and fornicated the night and morning before, the longer the home run he hit the next day. If he momentarily faltered, his resurrection to supremacy simply took a few weeks. These stories seem to be the ultimate in the male dream.

This is a book about Ruth and money. In our time, not his, corporate baseball has learned to adopt many advertising strategies, not the least of which is nostalgia. One of the virtues of nostalgia is that it alters memory into sentiment and changes sentiment into dollars. So while it is true that in the middle of Ruth's professional career, one sportswriter, F. C. Lane, wrote that a "haze of inaccurate, almost meaningless bunk endowed Ruth with virtues utterly alien to his nature ... exaggerated beyond all the bounds of sanity," the bunk too could be changed into cash.[7] And still may. For example, from 2012 to 2014, auctions of Ruth's clothing, bats and other items brought in $10,255,320.

In his own time, there appears to be no doubt that Ruth rarely showed his public an unfriendly side. Except in matters of money, his approach to being displeased was to distance himself from whatever—or whoever—unsatisfied him. It is now impossible to know the reasons why he chose not to deal with problems. Genial and eager to please and entertain, he is almost always portrayed as likeable. And, of course, he came across as not contentious, because only infrequently was he denied. Many times he got what—or who—he wanted by buying it.

Of all the words used to describe Babe Ruth since he played his first professional game over 100 years ago in 1914, the word "shrewd" never has been written. Once he was traded to the Yankees, the reader sees Ruth demanding a part of his sale price from his former employer, and within a year hiring a very clever man—Christy Walsh—with whom he partnered through many years and many deals. Through Walsh, Ruth's name and face not only made money for him and for Walsh, but in fact made money for, and created jobs in, firms who signed Ruth to endorsement deals.

Ruth's salary dazzled many people and seemed to anger very few. He became a national product almost before any other in America. Before Coca-Cola, before Juicy Fruit gum, the name and the photograph of Ruth was not only set before the American consumer, Ruth himself went from Maine to California, to small towns as well as small cities and major metropolises. There he showed himself in barnstorming games and on the vaudeville stage. He was, in fact, selling his name, his brand, to the American buyer. This book carefully follows how Ruth became the product that he is to this day.

That Ruth pursued his pleasures is indisputable. Many have concluded that this austere childhood led him on that pursuit. Whether or not that is true or just one reason, it seems clear that his mostly harmless fleshy pleasures caused him no guilt or shame, but then he seemed not to have spent much time on self-examination. That he needed to pay for his pleasures is undeniable. Ruth would not be denied his own pleasures, and he sought out fun in hundreds of places. Revealed now for the first time is how that money was made and displayed, as well as the extremes Ruth was willing to go through to put that money into his pockets. An excessive man, a careless man during more than half of his career, he made a success in the field out of his baseball talent and his own honed skills. But he was famous as much off the field as on, and he was able to generate secondary success measured, as Americans often prefer, in money.

Success is often dependent on timing. The timing of Ruth's career could not have been better for his bankroll. Four things in particular, as this book repeatedly examines, saw to it that Ruth succeeded: the growth of the American media, New York City becoming the greatest metropolis in the country, the emergence of national products (like Coca-Cola), and the expansion of the importance of sports news to American newspapers. This book sees Babe Ruth as both conspicuous consumer and moneymaker. Alive today, he might be called a job creator, making money for others. His presence in person, in print or on the radio created products and sold products. He was Babe Ruth, Incorporated.

No matter how large the salary, it was not enough money or praise for Ruth. His appetite for food, drink and sex has become known from many biographies of him written over a span of three decades. The authors of those books—many of them published in the same year as Henry Aaron broke Ruth's record—and the writers of articles since his death seem to be admirers of baseball, admirers of Ruth's masculine qualities of power and bluntness. Many of those books have concentrated on depicting what has been admired in the most positive light possible, while mentioning but not judging his negative qualities. Apparently written in a rush, they remain books mostly intended to entertain. (While it is also true that a more modern researcher had many more ways to investigate the validity of the Ruth stories, both the Seymours and Professor Smelser produced earlier works of fine scholarship.)

The hundreds of works cited in this book are heavily weighted in three ways. First, the pieces of writing at the time, rather than the memories of kindly old men, are used in this book to get a sense of what really happened, and to examine what can be seen as the truth after so many lies through exaggeration have been written.

Second, those writers not beholden to Ruth or his agent Christy Walsh, many of them local historians removed from Ruth's career by many decades, tend to be more interested in the narrative rather than Ruth himself.

Third, the ideas of those writers who see baseball as sport, entertainment and business combined, three aspects joined, rather than separate, have been included in this book.

Therefore, this book has three pieces working together to show how and why Ruth became both product and factory. He was a product because his image was created and promoted the same as any other piece of merchandise. He was a factory because for many businesses, his image turned into a kind of raw material from which corporations might manufacture merchandise to be sold for a profit. During the season, his performance on the field drew admirers to him, admirers who wanted what he had ... or at least would pay for something that might connect the admirer to Ruth. His salary from the Red Sox and the Yankees made him famous. His bad boy image, tame though it was, added to his appeal. Babe Ruth didn't just change the way the game of baseball was played. He changed the way it did business. This is the first piece.

Next, his appetite for fame, for applause and for the money that comes with those less tangible delights have remained less well known. The second piece in this book is the barnstorming tours, tours which kept Ruth sated with praise and cash. Every year from 1914 to 1931, he played in post-season games to make even more money, and to have some fun in sightseeing, often playing 20 games in 20 places. As he played, he would be paid even more in each town to visit a local business and be photographed in it, including visiting shops where products bearing his name or image were sold. When Ruth came to town, it was not uncommon for schools, factories, and even coal mines to shut down for the game. The story of his barnstorming in towns as small as Sleepy Eye, Minnesota, or as large as Los Angeles has never before been told.

The third piece of this book shows how many aspects came together just as Ruth reached true fame as a hitter. It is no coincidence that his cash flow increased when he came to the center of wealth in America, New York City. The book explores the interaction between Ruth and advertising and the growth of newspapers, radio and magazines. The book explains how many different factors of the society he lived in, even though he mostly ignored it or even scorned it, helped him to become even richer and more influential in the world of commerce. The book probes how Christy Walsh, through his New York syndicate, collaborated with Ruth to mold his image and add to his heroic stature. Sportswriters, for example, cooperated with Walsh to portray Ruth as an American ideal: strong, noble, loving. The sportswriters earned extra money from Christy Walsh not only to ghostwrite for Ruth during the baseball season but to be given jobs in the off-season writing for the syndicate. The book also shows the relationship between owners of teams, that is employers, related to the players, or employees. It looks at Ruth's interaction with children and with Johnny Sylvester in particular. It sees how the maturing of train travel helped Ruth to earn money and sees his influence on sports collecting.

The book ends with a look at Ruth's lasting, though recent, ability, 100 years after he played his first game, to make money for his family, for companies, and lately for auction houses. In 2012, a jersey he wore in 1920 was auctioned for $4,415,658. Almost 100 years to the day when he first took on the job of professional baseball player, on February 8, 2014, newspapers ran a story that read "a baseball of legendary proportions, signed by Babe Ruth with a promise to a sick child [Johnny Sylvester], was recently auctioned for more than $200,000." In the last 16 years, Ruth material in auction has sold for more than $15,000,000 in the higher priced items alone.

At his funeral mass in the religious faith that Ruth barely paid any attention to, a Cardinal said he felt sure that the memory of this baseball player would "continue to inspire the young to live chaste, sober and heroic lives" and asked God to treat Ruth not merely with forgiveness but with "especial love."

Even at the end, something extraordinary for this baseball player—a Roman Catholic Cardinal pleading with his god for extraordinary love to be bestowed on a celebrity equally well-known for his relentless pursuit of his own pleasures and the American dollar.

1

Reformatory Farewell
(1914)

In 1912, an article appeared called "The Business of Baseball" in which the sport's financial aspects were made specific: "Fifty million people pay $15,000,000 a year to see baseball games. One hundred and seventy-nine thousand people paid $350,000 to see one series of baseball games. Baseball magnates pay salaries of $10,000, $12,000, $15,000, and $18,000 to their managers and players."[1]

In the same year, at the dreary facility at 3225 Wilkens Avenue in Baltimore called the St. Mary's Industrial School, salaries were also being paid. Some of the boys were being trained as tailors and shirt makers. One boy, George Ruth, Jr., labeled for years as incorrigible, had reached age 17. A decade earlier, on June 13, 1902, George Herman Ruth, Sr., had taken his seven-year-old to St. Mary's. The boy had "spent most the first seven years of [his] life living over [his] father's saloon at 426 West Camden Street, Baltimore."[2] Sometimes he would be released to his father's bar when help was needed there. He would be an unpaid employee, someone who contributed to the family upkeep. Otherwise he could take to the streets free and unfettered to swim, to throw fruit at wagon drivers, to steal, or to do what he wished.

A book with Ruth named as the author remembered, "My folks lived in Baltimore and my father worked in the district where I was raised. We were poor. Very poor. And there were times when we never knew where the next meal was coming from."[3]

At the reformatory, he was being prepared to enter the working world. There, for his skilled work attaching collars to shirts, as Smelser reports, Ruth might make some credits at the school's store. He is said to have spent some of those credits on candy, which he gave to some of the smaller children.[4] But after the sewing was completed, one of the activities the boys eagerly sought was the baseball games being contested in the big yard. At St. Mary's, baseball-mad as the rest of the country, at least 40 teams played— the uniforms made at the tailoring shop.

The games, however, were not confined to the school grounds—a team of stars from St. Mary's might take on another institution or local challengers, for example—and Ruth stood out among all the rest in liking the respect he received for his skills, later saying, "the thing to hold my interest and keep me happy … was baseball."[5] When he reached the age of 14, the time when his formal schooling would end, Ruth continued to work as a tailor "partly for the income."[6] But he was still part of the strongest baseball team at St. Mary's and apparently made an impression against the team from Mount St. Joseph's.

Both money and renown came to young Ruth in 1912 and 1913, when he played some games for the semipro Bayonnes.[7]

Jack Dunn, 42, owner and manager of the International League Baltimore Orioles baseball club, visited the reformatory in the winter of 1914 in search of the 19-year-old who had been in the care of the Xaverian Brothers at St. Mary's. Dunn had heard about the six-foot, two-inch youngster and had been watching him in action. The stock of new, qualified baseball players was being contested by a new league and a new local team—the Federal League's Baltimore Terrapins—who had the temerity to play their home games in a park—Terrapin Park—right across the street from Orioles Park. The competition among teams was not simply for attendance. Team owners like Dunn regularly made huge profits by selling players' contracts to other teams. Ruth, a powerful young man, filled out his 6'2" body with 185 pounds of muscle, and so was of larger proportions than most men of his time.

Dunn knew he might have a valuable athlete in his sights with Ruth and offered the young man a contract for $600 a season, a salary about 25 percent of a skilled major leaguer's. During the season, that meant cash of about $30 each week. So he was making what was considered, in American industry, as the extraordinary $5 a day salary that Henry Ford introduced in 1914. After all, "Between one-fourth and one-third of the male workers 18 years of age and over, in factories and mines, earn less than $10 per week; from two-thirds to three-fourths earn less than $15, and only about one-tenth earn more than $20 a week."[8]

If he made the big leagues, he might earn what other pitchers, the big stars of the time, took home in salary. While Walter Johnson pocketed $7,500, Christy Mathewson's salary was 25 times larger than Ruth's at $15,000. Both were clearly exceptions, since the 1914 average player salary amounted to $1,200.[9]

Though St. Mary's School was just six miles northeast of the Orioles' ballpark, the new job offered Ruth much more money than sewing collars might have brought him. On March 2, 1914, the first squad of Orioles left Baltimore by train, bound for Fayetteville, North Carolina, to begin training. Never having been outside of the city of Baltimore, after living in a dormitory for so many years, Ruth found himself riding in a train car for most of a day. With manager and owner Jack Dunn now serving as his custodian if not his legal guardian (yet exercising complete control over his legal matters such as signing contracts), we can imagine Dunn seeing to it that his new recruit was fed lunch before he boarded the two o'clock train south. Since the train would take about seven hours to reach Fayetteville, at least one meal would have to be consumed on the train, probably a box lunch. Ruth had been assigned a watcher: Rodger Pippen, sports editor of the *Baltimore News-American*. About seven years older than Ruth, he and Ruth would remain acquaintances for years.

After what was then called "the training season," the International League season opened on April 21, and the next day, April 22, 1914, Ruth pitched his first game, a six-hit, 6–0 win for Baltimore over Buffalo. Ruth had two hits that day. Just 200 fans showed up.

The Baltimore team was the southernmost team in the International League, while Ruth's club had to travel as far north as Montreal and Toronto. Since the team would also play in Newark and Jersey City, Providence, Rochester and Buffalo, and since a player's time on the field would be limited perhaps to the hours between noon and five—the games themselves typically taking about 90 minutes during that era—the 19-year-old

Ruth would be exposed to new places full of new opportunities for fun. In Montreal, a new language as well. After being confined to the city of Baltimore, and then to the grounds of St. Mary's, the long train trips—550 miles to Montreal and another 400 miles to Toronto—could have been very exhilarating. What he ate on the train he did not pay for. The money he was paid was just for his pleasures. And he had money in his pocket.

By June, partly out of fear of having Ruth stolen away by another team—Ruth would go on to win 22 games that year—Dunn raised the young man's salary to $1,800 for the season, perhaps due to an offer tendered by the Federal League Terrapins.[10] Ruth said later bitterly, "I turned it down because we were told by organized baseball that if we jumped we would be barred for life. But nobody was barred for life and I just got jobbed out of $20,000 without a thank-you from anybody."[11] If another team owned his contract, that other team could sell (the rule said "assign") his contract. (In much of sports writing, there is a shortcut when describing the sale of a player's work contract. The phrase "sold the contract" disappears, and the expression "sold the player" is used in its place. It remains an odd expression.)

During that five-month season, every two weeks Ruth was to be paid $150. That bi-weekly amount was almost a year's pay to an employee who had no high school diploma. For the more skilled worker, it equaled about 14 weeks' pay. Some sources say an average year's salary in 1914 was $550, or about $20 every two weeks. Movie star Charlie Chaplin was then earning $150 a week. It was possible for the young man, now called "Babe," to dream of equaling Ty Cobb's baseball salary of $15,000 for a single season.

Before long, the baseball world, and Ruth, found out more about Baltimore and baseball money through syndicated stories: "Dunn ... can parcel his players to National and American League clubs at good figures.... [The Orioles] have a great pitcher, apparently, in the person of Babe Ruth, a left-hander, who was secured from a local reform school. Ruth could command a fancy figure and ... would fit in well in any big league club."[12]

"In 1914, with Baltimore, he had a tremendous rookie season. He won 14 games in less than three months for the Orioles before Dunn sold him to the Boston Red Sox in July."[13] Manager and team owner Dunn cashed in by selling Ruth's contract to the Boston Red Sox for $16,000 on July 8, 1914. Dunn also sold fellow pitcher Ernie Shore, 23, and including the sale of Ben Egan, a catcher, Dunn profited more than $20,000. Within 100 days of Ruth being a paid professional, someone else was making considerable money from his talent. Dunn would not be the first person to make money off of Ruth. (Dunn was able to purchase a pitcher named Grove for the bargain price of $3,500 and in 1925 sold Lefty Grove to the Philadelphia A's for $100,600.)

Now often called Babe ("There goes one's of Dunn's 'Babes,'" as the story is told), Ruth received a shock upon sitting down with the Red Sox management. Boston actually lowered his salary to $1,300 with the major league team. But he was not with them very long.

After starting and winning his first major league game on July 11, 1914—"'Babe' Ruth the Red Sox' new $20,000 southpaw in a debut stunt"—was the typical headline, one that emphasized money), he lost his second. Though he remained with the big club for little more than a month that summer, he was used only in a Manchester, New Hampshire, exhibition game on August 17. But then, for complicated reasons that Creamer's biography sets out in detail, Ruth was optioned after one month with Boston to the minor league Grays of Providence, Rhode Island, for the rest of their season.[14]

On Saturday, September 5, 1914, Ruth hit the first home run of his professional career and shut out the Toronto Maple Leafs, 9–0, at Hanlan's Point Stadium. It was the 19-year-old Ruth's only minor league homer. Behind Ruth and pitcher Carl Mays, 22, the Grays won the International League pennant. Babe Ruth played in 46 minor league games for Providence and Baltimore combined, recording 22 wins against nine loses. It is claimed by Creamer that "Ruth almost single handedly kept the [Providence] club in contention" and that he once "won four games in eight days."[15] The team schedule included at least 156 games; Ruth appeared in 46 of the games in the minor leagues, 30 as a starter, five as a reliever. Ruth had seen further evidence of the business aspect of his profession. He started playing with Baltimore in 1914, and before the year was over he was playing against Baltimore in the same International League where he had begun. No loyalty here.

Back in Boston for the October 2 game, the *New York Times* reported that "Boston's rangy left hander, Ruth" pitched a complete-game, 11–5 victory over the New York Yankees. He also doubled. By season's end, October 7, Babe Ruth had pitched 23 innings for the Red Sox in 1914 with an ERA of 3.91; with ten at-bats in five games, he made a single, a double and scored one run. The team finished second.

During that brief time with the Red Sox in 1914, Ruth met Helen Woodford, a 17-year-old waitress. Ten days after the season ended, on October 17, 1914, the couple married at St. Paul's Roman Catholic Church in Ellicott City, Maryland, 12 miles west of Baltimore. It was decided that the newlyweds would spend the winter in Baltimore with Ruth's father. His mother had died earlier that year. It is likely that Ruth needed to work through the winter and live cheaply in his father's apartment. After all, as *Sporting Life* for October 24, 1914, headlined, "Players Now In Winter Quarters Without Any Post-Season Money To Help Pay Coal Bills."

Since cold weather had not yet arrived in the major league cities, there was still money to be made from baseball by major leaguers. In Chicago, as one example, on October 15, 1914, the White Sox won the final game of the intra-city series over the Cubs. (Post-season city series had also taken place in New York and Philadelphia that year.) Each White Sox player took home $527.30, and every Cub pocketed $398 to help them get through the winter. Their next baseball paycheck would not come for six months, on April 15, 1915. With the Boston Braves in the World Series that year, no city series was possible for the Red Sox.

In Baltimore, hometown major leaguer Fritz Maisel of the New York Yankees won with the Catonsville Volunteer Hose Company. The *Baltimore Sun* of October 23, 1914, covered the first game between the Albrecht A.C. and St. Mary's (Ruth's old reformatory) all-stars. Ruth was hired to pitch in that semipro game which attracted 8,000 spectators.

Meanwhile, major league professional baseball had become such profitable business by 1914 that a third league, the eight-team Federal League, had played a 154-game schedule in eight cities; four of those cities had National or American League teams. The success of baseball corporations may have had something to do with the rise in advertising expenditures in the country. For instance, in 1914 total advertising volume in the United States rose to $682 million.[16] In addition, the introduction of the teletype machine allowed the *Associated Press* to transmit words by wire from keyboards to distant printers, allowing baseball fans to receive immediate news of their teams. Both of these contributed to the 1913 conclusion that "the game of professional baseball no longer is a mere athletic contest as it was in the early days; it has come to be a great 'show business' analogous to the theatrical business."[17]

2

A Pitcher Leads
(1915)

A rumor appeared in the *New York Times* of February 3, 1915, claiming that Babe Ruth's Boston contract would soon be sold to the New York Yankees. But not so. As the new year began, there were excellent reasons for maintaining the Red Sox team as it was constituted. For one thing, the team had won 91 games in 1914. The Red Sox had added not only the finest pitchers in the minor leagues, Ruth and Carl Mays (24–8 at Providence) to start games, but also Ernie Shore, a full-time player in 1914 who would win 19 games in 1915. The team's 1915 roster showed plenty of superior talent. Future Hall of Famers included Herb Pennock, Harry Hooper, and Tris Speaker. (That year's lineup also saw five front-line players who eventually wore the uniform of the New York Yankees.) With these additions and the continued presence of the rest of the second-place finishers in 1914, the tenants of Fenway Park were about to begin a very successful four years.

Ruth's presence on the team was hard to ignore. At six feet, two inches and 190 pounds, Ruth clearly contrasted with most of the other players in the Sox lineup: an average of five feet, nine inches tall and 168 pounds.[1] That year Ruth was paid from Opening Day to closing day (165 days) at the increased salary of $3,500, or $21 per day for the five-and-a-half-month season. (Had he been back in Providence, for example, his salary would have come out of the entire *team's* monthly payroll of $5,000.) Ty Cobb's pay in 1915 reached $20,000, while infielder Roger Peckinpaugh's was $7,000 with the Yankees. Another contrast to be seen was the weekly salary of movie star Douglas Fairbanks—$2,000 for as long as it took to complete the movie *The Lamb*.

For any distant away games (St. Louis, Detroit, Chicago), Ruth and his team rode in Pullman cars whose porters were making a very high salary (or so thought Congress) of $27.50 per month even while "The porters were required to work 400 hours per month or 11,000 miles—whichever occurred first to receive full pay."[2] Had Ruth been a tailor, as trained, he would have been on strike in April 1915 and without pay. The strike failed, forcing the workers to go back to their 59 cents an hour pay.[3]

Ruth became aware of his fame and felt a need to have someone take care of his life outside of baseball. These tasks included culling various requests through the mail or sifting through arrangements for appearances at events like communion breakfasts. The need reflected an approach to some orderly ways to generate more money for himself, and so sometime in 1915 Ruth hired John Igoe, a Boston druggist—Igoe later owned the Harvard Drugstore on Huntington Avenue—to serve as his business manager, perhaps the first athlete to have that kind of employee. Johnny Igoe, born circa 1873 in Ireland, was Ruth's senior by 20 years. "Igoe was working at Fenway Park when Ruth came to Boston in 1915.... They became good friends and when Ruth's fan mail began to arrive Igoe acted as secretary and answered letters when he thought necessary. Later he managed Ruth's out of season tours."[4] He also served as a kind of secretary and companion for various speaking engagements in the Boston area.

By the time mid-season in 1915 rolled around, the press took more notice of Ruth.

> Ty Cobb Has Rival In Southpaw Babe Ruth ... that Ty Cobb the Georgia Peach is not the only pebble in the American League. Ruth made four trips to the plate yesterday afternoon and all he did was slam out a home run, a pair of two baggers, and a single. The home run ... was one of the longest drives ever witnessed at Sportsman['s] Park, the home of the Browns. The ball went clear over the right field bleachers, across Grand Avenue, and landed on the far side of the walk.[5]

That year Ruth hit four home runs in just 92 at-bats, three home runs fewer than league leader Braggo Roth, who came to bat 240 times. The entire Boston Red Sox team hit seven home runs. As a pitcher in that low-scoring era, his earned run average was 2.44, the highest among Boston starters.

In addition, the young pitcher finished the year at 18–8, helping his team to a pennant and a record of 101–50, and contributing to a league leading attendance of 539,885 at a time when the primary, if not sole, source of team income was ticket sales. (In the National League, the pennant-winning Philadelphia sold 90,000 fewer tickets.)

Ruth continued to be the object of attention in the papers. The *St. Petersburg Evening Independent* of October 2, 1915, stated, "Babe Ruth is one of the best hitters on the club and certainly the greatest slugger." The *Pittsburgh Press* took note that "Ruth has batted in 19 tallies. [Red Sox catcher] Forrest Cady owns the same number and he has been in double the contests that the Babe has."[6]

Thanks to winning the pennant, Ruth also earned $3,750 that year when his team played their home World Series games not at Fenway but in the Boston Braves' field. That park, much larger than Fenway, hosted games that drew on average 20,000 more paid than did the games at the home park of the opponent Phillies, Baker Bowl. Ruth, despite his 18 victories was limited to one appearance, as a pinch-hitter for Shore. Even so, the Red Sox won the championship in 1915, beating the Phillies four games to one, with Foster, Leonard and Shore doing the pitching in the five-game series.

For this year, Ruth seemed willing to survive on the baseball money supplemented by income from his events scheduled by Igoe and from his father's saloon. He did play a little post-season baseball, three games in October, but his major post-season play would not begin in earnest until 1919.

Once more the married couple spent the winter in Baltimore with Ruth's father; in fact, Ruth invested in his father's saloon and worked the bar in the winter of 1915–1916. Three days after the Series ended, Ruth, for the joy of playing baseball or to get away from the wife, or for whatever combination of reasons, decided that though he had made $7,280 in 1915, he would play more games. And why not? Others were. Twenty-two major leaguers were organized into the 1915 Trans-Continental Tour of the American and National League baseball stars, a tour that had been planned to take them from the Midwest all the way to San Francisco, playing 27 games in 28 days. Those game between the All Nationals and the All Americans featured such stars as Walter Johnson and Grover Cleveland Alexander.

Meanwhile, there was one fewer major league. In December, Organized Baseball agreed to a formal "peace treaty" with the Federal League, ending a two-year political war. The Federal League officially dissolved on February 16, 1916.

There would never again be more than two major league leagues in baseball. Organized Baseball was even more of a cartel now, though the cartel's monopoly continued to be challenged in the courts by the old Baltimore Terrapins, who would win their case, then lose it on appeal. In 1922, the Supreme Court decided to hear the case.

For players like Ruth, the death of the Federal League meant that now more than ever, he would be at the mercy of his contract's owner.

So when called on by Irvington, Massachusetts, a five-cent trolley ride away, Ruth said yes to a Saturday game on October 17, when he might pocket $50 or $100. Playing with or for a semipro team was not unknown to Ruth. After all, his Red Sox on August 30, 1915, played an exhibition game against the semipro Toledo (Ohio) Rail Lights club. Playing at the Mount St. Joseph's College grounds, Ruth pitched the first three innings and then became the catcher when catcher Doc Knell was injured in the third inning. (Ruth had to use a glove made for a right-handed player, he being left-handed.)

The second post-season game Ruth played, this one on a Sunday, took place on the diamond at St. Mary's Industrial School before a crowd of 8,000. (On that October 24, the All Nationals and All Americans were playing in Omaha, Nebraska.) "Babe Ruth Is Hero Of Hour. Band Plays In His Honor And Former Associates Cheer," the *Baltimore Sun* reported. Also playing were present and former major leaguers from the Maisel family of Catonsville, MD. Ruth walked two, struck out 14, and made two hits and a sacrifice in the 12–2 win against the local Albrecht Athletic Club.

Though Ruth made money, probably $100–200 for the two games, he also lost a $500, two-and-a-half-carat diamond ring paid for with part of his World Series bonus. Though November arrived, "baseball has not yet been dealt a knockout wallop," said the *Baltimore Sun* with Ruth and the Maisels—the "celebrated knights of the national game"— playing once more on the St. Mary's field.

Some papers continued to caution players about the dangers of post-season play, citing Tex Russell's decrease in wins for two years after his play in the California Winter League in 1913. As for the high-salaried Ty Cobb, though his contract like all others in Organized Baseball ended with the end of the season, he was not a free agent because his contract had the reserve clause, which said in effect that he either signed with his current team—when it was ready to sign him to a new contract—or the team disposed of him through trade, sale or release. The team decided his fate as a professional baseball player. If he wanted to be paid to play baseball, it would be with the Tigers; he could not sign with any other team, major or minor league. Though not by law under contract, he was still held to be an employee who needed to obey his boss and not play in the post-season.

3

Stardom Arrives
(1916)

Ruth's 1916 Red Sox salary called for $3,500. In that same year, Walter Johnson earned $12,500, while another pitcher, Herb Pennock, then a below-average pitcher with Boston, collected $1,200. Ty Cobb's income came from both his $20,000 salary with Detroit and his endorsement: "Ty Cobb 'Comes Back.' Nuxated Iron Makes Him Winner."

Outside of major league baseball, the net annual income for Americans in the medical professions averaged $3,000.[1] In Worchester, Massachusetts, the mayor counted on a salary of $4,000, his clerk $1,700; the President of the U.S.'s salary was set at $75,000 a year, the Vice President at $12,000. In the new film industry, there was plenty of money. Charlie Chaplin signed a contract in 1916 that the *New York Times* said paid him $670,000, and both Mary Pickford and Douglas Fairbanks' salaries rose to $10,000 per week.

Ruth used some of his money to lease an eight-acre farm at 558 Dutton Road in Sudbury, 30 miles from Boston. Some biographers suggest that investment freed him to carouse in Boston while his young wife stayed on the farm.

Looking to ease the burden of Tris Speaker's salary, the Red Sox traded the outfielder to Cleveland on April 9, 1916. There Speaker led the league in hits and average plus five other offensive categories. This deal may have hurt the team, but it saved the owner about $15,000.

Winning ten fewer games than in 1915, the 1916 Red Sox still finished in first place in the American League. Ruth hit three home runs in 1916, while the league leader with 12 was Wally Pipp, who came to bat for the Yankees 617 times, four times more than Ruth. As a pitcher, the 21-year-old Ruth won 23 games, third in the league, and led the league in ERA at 1.75, in games started, and in shutouts. For this year of achievement, Ruth was selected to be one of two American League pitchers on the All-American Team. The other pitcher—the right-hander to Ruth's left-hander—was Walter Johnson.

Once again the Red Sox played their World Series games at Braves Field, a park with 5,000 more seats than Fenway. Ruth's best-known game in the Series against Brooklyn of the National League was Game Two, when he drove in the tying run and pitched a 14-inning, 2–1 win. When the Red Sox won the World Series in five games, Ruth was able to add another $3,826.25 to his bankbook, taking his yearly earnings to more than $7,400 and placing his income at $2,500 more than the United States' Assistant Secretary of War's salary.

Baseball changed in two major ways that year. With the collapse of the Federal League, many salaries went down, the lack of competition from a rival league the reason.

The other was the immediate transmission by the *Associated Press* of play-by-play to member newspapers directly from Braves Field in Boston during the World Series.

Ruth and the other World Series participants were warned by National Baseball Commission head Ban Johnson not to barnstorm; they said they were going hunting. As for others, the Pirates barnstormed in Ohio, the New York Giants met the Paterson, New Jersey, Silk Sox semipro team, and, in a match in Kansas City, Zach Wheat's team opposed a team featuring Grover Cleveland Alexander, Hal Chase, Casey Stengel and Max Carey.

Ruth was now part of a team, and an important part, that had just won two championships in a row and three within five years. Who might pay to see him play in October outside of Boston? Teammate Jack Barry arranged a game to be played on Sunday, October 15, 1916, in New Haven, Connecticut, meeting the semipro Colonials. Since Connecticut still subscribed to blue laws, the game was staged outside of New Haven proper. New Haven native and team owner George Weiss, according to his biography at Baseball Library.com, "gave the fans what they wanted: big-name stars and Sunday baseball. Ty Cobb demanded $350 for his first game; Weiss gave him $800, and Cobb returned to New Haven frequently."

Lighthouse Point, five miles south of the city, was chosen for the game. Many of the 3,000 fans arrived by trolley, so this amusement area became known as a "Trolley Park." The fans at the game got their money's worth. Ty Cobb managed the home team. Ruth and Hick Cady were the battery for the Red Sox team that also fielded stars Duffy Lewis and Everett Scott, along with Jack Barry. For Cobb's home team, New York Yankees pitcher Ray Keating pitched eight innings. Ruth pitched all nine innings and "made one of the longest drives ever seen at the grounds," which was merely a double to center field. Cobb, playing first base, also made two hits.

Two days after the New Haven game, October 17, 1916, a "party [of players and others were] invited to Lake Squam, New Hampshire by Ed. Maynard of the Draper-Maynard Co. Maynard makes it an annual hobby to carry a bunch of players to his beautiful camp for a week-end hunting outing." This outing showed itself to be an excellent example of a number of things, as covered by *Baseball Magazine*, the story appearing in its December issue.

The party, comprised of six other players besides Ruth, left Boston by automobile on October 16. In the caravan of cars were the Red Sox trainer, a few friends, and relatives of several of the players, and "the party included also Arthur Duffy, the one time champion sprinter, and Mrs. Duffy; Tim Murnane, the Boston baseball writer; Paul Shannon of the *Boston Post*, and a member of the *Baseball Magazine* staff, accompanied by a 'still' photographer and a movie camera man."

Typical enough for a post-season game of its time, the trip to Laconia combined a vacation with a barnstorming game and a hunting trip. For the baseball game part of the trip, "The City Band met the all stars," the *Boston Globe* reported, "and escorted them to the grounds. All the schools and a number of mills and shops were closed during the game." After the game, attended by 2,500, the Red Sox party, now 40, reached Squam Lake, where they were served very large steaks and also fed on "Six roasted suckling pigs.... The players slept on beds made of limbs of birch trees, with covers of army blankets and genuine sheep skins.... [After] the bear hunt was followed by wrestling matches, tango dancing in the camp house and boxing bouts." Meanwhile the National Commission still could not make up its mind about barnstorming by World Series players. "In 1916, the Commission had also tried to withhold the Red Sox's emblems because of a barnstorming tour. After intense criticism, they reversed the decision, but fined each player $100, the approximate value of the emblems."[2]

Though "The 'no barnstorming' rule was formalized in 1914 by adding a clause to the standard players' contract, the rule was mostly ignored and the Reds, Pirates, Cubs, and Federal League Whales, all barnstormed."[3] On a larger scale, and in a sanctioned series, the barnstorming games labeled "The Tour To End All Tours" had begun in at 1913 and ended in 1914. This was barnstorming controlled by team owners.

Around the same time, speculation arose about Ruth's future as a hitter. An article appeared in the *Fort Worth Star-Telegram* titled, "Job in Outfield Awaits Ruth When Pitching Days End."[4]

4

Best at His Craft
(1917)

Though there remain many tall tales about his hedonism, Ruth, along with manager Jack Barry and Heinie Wagner of the Red Sox, worked out in the gym at Holy Cross College in Worcester before training season officially began.[1] The preferred version of Ruth's life for about his first ten years in baseball remains one of dissipation on a massive scale. Writers do not wish to portray him exercising, selecting bats, working on his fielding, studying pitchers, or asking questions of more experienced players. Whorehouses, pranks, and traffic accidents read as far more interesting.

Players of the time had found ways to add to their baseball salary. Ruth's teammate in 1915, Tris Speaker, received $50 each time he hit the Bull Durham outfield sign, first at Huntington Avenue and later at Fenway Park. He endorsed Boston Garters, had a two-dollar straw hat named in his honor, and received free mackinaws and heavy sweaters. Hassan cigarettes created popular trading cards of Speaker, depicting him running the bases.[2]

Ruth could add to his salary as many players had. In 1917, he signed a $100 contract with bat manufacturer J. H. Hillerich in exchange for endorsing the company's bats. Even while he was still a pitcher, not a hitter, the company thought it could likewise make money from Ruth's fame. Then too, around this time, Ruth's picture appeared on a nickel cigar wrapper, the company that produced them partly owned by Ruth. Ruth, or Igoe, or both, saw to it that Ruth was photographed, face toward the camera, rolling cigars himself.

Money and ownership changed hands when Harry Frazee bought the Red Sox on November 1, 1916, for $675,000. Seemingly a wise investment—the team had just won the World Series twice—Frazee improved the team with trades and paid his players salaries that were reasonable for the times. Ruth signed a contract for $3,500, while Everett Scott, clearly the American League's best shortstop, drew about $4,500. Outside of major league baseball, the average year's salary stood at $750.

On May 18, 1917, the Selective Service Act was passed, authorizing the President to temporarily draft additional men. Ruth registered as he was bound to do on June 5, but he was considered as the sole support of his wife and so not listed very high for possible induction.

On June 23, Ruth, starting for the Red Sox, walked the first hitter, Eddie Foster, on pitches Ruth thought were not off the plate. The umpire, Brick Owens, obviously thought his calls correct. The two began to argue, Owens ordered Ruth out of the game, and Ruth attacked Owens, punching him on the left ear. Police came on the field to restore order. Manager Jack Barry chose another Red Sox starter, Ernie Shore, to take Ruth's place. Foster unsuccessfully tried to steal second, and for the rest of the game no one reached base. Ever since, arguments continue about whether Shore should officially be credited with a "perfect game."

What happened next could be viewed in strong contrast to what might happen now. For punching the umpire, on July 1 Ruth was suspended for a week and fined $100. Even so, baseball seemed to be struggling with the way to deal with misbehavior on the part of athletes. The year 1917 marked the time when official sanctions were published "warning that players 'guilty in public of gross misbehavior, including intoxication, fighting, quarreling, indecency, or any scandalous conduct' would be penalized with fines, suspensions without pay, or both."[3]

A benefit game also seemed to be outside the rules. On September 27, 1917, at Fenway Park, the Red Sox played a benefit game against an American League all-star team during which Ruth and Rube Foster combined for a 2–0 shutout. The squad featured Ty Cobb, Tris Speaker, and Joe Jackson in the outfield. Ruth won the fungo hitting contest with a drive of 402 feet, while Joe Jackson had the longest throw at 396 feet. More than $14,000 was raised for the family of sports writer Tim Murnane, who had died on February 7. [Murnane had vacationed with Ruth in Laconia just the year before.] "Actress Fanny Brice helps sell programs and former heavyweight champ John L. Sullivan coached third base for the Sox."[4]

Murnane and Ruth lived at a time when it was a rare employer who concerned himself with employee benefits. Few industries provided workers with insurance, health care coverage or a pension. Almost a third of the American population still made their income from farms. When you died, your family paid for funerals, medical supplies, and doctors' bills without recompense from an insurance company. If the family could not come up with the money, they might borrow it and, since they were then broke, almshouses or poorhouses still existed in those days. Unless you had completed military service or worked for a railroad, your chances for a pension were slim. (Federal civilian pensions were offered under the Civil Service Retirement System formed in 1920, and the first Social Security payments were made in 1940.)

Organized baseball encouraged some kind of recognition to the war when on October 3, 1917, a Fenway Park benefit game was scheduled for the bat and ball fund of the 101st Regiment of the Army, matching the Red Sox and Washington, with Ruth and Walter Johnson as the starting pitchers.

The 2,070 who showed up for that game seemed like a mob compared to the last game of the Red Sox season. On October 5, 1917, "less than 400 persons turned out to see the final game" of the season, said the *Globe*. The Red Sox had won the pennant in 1916 with 91 wins. Producing five more runs and allowing 25 fewer runs in 1917, they won 90 games but still lost the pennant by nine games to a White Sox team that won 100 games.

Ruth once again found himself chosen for *Baseball Magazine's* annual "All America" team for 1917 as the left-handed pitcher. With 24 wins, 35 complete games, six shutouts and an ERA of 2.01, he had certainly earned that rating. He hit .325 in 123 at bats. (He had hit nine home runs in 361 at-bats from 1914–1917.)

Ruth's only barnstorming game for 1917 was contested on October 7, 50 miles south of Boston in Woonsocket, Rhode Island, from which part of the proceeds were earmarked for soldiers' welfare centers in the U.S. and abroad in a game promoted by the Knights of Columbus. This Catholic men's group was the first of the many fraternal orders Ruth would join. Ruth was already a member, affiliating with the Pere Marquette Council 271 in South Boston.

"Ruth as manager of the invading Red Sox contingent has promised to bring only genuine major leaguers." The *Woonsocket Call* also noted that Ruth managed the team, "and he will have the double task of caring for both the mound work and the men." Ruth doubled, stole a base and struck out four in a 4–2 win that consumed one hour and 40 minutes. He walked seven in the 4–2 loss. Bill Jenkinson reported that 3,600 paid to see the game. The game marked Ruth's first stint as manager of a baseball team.

Others were busy adding to their bankrolls to take them through the winter. The two World Series teams, the White Sox and Giants, played an exhibition at Camp Mills in Mineola, NY, for 600 soldiers. Two days later, the Negro Indianapolis ABC's played a team of All-Stars, including Ownie Bush and Hooks Dauss. The ABC's roster listed Oscar Charleston as one of their players. Two weeks later, on November 2, at New York Olympic Field, another black-white game was staged, this one between the Lincoln Giants and pitcher Chief Bender's Leaguers. There would be no mixing of races on either of these teams.

The National Commission once more exercised its authority late in October 1917. Twelve White Sox players had agreed to play for a Chester, Pennsylvania, millionaire for $10,000, meaning that the starters and pitchers for the team would take home $833 each. For pitcher Eddie Cicotte, this amount equaled 16 percent of his 1917 salary. But "the National Commission stepped in with its threat to withhold $1,000 for each player's share of the World's Series money until January 1.... Later the Commission broadened its order to include all players under contract to the major league clubs." *The Sporting News* of October 25, 1917, placed this story on its front page.

Around the same time, Red Sox teammate Harry Hooper, a nine-year veteran of the team and team captain, suggested to management that Ruth might be more valuable in the lineup as an everyday player. Ruth had hit .325 that season with the most at-bats of any pitcher on the team, 123, less than a quarter of an everyday player. With a new manager, Ed Barrow, about to take charge, the timing might be right to make the change.

Reports surfaced that Ruth had been in a car crash in Boston in November. A woman, not his wife Helen, was also in the car.

5

Labor Relations

Baseball, an enterprise that Robert Burk calls "a high skilled labor-intensive entertainment business," for most of its history held two advantages for its owners.[1] First, "The reserve clause … gave the club an exclusive and perpetual option on the player's services."[2] Second, "each [team had] a monopoly of the area in which it operated."[3] It became very clear very early in the history of Organized Baseball and continuing for 100 years, that the player was thought of "as commodity. He is both employee and product; a resource that is usable until his value depreciates, at which point he is discarded."[4]

While this attitude toward employees remains in force today in many enterprises, in Ruth's time some things had begun to change outside of baseball. Certainly the Boston police strike during Ruth's last year with the Red Sox, 1919, can stand for the times. In this circumstance, with "new officer pay" of two dollars daily not having "risen … since 1857" and with "officers work[ing] between 73 and 98 hours weekly," at a rate averaging 29 cents per hour, a union had to be put in place to bargain new terms of contracts.[5] Workers' compensation wasn't enacted in this country until 1911, as payment for "industrial accidents." Most states passed these laws in the 1910–1915 period, and some major U.S. companies established pension plans prior to 1930.

Yet "when players engage in salary disputes … fans become aware of a less romantic facet of the professionals' lives. And the fans are not always pleased at the spectacle."[6] "Greedy players" was the cry of the sportswriters. Baseball was seen as a sport, an entertainment, a pastime. And it was in baseball's interest to keep it that way.[7] For fans, it was a glorious, glamorous pastime, a way to pass time. The players were not police, not in a vital occupation.

If you take Ruth out of the payroll statistics listed by Baseball-Reference.com, then the average pay for the 1927 Yankees was $7,989. Again, excluding Ruth, 25 players appear on Baseball-Reference.com as being Yankees that year. In New York State, average net income, based on tax returns filed, equaled $3,847. Thirteen of the 1927 Yankees were paid salaries below the average. U.S. Senators and Congressmen were making $10,000 in 1927, and Congressmen also had a pension plan.

But regarding most of these players, that is, not the few stars, at the time no one was even guessing at their salary. All the fans heard of was Ruth's and Hornsby's pay. For the fans, with pay that high, there was no room for complaint for doing work that many fans considered, at the least, as a part-time job, like a schoolteacher.

Did the players complain, or did they try solutions to fix their problems? In 1923, "The players can look back over the first half-century or so of major league baseball and see that they have organized a union roughly once every dozen years (1885, 1900, 1912,

1922), and disbanded or abandoned each of them within five years or less."[8] But conditions remained the same.

Players were children who needed to be watched and disciplined. A team member typically would be required to eat at the team table, to submit to a curfew, and to have his bedtime checked. At the same time, in this labor-intensive industry, "by 1929 aggregate major league team salaries amounted to only 35.3 percent of total major league expenses … 22.1 percent in 1950."[9]

Important to remember, too, was that for most employees of the time, there was no health insurance, there was no unemployment money, and there were no savings. A player had no pension and, if he were hurt playing baseball, he was on his own.

Even for a player who did not cause trouble for the owners, if he were hurt and could not play, his pay stopped until he was ready to take the field again. Other weapons in the arsenal of the owners included suspending or fining a player, creating fees for washing uniforms (uniforms you were required to rent, leaving a deposit), or charging you for Cokes in the locker room. And, of course, determining your salary.

Under the rules of the reserve clause, Leo Durocher, a man of strong opinions, was paid $6,500 in 1934 by the Cardinals after being in the professional ranks for ten years. During that "Gas House Gang" year, should Durocher have displeased his employers, he could have been traded to the notorious Phillies, who often paid their wealthiest employee what other teams were paying their lowest-paid man. Or he could be sent to the minors, where his pay might easily decrease from $1,180 per month to the money that Elbie Fletcher made that year—$250 per month. Durocher's only other choices, under the reserve clause, were to accept the owner's decision to trade him or send him down, or to quit baseball and go back to Springfield, Massachusetts, and find himself a job at the firearms factory. He would be blackballed from playing sanctioned baseball—declared an outlaw—if he chose not to obey his owner's wishes.

A player could lose his place in baseball if he was declared ineligible for almost any reason. Owners had declared some leagues "outlaw" because the new leagues refused to abide by the reserve clause or because they raided other teams and lured away players with the offer of higher pay. Playing in an outlaw league, against a player who had had played in an outlawed league, or against a team from an outlawed league like the Players' or the Federal League, might end your upper level professional baseball paydays.

What good came out of players' complaints? "Summer 1923: Under a barrage of threats and promises from the owners, the Players Association dissolves without achieving anything for the players. One of the owners' unkept promises—a fund for needy former players—does take shape the next year."[10] A pension plan, money paid to players during spring training—these and a few others—would have to wait 34 years for minor changes and 53 years for major alterations.

"Although we prefer to see baseball as a game we play or watch for recreation, from almost the beginning it has been a labor-intensive industry whose on-field personnel constitute both the entertainment product we enjoy and men engaged in doing their job."[11]

6

Home Run King
(1918)

Sporting papers complained in early 1918 that some baseball organizations did not make money in 1917, and it remained true that the demands of World War I would affect attendance in 1918. From a high attendance for the Red Sox of 496,397 in 1916 to the low that would be reached in 1918—249,513—team owner Frazee saw his revenue drop by half. Part of the 1918 decrease was tied to the wartime short season lasting from April 15 to September 3. Naturally, if you play 28 fewer games you would draw fewer fans in 63 home games instead of 77. The decrease in ticket sales might also be attributed to the entry into military service of Jack Barry (also the team manager), Duffy Lewis, Mike McNally, Ernie Shore, and Chick Shorten: in all, five starters and a backup catcher, as well to the absence of the traded Tillie Walker.

The business downturn was examined by Harold Seymour, noting that the owners "saved an estimated $400,000 in payrolls" through "the simple subterfuge of 'releasing' all of them with ten days' notice" while at the same time conspiring not to steal players while they effectively were free agents. When players sought legal recourse, they were traded or, as one player was labeled by a reporter, "something or other turned him 'Bolsheviki.'"[1]

Athletes' salaries have always attracted attention. Burk's study shows an average major league salary to be about $1,300 for a season while an average workingman's 1918 salary reached about $1,000.[2] But it is unfair to compare the two. A major league baseball player is at the top of his profession. He is not being paid an "average" worker's salary because he is not at the bottom nor in the middle of his occupation.

Business elsewhere in baseball remained brisk. The National League Boston team, the Braves, had been bought in 1913 for $187,000 and sold in 1916 for $500,000. The Cubs were sold for more than $500,000, and the St. Louis Cardinals were sold for $375,000. Nevertheless, the press, as usual, came down on the side of the owners and against the players. "The players, many of whom have no regard for the welfare of the club owners, should be made to deliver the goods without receiving additional inducements."[3] Ty Cobb put $20,000 in his pocket, while movie star Mary Pickford's salary equaled $1,230,000 for two years' work. Another actor, Francis X. Bushman, not at Pickford's level, as the *New York Times*, reported on November 5, 1918, made $160,000 a year. In contrast, for those in the military it was typical that a private's pay would equal $15 per month.

Ruth would earn more than the mayor of Boston. Ruth's deals with the owner incorporated a salary of $7,000 with "a $1,000 midseason raise, plus another $1,000 upon winning the pennant, and a $1,000 World Series bonus."[4] Frazee, the owner, did not seem to mind Ruth's salary. Frazee, as usual, needed the money made from increased attendance.

The Red Sox's season, though damaged, was soon repaired. First, a baseball man with experience at every level of baseball, Ed Barrow, was hired as manager. Barrow became available because his salary as president of the Eastern League had been slashed. Barrow saw that Connie Mack was dismantling the last-place Athletics, who averaged just over 2,400 paid that year. On December 14, 1917, Barrow dealt three players plus $60,000 in cash to Mack's team for the contracts of Amos Strunk, Wally Schang, and Bullet Joe Bush.

Looking at his pitching staff in 1918, Barrow saw quality throwers: Carl Mays, Sam Jones, Joe Bush and Dutch Leonard. Ruth might be spared from too many pitching duties and add his hitting to the lineup. Barrow began to think that Ruth could be played in the outfield as well as pitch—he had shown his hitting ability—so Ruth worked especially hard as a hitter in spring training. (Besides starting and relieving, he played three other positions that year.)

Ruth made five hits on May 5 against the Senators. After seven games that season including five starts as pitcher, Ruth made his first start as a non-pitcher on May 6, 1918, assigned to first base and batting sixth against the Yankees. The next day, he tied a major league record with a home run in three consecutive games.

On May 18, 1918, Secretary of War Newton Baker issued the Work or Fight order: serve in the military or some war-related industry by July. It did not take long for this to affect the Red Sox. Pitcher Dutch Leonard, to avoid the draft, signed up for a shipbuilding job in Quincy at the Fore River Shipyard. And to pitch in the Shipbuilders' League.

Ruth, feeling his stardom and chafing against Barrow's St. Mary's-like curfew as if he were still an incorrigible boy, soon was ignoring the hours set for players. Barrow could do little to curb Ruth's tomcatting; Ruth would have his way, but as a middle ground Ruth agreed to write Barrow notes on what time he came in each night, and no more was said concerning curfew.

But Ruth was still pushing back. On July 2, 1918, Ruth ignored a sign from Barrow during an at-bat that led to a heated verbal incident. Barrow fined Ruth $500—five percent of his salary. Ruth quit the team, and it was reported by the *New York Times* the next day that "Babe Ruth Jumps Red Sox…. Babe Ruth announces that he has joined the Chester team of the Delaware River Shipbuilding League." The management of the Red Sox was furious. It owned Ruth's baseball contract, and that document was still in effect. Though Ruth's work in the defense industry might look to be patriotic, nevertheless the contract stood.

Dispatched was veteran player Heinie Wagner, then 37 years old, who tracked down Ruth in Baltimore and convinced him to return to the Sox. When Ruth returned, "after renegotiating his contract on July 12 with Frazee to include some hitting related bonuses, he took time to make his peace with Barrow."[5]

The *New York Times* began to refer to Ruth as the "Home Run King" around this time.

"He scoffs when he hits a single, merely lifts his eyebrows at a double, begins to take a little interest in life when he hits a triple, and only begins to have a good time when he slams out a home run. That's George Babe Ruth, the caveman of baseball, who is whaling away to fame this season with the Boston Red Sox."[6]

Ruth considered the business aspect of his fame, a fame that labeled him both "King" and "caveman," saying, "My main objection to pitching has been that pitching keeps you out of so many games…. I'm young and strong and I don't mind the work but I wouldn't guarantee to do it for many seasons."[7] Ruth had, as an exemplar, Smoky Joe Wood's career as a Red Sox pitcher. At age 25 in 1915, Wood won 15 games, but he never won another and pitched just 18⅓ more innings in the big leagues (although, unlike Ruth, he had blown his arm out).

Ruth showed he was not simply a slugger. Ruth would steal home ten times in his career. Even so, slugging was important; the tenor of the game was changing. For example, Zach Wheat in 1918 became the last player to lead the National League in batting without hitting a single home run.

Another wartime announcement came early in August: there would be no major league baseball after September 1, the new date set by Secretary of War Baker for the ball players within draft age to get into essential work.

In late August, Ruth's father, George Herman Ruth Senior, died, and once more Ruth left the team to attend to the funeral. "It was his last extended visit to Baltimore, which he never again thought of as home. His father and mother were dead, his only sister was eighteen, a grown woman, and his stepmother had the bar. He was Babe Ruth of Boston now."[8] He missed three home games but was back in time for the Friday, August 30, game against the Athletics. The next day, the box score showed Ruth as the winning pitcher. Two days after that, the season ended.

The champion Red Sox won the American League championship after 126 games with a 75–51 record. Ruth's at-bats rose from 123 in 1917 to 317 in 126 games, averaging 2.5 at-bats per game. Four starting pitchers—Mays, Bush, Jones and Ruth—won 65 games. In 1917, Ruth had pitched 326⅓ innings, but in 1918 just 166⅓ due to his 684 innings as a position player, and he became the only ballplayer in history to win ten games (13–7 with a 2.22 ERA) and hit ten homers in the same season. After 1918, he would not come to bat fewer than 426 times until 1935.

The 1918 World Series would have a number of odd aspects. As many had before them the champion Cubs' owners chose to play on another, bigger grounds, Comiskey Park, which accommodated 14,000 more seats than the Cubs' home, Weeghman Park. For another, attendance would average only 21,413 for the six games. Lastly, the winners' and losers' shares would be lower than ever before due to two changes: the new plan to distribute the attendance receipts to eight teams instead of two, and the ten percent war tax imposed by the government.

The first three games were played at Comiskey Park. In Game One, Ruth shut out the Cubs, 1–0, and extended his consecutive scoreless World Series innings streak from 13 to 22 (and then to 29 in Game Four). He hit a two-run triple in the fourth game as well. The pitching and hitting helped his team to a 3–1 lead in games. A New York City newspaper headline emphasized Ruth's role: "Ruth helps Red Sox to drive within one victory of world's baseball title…. Ruth still untamed hero…. Tarzan of Boston tribe triples with two on bases in early effort."[9] In the same article, Ruth ("a colossal figure") was likened to Banquo's ghost, who in Shakespeare's *Macbeth* appeared at the title character's banquet and "cast a sinister shadow over the Chicago club."[10]

Yet money again took over baseball. Major League Baseball's web site explains, "The Series was threatened by a player strike in Game 5. When the players' demand for larger World Series cuts was rejected, it took an appeal from A.L. President Ban Johnson to convince the players to take the field."[11] The appeal was really a threat not to give any money at all to the players, but to donate all of the players' share to the Red Cross. "Some of [the players] were wondering if they had enough money to pay their way home."[12]

How did the owners justify not increasing the amounts later, in a more sober moment? "Although the players on the Boston Red Sox and Chicago Cubs objected to the other clubs getting any money at all until they received their full share of the spoils," explained the *New York Times,* "the National Commission did not see its way clear to change the rules all over again at such short notice."[13]

How did the owners and the National Commission keep their promise not to punish the angry players? By denying them their championship emblems, which were not distributed until a ceremony 65 years later.

The Red Sox won Game Six at Fenway Park, and that ended the Series. Now the money part of the game: the 1910 World Series, drawing almost the same number of attendees as in 1918, showed the winners' share to be $2,062. The winner's share in 1917 had been $3,669. But the 1918 winning share was $1,102.51, the least ever, and the losing share was $671.09, next to the lowest. But Ruth's total income from the Red Sox in 1918 reached $10,102.51.

Befitting the times, the perennial barnstormers, the Cincinnati Reds, "will disband immediately after today's game [September 2, 1918] and nearly all of them have secured employment of an essential nature," reported the *Cincinnati Enquirer*. Team members on the Boston Americans played a number of in-season exhibition games in 1918—receipts to the owner—as part of their contractual duties: in Bridgeport; against the Doherty Silk Sox in Clifton, New Jersey; in Woonsocket; and on August 18 against the New Haven Colonials. October began and ended with two notable games. On October 5, the Negro Chicago American Giants played a squad that called itself the Major League All-Stars in Chicago; the other game matched the All-Nationals and the Giants on a Sunday in New Jersey. Rube Marquard pitched for the Giants, and Red Causey and Al Demaree played as well.[14]

For the 1918 season, Ruth had not only led the league in home runs, but he also had been picked for the *Baseball Magazine* annual "All America" team as the American League's best left-handed pitcher. It is easy enough to understand how Ruth might have counted on the same amounts of money he had taken home from the World Series games in 1915 and 1916. But in 1918, Ruth earned almost a third of what he had taken home in those other years.

Some of these post-season games had limited, and confusing, newspaper coverage. Some would only be referred to in a vague way. But we can see that Ruth perhaps played in as many as seven games beginning on September 14, although the reports of his pay ranged widely.

The first game Ruth agreed to was to be played in New Haven, again involving the New Haven Colonials because George Weiss "realized that the soon-to-arrive Cubans" were very good. Weiss arranged for them to come to Lighthouse Field but was worried that his Colonials might be badly outclassed.[15]

Weiss knew that Ruth would provide good attendance at the game, since the *New Haven Register* said Ruth "is truly the miracle player of baseball" and added that Ruth was "unquestionably the biggest baseball sensation of the year." Weiss, later to make his mark in the major leagues, counted his box office receipts and watched as the Stars "whipped the Colonials handily, [as] Ruth provided the only bright light in the 5–1 defeat with a mammoth homer beyond the flagpole in left centerfield."[16]

The next game's activities, or advertising, began early. The *Hartford Courant* reported that Ruth arrived the night before the game, lodged at the Bond Hotel, and with a fee of $1,300 part of his duties was to give "an exhibition of fungo hitting…. A band has been secured to keep the crowd entertained."

Hired probably by the wealthy theatrical magnate Sylvester Z. Poli, Ruth played for Poli's baseball club in a championship game, called the semipro championship of New England, on September 15. A crowd of 5,000 (the Red Sox had averaged 3,960 per game that year) attended the game to see stars other than Ruth, yet the *Courant* believed that "all eyes were focused on Babe Ruth…. After being given a rousing ovation," he hit a long double off the top of the Bull Durham sign in center field. The only run scored in the game came on an Agnew single in the ninth inning. Pitcher Ruth gave up only three hits for Poli, and only two rival Red Tops made it as far as second base.

After a $300 game in Springfield, Massachusetts, his fourth post-season game, Ruth returned to Hartford with the Poli team to play a doubleheader on September 23. The *Pittsburg Press* wrote that he made $350 for the game.

But then it was time to travel 275 miles south to Lebanon, Pennsylvania, where he would play for Pop Kelchner, who managed Lebanon's team in the Bethlehem Steel League, a shelter for big-league players trying to stay out of the First World War. CEO Charles Schwab formed the league in 1917 with instructions that he wanted "some good wholesome games that will furnish amusement and entertainment for the Bethlehem Steel Co.'s employees, and don't bother me about details of expense." One example was Shoeless Joe Jackson, who worked at Bethlehem Steel's Harlan Shipyard in Wilmington.[17] Kelchner's roster that fall included, among others, Rogers Hornsby. Other major league players on that team were Ruth's teammates Sam Agnew and Ernie Shore.

"One morning," Kelchner wrote in a letter quoted by Mike Drago of the *Reading Eagle*, "Babe broke up a practice session with his fungo hitting. Every time he hit the ball it went out of the park with the result that soon we were out of baseballs and practice for that morning had to cease…. Later on I discovered there were scores of his admirers outside the park to whom he had promised baseballs, and he chose this as a means of supplying them!"[18]

The only game Ruth played for Lebanon was his fifth post-season game on September 28, while he continued his employment at the Lebanon plant of the Bethlehem Steel Corporation. At first base, Ruth made no hits in the game and his team lost, 4–2, before 1,500 fans.

For Ruth's game six, on September 30, 1918, the player traveled to the home of the Reading Railroad, Reading, Pennsylvania, to Lauer Park on Second Street. Almost all the players on both squads were major leaguers, and the crowd was counted at 12,000. When Joe Jackson homered, he was handed a bonus $20 bill on the spot.

For all this play, there was still a war going on, and the Spanish flu epidemic was just beginning to pick up its deadly speed. It would kill 600,000 Americans before it was through.

As in much else in baseball, there was no way to change the mind of the National Commission, the ruling body that served as the owners' mouthpiece. Before many days had passed in 1918, it felt the need to "criticiz[e] the shipbuilding and steel corporation industrialists, who effectively lured valuable resources [players] from another essential industry [baseball]."[19] The Commission, and most times that meant just one man, Ban Johnson, could punish anyone in the Organized Baseball.

The *Baltimore Sun* announced plans for a game to be played, probably on Sunday November 10, with a headline "Former Birds To Play. Babe Ruth And Eddie Murphy [White Sox outfielder] Will Oppose Dry Docks." The contest was apparently played, since the *Baltimore American* reported that Ruth was back in Lebanon, Pennsylvania, on November 18 on crutches, from the injury occurring during that underreported game in Baltimore. Yet a book by Allan Wood claims that Ruth played in Lebanon on the 17th against "the ersatz Red Sox."[20]

Not long after, since the Armistice had been declared, Ruth returned to Sudbury, Massachusetts, to his 12-room house with outbuildings that, according to biographer Kal Wagenheim, cost $12,000.[21]

7

Magnates

Early in Ruth's career, Yankees co-owner Tillinghast L'Hommedieu Huston, perhaps thought of the purchase of Ruth, or any other employee, this way, telling the *New York Times,* "If I pay $8,000 for a bull, just think what I'd pay for a good pitcher or a lad who could hit plenty of home runs."

Huston was one of those persons of wealth and power who in the Progressive Era were referred to as magnates. For some baseball historians, the argument between owners and players is about economic class. The owners, like Jacob Ruppert, might be wealthy men, wealthy from revenue outside of their baseball holdings. The owners knew their authority and were mostly confident in their knowledge. For everyone else, professional games in many countries still exist as ways of social and economic upward movement while the player is working in the sport. In Ruth's time and before, few professional baseball players could survive the entire calendar year without more than one source of income, more than the baseball paycheck.

The wishes of the magnates can be expressed best in the statistic that in professional baseball, a labor intensive industry, the percent of salaries "as a share of club receipts" in one of Ruth's highest paid years, 1929, equaled 35.3 percent.[1] In contrast, "Education is a labor-intensive industry [and] according to some estimates, 85 percent of the costs of public schools are spent for salaries and fringe benefits."[2] In other occupations, "73 percent in public transit; even in a hospital with a great deal of maintenance and equipment costs, 50 percent goes to nurses."[3]

In Ruth's time, if players looked carefully at their contracts, they might see these two items: even if during his performance as an employee of the club, "Should the player become disabled or his ability to perform his duties be impaired" in "excess of 15 days," the contract could be terminated," and second, "Should the player's services" not be "of sufficient value to the club ... the club may ... terminate this contract."

The players had little bargaining power and were powerless faced with the owners' authority. The players in Ruth's time and until about 1947 had few if any weapons, nor did they have anything to fall back on. By 1950, players' salaries equaled just 22 percent as a share of club receipts. The employers offered no insurance, no health plans, no pension, no winter money, and no spring training money. If you refused to sign the contract or "held out" for more pay, you might have some success.

Was owning a team profitable? Though the owners in the past rarely revealed the prices when selling teams, some data is known about the Boston baseball teams. James E. Gaffney bought the Boston Braves in 1913 for $187,000 and then sold the team on

January 8, 1916, to Percy Haughton for $500,000. In 1935, Braves shares were worth $420,000, a sale of a last-place team.

As for the Red Sox, who went through a series of owners in early years, in 1913 the team was sold to Joseph J. Lannin for a secret price, and three years later Lannin sold the team—Fenway Park, players' contracts and the franchise—for $675,000 to Harry Frazee. Seven years after that sale, Frazee sold the team to J. Robert Quinn, the team having been stripped of players, for $1,200,000. Ten years later, longer ownership came in when on February 25, 1933, Quinn sold the club to Thomas A. Yawkey, a 30-year-old New York millionaire and son of a former owner of the Detroit Tigers. The selling price for the last-place team was put at $1,000,000.[4]

During some Great Depression years, when failed businesses could be counted in the tens of thousands and failed banks in the thousands, not one baseball team then—or ever—has failed, even the St. Louis Browns, who averaged just over 1,000 paid attendance in 1935.

In "The Babe Ruth Story," the 1948 movie, the Ruth character is advised that he ought to take legal action against the Boston Braves for their treatment of him. Ruth refuses, saying that would be like "suing the Church," a sentiment more influenced by an owner than a player.

The hierarchy among owners in baseball during Ruth's early time was headed by its own Vatican: The National Commission. This group was supposedly a three-person committee in charge of organized baseball—that is, the major leagues and all the approved minor leagues—from 1903 to 1920. The Commission, a product of the National Agreement of 1903, "gave it the power to interpret and carry out the terms and provisions of the National Agreement, as well as the ability to enact and enforce fines and suspensions."[5] The commission, like other groups, saw a struggle for power. In addition to its other functions, it served as a high court.

This first "court" judged itself as one whose "history is a page of the fairest and most just decisions which have been handed down by any tribunal in the history of sport in the world," so spoke the voice from on high in the 1911 *Spalding Baseball Guide*, just eight years after the Commission's founding. The owners may have said the system played fair but in 1914, a state court said the baseball contracts "lacked mutuality of obligation."[6] True courts have the authority over true crimes. Owner-player disputes over salary, working conditions, and the like were placed in the hands of the Commission, supported by the owners. And even though Garry Herrmann, President of the Cincinnati Reds, had been named as the chair of the Commission, the Commission's de facto boss was Ban Johnson, the founding President of the American League. Baseballreference.com says plainly, "Herrmann was a friend of Johnson's from his days in Cincinnati, and would regularly side with Johnson over the coming years." The third member of the Commission, typically the National League president, changed often during the 1903–1920 period. Thus we see that, "Thanks to his control of the National Commission, Ban Johnson became the most powerful man in baseball over the next decade and a half."[7]

With the ratification of a new National Agreement in 1921, new Commissioner Landis was given broad powers in such areas as owners terminating a player contract just with ten days' written notice. If the player objected, "in case of dispute between the Player and the Club … the same shall be referred to the Commissioner as an umpire, and his decision shall be accepted by all parties as final." Also made final was the reserve clause, which "in every player contract bound players to their teams, prohibiting them from playing anywhere else…. They could accept the contract offered or find a different line of work."[8] Landis's secretary, Leslie O'Connor, found it necessary to issue a special edict warning players that if they "still failed to show up within ten days, they would be placed on the ineligible list and would have to apply to Landis for reinstatement."[9] For example, Joe DiMaggio, Yankees outfielder, refused the 1938 contract offered, seeking $40,000. When forced to sign for $25,000, he was penalized a day's pay until the owner decided he was ready to play. Each day out of the lineup cost DiMaggio $148.81.

The owners drew on their power from the vague and nebulous language of the updated Agreement of 1921, which was filled with phrases that could be interpreted any way an owner or new commissioner Landis pleased. The job security of players had very little if any consideration in the final document, which allowed employees to lose their job by way of phrases like the following:

—"conduct detrimental to base ball"
—"in the interests of the morale of the players and the honor of the game"
—"wholesome and high-class professional baseball"
—"conform his personal conduct to standards of good citizenship and good sportsmanship"

With this ambiguous and vague language, owners were free to deal with their players under contract as they wished. The commissioner, selected and hired by the owners, knew that in case of a "dispute between the Player and the Club … the same shall be referred to the Commissioner as an umpire, and his decision shall be accepted by all parties as final."

The third court for the players is the highest in the land, the U.S. Supreme Court. In its May 22, 1922, decision as written by Justice Oliver Wendell Holmes, the court decided that professional baseball was not "trade or commerce in the commonly accepted use of those words." The authority of the professional baseball cartel, from now on, would be absolute. The owners continued to hold onto the Supreme Court decision of 1922 and nothing prevailed against it. Not labor unions, not groundbreaking federal labor legislation such as the Norris–La Guardia Act, and not the National Labor Relations Act of 1935 changed that policy.

Baseball gave financial assistance to the sporting paper *The Sporting News* to be sure the paper sided with the wishes of the magnates.[10] Perhaps owners were content with executive performance "because they took their gains as much in psychological income as in money. They seemed to enjoy ownership for the pleasure of being arrogant, as when the Pittsburgh management in 1909 scolded the customers for their failure to encourage the players…. Owners liked to treat their players as children at best and as domestic animals at worst."[11] Almost everyone who was not a player trumpeted the power of the magnates to conduct business as they saw fit. *Baseball Magazine*, in 1914, warned players not to behave so that people would think them spendthrifts. "A very glaring instance of this among baseball players is the recent evil tendency to purchase and maintain automobiles."[12] Thirty-five years later—April 6, 1949—the *Christian Science Monitor* wrote, "American baseball is big business with a $300,000,000 to $400,000,000 investment in ballparks and talent. All its top men say it must have the reserve clause to live." With the support of the press, the owners stood firm for the most part. "Perhaps owners were self-righteous because the sporting press usually sided with management on controversial questions."[13]

"Though the owners wanted to believe themselves acting, as the banal phrase goes, in the best interests of the game, Charles Weeghman of the Cubs was a friend of Mont

Tennes, a leading figure in Chicago's gambling world."[14] Before Ruppert, and some commentators would say typical, were Yankees owners were Frank Farrell and William Devery. Farrell was a gambling tycoon, and Devery was a police officer who (it was said) found the secret of making crime pay. The organization headed by the two was thought to make about three million dollars a year from prostitution, gambling, and civic corruption."[15]

Concerning the trials of the Black Sox: "The owners recognized that airing the game's dirty linen was not in their best interests. Therefore, they decided to provide good attorneys to aid in the players' defense. Later, baseball would punish its sinners by extralegal weapons in its arsenal."[16]

In the newest Yankee Stadium, there is a section against the center field wall on the playing field called Monument Park, with markers for Ruth, Lou Gehrig and others. For all but one monument, the markers measure about 75 inches high by 24 inches across. For a more recent owner, George Steinbrenner, a monument/plaque hybrid measures 84 inches across and 60 inches high, weighing 760 pounds, showing 5,040 square inches across its face.

8

A New Record
(1919)

"Babe Ruth's resolution for 1919 was simple: make more money."[1] Red Sox team owner Frazee agreed. "Babe Ruth likes to get what is his due.... Ruth is what I call a good business man and he likes to work on a basis that will net him an increase according to what he does to earn an increase."[2]

There existed some odd business relationships in Ruth's time. For instance, Connie Mack of the Philadelphia Athletics sent eight players to the Red Sox in fewer than three years, including the 1918 season. Just as the Red Sox had been receiving players from the Athletics, Frazee, working with manager Edward Barrow, seemed to have the same kind of arrangement with the New York Yankees. The Red Sox traded pitchers Dutch Leonard, Ernie Shore and outfielder Duffy Lewis to New York on December 18, 1918. It was just the first of many deals between Frazee and the Yankees owners. Once first string catcher Sam Agnew's contract was sold in January 1919, to Washington, Frazee was able to realize $54,000 from sales.

If, before the trades, Frazee's Red Sox needed money, the New York Giants, on the other hand, were prospering well. Around 1910, then team owner John T. Brush's profits on the Giants range from $100,000 to $300,000 annually.[3] The franchise that sold for $100,000 in 1905 was sold for over one million dollars in 1919.

Ruth, assuming Frazee was now well financed, demanded a salary of $15,000 for 1919. With Duffy Lewis traded, "The Boston fans sided angrily with Ruth against Frazee. There were published suggestions that other American League owners might chip in to make up the difference because Ruth filled their parks for them."[4]

The constant quarrels about salary provided a continuing conflict. "The gritty facts are that ballplayers like to think they are paid for skill, and management says its high resolve is to field great teams. The gritty facts are that ballplayers are paid for their drawing power, not their artistry, and management ... wished only [to] sell tickets, food and drink at its ballparks."[5]

As things stood for so many decades in major league baseball, you played for whoever your contract owner said you played for—even if you had not yet signed a contract for that year—and you were paid at whatever rate your employer chose to pay you. Peculiar a system as it may have been, "Professional baseball is bound to be a business from its nature," The Outlook magazine noted in 1920.[6]

Ruth could see the salaries for police in Boston, who went on strike "against pay scales of 21¢ to 23¢ per hour for 83 to 98 hour weeks."[7] He could know that Eddie Collins, whose baseball excellence was confirmed by his winning the Chalmers Award, the league's Most Valuable Player prize in 1914, was being paid $15,000.

In other lines of work, opera singer Enrico Caruso took home $3,000 to $5,000 per performance, and movie queen Mary "Pickford was lured away from Famous Players by First National, which offered her a $675,000 per year salary and 50% of the profits made by her movies."[8]

After more than three months of wrangling, Ruth accepted a contract for $27,000 for three years.

Harry Frazee was still talking money. He admitted, "the war has cut into my amusement business of which baseball is a part."[9] Asked if some things he owned were for sale, Frazee replied, "Anyone who wants them can have them at a price."

Historian Gene Carney observed:

> Baseball was seen as a sport, an entertainment, a pastime.... In fact, baseball was also a business, and a big one. Franchises in 1919 were at or approaching the million dollar mark in worth. Baseball was also a monopoly.... Players signed a standard contract containing a reserve clause tying players to their teams, prohibiting them from playing anywhere else. This meant that players had no bargaining power at all. They could accept the contract offered or find a different line of work.[10]

The excitement of baseball fans was not tempered by the dollars and cents aspect of the game. Ruth hit his ninth home run on July 5, 1919, two fewer than he had hit all year in 1918. Although September 8 was scheduled as a regular season off-day, the kind of rave write-ups Ruth would be getting for more than a decade can be seen clearly as Ruth showed off all of his skills as a baseball player during an exhibition game. "Ruth hit two home runs before a home town crowd of 10,000," the *Baltimore Sun* reported. "An overflow crowd, estimated at more than ten thousand fans, turned out yesterday at Oriole Park to greet the slugging Babe Ruth, and, after nearly two hours of thrills, left for home and supper firmly convinced that the former Industrial School player deserves all the nice things that have been said."[11] Whether Ruth deserved more pay might depend on Frazee's percentage of the gate that day.

The *San Jose Evening News* of September 15, 1919, summed up: "Babe Ruth is now pronounced the greatest attraction in baseball. Vaudeville managers are now bidding for him. Boston pays him $12,000 a year to bust fences and the theatrical people are ready to double his salary." The *Evening News* was wrong about Ruth's salary—it was $9,000. Still, anything concerning Ruth made the papers. The *New York Times,* on September 21, 1919, noted, "Perfumed Notes For Ruth; Home Run King a Victim of Souvenir Seekers— Needs a Secretary," and referred to him in mock heroic terms: "Babe Ruth, the mastodonic mauler of Boston."

These accomplishments did not seem to impress owner Frazee, as Ruth would soon recount. But for now, on September 20, Ruth accepted what he was quickly coming to consider his just due. The Catholic men's fraternal organization, the Knights of Columbus, oddly enough decided to give Ruth even more cash, and a gift too. (It may have been their way of claiming him as their own.) On this "Babe Ruth Day," the Boston Knights gave him $600 in treasury savings certificates and a traveling bag. Ruth hit home run number 27, and baseball writers began searching for the record for home runs in a season.

The Red Sox moved to New York for games against the Yankees, where the *New York Times,* ignoring the fact that professional baseball was only played in America, said, "A new world's batting record was made up at the Polo Grounds yesterday, when Babe

Ruth … boosted his twenty-eighth home run of the season." However the *Times*, was not merely impressed with the number. It was impressed with the kind of home run Ruth made. "Ruth's record-making home run went so far that Ruth could have whirled around the bases and scored a dozen runs before the ball could have been retrieved."

Near season's end, the Red Sox found themselves with a two-day break before ending the season in Washington with three games beginning September 27. Ruth seized the opportunity for another payday. The *Wilkes-Barre Times* of September 26 reported that on September 25, the "Red Sox," or at least Herb Pennock, Roxy Walters, and Ruth, played in Lebanon, Pennsylvania, against the Klein Chocolate Company team. Ruth pitched the seventh inning.

When on September 27, 1919, Babe Ruth hit his 29th home run, columnist Ralph Davis of the *Pittsburgh Post Gazette* wrote, "It is doubtful whether his modern record will ever be surpassed." Part of the astonishment on the part of sportswriters was that the National League leader hit 12 home runs all year, and that the second-best home run hitter in Ruth's American League hit ten home runs. Another way of seeing what this accomplishment meant to baseball fans is that the Ruth's Red Sox record for home runs would not be broken for 17 years.

But the team finished more than 20 games behind the Chicago White Sox. Ruth was picked again for the annual *Baseball Magazine* "All America" team in 1919, but that year not as a pitcher but an outfielder.

With the season over, with no more money coming in until next April, many players were going out on what was sometimes called the "Pumpkin Circuit"—barnstorming in the Fall—that year. *The Sporting News* of October 19, 1919 noted, "The Cincinnati Reds in their late exhibition games in which the players shared 50–50 with the club took in over $10,000 and the players who took part netted over $200 each."[12] For an average player, these post-season games could provide an additional 15 percent above a yearly salary.

It did not seem that the size of the town or city mattered to Ruth, only the percentage of the gate or the guarantee that could be negotiated; that is, whoever wanted him the most. In 1919, just three cities in the U.S. counted one million or more inhabitants, while there were 9,500 places with fewer than 1,000 residents. Classified as urban territory in the 1920 census were 2,722 cities; classified as rural places—that is with a population of under 2,500—were 12,855 towns and villages. A full 48 percent of the population in 1920 lived in rural areas.

By now Ruth understood the advantages of barnstorming, or at least playing in post-season games. Before Christmas, Ruth would play in 20 games from Hartford to Los Angeles—3,011 miles—and see what else might be out on the West Coast that he could find to cash in on from his celebrity.

For that first game on September 28, Ruth needed to come up the day before from the District of Columbia to Hartford, to once more play with the Poli team—Mr. Poli must have paid very well—even as the Red Sox were playing that same day in Washington. He would be paid again even though he must travel 550 miles to the north of Boston—Portland, Maine, population 70,000.

After the game at Portland's Bayside Park, smart scheduling required Ruth to travel just 35 miles to begin October in Sanford, Maine. The local paper also did a fine job of establishing the sense of the event, according to the Sanford Mariners' current web page. "A song, written somewhere, sometime, by somebody was sold in the grandstand and along the sidelines during the game. The chorus was sung at intervals by a man with a

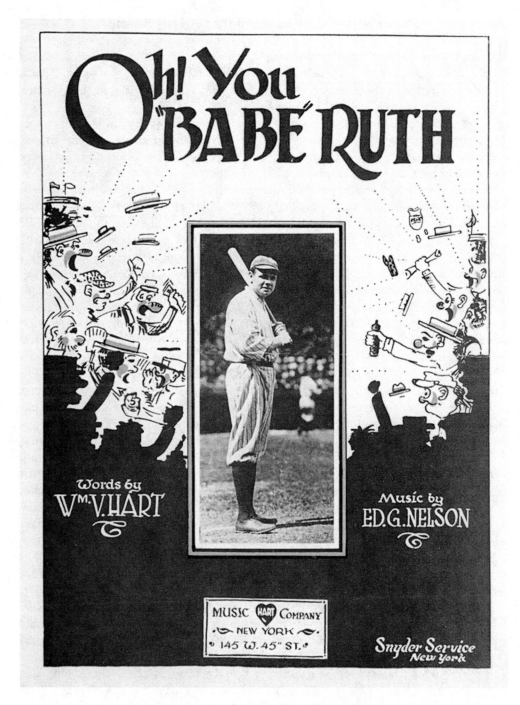

Sheet music for "Oh! You "Babe" Ruth," 1919.

megaphone, and a younger man did the selling act [of the sheet music]. The song was all about Babe Ruth's batting prowess."[13]

Ruth's three-run home run helped the Red Sox to a come-from-behind, 4–3 victory. Right after the game, Ruth's squad drove 80 miles to Lynn, Massachusetts, where Ruth played for the Coronet Stars against the Red Sox at Little River Park at 4 p.m. The city was home to one of two General Electric factories, and the *Lynn Daily Evening Item* thought, "The coming of Big Babe this afternoon to Little River is the greatest attraction ever staged on an open lot in this city.... His record [of 29 home runs] is likely to stand the ravages of time for there never was another slugger who could wield that magic mace, and there is likely never to be such a one again."

To see Ruth, "15,000 fans had come thither" and "sensing the crowd's desire to see Ruth try once more to hit a home run, in the ninth, Stuffy McInnis deliberately dropped a double play relay so that Babe could bat one more time." The large crowd witnessed two Ruth home runs in a game played in 87 minutes.

For his sixth post-season paycheck, the one on October 4, 1919, Ruth traveled just 50 miles to play a game at Columbia Field in Attleboro, Massachusetts. He had signed on to take part in what the small city of 20,00 had just decided to call the Little World Series. Previously, while Attleboro and North Attleboro had played their series only with amateur players, in 1919 "every man who ever donned a uniform will be eligible," the *Attleboro Sun* reported on September 2. Showing up in 1919 alone were Zack Wheat, Walter Johnson, Rabbit Maranville, and Jim Thorpe. There was clearly money to be made for the players. North Attleboro manager Frank Kelley reportedly was furnished "with a bankroll so large it couldn't be held in a single pocket" by local businessmen. Another account says Attleboro manager Dan O'Connell was assured by textile mill owner Oscar Wolfenden that "money would be no object" in the quest to bring in top players.[14]

Ruth was paid $500 to play in the final game of the series for North Attleboro. "Outfitted in his Red Sox road uniform," he was honored by "the North Attleboro Knights of Columbus … in a pre-game ceremony, presenting him with yet another diamond ring."[15] Ruth played left field for North Attleboro and batted a single.[16]

As seen in the pages of the SABR Baseball Biography Project of Elmer Bowman, Rutland manager Harry Shedd had booked an exhibition game at the Rutland fairgrounds against the Boston Red Sox. The Boston team had been booked to play in Providence, Rhode Island, but Shedd lured them to Rutland by promising half of the gate receipts and a guarantee of $1,500, reportedly one of the largest ever paid a baseball team in New England. The chief reason for all the expense and excitement was the coming of Babe Ruth,[17] which the *Rutland Herald* described as "probably the greatest baseball attraction ever brought into Vermont." Moneyed citizens could be found in Rutland because "The Vermont Marble company … combined the various Rutland marble interests into the world's largest marble industry."[18]

While Ruth was pocketing money on the road, back in Boston a certificate for the label and trademark for his company's cigar brand was officially registered. Alert as Ruth often was to money-making deals, the Babe Ruth Cigar Company was one of Ruth's investments and certainly an early (1917) example of attempting to cash in on his name.

After taking five days off, he traveled to Beverly, Massachusetts, where, according to a story in the *Beverly Evening Times*, more than 1,500 fans showed up for the game against Marblehead and saw Ruth homer. Game nine was played on October 11 in a former major league city, Troy, New York.

Ruth's tenth game of the 1919 post-season, on October 13, 1919, featured a contest between "Babe Ruth's American League Stars" and the "International League Stars" at Ebbets Field. The game was covered by the *Brooklyn Daily Eagle* in fine detail. For Ruth's game, the prices were raised to 55¢ for the bleachers; 85¢ for the grandstand; $1.10 for reserved seats and $1.65 for the box seats. The *Eagle's* coverage claimed that 1,100 fans "want to see Ruth … come up three or four times in each inning of a game. If he hits anything less than a home run he will be out." Even so, the crowd witnessed "a couple of baseball games really worthwhile…. Ruth ran himself into popular favor by racing from first to third on Stuffy McInnis' sacrifice bunt." The two games took an average time of 91 minutes to complete. The *Eagle* also took note that Ruth had pocketed $200 for the game in Lynn, Massachusetts, on October 3. The star had also been in negotiations with Putnam, Connecticut, to play there, but Ruth refused to play for less than $500. Putnam offered $300, and Ruth turned it down. He may simply have wanted some time off, his next appearance to be three days hence on October 17.

The area around Scranton, Pennsylvania, would see Ruth appear many times in his barnstorming career. This game, organized by attorney Leon Levy for the benefit of "Jewish War Sufferers," recruited other major leaguers. Ruth gave a batting exhibition before and after the game, and The Sirens Orchestra played during the game.

Whether or not Johnny Igoe, hired by Ruth in 1915, was involved with the 11 games played in early October remains unknown. Identified by Robert Creamer as "an agent of sorts, a Boston friend," and by Kal Wagenheim as "druggist-manager,"[19] the *New York Times,* chose to label him the "business manager" of Ruth on May 25, 1919. But his name again appeared after the Scranton game. "It is Igoe who arranged a postseason tour for Ruth that took him through the west and eventually to Los Angeles, where he appeared in exhibition games."[20]

Ruth, his wife Helen, and Johnny Igoe departed from Boston on October 24, 1919, and traveled 2,800 miles by rail to Los Angeles, where he was to be paid $500 per game plus expenses. The trip had four advantages for Ruth. First, he continued playing and earning where the weather would not turn ugly, or at least stay predictable, conditions not to be found in Rutland or Scranton. Second, on the way West, he could rest in his Pullman car for almost four days, changing trains only in Chicago. Third, the Hollywood district was firmly establishing itself the center of the motion picture industry, and there might be money to be made there too. Fourth, there winter baseball had existed in the California Winter League since 1879, even though the slate of games might not ever reach ten. But, at the same time, games could be scheduled outside of the league. (The Winter League was, in 1919, gaining momentum. By the next year, a team might play 40 games in a season and feature Negro League teams.) Listing six teams playing a 182-game season, the Pacific Coast League was contested at a high level, then in its 15th year of operation. Since no major baseball was situated west of St. Louis, the league became very popular in California, Oregon and Washington.

Even as Ruth was arriving from the East, two teams were forming that could play each other a few times. These two teams were named after their most dominant player: the Red Killefer All Stars and the Buck Weaver All Stars. (Weaver had just finished losing the 1919 World Series, with some White Sox, including Weaver, soon to be labeled the "Black Sox.")

Ed O'Malley, in the *Los Angeles Times,* wrote, "The world's champion hitter of all times in the diamond sport arrived here last evening [October 27] on the Santa Fe Limited, accompanied by Mrs. Ruth and his secretary."

From two games at the start of November, and from all of the others in California, money was out there for the taking. The size of the payday would, to a great extent, depend on Ruth's presence on the field. Almost 2,000 miles from the nearest major league city, baseball fans in California would want to see this newcomer who hit so many home runs.

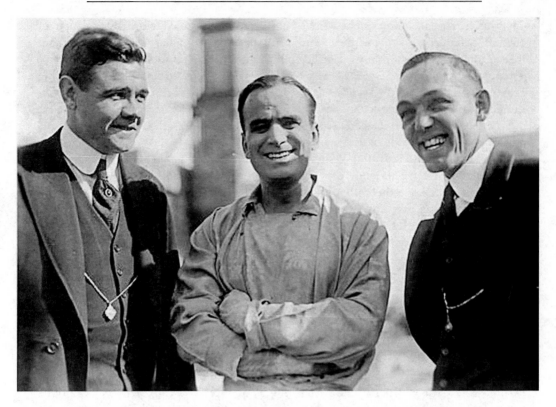

Left to right: **Ruth, Douglas Fairbanks and Buck Weaver, Los Angeles, 1919.**

Who would make money from the presence of Babe Ruth in California? Johnny Igoe would earn a percentage of his player's income. The promoter was in line for paydays. The players, umpires, and concessionaires would earn money. The people who printed and sold the scorecards would be in on it. Over and over, when Ruth came to town there were paydays for many people

The next day, Wednesday. October 28, the Ruth group visited the movie studios, and while there Ruth was approached to debut in a feature film for a promised $50,000 fee. Such a payday represented an amount several times his annual baseball salary. Ruth was receiving the kind of respect, in the form of economic value, that he soon came to expect and demand. In fact, ads in that day's *Los Angeles Times* stressed how wealthy a ball player Ruth remained: "First Appearance on Pacific Coast of Babe Ruth World's Greatest Home Run Hitter And Highest Priced Ball Player, The $20,000 King Of Sluggers, General Admission .50, Grand Stand, $1.00. Games Called 2:00 P.M."

The vast majority of these games' lineups was composed of past, present and future major league players. Certainly baseball enthusiasts would know these names and be eager to see them play together against such skilled opposition.

Continuing with a schedule that seemed to produce the most money, games 14 through 16 of 1919 were lined up on Saturday and Sunday. In fact, three games in two days in two cities caused Ruth's next stop to be San Francisco, where there were two Pacific Coast League teams in the area, the Oakland Oaks and San Francisco Seals. The two teams, of course, meant that they both had ballparks that could accommodate a goodly crowd of paying customers. The three games averaged about 5,000 customers each.

For Ruth's 17th barnstorming game, he traveled to Sacramento's Buffalo Park, named after the Buffalo Brewing Company. Even though the park was listed as seating 5,000, Ruth's presence filled it to 1,000 beyond capacity. He pleased the fans, making two hits, a double and a home run over the center field fence, in a 5–4 loss. Biographers Leigh Montville and Smith point out that Ruth continued to pocket $500 for each of the 17 games plus expenses for Ruth, wife Helen and business manager Igoe.

Ruth found out that people literally from coast (Portland, Maine) to coast (San Francisco)—not just in the eight major league cities—would pay him a great deal of money to see him perform. "On this trip to California, Babe Ruth discovered ... that he was a virtuoso performer who could amaze people in one moment with his tremendous power and make them laugh in the next instant with his natural comedic tendencies."[21]

But there was nothing comic in his determination to make more money from his Red Sox contract, more than the $9,000 he had agreed to be paid for the next two years. The very fact that he was daring to renegotiate a contract seemed to horrify many writers and most owners. It has always been part of the oddness of the attitudes of baseball people that players—actually employees or workers—ought to be satisfied with whatever their bosses decide on for a salary. The player ought to keep quiet about his salary and depend on the fairness of the owner. "The club owners feel that the salary question is one that involves only the player and his employer and that the players should refrain from making the issue public."[22]

The attitude on the part of fans seemed to have something to do with the mistaken idea that many fans have about baseball—that it is some sort of idyllic world to spend your time in the company of other highly skilled men playing a game, as if that fact alone ought to make you just happy to be playing for money at all. Athletes have been known to say that they would play for nothing, yet no one has met a professional player who has played for nothing.

But Ruth knew there was something special about 1919. Though most biographers think it unlikely that Ruth read anything in regular newspapers, it is likely that he might glance at *The Sporting News* headlines like this one: "In 1919 Estimated 6,000,000 Persons Attended Games in National and American Leagues. Most Prosperous Season. Money Rolls in." The prosperity was not a new thing either. The Detroit Tigers made $365,000 in profits over five years beginning in 1908; the St. Louis Browns profited by $168,000.[23]

One newspaper thought there was something wicked about Ruth's desire for more money, as he announced his demand for a raise of $11,000, when he had signed a three year contract for $9,000 per year. The *Oakland Tribune*, in its editorial page of November 14, 1919, thought that the $20,000 Ruth was demanding "would be bad for Ruth. It would destroy his moral vision.... If he does not get his $20,000 he can retire now and that might be a good thing for baseball."[24] It certainly might cause trouble for the owners. "Leaders Prepare To Combat Drive For More Pay; Babe Ruth Starts Idea," wrote one paper, while another reported "the magnates ... realize that the players know the owners prospered and know, too that the clubs anticipate a big season in 1920."[25]

Back and forth went the debate. "Babe Ruth's Trick Leaves Ugly Taste. Method of Boost in Salary in Vie of Effective Contract Smacks of Poor Judgment. Many Players Are Unappreciative [and do not] seem to consider the tremendous investment of the men who own the franchises," said the *Pittsburg Gazette Times* on November 2. Syndicated writer N. E. Brown saw the quandary from all angles:

Frazee cannot expect the other moguls to help him boycott Ruth if Ruth becomes obdurate.... The movies await Ruth. Two or three hundred thousand dollars await Babe for his first venture in that game. There are a half dozen other business venture which would bring in gold for Ruth because of his fame and popularity. To sum it all up, baseball needs the man more than the man needs baseball. And because the thing is this way Babe can ask anything short of the combined profits of the two leagues and get away with his request.

Still, there was money to be made yet in California. Perhaps not as much as with Weaver and the other stars, but a few paydays. Now halfway through December, Ruth signed on to "box an exhibition match with Jack Dempsey" for an orphan fund staged by the Knights of Columbus.[26] Three days later, on December 21, a baseball game for orphans was staged against the Dyas Stars. "In the name of sweet charity Babe Ruth tried in vain to Swat the pill over the fence but couldn't connect. Babe's team copped 4 to 1 in the game."[27] Ruth played first base in that game, teaming with the Meusel brothers. He finished his California baseball in a game at San Diego on December 28. Since it drew 3,500 fans, Ruth would be likely to be highly paid for that game. Jenkinson says, "During the off season months (until February) Babe had earned $15,000."[28] Later statements by Ruth suggest the money was spent quickly, no matter how much it was.

Playing many rounds of golf, often with Buck Weaver, Ruth enjoyed the warmth of the California winter as he awaited movement from Frazee. He and Weaver learned some useful things about the business of baseball. In the meantime, a typical headline might read, "Babe Ruth May Make World Tour; Babe Ruth, the Slugger, May Become Pugilist; May Stay with Movies. 'Babe' Ruth Will Quit Baseball Unless His Terms Are Met."

The noises from Ruth (and Igoe) became louder. Ruth remembered he had hit all those home runs in just 130 games, due to the shortened schedule that year. What might he do with more games?

9

New York City and Fans

By the time of Ruth's arrival in the winter of 1920, New York was becoming "the most commercially and culturally creative place on earth—committed as never before or since to the intoxicating dreams of capitalism and commerce."[1] Certainly many of the eight million people who occupied the metropolitan area, a 20.5 percent increase in population in a decade, had been drawn there to have their dreams fulfilled.

And the city seemed ready to keep the commerce that fueled those dreams moving at high speeds. After New York City's first subway system opened in Manhattan on October 27, 1904, and later extended into Brooklyn and Queens, workers could be transported at speeds between 25 and 45 miles per hour. The subway system carried five million passengers per day.

Since 1915, the Eighth Avenue line took customers to the Polo Grounds, but Yankee Stadium was built on the other side of the Harlem River, to the east and north.

In the nine years from 1920 to 1928, professional baseball looked to be centered in New York City, centered because either Brooklyn, the Giants or the Yankees won a league championship in every year except 1925. Since in those eight years Ruth's team dominated six of them, Ruth "thrived both personally and financially on the attention available in New York City, America's entertainment and media epicenter."[2]

The Stadium

Financially, team owner Ruppert's thriving was stilted since the paying public who came to the park provided almost the sole source of income for Ruppert's Yankees holdings. The contract between the Yankees and the Polo Grounds owner, the Giants, insured a disproportionately lesser amount of revenue going to the Yankees. On February 6, 1921, the Yankees issued a press release to announce the purchase of ten acres of property in the west Bronx for the erection of a new baseball facility "directly across the Harlem River from … the Polo Grounds, which they shared unhappily with the landlord Giants of the National League since 1913."[3] The land cost $675,000. The Yankees ledger showed that their 1920 profits equaled 55 percent of the parcel's price, or $374,079. This decision came out of necessity. "The Yankees … [being] tenants … did not have any non-baseball income earning ability," while paying annual rent of $55,000 "at first but increasing to $100,000 per year in 1921 and 1922."[4]

The stadium would be ready for games at the beginning of the 1923 season. By then the subway system reached four boroughs, while the ferry moved people onto Staten

Island, and railroad moved workers from the nearby states of Connecticut and New Jersey, as well from Long Island. Elevated station stops for the new ball park were finished as early as June 1917, and three stops were within a short walk of the stadium. This also meant that construction workers for the new Yankees park were able to travel to work easily.

The stadium was constructed on a site favored by baseball men more than once since 1890. Part of what made the building of the park appealing—in addition to the size of the market then present in the metropolitan area—was the decision by New York State in 1919 to allow admission-based baseball to be played on Sundays. (Massachusetts, home to two teams, and Pennsylvania, with three major league squads, did not alter their blue laws for ten years more.)

The three-million-dollar stadium had been planned for since 1915. A new stadium attracts crowds. Yet what does seem to be true as well is that many fans attracted to the park, begun at a time when the Yankees team had never even won a pennant, were drawn to it partly at least because of Ruth. Because of the crowds he drew, people made money: ticket scalpers, parking lot owners and attendants, retail stores in the area such as speakeasies, along with the stadium concessions owners and employees.

Fans

Ruth, and other players, showed the owners' seriousness about building a championship team. Some writers spoke about the fact that some people paid no attention to baseball or to Ruth. Some fans had only a passing interest in him. Some fans preferred the baseball of Cobb, the baseball built around bunts and steals, and might come to the game to see George Sisler. Ruppert seemed to be certain that Ruth was the key to the team's success, the filling of Ruppert's coffers, and the chance of the large stadium investment paying off.

Ruppert knew the drawing power of Ruth; he needed to extract the maximum amount of money from his investment, an amount that the new stadium would multiply. "People with no interest in baseball traveled hundreds of miles to get a glimpse of the Babe."[5]

The times had changed so that "The streetcar, the telegraphic news service, the regular and predictable hours of factory work, the boredom of occupations which, unlike farming, had no work-changing seasons—all inclined city people to watch professional athletes."[6] Some fans came to Ruppert's stadium to socialize with other fans. Some fans paid to gain entrance to the stadium to marvel at its size, like visiting the Woolworth Building. Some came to be amused and entertained. Some came because of a kind of envy for those in the baseball uniforms, fans who "realize that they would trade a great deal to step into one of the major league ballplayers' shoes for just one day."[7]

Some came to see Ruth hit a home run and to be able to say they saw Babe Ruth play.

Famously, Red Sox teammate Harry Hooper said in 1965 that in his opinion Ruth was "a man loved by more people and with an intensity of feeling that perhaps has never been equaled before or since."[8] Did Hooper mean a love that lasted beyond a baseball season or a baseball career? Hooper was in his 77th year; Ruth had been dead for 17 years. Hooper had lived in California, Ruth in New York.

If Hooper's evaluation is not hyperbole, why is it so? Though "loved" is a bit overboard, and though it is difficult to pin down the feelings of a myriad of fans, it is not so difficult to see how Ruth thought about his fans. He knew, for instance, that fans were interested in the production of home runs, and he "liked to show off his great strength."[9] In fact, near his life's end, ghostwriter Bob Considine had Ruth declare, "I always felt I had an obligation to my public."[10]

Certainly the most articulate of Ruth's teammates and one of the ones who had played with him on both the Red Sox and Yankees was Waite Hoyt. The pitcher (and later broadcaster) knew that part of Ruth's appeal was how uncomplicated the man seemed to be. "Never in Ruth's career was he tormented by conscience, or by the physical distress [he brought] to others.... In his philosophy [people] were all fine. Everybody was a 'good fellow.' but as for their reputations, their troubles, that was their business."[11] The result of this attitude, combined with Ruth's constant desire to keep moving, to keep traveling, must be a lack of friends. No teammate was invited to his wedding with Claire. Those who formed a circle around Ruth after baseball were mostly sportswriters, businessmen and lawyers. Ruth's granddaughter is blunt: "Babe didn't have a family per se. He had a father, but, really, he was abandoned. His family was his fans."[12]

In addition, as Hoyt said, Ruth possessed a "childish desire to be over virile," a virility that might seem very attractive to outsiders. Certainly newspapers emphasized his strength, his power, the height and distance of his home runs. While recognizing his teammate's "need for intimate affection and respect," Hoyt saw that Ruth traveled separately from the team, lodged separately and ate separately, mostly out of necessity. Otherwise, he would be continually bothered by his fans. When he had to be on stage with his fans close by, Ruth was genial, accommodating, and outgoing. He was a performer and knew it. If Ruth chose to live in a whirlwind, the choice led to "a life he didn't and couldn't take time to understand."[13] Applause meant a great deal to Ruth, and he went many, many places in search of it.

Even retired, he wanted to spend time on "a tour of the baseball camps," places where he would be comfortable, well known and accepted. This was March 1948, with fewer than six months to live. The visit would be in conjunction with "his job as consultant with American Legion junior baseball for the Ford Motor Company" the *New York Times*, reported. By accommodating every team and a major corporation, he was simply being Babe Ruth.

Amiability has a price and a cost.

10

New Team, New City
(1920)

There were three urgent money needs for four baseball men at the end of 1919. Ruth needed to get out of his Boston contract, so he might be paid the kind of money Ruth calculated he deserved. The two owners of the New York Yankees needed a star player and a productive outfielder to produce a winning team and thus raise attendance and receipts. Harry Frazee, the Red Sox owner, was in desperate need of cash for his theatrical projects and for his Red Sox debts.

By the end of 1919, Ruth tried many strategies to force Frazee to pay him what he wanted, what he felt he had earned. As his support, Ruth could remind the Red Sox owners that "All-Star Baseball Nine Picked by J. J. Corbett. Babe Ruth Most Valuable Man for All American Team" headlined many papers in late December 1919. In the *New York Times*, a headline said that Ruth did not like his contract owner, partly because "Frazee made him pay for wife's ticket at a big game in his honor."[1]

Back in July 1919, Ruth's teammate, pitcher Carl Mays, quit in the middle of a game and was later quoted as saying, "I'm convinced that it will be impossible for me to preserve my confidence in myself as a ballplayer and stay with the Red Sox as the team is now handled.... The entire team is up in the air and things have gone from bad to worse. The team cannot win with me pitching so I am getting out.... Maybe there will be a trade or a sale of my services."[2]

Frazee wanted some recompense for Mays' rebellion and tried to sell his services to the Yankees on July 29. He succeeded. By the next day, Frazee sold Mays' contract along with two others for $40,000. This case was almost the model for Ruth, as Mays' SABR biography explained:

> Several days before Mays was dealt, Johnson had privately suspended Mays and issued a secret order to all eight American League clubs prohibiting them from acquiring the pitcher until his suspension had been served. Johnson feared that Mays's actions could set a bad precedent for the league, by giving players the power to subvert the reserve clause and force trades simply by refusing to play for their clubs.[3]

Ban Johnson's efforts at collusion did not work, however, and the trade went through, the Yankees gaining a strong pitcher. Could Ruth also help to move a trade along? Eliot Asinof's musing on Buck Weaver helps.

> By the end of March [1920], ... Weaver ... knew the Yankees wanted him. Colonel Ruppert was spending a lot of dough building a club. Weaver ... recalled how, last fall, he had played exhibition ball with Babe Ruth, and Babe had never stopped complaining about the Boston Red Sox being a

lousy outfit. It was a way of getting Harry Frazee's goat, a technique Ruth had learned from Carl Mays.[4]

Ruth started making plans, figuring out how he could get himself transferred. The Yankees were certainly looking for more production from their outfield. Ping Bodie, Sammy Vick, and Duffy Lewis, the 1919 New York outfielders, had averaged only 58 RBI. When Ruth announced, "I am not stuck on the idea of going to New York. My heart is in Boston," the syndicated columnist Neal O'Hara, skeptical at hearing this, responded, "He means that's where his cigar factory is."[5]

As for the Yankees' owners, Ruppert and Huston, their ambitions quickly had become known. Even before the sale of the team franchise was made final at the end of 1914, Ruppert said he intended to spend millions on his own new ballpark; before long the land for the structure would cost $565,000 and the plant $2.5 million. It would seat 58,000, with the next largest park, Chicago's Comiskey, at 35,000. No doubt the New York owners were looking for players to help them with the financing of their plans, quality players who had fan appeal. In all their years, since 1903, the New York Americans had never won a pennant. A mediocre ball club, they finished the season in second place only twice while finishing last three times. In 1919, while finishing third, they counted 619,164 paid admissions. The pennant-winning White Sox drew 627,186. More than six million had paid admission to major league parks in 1919.

Was there money available to buy the contracts of other players? "A heavily invested real estate toomler as well as the head of the most powerful brewery in the world, 'Colonel' Ruppert's wealth kept increasing, making him one of the world's richest men with an estimated fortune of nearly $50 million."[6] Huston, the other team owner, had paid, in cash, $260,000 for his share of the team. (Huston would multiply his money by a factor of 5.7 from this investment.)

Frazee knew that his vending of Ruth might make him and the team unpopular in Boston. But there were precedents for the selling of star players. The Red Sox owner before Frazee sold star outfielder Tris Speaker for $50,000. There was another precedent—specifically the Philadelphia Athletics' Connie Mack selling players to save his franchise, such as the contract of star Eddie Collins to the White Sox for $50,000.

Frazee already had a cozy history with the Yankees, so much so that before very long he would trade to the Yankees his starting catcher, shortstop, third baseman and three more pitchers. The ease of these sales was assisted by the fact that for some time now, Frazee had been "a good friend of Yankees owners Colonel Jacob Ruppert and colonel Tillinghast l'Hommedieu Huston."[7] In fact, "Frazee and Huston were not only friends but Broadway drinking buddies."[8] The Yankees had already demonstrated their relationship with Frazee in the Carl Mays deal. Frazee, Ruppert, and Huston were "'as close as three fingers on the same hand.'"[9] How close? Once, At New York's Hotel Martinique, "Huston and…. Harry Frazee, [were] passed out cold, fully dressed, liquor bottles everywhere … not an uncommon sight where Messers. Huston and Frazee were concerned."[10] After all, the Frazee offices were in New York, not Boston; he kept his headquarters at 145 West 54th Street, just a short stroll, or a five-minute taxi ride, from the Yankees' offices at 30 East 42nd Street. "I believe that it was over a few glasses of beer that Huston first learned of Frazee's need and that if the amount was right he could obtain me for the Yankees," Ruth, or his ghost writer, said in 1948.[11] Later, in February 1920, Ruppert, Huston and Frazee would board a train together in New York to travel to league meetings in Chicago.

Just to protect and justify himself, Frazee began to disparage Ruth, complaining that "Ruth had simply become impossible and the Boston club could no longer put up with his eccentricities. While Ruth, without question, is the greatest hitter the game has ever seen, he is likewise one of the most selfish and inconsiderate men that ever wore a baseball uniform."

Frazee was even willing to say that it was Ruth's fault for the team's second-division finish in the league. "[T]here is no getting away from the fact that despite his 29 home runs, the Red Sox finished sixth last year," Frazee said. "What the Boston fans want, I take it, and what I want because they want it, is a winning team, rather than a one-man team that finishes in sixth place."

Frazee also called Ruth's home runs "more spectacular than useful."[12]

But Frazee had three real crises to deal with: first, he was primarily to his mind a theatrical person—a theater owner and a theatrical producer. Frazee could not afford to carry both his ball club and his theatrical productions. For example, after Frazee fell into financial difficulties, the Longacre Theatre at 220 West 48th Street, built by Frazee in 1913, changed hands many times before being sold to Astor Theatre Incorporated, a Shubert subsidiary, in 1919. As Dan Levitt points out, Frazee was then buying a theater in New York, the price of which is unknown but which had cost $500,000 to build.[13]

Second, he was looking at a demand for immediate payment of a debt he owed to previous Red Sox owner Joseph Lannin, money that had already come due in November of 1919. No small debt, Frazee owed more than $260,000. Part of this debt seems to have been connected to the ownership of Fenway Park. If Frazee did not pay Lannin, Frazee might not only lose the team's revenues, he might even lose ownership of a place to play his games.

The bargain trade for Ruth was signed in early January 1920. For Ruth's services, Ruppert and Huston paid $100,000—$25,000 down and then three installments of $25,000, and Ruppert agreed to personally lend Frazee $300,000 to be secured by a mortgage on Fenway Park. Would Ruth go along with this arrangement? In an e-mail, Professor Michael Haupert explained the finer details. "When the Yankees bought Ruth, the Red Sox agreed to pay 50 percent up to $5,000 of any salary increase for Ruth each year in 1920 and 1921, if the Yankees had to renegotiate Ruth's contract. The Yankees did increase Ruth's salary each of those years from $10,000 to $20,000. These were the last two years of the three year contract Ruth signed in 1919 with the Red Sox."

Creamer's take on the sale stated, "Technically, he would continue under his old contract—$10,000 a year for 1920 and 1921—but he would also receive an immediate bonus of $1,000 and $20,000 more ... in $250 lumps over the next two seasons."[14] And so "Ruth's good will was won over by ... a bonus arrangement," said the *New York Tribune* on January 7.

From Los Angeles, the *New York Times* reported that "Babe Ruth, the Colossus of Swat, has signed his name to a document agreeing to play with the Yankees next season. Manager Miller Huggins, went to Los Angeles to sign the player."[15] The cross-country trip by Huggins must be considered unusual, and for Ruth just one more indication of his pre-eminence in baseball. While he "agreed to the Yankees' terms, Ruth ... said ... that he wouldn't agree to anything until he got a slice of the money which had been paid to Frazee."[16]

Ruth got a slice too, an extra $5,000 paid for 1920 for exhibitions—probably the approximately seven intra-season exhibition games per year that most teams played—

along with $50 per home run.[17] To some, New Yorkers' spending patterns had long been known. An article as early as 1894 explained, "The liberality of the New York Club in spending money freely for star players has awakened the public from its lethargy and as a result the games at the Polo Grounds are patronized by vast crowds."[18]

In the next day's papers, Red Sox president Harry H. Frazee continued to rationalize the trade. To the *New York American,* Frazee said, "I sold Ruth for the best interests of the Boston club. The Babe was not an influence for good or for team play. He thought only of himself, whether the question was one of breaking contracts or of making long hits.... Ruth was sold for the good of the Red Sox."[19]

Chiming in to the *New York Times,* Frazee said he had sold Ruth to the New York Americans because he thought it was an "injustice" to keep him with the Red Sox, who "were fast becoming a one-man team. Mr. Frazee said he would use the money obtained from the New York Club for the purchase of other players and would try to develop the Red Sox into a winning team."[20] The *Journal* reported: "The Red Sox President said he felt certain the team never could have won a championship with Ruth as a member, but that he felt the team as it stood today without him and with certain prospective additions would be 25 percent stronger." The truth? "With the money from the Ruth sale Frazee could meet his immediate financial obligations but showed little interest in reinvesting in his ball club."[21]

Up until this contract sale, notable sales of the contracts of players included, in 1919, Arthur Nehf—$40,000; in 1915, Eddie Collins—$50,000; in 1914, Johnny Evers—$25,000; in 1913, Larry Chappell—$18,000. If you put all the money in the Ruth deal together, a sum is reached of $400,000. By contrast, Huston and Ruppert had paid $450,000 for the entire New York Yankees team at the end of 1914. The previous owners had bought the club for $18,000.[22]

When Harry Hooper, Ruth's Red Sox teammate, was traded to White Sox early in 1921, it became clear that owners, including Frazee, would continue to employ a player "until the player had been used up in their service."[23] At least Frazee might have included that in his thinking. Or, since Hooper had five productive years with his new team, the White Sox, Frazee just wanted the money for himself without caring much about the quality of his team.

It is of some interest to speculate about Frazee. If he was so intent on financing a show as alleged, he could have sold the team and made considerably more money than selling a player or two. The team had clearly been a success over the decade. But what to think? Did he enjoy being an owner and an impresario too much to give either up? Since he did not sell the team for almost six more years, it seemed he wanted to be both.

The writers contributed their take on the sale: the *Baltimore Sun* suggested, "If the owners are sincere in their desire to win a pennant, is no better illustrated than the purchase last week of the release of Babe Ruth by the New York Americans from the Boston club at what is believed to be a record price" The *New York Herald* considered the trade a sound investment due to Ruth's overall performance in 1919: "Ruth led the league's outfielder with only two errors in 258 chances, the league's leading left fielder in percentage. He also had 26 assists. Of his 139 hits, 75 were for extra bases." He scored 103 runs walked 101 times.[24]

Once again Babe Ruth showed his business acumen in his demand that he be treated as the important star that he was. That February, he went to Boston to demand the money from Frazee. In early February, the *New York Times* revealed Ruth's financial plans. Leaving

California, Ruth was determined. "Outfielder George H. (Babe) Ruth … said he would reach Boston Sunday night and would go to New York Tuesday to confer some more with Miller Huggins of the New York Americans." He had agreed mostly to the terms of the contract but had not yet signed. "Ruth insisted he would not sign a contract … until he receives a part of his purchase price."[25] Ruth asked for $15,000 of the purchase price."[26] When that did not work, he rode down to New York and at the Yankees office, Ruth asked Ruppert for $15,000 of the purchase price.

Concerning this demand, there existed a history that went back at least three decades. Deacon White, traded to the Pirates in 1889, told a Buffalo reporter: "No man sells my carcass unless I get half."[27] Then too, another Ruth teammate, Tris Speaker, got a part—$10,000 of the $55,000 deal—of the selling price when sold to Cleveland in 1916.[28]

Summing up and comparing, an article titled "Plutocratic Incomes Of Modern Athletes" noted

> The total cost of his [Ruth's] services will be $190,000 in two years, and the business men, Colonels Rupert and Huston, who are paying the money regard it as a sound investment…. When John McGraw, now an owner of the New York Giants, was the salaried manager he got $30,000 a year and, being a showman as well as a baseball man, was deemed well worth it to the box office…. Benny Leonard, lightweight champion of the world [counts an] income estimated at something like $120,000.[29]

In 1920, doctors at the top of their profession made $25,000 to $30,000. Not yet at the top? Graduates of the Harvard Medical School expected their peak earning to reach $4,680.[30] Physicians in Gettysburg, Pennsylvania, announced that they would raise their fees to "$2 for house calls, $1 for an office visit and $3 for calls between 8 in the evening and 8 in the morning."[31]

Ruth, now at the top of his profession, could claim a very high salary. "Fill the seats and fill your pockets. Be known as a bit player in 1920 and your mean player's salary was $5,000."[32] For those who did not fill seats, nor have such a profession, these salaries were being paid: salesmen with a college education were offered $65 per week; a typist $1,040 a year to start.

Endorsement offers began to arrive for Ruth. United News paid Ruth $1,000 a year with a bonus of $5 per homer if the slugger described the homer by telegram to Fred Ferguson. As Ruth signed for $10,000 from Home Run cigarettes, Ruppert and Huston paid premiums for a $150,000 life insurance policy on Ruth.

Just as baseball found itself transitioning from a game of singles to a game of power, a series of changes were put in place that could not fail to help Ruth's reputation as the premier power hitter. First, a change was made in credit for a home run. For some time, if a team was behind by one run and the batter hit a home run with two runners on base, once the runners scored, the game was declared over. So the batter might be given credit for only a single. Now the home run counted as a home run.

Baseballs began to be made with better quality yarn on a machine that wound the yarn more tightly than before. Bill James discounts this idea, writing that a "better quality of yarn was available after World War I, and this may have increased the resiliency of the balls, but that was incidental, and its effect was not dramatic."[33]

Third, dirty or scuffed baseballs were not to be kept in a game any longer. Baseball's justification for the change was the fatal head injury of Cleveland shortstop Ray Chapman by Yankees pitcher Carl Mays, which many blamed on Chapman's inability to see a worn, discolored ball as it sped toward his skull."[34] Whiter balls meant that they would be easier to see as they sped from the pitcher's hand. "The National League revealed a startling statistic by reporting the use of 27,924 baseballs during the 1920 season, which represented an increase of 10,248 over 1919."[35] By 1924, writes Harold Seymour, the number approached 55,000 baseballs.[36]

Fourth, another rule change for the 1920 season had a huge effect on hitting. It stated that the spitball and other unorthodox deliveries were outlawed, except for the few pitchers who were using those pitches and were currently major leaguers. The Joint Rules Committee voted to ban the use of all foreign substances (saliva, resin, talcum powder, paraffin) as well as any other alterations (sandpaper or emery) to pitched balls.

Quickly, the Yankees began to cash in on their new purchase. "The Yankees, with Babe Ruth as the headline attraction, are going to be billed through Florida like a circus. The Jacksonville Tourist and Convention Bureau … will launch an extensive advertising campaign to bring visitors to the city during the time that the two ball clubs are training there."[37]

Back home in the Polo Grounds (the Yankees were still three seasons away from having their own home field), fans each paid between $.55 and $2.20 admission. The accepted way of translating a 1920 price into today's money is to use the Consumer Price Index, which tells us that the multiplier for 1920 equals 12.2. So a $2.20 seat at the Polo Grounds in 1920 should cost $26.84 today. Ruth's $20,000 salary equaled $244,000 in 2014.

Ruth had truly become a money machine not only for his employers but for many, many other people and corporations for the rest of his life. And rapidly, too. In 1914, the A.P. introduced the teleprinter, which transmitted directly to printers over telegraph wires. Eventually a worldwide network of 60-word-per-minute teleprinter machines was built. "Thus in less than a minute from the time 'Babe' Ruth swats the ball a primitive bang, sending it over the fence for a home run, the entire American people is aware of the fact."[38]

Ruth began to settle in to his new home city, using the Ansonia Hotel's 11-room suite at 2109 Broadway and 73rd Street. The Ansonia was a fabulous luxury hotel featuring a maze of pneumatic tubing snaked through the walls, delivering messages in capsules between the staff and tenants. In the summer, freezing brine was pumped through steel flues in the walls that … kept the building at a uniform 70 degrees…. In the basement was the world's largest indoor pool … and Turkish baths.[39]

To travel 80 blocks uptown to the Polo Grounds, he bought himself a 12-cylinder Packard. There were few traffic lights at the time to slow him down. In New York, a new city for him to live in, Ruth "wanted to go to all the parties. Helen was a little girl, just not up to it," as Ruth's daughter Julia remembered.[40] If the parties included lots of alcohol, Ruth drank. If there were willing women, so much the better. On the road during the season, old teammates told writers, he would often use other players' rooms to have sex with women while his wife remained in another room in the same hotel. Ruth "had developed an attitude to match his celebrity, his uninhibited behavior from Boston now wrapped in a true sense of privilege. The rules for everyone else didn't matter," especially if you had all that money to provide the privilege.[41]

Ruth did not live a fantasy. He knew his gate appeal. "By early May we find him packing ballparks wherever he goes … gates locked—reserves called to handle the mob outside…. Vast crowds not only gather to see him play, but in addition these vast crowds frequently hiss and hoot the home pitcher for not giving Ruth the chance to hit the ball and beat the home club!"[42]

Such stories appeared particularly in Ruth's early Yankees years, stories like this one from early in 1920 in the *New York Times*: "Throng Of 38,600 At Polo Grounds; Crowd Shatters Attendance Record Made in 1911, and 10,000 Are Turned Away."[43]

On June 18, the day of the 57th game of the year, he was hitting .345 with just ten fewer homers than in all of 1919. In Washington in July, Ruth drew the largest crowd on record for that city. The power hitter made money not just for his employers but for every owner where he played. "Of the approximately 85 percent of revenues that came from gate receipts, about 65 percent came from the home gate and about 20 percent from the road gate."[44] He generated income for the road games for Ruppert and Huston and for the home team owners as well. Everyone connected with the games made money: the other team employees, the rival team's workers, the public transportation systems to carry fans to the ballpark, the vendors in and outside the games. The increase in fans meant an increase in hiring and even an increase in salary for everyone involved.

Pitcher Walter Johnson understood the effect Ruth had. In 1920, the 32-year-old pitcher contemplated "Ruthmania," excerpted in *Literary Digest* for September 18, 1920.

> There was an odd angle to the Memorial Day games which illustrate what a curious sport baseball really is. In the first encounter, Duffy Lewis smashed a home run into the stands, which tied up the score. There was very little commotion. A minute later, Truck Hannah drove out another homer, which won the game. The excitement was nothing unusual. Then in the second game, Ruth hit his home run when the game is already won, and there is particularly nothing at stake, and the crowd gets so crazy with excitement, they are ready to tear up the stands. Strange, isn't it?

Perhaps the sight of big man Ruth with his large bat stirred fans. The *New York Times* headlined, "Ruth Swings a 54-Ounce Bat; All Others Weigh Under 45."[45] Tom Meany judged that the home run "was like the lethal knockout punch of Jack Dempsey … the broad, direct approach to victory, the shortcut so esteemed by Americans in sport and in business, in recreation and in war."[46]

More home runs. "A social session of the Knights of Columbus was held at the Polo Grounds yesterday afternoon, the lion of the occasion being Knight Babe Ruth, who entertained with his twenty-fifth home run of the season, a monster bang." Not just home runs either, because Ruth had recently hit in 19 straight games. The gifts kept coming, though the choice was odd. To a man who bought the biggest Packard, this present may confound some people.

The Knights of Columbus in Boston gave him diamond-studded cuff links in 1920; they had given him a diamond ring in 1919. The K of C's in Baltimore presented him with a diamond ring and a diamond studded watch fob. Ruth received dozens of these tokens every season, and he couldn't possibly keep them all.[47] The conspicuous consumption of the era apparently even applied to gifts for Ruth.

The fans kept buying tickets. "Yankees Play before 108,200 Fans in 5 Consecutive Days" Seven home games in five days drew 108,200 fans to the Polo Grounds in early June. Ticket sales alone in those five days could pay the salary of five Babe Ruths. In July in Chicago, certainly not a time to settle a pennant race, four games attracted 129,000.[48]

The numbers continued to pile up in support of Ruth's popularity. August began with "a crowd estimated at forty thousand, the largest which ever witnessed an American League game in Chicago, Greatest Gathering Ever Seen at Pennant Game Babe Ruth the Magnet. Fans Scale Ten-Foot Wall. It was a record breaking crowd for Chicago or any other place, outside of a world's series contest."[49] With the Yankees in second place and the White Sox in third, clearly, the home runs drew the crowds. On August 2, the *New*

York Times concluded, "Yankees Greatest Drawing Card in Baseball History." Extrapolating from Ruth's home run production, the paper predicted that "Ruth should go beyond the half century mark in circuit drives" before season's end.

Fame was yet another commodity Ruth turned into cash. Earlier, while in California, he signed on for a movie with a $15,000 advance, to be filmed in August. So each morning, at a point during the season, he drove up to Haverstraw, New York (about 25 miles each way), and Fort Lee, New Jersey, to film *Headin' Home*. Who else would he portray but Babe Ruth, from a script written by sportswriter Bugs Baer. Ruth began to be famous for his energy level, though one day during shooting, a wasp stung him on the right forearm, enough to slow him down. The wound became infected and had to be lanced. Ruth sat out six games nursing the injury.[50] Signed on to make $5,000 a week for ten weeks' work, the movie was finished but the company went bankrupt before Ruth cashed the check.

"In 1920 he received $500 for sitting at a prominent table in Edelweiss Gardens, Chicago, for two evenings and making a speech, the gist of which was, 'I haven't much to say and I hardly know how to say it, but I hope you all have a helluva good time.'"[51]

Even presidential candidates wanted Ruth. In 1920, when Republican Warren G. Harding sent an emissary to request Ruth's participation in his "front-porch campaign" for President, the ballplayer's first response was, "Hell, no, I'm a Democrat." His second response was in reaction to the offer of $4,000 if Ruth would join Harding at his home in Marion, Ohio. Sportswriter Fred "Lieb would get $1,000 for delivering Ruth to Harding's porch. Ruth bit, but was unable to find a time."[52]

"He has become a national curiosity," reported the *New York Times* as early as 1920, "and the sightseeing Pilgrims who daily flock into Manhattan are as anxious to rest eyes on him as they are to see the Woolworth Building."[53] But not everyone enjoyed Ruth's power game. "It may be a triumph of brawn over brain. It may suggest the dominance of mere brute strength over intelligence. It may show a preference for the cave man over the finished artist."[54] Even with his detractors, Ruth kept finding ways to make money. From the catalog of the A. L. Burt Company, the *New York Times,* edition of November 7, 1920, listed a book, *The Home Run King,* with the author named as Babe Ruth. (The use of that title "King" had appeared before but Ruth could already lay claim to the title belonging to him alone.)

Babe Ruth found himself such a powerful drawing card in 1920 that "he pulled 20,000 fans to Connie Mack's ball yard the last series of the season." The 20,000 fans who bought tickets to Shibe Park from September 27–29 represented 14 percent of year's total home attendance for the Athletics. Earlier that month, Ruth and the Yankees, who would finish third in the league that year, drew more than 25,000 to an exhibition game with the Pirates. Ruth was unmatched as a baseball gate attraction. Overnight he became a national baseball hero, idolized wherever he went. In that same month, a Cincinnati businessman wrote: "Ruth is now known all over the country if not the world. The opportunity to let the fans here see him 'in action' would be a treat and incidentally a financial success."[55]

Money was everywhere for Ruth. "There was one time in St. Louis," as Ernie Shore recalled, "We got into the locker room and someone handed Babe a pile of letters and he landed them to me to sort out. They were checks—one hundred and forty goddamned checks, anywhere from one dollar to five dollars. They were for his autograph. The fans figured he'd be sure to endorse something that meant money, and then they'd have his autograph."[56]

He made money for himself and his employers. The Yankees doubled their attendance of 1919, setting a league record of 1,289,422; the New York team would not surmount that number until 27 years later. All the sportswriters—save one or two—approved of him and praised his abilities. These writers did not mind at all being nice to Ruth, showing him in the best possible light. When Ruth decided to help out St. Mary's, which had been destroyed in a 1919 fire, he arranged to have the school band come with him on the last road trip of the season and generate $2,500 for the school.[57] A 1920 magazine called him "A New Hero Of The Great American Game" and began to invent a story that might make the public think kindly of Ruth. The story stated that Ruth once lived as a "waif on the streets of Baltimore," and yet his name was "on the tips of more tongues than any living American." Rags to riches, the American story. Not only was he generous, not only had he triumphed over adversity, the slugger remained "possessed of shrewd business sense as well as a sense of humor."[58]

If numbers do not lie, at season's end, the truth accumulated for Ruth: his 54 home runs totaled more than any team total but one; the runner-up to Ruth in home runs was George Sisler, 35 home runs behind.

It did not seem to make any difference who was pitching—"Ruth Has Hit 12 Homers off Left-Handers, 13 off Right," the *New York Times,* took note in mid–July.

As his celebrity grew, writers began to construct the narrative about his reputation that would be most pleasing to their audiences. Ruth's behavior as a child started to be sanitized. "No one should get the impression that he was incorrigible or a bad boy," an article insists.[59] The piece from *The Independent* called "Meet the American Idol" nominates Ruth as the new hero of the Horatio Alger school when it says "he is about as self-made as man can be."[60] The only photo in the article shows Ruth assisting his wife from a cab. What are we to make of this idol-making? It is hard to say, but easier to say that this sort of construction would go on for much of Ruth's career, hit some low spots in 1922 and 1925, intensify after the 1926 season and culminate in asserting Ruth to be the kind of god-like person who could heal terribly sick children.

This personal reputation, as well as his professional image as a person of power, or achievement, was being translated into cash, with much, much more cash to come. But first, Ruth needed to take care of his coverage of the World Series. That is, he needed to find someone to write the pieces for him, ghostwrite for him, even though Ruth had the byline. His choice was an odd one. Sidney Whipple, age 22 to Babe's 25 years, was not really a sports writer. Later, he gained some fame for covering the Lindbergh kidnapping and for reviewing drama. Presumably Ruth sat in the press box and watched Whipple type.

The true source of money for Ruth after the World Series was going to be more barnstorming. Advertised in the *New York Times* as a "Special Tour, Babe Ruth, Carl Mays Stars," the tour was promoted by Savage Enterprises, "Connie (Cornelius J.) Savage … [being] part of the sporting life in New York City."[61] Savage was also known for his promotion of a team called Jeff Tesreau's Bears, and Tesreau and Ruth would travel together in 1920, though not for every game.

The first game was lined up to be played in Springfield, Massachusetts. Ruth drove into the city in "his $15,000 Packard," wearing "his New York traveling uniform and a green golfing hat." Players in Ruth's time only rented their uniforms, and with the strongly corporate side of all aspects of the sport not yet in place, there was not yet any prohibition from exhibiting yourself in a major league uniform.

When Ruth flied out in his fifth time at bat, "youthful rooters … suddenly stormed the field ... swarmed in droves around to where Ruth was making his way back to the bench ... surrounded Ruth and hurrahed him.... Ruth good naturedly fought his way through the mob scene till he was helped out by the strong arm of the law," after the 3–1 win. Three thousand people attended the game that ended after just 97 minutes of play. This swarming by children would be repeated many, many times in barnstorming games, at times dangerously repeated.

Yet Ruth is always described as happy to be mobbed, grinning, and good-natured. Over and over again through the years, he seemed to delight in people's adoration of him, a mad kind of love. This affection alone goes a long way to explain not only why he barnstormed, but why he considered himself an entertainer, a person who pleases the public in return for their affection.

The next stop was the "Bell City," so-called because of its history of manufacturing innovative, spring-driven doorbells. To get to Bristol, Connecticut, a city of 20,000, required a drive of just 44 miles for Ruth. There he played at Muzzy Field, putting on quite a show. Many of the spectators who paid either a dollar or 25 cents for their tickets at Walsh and Holfelder's smoke shop doubted that Ruth could drive a ball out of the spacious ballpark, which measured 388 feet down the left-field line, 441 feet in center field and 322 down the right-field line. Babe hit four balls out in his batting practice demonstration.

The game itself, which matched the New Departure ball bearing semipro or company team vs. Poli's, was umpired by lightweight boxing champion Benny Leonard. The next day's game report began on the first page of the *Bristol Press* for October 4, 1920, and commented that "The Yankee star made a host of friends by the manner in which he attempted to please them." He played every position on the diamond except pitcher and hit two singles and two doubles in the 95-minute game.

Quickly an article appeared claiming that Ruth signed a contract calling for $35,000 for 15 games with the Tesreau Bears. Ruth, and a few Yankees—and Tesreau—were under contract for the game. A United Press story in the *Eugene Register-Guard* on July 14, 1962, related that Ruth insisted that year on a guarantee of $3,500 for weekdays, $5,000 for Saturdays, and $6,500 on Sundays.

Wagenheim's book says the gate receipts were kept in a cigar box. When attendance was low one weekday, the promoters had to take $600 from their own pockets to make up Ruth's agreed-on $3,500. But, to be fair, Ruth just grabbed the bigger bills in the cigar box, leaving the men $1,300 divided by the professionals Fred Hoffman, Carl Mays, and Wally Schang. Since Hoffman's Yankees salary was $2,250, his cut of $433 equaled almost 20 percent of a season of 154 games for one barnstorming game. We can understand why so many players would remember Ruth fondly.

Beginning in 1920, three different Negro leagues were established. The Negro National League was formed of teams from the Midwest, and the Negro Southern League included teams in Atlanta, Birmingham, Nashville, New Orleans, Memphis, and Montgomery. The Negro Eastern League did not come into being until 1923. Nevertheless, there remained in the Philadelphia area well-organized teams that Ruth could play against and make money with.

One of the reasons that attendance would be high for barnstorming games in the city was the segregation of Organized Baseball in specific and the racism in the country in general. In 1920, black men were lynched on an average of one every week. (The number was even higher in 1921.) In Philadelphia, black citizens decided, for example, not to have their newspapers cover the all-white World Series, as if it did not exist. But the Negro games received better coverage, particularly because the teams were examples of successful black-owned businesses. Early in October a white team made up mostly of Athletics, including Pep Young, Jimmie Dykes and Joe Dugan, played the black Hilldale club and won, 2–1. The Athletics would not have played had the money not been acceptable.

Because the national black newspapers came out weekly, the reports sometimes tend to be confusing about exact dates. Game details were often limited to a few lines. Particularly noticeable is the absence of lineups, so narratives of some of these games must be simply best estimates. Ruth, it was rumored, was offered $5,500 for three consecutive games to be played in the city.

There appeared to be some optimism about attendance for the three barnstorming games that were played in Philadelphia, seeing that they all were scheduled in major league parks. For example, the *Baltimore Afro-American* of October 8 sets the date at October 6 in the American League's Shibe Park for Ruth's first Philadelphia game against a black team, the Atlantic City Bacharach Giants. Dick "Cannonball" Redding was player-manager of the 1920 club. Dick Lundy played shortstop. In 1920–1921, the club played briefly in the Cuban Winter League.

Playing again the next day, Ruth moved to Baker Bowl, the National League park, to meet the Hilldale team, who were based in Darby, Pennsylvania, west of Philadelphia. Star player Louis Santop was with them in 1920; in 2006, Santop was elected to the Baseball Hall of Fame. In this game, Pud Flourney, the Hilldale pitcher, not only kept Babe Ruth from getting one of his famous home runs, but struck him out twice while throwing a three-hitter.

There are those who think that Ruth was given good pitches to hit in barnstorming. There may have been times like that, for show business purposes. But, said the *Hartford Courant*, as well as Ruth's performance so far in Philadelphia in 1920, the opposite seemed to be true. "Before the end of segregated baseball, an estimated 438 games were played between black and white teams. Black teams won 309. 'That's when we played the hardest,' one black player said. 'We wanted the public to know that we had just as much talent. Maybe even more.'"[62]

Little data came out of the October 8 game, again played at Baker Bowl against Hilldale. To add to the confusion, the *Chicago Defender* with a dateline of October 8, 1920, said Ruth's team faced Tesreau's before 12,000 fans in New York City on the same day.

An October 10 game was played at northern Manhattan's Dyckman Oval, a game that had been arranged between Ruth's squad and the Bronx Giants, a white semipro club. Since the Bronx Giants were not a first-rate club, they did not see much coverage in the New York City papers. Only those particularly ambitious semipro team owners, like Max Rosner of the Bushwicks, might slip some money to a newspaper writer to have his games mentioned. Ruth took a few days off after that game, during which he might have read World Series reports under his byline. "Ruth has not been seen at any of the games," making him "apparently as good a long distance reporter as long distance hitter."[63]

Then, with Mrs. Ruth, he likely boarded a New York Central train for games in upstate New York. Then he traveled to a city, Oneonta, that listed fewer than 12,000 inhabitants. That same day as Ruth's 11th game, October 15, 1920, a subpoena was issued for gambler Arnold Rothstein concerning the 1919 Series. Later known as the Black Sox, players from the Chicago White Sox had conspired to lose games in the 1919 World Series.

The story would stay in the sport headlines for years to come. Ruth's opinions about the scandal cannot be found, although gambling had been and always will be one of the chief attractions of any game.

The Oneonta newspaper, the *Daily Star*, covered the game in detail, during which about 3,000 fans saw a lineup that featured Fred Hoffman and Lefty O'Doul, with Ruth at first base and in right field; Carl Mays, the pitcher, in left field; Jeff Tesreau in right field and at first base (a switch with Ruth). Retired spitballer Big Ed Walsh pitched three innings and gave up six hits and two runs.

The opposition was a team from Endicott-Johnson, near Binghamton, New York. "As Ruth came up to bat in the first frame, representatives of the local council Knights of Columbus walked to the plate bearing a silver tea set which they presented to the swat king; they also carried cigars for other members of the team."

Once three more games had been played, Ruth and his team caught a train to Medina. The village, about midway between Rochester and Niagara Falls but north of the main New York Central tracks, hosted Ruth's 14th game. Ruth hit 15 home runs in batting practice, leading the *Lockport Union Sun and Journal* to report that Ruth "gives one the impression that he could pull a tree up by the roots. In the sixth with one on, Ruth had a count of three and one. The next pitch was high over Ruth's head. Umpire Cleary called 'Strike Two.' He knew the crowd wouldn't stand for a pass as they wanted to see Ruth hit. On the next ball, Ruth lifted it with a sharp crack and it traveled clear beyond right field, scoring Mays ahead of him."

When the time came for money to exchange hands, "Medina paid $2,000 for the New York quartet yesterday, but ... the gate was $400 short of the amount." The blow may have been softened somewhat by the invitation to a banquet afterwards by the Medina K. of C.

After completing 19 games, Ruth traveled back to New York City in order to pack for his trip to Cuba on October 27 for 20 games with the New York Giants and its standouts. Since reports of these games have a number of things working against them, this trip will be mentioned only briefly. For one, some reports of these games are in Spanish. Second, they took place out of the country. Third, the reports may be of a game or two but not complete, including one story which both Jorge S. Figueredo and Manuel Márquez-Sterling later repeated.

The article, "Visita del 'Bambino' a Cuba," read,

> Igoe and Ruth asked for two thousand dollars a game and all expenses paid for three people, including wife Ruth.... A Japanese promoter offered to pay $40,000 for 10 games. After two conversations with John Igoe gave him $10,000 in cash upon signing the contract and a week later I sent another similar amount, and the three plane tickets. Ruth went on to play in ten of the 20 games the Giants took part in.

The Cuban games were played at Oriental Park, a ball field owned by the owner of the Giants, Charles Stoneham, and the manager of that team, John J. McGraw. The ball field was part of a complex that also "consisted of a race track, [and] gambling casino."[64]

Ruth's losses at the racetrack have often been reported, and he came home essentially broke about November 12. At about the same time Ruth's ship was docking, Ruppert hired Ed Barrow to be secretary and executive manager of the team. Ruth knew him as the field manager of the Red Sox in 1918 and 1919. Now called the team's general manager, Barrow would almost completely revamp the Yankees at least twice during Ruth's years with the team.

Coming to New York as business manager, a position now called "general manager," in mid–October 1920, Barrow knew the talent that remained on the roster of the Red Sox as clearly as he knew the way Frazee had decimated the team even as the Yankees with Ruth thrived. "In 1920, Boston drew a total of 402,445 fans to its home games; astonishingly, the Yankees accounted for 125,381 of these.... Looked at another way, Boston averaged 11,416 fans per game against New York; against the rest of the American League they averaged only 4,260."[65] Ruth might have thrown away his money, but he was a cash generator for the Yankees and for anyone who played the Yankees. And he knew it.

Wagenheim calculates that "Ruth earned a fantastic $90,000 during that fall tour, acting as his own business manager for most of it."[66] He remained so newsworthy that writer Sidney Whipple followed him and reported his activities every day. The praise for Ruth, and the cash that accompanied that praise, affected Ruth in expected ways, according to biographer Leigh Montville.

> He had developed an attitude to match his celebrity, his uninhibited behavior from Boston now wrapped in a true sense of privilege.... He often didn't even stay in the same hotel with the rest of the team, choosing to rent his own suite somewhere else for $100 per day.... On longer trips he had his own compartment on the train.... He was living the same life as his teammates, but on an entirely different plane. If there was any resentment about any of this, he never heard it.[67]

11

Train Travel

From 1914–1934—from spring training to at least October 1—and beyond, to even February 1 of the next year, Ruth lived in a hotel or on a train. In 1920, for example, just during the season, one "western" road trip would have him traveling 824 miles to Detroit (12 hours) in June and ending in St. Louis. By train, St. Louis to New York City would take 24 hours. A so-called western swing of ballparks might cover 2,500 miles or more in 17 days. On one of his last barnstorming tours, in 1928 when he was 33, during a tour that did not reach the West Coast, Ruth with Gehrig covered 4,600 miles on the way out and 1,800 miles to get home to New York from Denver.

This frenetic movement was not at all unusual for Ruth. He seemed to prefer constant movement. "He was a rootless man of the wardrobe-trunk culture," declares Smelser. "Like circus artists and touring actors, he lived his life in railroad cars and hotels, and it suited him well."[1] Part of the reason it "suited him well" was the comfort of his travels. During the season, the arrangements for regular season travel for the Yankees included two sleeper cars. The lower center berths accommodated eight regulars and four pitchers, with the upper berths being assigned to the rest of the squad. The 12 writers who traveled with the team were given their own, third car. The team manager had his own drawing room, as did the traveling secretary who had arranged the travel.

But as Montville points out, "Babe traveled in style, settled in his own drawing room where he could play records on his portable Victrola, or sing tunes to the accompaniment of his ukulele or even play the saxophone. He often relaxed in "his satin smoking jacket and slippers…. That didn't mean he stayed away from the noise in the rest of the Yankees' Pullman car. He would play cards, and he played a lot of bridge with Gehrig as his partner."[2]

During barnstorming trips, Ruth frequently traveled this way as well, depending on the length of the jump.

It is important to realize that the trains of about 100 years ago were constituted at a level of availability and luxury not since available to the ordinary American traveler. First of all were the quarter million miles of tracks that stretched out across the country in the 1920s, 100,000 more miles than in 2013. Amtrak brags of its new record for Fiscal Year 2011, saying it "carried nearly 30.2 million passengers" that year; in 1920, railroads in America carried 127 million passengers, on 9,000 inter-city trains.[3]

On board many long distance trains was "a stenographer, who will take down your important letters, typewrite them and see that they are mailed at the next stop; a barber-valet who will shave you, cut your hair, press your clothes while you sleep, prepare you a bath; maids who will serve you five o'clock tea." In 1925, the Broadway Limited of the

Pennsylvania Railroad publicized that it could take passengers from New York City, leaving at 2:55 p.m., and arrive in Chicago at 12:55 p.m. the next day. On board there was an "observation car, a club car, and a dining car." Services available on this train included "Stenographer, Barber, Valet, Maid, Manicure," and "as always, carnations were given to men and perfume and flowers to women boarding the train."[4] Before air conditioning, Pullman porters placed wet towels over open windows to keep out smoke and dirt. Each porter was furnished with a call card which listed the destination of each of his passengers and showed the time each wished to be awakened."[5] The porter was lectured on the correct way to wake his traveler gently.

Of the meals on board, the 1927 Pennsylvania Railroad dining car menu listed a Chicken salad sandwich for .50, Fried Chicken $1, Roast Loin of Pork .85, cup of soup .25, and a cup of coffee .15.

In other words, the train was a full-service hotel. Ruth, choosing hotels, always had two options. Choice one was the best and newest hotel, where he booked a suite. Choice two was to accept the free suite a hotel offered him for the privilege, and business move, of saying Ruth, like George Washington, had slept there.

Those free hotel stays sometimes came as he barnstormed, and it was the comfort and availability of good hotels and great trains that had something to do with how many times he went out on tour. More importantly, perhaps, was a publication of the times that made traveling on trains easy to schedule. *The Official Guide of the Railways and Steam Navigation Lines of the United States, Porto Rico, Canada, Mexico and Cuba* was printed from 1900 to 1973. The guide, crammed with timetables, also listed which trains would have diners, sleepers, all-male club cars, and lounges. Having that *Official Guide* in hand meant that Ruth or his travel manager could make the barnstorming travel arrangements. They could write a telegram on the train and have it sent from any station, a telegram identified, for example, by this signature: "Babe Ruth—Car 147."

Ruth could even order up a Pullman car. "Even tiny lineside communities received their own Pullman service via an innovation known as the 'set out' sleeper. Patrons could board or alight their Pullman car set out at their local station. Asleep in their berths … their car … was added to … a train."[6]

If communities had no train service, they might have interurban service. "The interurbans … ran far more frequently than the steam trains, for one car made a train. Once in town the cars usually operated through the streets and went right downtown."[7] Once in town, Ruth or his manager would often collect a fee from a hotel, including its services, like a barber to shave Ruth.

Until his first wife died and he married Claire, and even after, Ruth did live a "rootless" life, seemingly happily, moving from his hotel, to a hotel-like train, to a hotel at the next stop.

12

The Yankees, the Judge and the Agent (1921)

This was to be the year of the dollar for Ruth, Ruppert, the American League, and the new baseball commissioner, Judge Landis, on the job since November 1920. And profitability not just in baseball. One writer, Jim Waltzer, proclaimed the "Birth of Modern Promotion" when he wrote about the Dempsey vs. Carpentier fight in 1921, an attraction from which the two boxers and the promoter split one million dollars. The fight engrossed 300,000 radio listeners.

The profits, from Ruth, for Ruppert now seem clear. "Never before in the history of baseball and seldom in any other sport has arises such a colossus of wonderment and veneration as the big fence breaker ... the Yankees [have become] the greatest gate attraction ever known to baseball history."[1] This was high praise for the 1920 second-place team.

Since, as Seymour tells us, road receipts equaled 20 percent of the gate in the other seven cities, the books for the Yankees would show gross receipts at home of $864,829.77 (or 67 cents per ticket) and for the road at $273,176.37. The net profit for 1920 equaled $374,079. Yankees attendance at home totaled 25 percent of the attendance of the entire league.[2] Their average home attendance increased by almost 5,000 customers per game.

Exhibition games brought in $21,972.77. Some researchers believe Ruth was given 25 percent of the exhibition revenue, so that means he added almost another $5,000 to his salary. It is also thought he would be paid $50 for each home run. The range in the estimates, therefore, of Ruth's 1921 income from the Yankees alone ranged from $27,000 to $36,688.

Meanwhile, as Norman Macht writes, "In Chicago the Board of Review allowed the White Sox to classify players as merchandise."[3] Hugh Fullerton had something to say as well. "Baseball, America's national sport, has become more than that: it has become the third largest amusement enterprise in the United States. Last season, in which the sport enjoyed its greatest prosperity, professional clubs in 'organized' baseball played before more than twelve million spectators."[4] If Ruth demanded respect and money, he was asking for a reasonable piece of what he had generated.

The entertainment business, whether sports entertainment or not, wallowed in money, such as $1,250 a week paid to Rudolph Valentino.[5] Mabel Normand's salary had shot up to $4,000 a week by 1921. Even a minor movie actress such as Gaby Deslys might command $15,000 for appearing in one picture. Commissioner Landis' yearly salary was $50,000, while a minor leaguer like Goose Goslin in Class A, two levels below the major leagues, could count on $58 per month, but only for five months. Outside of baseball, some estimates say an average month's salary totaled $84.

Ruth had the advantage of having money arrive from both the team that held his contract and from many, many outside sources. If his employer, Colonel Ruppert, paid him about double the 1920 salary, he had generated much more revenue: "He has drawn more fans to the ball park in one year than any two teams have in two years."[6] Ruth's homers drew fans not just to the Polo Grounds, but to all the pre-season and intra-season exhibitions which Ruppert recognized. Team owner Ruppert understood Ruth's importance to his corporation. "'Babe' Ruth, the home run king, is insured in favor of his employers to an aggregate of $200,000."[7]

Ruth was not being paid in 1921—by the Yankees—from February 21 until April 12, though he was obliged by his contract to report for work for training. His contract read, "In order to enable the player to fit himself for the duties necessary under the terms of this contract, the club may require the player to report for practice at such places as the club may designate, and to participate in such exhibition contests as may be arranged by the club for a period of 30 days prior to the beginning of the playing season."

Luckily, Ruth had an entire press corps working for him. Typical enough was Grantland Rice, who often remarked on his friendship with Ruth. To Rice, Ruth at 26 "is still a kid, a good natured kid who is rarely inclined to sulk or lose his temper."[8] At one point in the season, Ruth's manager, Miller Huggins, the player's supposed antagonist, supposedly said, "You've got this country goofy, Babe."

Ruth's celebrity, combined with the fact that he espoused Roman Catholicism, showed up when fire decimated Ruth's old reformatory home. Catholic Cardinal Gibbons wrote on January 6, 1921, saying that St. Mary's needed to be rebuilt "as a national testimonial to Babe Ruth."[9]

That stature kept manufacturers knocking on Ruth's door, still in a very small way for the most part. The number of knocks had been curtailed by the absence of Johnny Igoe, still back in Boston. For example, the $100 contract Ruth signed in 1917 with Hillerich & Bradsby to have his name of their bats was not a great deal of money. Worse for Ruth, "the bats quickly were outdistancing the sale of any other bat."[10] There exists no evidence that he was being paid more as sales of his bats rose. Control of business dealings like this were needed.

Another problem arising from Ruth's fame was the unauthorized use of his name and likeness. The "Boyish Babe" cigar box featured an illustration of Ruth on its top. A slapdash movie of Ruth hitting called "Over the Fence" appeared in theaters, and Ruth tried to force an injunction against its showing, unsuccessfully, the court ruling that Ruth was a public figure. That suit over, the film makers put out another short called "Babe Ruth: How He Makes His Home Runs." Ruth, with a reputation for being indifferent to his money, did not seem here to be so blasé; he seemed very, very careful. But the tending to his money was slapdash, and without a watcher, Ruth would continue to have headaches, lawyer's fees, and lost income. There eventually came enough "promoters and schemers" to occupy all of his free time.

But then, as Ruth was leaving Pennsylvania Station for spring training (the story goes), he signed with Christy Walsh as his business agent. Ruth had been making $5 to describe to the Associated Press each home run he hit. Walsh promised him $500 for each. Walsh handed Ruth a check for $1,000 on Opening Day to seal the deal.[11] The February 21, 1921, letter on Walsh letterhead that read "Syndicating Sports Cartoons and Features" was an agreement calling for a 50/50 split on "gross receipts." Ruth would come to count on a great deal of cash coming his way from the Walsh office in room 800, 50 East 42nd Street, in New York.

Ruth, now managed by Walsh, who lived at 570 Seventh Avenue in New York City, would become much more important to Ruth in many ways in the next 15 years. Walsh's syndicate was the first public relations company to represent athletes. (There would not truly be another sports agent until Mark McCormack in 1960, when he signed golfers Arnold Palmer, Jack Nicklaus and Gary Player.) In an age of mass consumption, Walsh saw that stories of great deeds in sports were a commodity which he could mass-produce."[12] That mass consumption year, 1921, counted $676,986,710 spent in the United States on advertising.[13] The Yankees slugger would be a significant part of that expenditure. Walsh knew too how ubiquitous Ruth's name and image had become, even without the help of an agent. "In 1921 more journalistic words were devoted to Babe Ruth than had ever before been accorded an athlete."[14] Ruth's involvement with the Walsh enterprises put the player in the top 5.51 percent for average net income in the country. A full 64 percent of Americans earned under $5,000 in net income, with earners in New York State placing second in average net income at $3,847.

Contrast is needed to see the revolutionary aspect of Ruth's signing with Walsh. Some time before 1921, it was only an actor who had a press agent. The two major leagues did not have a public relations arm—called Service Bureaus—until 1932. It was not until 1935 that a major league team had its own press agent, St. Louis reporter Gene Karst.

This would be a good year for Ruth, in large part because for the first full year, the effect of two important rule changes were felt. First, the prohibition against the use of doctored balls allowed the hitters to be more relaxed at the plate, knowing that the pitchers would have better control of their own pitches. Next, immediately replacing misshapen and dirty balls with new balls, balls rounder and brighter, had the effect of making the balls easier to see and therefore to hit.

Ruth had superior skills to use these changes to his best advantage. Taken to Columbia University's psychological department, perhaps by Christy Walsh, but certainly with a friendly sportswriter in attendance as usual, Ruth was hooked up to various machines to test his visual acuity, muscular reaction time, and what is now called hand-eye coordination. The results published in *Popular Science Monthly*—but written by a sportswriter—stated that

> in attention and quickness of perception he rated one and a half times above the human average. That in intelligence, as demonstrated by the quickness and accuracy of understanding, he is approximately 10 percent above normal.... The scientific "ivory hunters" dissecting the "home-run king" discovered brain instead of bone, and showed how little mere luck, or even mere hitting strength, has to do with Ruth's phenomenal record.[15]

After spending some time in February in Hot Springs, Arkansas, Ruth and some others traveled to the Yankees' spring training site of Shreveport, Louisiana. Ruth's heroic stature and celebrity status brought him an even higher level of adoration. The *New York Times* reported that on March 11, "Babe Ruth is having many an honor showered upon him by the citizens of this town. Among other things, he has been loaned an automobile during his stay here, and he has been granted the unusual privilege of driving it without a license. Instead of the customary numbered license plate on the car, there is the sign inscribed 'Babe Ruth.'"[16]

The Yankees had become stronger by their usual route—buying from Harry Frazee. Pitcher Waite Hoyt would average almost 16 wins a year for ten years; Mike McNally will appear in 50 games a year for four years, and catcher Wally Schang would hit .297 in 529 games. Later that year, Frazee sold more front-line players to the Yankees.

Some suspicious minds looked at whether the ball itself had changed, so as to be more lively, an argument refuted early in the 1921 season. National League president John Heydler launched an investigation to see if the league was being sold some "'rabbit balls.' He concluded that the balls in use were the same as always, and that the changes were due to the abolition of the spitball and other freak deliveries, plus the example of Babe Ruth who had shown that it was possible to hit home runs with much greater consistency than was previously thought."[17]

For good luck, as it was thought of then, veteran mascot Eddie Bennett, a hunchback who had been paid to sit in the dugout with the White Sox and Dodgers, signed with the Yankees and stayed with them for many years as a ballboy. But many observers did not give credit to luck. Now in Ruth's first year of playing every day—he would accumulate 540 at-bats, his first time over 500—by midyear he reached a milestone that was noticed by the press. Since 1876, the accepted founding of the first major league, the career record for home runs was held by Roger Connor, who played in the major leagues from 1880–1897. Connor had come to bat 7,797 times in his career; Ruth had not yet reached 2,000 at-bats. Nevertheless on July 18, Ruth hit his 139th home run, making him the all-time leader in two and a half years as a full-time player.

Something else of importance to baseball, and many think to Ruth too, was announced on August 3, 1921, the day the players accused of fixing the World Series for gamblers were declared innocent by a jury in Chicago. However, on that same day, Commissioner Kenesaw Mountain Landis announced that he had banished the eight players from baseball for life, despite the acquittal. Gene Carney points to the popularity of Ruth: "Baseball survived the scandal and then came along Babe Ruth and suddenly baseball fans were hooked on the game again."[18] Other observers disagree with Ruth's influence. By 1924, Henry L Farrell, United Press Sports Editor, in his syndicated piece called "Some Wonder as to What Will Take Place Now," examined the debate. "Baseball was saved in that crisis not as much by Landis as it was by Babe Ruth who came along with a home run craze that turned conversation away from the scandal."[19]

Marshall Smelser's 1974 biography declared, "From 1910 to 1918 baseball attendance did not increase as rapidly as the population. From 1919 to 1930 attendance increased at a much greater rate than the population. Until we know of some other cause we may credit the Ruth Game for turning the figures around."[20] The *New York Times*, eager to be rid of the fixing scandal, published Irwin S. Cobb's piece on the World Series, concluding, "It should be written that 1921 has wiped the shield of our hemisperic pastime clean of the befouling smear which 1919 put upon it."[21]

"Regardless of the verdict of juries, what Landis decided to do" sent the "status of the Commissioner of Baseball skyrocketing. Landis was hailed as a hero, a savior, a mighty power for the forces of honesty and clean sport."[22]

Yet, to the common mind, the easy answer for the survival of baseball—and to some there was doubt about baseball's survival—names either Landis or Ruth. Why Ruth? With the passing of the years, it is now known what the causes of the fix were. There was the parsimony of White Sox team owner Charles Comiskey, which kept the salaries of his stars so low. "Shoeless" Joe Jackson earned $6,000 in 1919, Jackson who had been in the top ten in his league in almost every offensive category since 1911. The players wanted to make some money. They were angry at Comiskey and knew there was no redress for their grievances. So they met in secret and schemed their strategy on how the fix would work, and the gamblers put the fix money under pillows in hotel rooms.

Ruth, as eager for money as any of the Black Sox, had been paid $10,000 in the fix year, 1919, but his Boston team did not make it to the World Series. Ruth showed his cleverness to redress his own frustrations with owner Frazee by balking at contracts while having, at the same time, the knowledge of how much income from ticket sales he had created for his employer, and would continue to create.

But probably more important than anything else must be the way Babe Ruth's image had been constructed over the previous seven years. He was an innocent man-child—the nickname "Babe" never left him though he aged—incapable of scheming and working in secret. That he loved to play baseball had been made obvious to the most casual fan. That he was a creature of appetite, not cold intelligence, also became clear. The notation on his St. Mary's reformatory record—"free from guile and deceit of any kind"—had become evident over the years to his fans.

The establishment of the differences between the innocent Ruth and the conniving fixers was really unnecessary. The contrast stood out in bold relief. "If Landis was the image of its new purity, it was Babe Ruth who gave it excitement. In terms of dollars and cents—the measure of a magnate's mind—the great home-run slugger was worth a million."[23]

What was clear to see as well was the change coming over the sport of professional baseball. Up until Ruth's era, "Players won games by outwitting the other team and by trying to place their hits. They even practiced getting hit by pitched balls."[24] The highest paid star on many teams was the most accomplished starting pitcher. Before Ruth, the pitcher, standing alone in the center of the infield, remained the focus for the attention of the fans. Now Ruth, trotting around the bases, garnered both the attention and the cash rewards. Before Ruth, one-third of home runs had been the inside-the-park type. Exciting yes, but something different had happened when Ruth hit baseballs over the fence, home runs 29 or 59 times a season. Fans repeatedly saw the leisurely trot around the bases, Ruth accepting plaudits as his due, with straw hats often tossed onto the field in salute to this slugger's might. "[Ruth] liked to show off his great strength ... just to show off his gift, during batting practice Ruth used to hit balls into the lower right field deck of the Polo Grounds with one hand."[25] In fact, as Bill Jenkinson points out, Ruth behaved like "a trouper, the show must go on," seemingly as his motto.[26]

Before the 1921 World Series began, there was a benefit game for Christy Mathewson on September 30, 1921. Mathewson, 17 years in the major leagues, had been diagnosed with tuberculosis, and in fact had but four years to live. Mathewson's reputation stood as that of a Christian gentleman, and he was well-paid for his services to the Giants, averaging about $7,000 a year. Not unlike Ruth, but years before, "Mathewson was the toast of New York. Endorsement offers poured in, with Matty 'pitching' Arrow shirt collars, leg garters (for socks), undergarments, sweaters, athletic equipment, and numerous other products."[27] Yet, a benefit game was needed for him to have his disease treated. Such was the system in place in major league baseball for the benefit of the players the fans paid to watch.

"BABE RUTH"
WITCH-E BASE-BALL GAME
(PATENT PENDING)

MANUFACTURED BY
BALTIMORE NOVELTY CO., INC.
215 N. FREDERICK STREET
BALTIMORE, MD.

Above and opposite: Ruth's name and likeness were used to sell a vast array of products, from clothing to sporting goods to novelties to life insurance.

Praise for Ruth flowed from many sources as the season neared its end. The editors of the *1922 Spalding Guide* were willing to state, "The greatest individual record of the year, attracting more interest than anything that has heretofore occurred in Base Ball, was the performance of George H. Ruth." What had he accomplished in 1921? Ruth hit .378 with 204 hits and 59 home runs, 168 runs batted in and 177 runs scored. He was the league leader in six categories. He had hit 17 more home runs than the entire second-place Cleveland team. He had hit 35 more home runs than Ken Williams or his teammate Bob Meusel.

His performance had helped provide the New York Yankees' team owners with their first pennant since the franchise received approval as a member of the American League in 1903. The Yankees' pitching had led league in ERA, and the offense led in runs scored.

New York City, by now the king of American cities with a population of more than 5.5 million, would be central to its first World Series, a best-of-nine series played at one ballpark, the Polo Grounds, between the Yankees and the Giants. The mob of New York City sportswriters began looking for evidence of the vital importance of the games. First, of course, the money. "Many Tickets Reach Speculators' Hands; Lowest Price for Strip of Four Is $44." These tickets had been known to bring $22 for four. The *New York Times* continued, "$230,000 Bet On The Series." More numbers served: "For two hours yesterday afternoon Times Square was devoted exclusively to baseball. At least 13,000 persons ... watched the reproduction of the first world's series game on the *New York Times* miniature diamond, the Star Ball Player Board, operated by expert from a balcony on the north side of the *New York Times,* building."[28]

Radio began its coverage of the series in 1921 this way: a newspaper man would telephone from a box seat to station WJZ in Newark, "where Tommy Cowan repeated the information over the air."[29]

Once the money numbers had been printed, the fan aspect got some press. "By Midnight Nearly 100 Are Ready for Gates to Open." And "New York on the eve of the first of the world's series contests gave itself up to mounting baseball fever." The games seemed to be thought of not simply as baseball games, but as the event of the year: "Notable Throng To Witness Game; Leaders in Finance, Society, Politics, the Theatre and Sports." That statement not sounding quite important enough, the *New York Times* went on, "The city fairly seethed with the discussion of the relative merits of the Giants and Yankees. On the eve of the opening battle between these rivals of nineteen years' standing, arguments of all." And as the first game approached, "This is the morning of mornings for the seething citizenry of the expansive city of which Manhattan is the core."

Ignored as of no consequence is the fact that many millions in New York—and around the country—had no interest whatsoever in the games. But, as in any other industry, there existed a narrowness of vision and an exaltation of the importance of that industry. Baseball had many daily writers working for it, whereas, for example, switchboard operators did not. That many millions had no interest in or time for the games sounded impossible in the sporting press. That millions in other countries might find it absurd to call the October games a "World Series" instead of, as George Carlin says, "the North American professional baseball championship for men" seemed of little interest to the sportswriters of New York and elsewhere in the country. The champion was to be the first who won five games, and not the four wins used now.

The Yankees began well, shutting out the Giants in the first two games. The Giants won the next two games. Ruth had hit a home run in Game Four. In Game Five, a bunt single and three strikeouts appeared next to his name in the box score, his weak performance due in some part to having deeply cut his right elbow during Game Two, a cut which then abscessed. In the last three games he came to bat just once, and in the Series just 16 at-bats plus five walks. His team batted just .207 in these games, losing the Series.

Even with a weak performance against the Giants, even with bandages and limping, a preacher singled him out in June. Dr. Straton "laments ... the State of the World" had not the same preacher in the same sermon found "Bright Spots in Longer Skirts and in 'Babe' Ruth's Two Homers." Hadn't Ruth been formally crowned in the clubhouse after the Series, a $600, tall, silver crown that "fans will be permitted to pay for?"[30] Hadn't he fulfilled his contract of $2,000 for covering the Series, just part of the $15,000 newspapers had paid him during the year? Hadn't Harry Weber, manager of vaudeville artists, signed Ruth "to Hit Home-Run Laughs on Vaudeville Diamond at $3,000 a Week?"[31] Did he think that the *New York Times* was talking about him when it wrote "that 1921 has wiped the shield of our hemispheric pastime clean of the befouling smear which 1919 put upon it?"[32]

It is easy enough to understand how Ruth knew he was set apart from the rest of baseball. The adulation, the crown, the money that put in clear terms how important he had become were rewards Ruth had come to expect as his due.

Rewards might again come Ruth's way from barnstorming, an enterprise he arranged long before the Series began by once more signing contracts with tour manger Connie Savage for 11 games. As far as he knew from experience, Ruth had a lot of money to earn, and from past practice the worst punishment would be a fine. Even when Landis forbade Ruth from barnstorming in 1921, Ruth chose to ignore the threat. After all, Ruth's thinking, as fathomed by Smelser, was "The fine for breaking the rule would probably be no more than Ruth's World Series share and he could make that much in two days of exhibitions."[33]

But Landis had weapons behind his threat. First, "Rule Numbered 691, dated January 7, 1911," the decision of the National Commission which stated that the "victorious team [was] required to disband immediately after the [World] Series has been completed." Yet more than 200 post-season games had been played between 1910 and 1919, with 48 contested in 1920 alone. Some, writers as well as owners recognized that the rule was being regularly ignored.

The second weapon that Landis was given by the owners was his absolute power over anything in Organized Baseball, as demonstrated by his banning of the Black Sox. The barnstorming question had to do with money. Owners made no money from barnstorming.

Opposite: **Barnstorming promotion, 1921.**

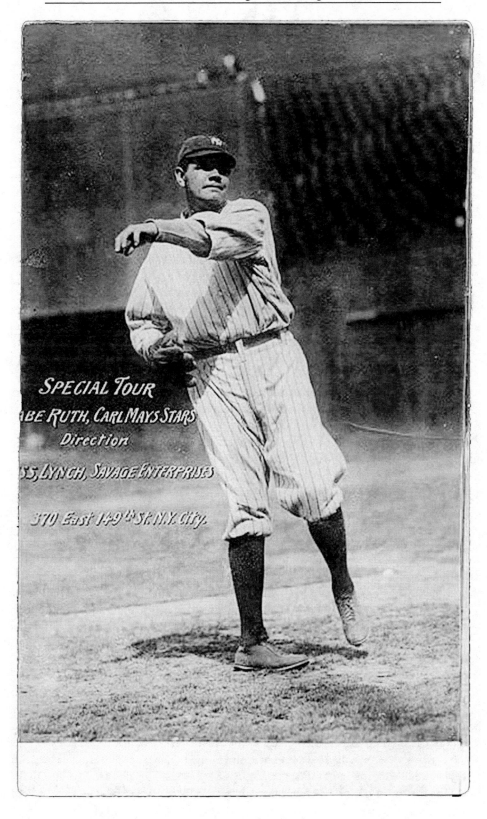

SPECIAL TOUR
ABE RUTH, CARL MAYS STARS
Direction
SS, LYNCH, SAVAGE ENTERPRISES
370 East 149th St. N.Y. City.

In addition, owners often claimed they feared barnstorming because players might be hurt playing on subpar fields. Of course, there had been many tours on subpar fields by now from which owners *had* made money.

Ruth did not like the totalitarian Landis. Many other players were furious that Landis overruled the Chicago court and took away the livelihoods of the Black Sox when the legal system had acquitted them.

Besides, by now Ruth seemed to feel little more than anger and contempt for almost anyone who told him what he could not do. Though some biographers think Ruth had not a shred of resentment about him, Ruth disliked Huggins, his field manager, because of his shortness. He also disliked Barrow, the general manager of the team, a man described as "a strict disciplinarian with an explosive temper, [who] ... even challenged Ruth to a fight once."[34] Even Landis' age annoyed Ruth. It was almost as if Landis searched for a fight with Ruth, the biggest name among players, to legitimize the extent of the commissioner's authority.

Never mind that the anti-barnstorming rule had as its genesis more to do with race than with any other aspect of the game. One worry of Landis went back to 1910 and the Philadelphia Athletics, World Series winners, who with the Chicago Cubs went on a barnstorming trip to Havana, Cuba. "To the dismay of [the] American League men, the Cubans proclaimed themselves 'champions of the world' whereupon the magnates passed the barnstorming rule which has been in effect ever since."[35]

Ban Johnson was quoted as saying, "We want no makeshift Club calling themselves the Athletics to go to Cuba to be beaten by colored teams."[36]

The papers jumped on what they quickly saw as an intense conflict—Ruth vs. Landis—red meat for them. "Players Threaten To Violate Rule" shouted the *New York Times*.

Ruth had his own point of view as well, declaring, "I am going through with it.... I don't see any reason why Judge Landis should pick on me and the rest of the fellows to enforce a rule which ... has never been enforced until this year."[37] Ruth thought that the Judge had tried to prevent him from fulfilling a series of legally binding contracts to barnstorm. So Ruth questioned three things about the rule.

First, why was it that others can play exhibition games and not be challenged by Landis? A winter league on the Pacific Coast featured players who were earning $10,000 for their work in that California Winter League and had a chance at $13,000 for just over ten weeks' work. Second, why should he *not* play. His New York contract itself said his obligation ended "on or about October 15," but who decides the ending date? Landis?

Third, why should World Series players be penalized for their success rather than being able to cash in on that success?

Landis' answer to Ruth's three questions encompassed three areas. First, "Commissioner Landis ... soon came to the rescue of those baseball executives who were tired of hearing about black players demonstrating their skills against major league players."[38]

The owners' point of view was partly stated, for example, in the *St. Louis Post-Dispatch* of October 18, 1921—"Ruth Case Viewed as Important Test Of Owners' Rights." Or at least so said the St. Louis Cardinals' executives. It remains important to see that it was *all* barnstorming that was objected to, not just touring by the World Series teams. No objections were raised when some barnstorming games were played from which the owners would be taking the profits, games such as the 1914 Connie Mack and Frank Bancroft tour that went out on the road, nor when in 1915 a series of 28 games between the

All Nationals and All Americans were played. Still, *The Sporting News* welcomed the authority of Commissioner Landis and his strictness.

The answer to Ruth's third question—and all of his questions—was really about money. "Some players were making more money from barnstorming than from playing in the World Series and the commissioner wanted to remove the temptation that they would not try as hard to win the pennant."[39]

Ruth was quoted in the *Buffalo News* of October 17. "It looks queer when a man who gets as baseball commissioner six times what a baseball player earns … attempts to reduce a player's income." Ruth let it be known that Huston and Ruppert offered "me a sum equivalent to my earnings" from barnstorming but averred that "I do not want to earn money I do not work for.… I want to earn money."[40]

As Ruth began his tour, he would feel Landis' authority before the very first game. Even as the four checked in to their Buffalo hotel, word reached them that the park they had booked had been forbidden them, by Commissioner Landis' fiat. With Buffalo's International League Park, where a team in Organized Baseball played, disallowed, they turned to Velodrome Park (also known as Legionnaire Park) to play the Polish Nationals. Later, Ruth told the press, "I look on this playing as for the good of the game as much as a benefit for my companions. I see no reason not to play, despite what Judge Landis' views may be." The use of the word "companions" and the balanced sentences of these words suggest they were written by Walsh.

In games in Buffalo, Elmira, Jamestown and Warren, Ruth was not drawing big crowds, largely due to bad weather for baseball. The pressure from Landis increased

Ad for barnstorming game in Jamestown.

almost daily. The team owners began to worry about the kind of punishment Landis was liable to impose on Ruth and how that punishment might adversely affect attendance and therefore receipts for all the American League. So as Ruth took trains 200 miles east and south to Scranton, Pennsylvania, Yankees co-owner Huston also came to that city. Ruppert and Huston had heard rumors that Ruth might be suspended for a full season.

Newspapers followed the Landis vs. Ruth controversy carefully. For example, "'Babe' Ruth Defies Landis" appeared in red ink above the masthead of the *Boston American* on October 17, 1921.

A crowd of 3,000 was on hand to watch Ruth at first base, Bob Meusel at shortstop, Bill Piercy at second base and Tom Sheehan pitching. Ruth's team lost, 8–6. Ruth doubled twice and singled. And that ended the tour.

The *Scranton Times* coverage concluded that Ruth gave up. "After a half hour's talk with Colonel T. L. Huston … in the Hotel Casey here early last evening…. It is believed that the New York Americans promised to pay whatever fine might be imposed by Judge Landis upon Ruth and the other players and also to pay them a price agreed upon in lieu of the profits they expected to gather from their remaining games."

The promoters for other contracted games were also paid off by Huston.

The *New York Times* reported on page 16, "Babe Ruth Repents; Quits Exhibitions; … Slugger To See Landis. Declares He Was Badly … Advised." The "badly advised part" is almost certainly Huston's words, since the *New York Times* report came directly from Huston once the co-owner returned to New York. "Badly advised" is language to help partly lessen Ruth's culpability, repeating once more the popular, child-like reputation of the star.

Ruth clearly refused to perform some act of obedience to Landis. The anti-barnstorming rule had just been enforced, as far as Ruth was concerned, to start a contest of authority between Landis and Ruth. Landis seemed to be the only person in all of baseball who thought barnstorming some terrible sin. So Ruth went off on a hunting trip and came back to New York City on October 27. Then he rehearsed his Keith Circuit vaudeville tour with straight man Wellington Cross. (Baseball players in vaudeville go back to at least the first years of the century, such as Cap Anson, and Ty Cobb, who starred in the play *College Widow*, for which theater patrons paid $2 each.[41]) Ruth's stage performances was billed as

BASEBALL

Athletic Park

FRIDAY, OCT. 21

George H.

"Babe" Ruth

And His All-Stars

Will play Scranton team of Inter-County League. Ruth will positively play in game. Contest starts at 3 P. M.

Ad for 1921 barnstorming game in Scranton, Pennsylvania.

"B. F. Keith's First Stage Appearance Of The World's Greatest Babe Ruth, the Bambino Himself and Wellington Cross in 'A Satirical Home Run.'"

Ruth did not go to see Landis. By November 10, fans could read about "Landis Waiting To Hear From Players; Offending Yankees Must Answer Questionnaire—Babe Ruth Mails Reply." Meantime, the vaudeville tour, arranged by Harry Weber, began in Boston on November 7, 1921, paying Ruth $3,000 per week (about the same amount in one week he made from the 1921 Series) and lasted from November to February (12 weeks). A press review of Ruth on stage was not flattering. "All lip-rouged like a tight-wire lady, with a voice as sweet as a furnace shaker in action, ... a grace of carriage somewhere between John Barrymore and an elephant."[42]

As for the continuing battle, the *Scranton Times*, not in its sports pages but in its editorial page on October 17, said, "It is a good thing for the game that Ruth has come to his senses and realizes that he is not bigger than organized baseball."

The text of the decision announced by Commissioner Landis, in early December thundered:

> There will be an order forfeiting their share of the World Series funds and suspending them until May 20, 1922, on which date, and within ten days thereafter, they will be eligible to apply for reinstatement.... These players ... willfully and defiantly ... violated the rule forbidding their participation in exhibition.... The situation involves not merely rule violation, but, rather, a mutinous defiance intended by the players to present the question: Which is the bigger, Base Ball or any individual in Base Ball?

"The mutinous defiance" cost Ruth $3,362 in World Series money plus, in 1922, 35 percent of his salary or $18,200, or nothing if the team kept its promise. Landis' "job was not merely to keep it honest but also to guarantee that the players were subject to the laws made by their masters. He did his job."[43]

That "mutinous defiance" language of Landis closely echoed *The Sporting News*: "The new attitude which considers above all else the general welfare of the game ... will make some players with Bolshevik tendencies hesitate in their hinted intentions of defiance of the rules ... who have arrogantly taken the stand that they are right and the rules are wrong."

The editorial staff of the *Chicago Tribune* suggested that Ruth's suspension was "merely justice to the hundreds of his associates in the game." Ever supportive of the magnates, newspapers demanded from the players "discipline," seeing a lack of discipline as the cause of "disintegration of loyalty to employer, teammates, and fans which produced the Black Sox."[44]

Were the rules wrong? The rules would be abolished in fewer than eight months. Were the rules "right" in the first place? But this quarrel was not a matter of law or morality; it was a matter of authority. Left out of all of this was the National Agreement of 1921, controlling the business of baseball. It mandated, "For violation by the player of any regulation the Club may impose a reasonable fine and deduct the amount thereof from the player's salary or may suspend the player without salary for a period not exceeding thirty days, or both, at the discretion of the Club."

But it was Landis, not The Club, imposing the penalty, and it was almost twice as long as the 30 days called for in the Agreement. The punishment was, in fact, illegal.

The Sporting News, as might be expected, stressed the money aspect of the suspension. The Landis ruling "deprived the whole American League circuit of a huge sum in gate receipts." Even so, the ruling must stand because "Ruth grossly insulted Commissioner

Landis in the Yankees' dressing room when told that he could not be granted permission to go barnstorming. Ruth openly violated the rules and then refused to send an apology." Ruth had to be made to "realize that he isn't bigger than the national game."

Ruth needed to be told who mattered in the entertainment industry of baseball. He played a child's game, a pastime; he was an entertainer, like a juggler or a clown. Baseball players in those days often were reduced to a juvenile status, as a method of controlling them, by not taking their demands seriously. Soon *The Sporting News* wrote, "Babe Ruth, as we know him, is a big spoiled boy ... simpl[e] and innocent as a child of six.... The spoiling that has been done by the men who should have taught the Bambino that discipline is the first lesson of the ball player, but who on the contrary gave the Babe the idea he didn't have to obey any rules."

The magnates may have made a mistake in their treatment of Ruth, but the magnates were serious men of business.

But the serious men of business did not seem to understand that if players were thought of as children, and treated like children, then the players would react to that treatment. Nine decades later, New York Jets receiver George Sauer, epitomized this complaint: "They know damn well that you were never given a chance to become responsible or self-disciplined. Even in the pros, you were told when to go to bed, when to turn your lights off, when to wake up, when to eat and what to eat. You even have to live and eat together like you were in a boys' camp."[45]

That Ruth was not only hurt by the suspension penalties, but according to the paper Ruth "will lose a $20,000 bonus for failing to break his home run record," somehow did not seem to be a business matter.

Landis and money? It was not until January 12, 1921, that Landis was installed in office. Landis, as eager for money as any barnstormer, insisted that he continue as a Federal judge as well, adding that $7,500 stipend to his baseball salary of $50,000. Why shouldn't Landis make a lot of money? He did not resign that judgeship until 13 months later.

The rightness or wrongness of the anti-barnstorming rule really was at stake here. "Landis knew" that by suspending Ruth the punishment would be enough to "dramatically strengthen his position as absolute boss of baseball."[46] Wagenheim notes that "there was a national uproar over Ruth's punishment. Fans sent petitions with thousands of signatures asking Landis to pardon the Babe. Ruppert and Huston, worrying about the financial consequences of Ruth's absence from the lineup."[47] Fans understood. Perhaps owners understood that they had erred in giving Landis so much power.

Prohibition now being enforced after the passage of the Volstead Act did not seem to hurt Ruppert's brewery business. His brewery made "near-beer," a concoction of beer that was below the Prohibition threshold of .05 percent alcohol, syrup and syrup by-products, as well as soda water bottling.

13

Ruth's Business Partner,
Christy Walsh

Christy Walsh espoused a flexible code of journalistic ethics and an equally flexible treatment of truth. In his thin book, *Adios to Ghosts*, Walsh admits, "a newspaper article, bearing the by-line of a baseball player and containing ideas or statements which have been written without his knowledge or approval, is deceitful to say the least…. I have never knowingly released copy that was 'fake.'" However, his next sentence says, "On the other hand, there have been emergencies where circumstances forced us to distribute a signed article that had neither been discussed with, nor approved by the author."[1] An "author," like Ruth, might be seated near a typewriter in the press box during a World Series, Walsh knowing the illusion was all. (Perhaps most telling of all the lies about Ruth are the failures to include Christy Walsh in any Ruth biographical movies.)

There was no suggestion that Ruth was recording the events of the game. Typewriters or telephones sat in front of his ghostwriters, journalists hired and paid by the Christy Walsh Syndicate. Walsh seemed to believe he was helping players out, explaining "Few baseball players have the time, the mechanical ability or the inclination to operate a typewriter."

The New Yorker decided in 1935, "Ghostwriting is ordinarily a kindly and harmless literary form."[2] To whom it was kind must have been Ruth, spared the distress of actually writing something, while being paid as much as $5,000 simply to lend his name. Kind, too, to the ghostwriters, glad of the kindness that flowed from a Walsh paycheck. (Walsh claimed that he had paid out over $100,000 to his syndicate members.) Harmless, too, these sportswriter lies, because they were written about players, about games.

Just as Walsh arranged lies in the service of commerce, so he created his own myths about himself and his own genesis, in his book, *Adios to Ghosts*. Many biographers have told a story of how Walsh signed Ruth to an agent contract. One biographer, Kal Wagenheim, tells how Walsh personified persistence and youthful optimism, writing that Ruth was pestered by a "young man" wanting to speak to the star. Walsh was then 35, Ruth nine years younger.

Making his attempts at speaking to Ruth, one writer made Walsh sound even more desperate, writing that in addition to his youth, Walsh was "an unemployed advertising man."[3]Wagenheim increases Walsh's admirable persistence by having him "camped on the doorstep of the Ansonia Hotel for days." Leigh Montville has a back-story to this, writing, "Walsh took out a $2,000 loan and journeyed to New York to meet his man."[4]

This picture was drawn by Walsh himself as published in a series of articles that

A sight-gag photo of a ghost writer taking dictation from Ruth.

began in the *Cleveland News* on September 21, 1937. Not much seems to be true about the story as it has been relayed over the years. In 1921, when Walsh went after Ruth's business, he was graduated from two colleges, one with a law degree, and had been employed in Detroit, Los Angeles and San Francisco as an advertising manager or director of publicity at various firms from 1915 to 1917, almost exclusively with automobile companies. He had picked up some money cartooning, but publicity was his main source of income.

A trade journal took note of his next career move, "Christy Walsh Joins Van Patten, Inc. Christy Walsh, editor of Punch, the publication of the Maxwell-Chalmers Automobile Company, Detroit, has resigned his position to go with Van Patten, Inc., New York."

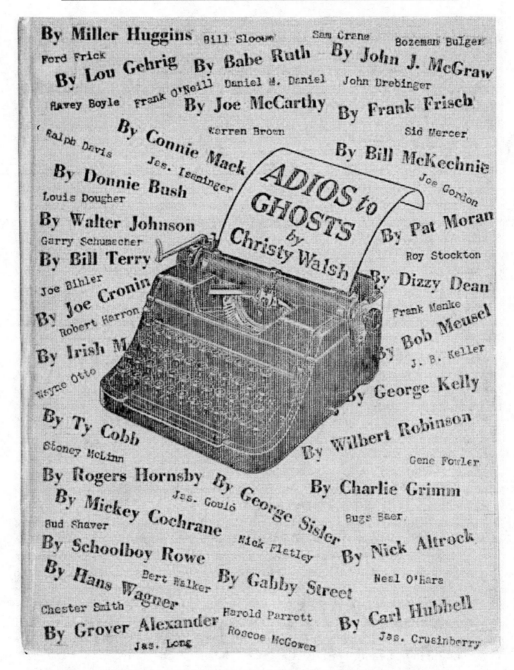

Cover of Walsh's autobiography with bylines from his syndicate's roster.

Walsh reported to the office of the advertising firm at 50 E. 42nd Street, New York City, on October 15, 1917.[5]

Still looking for extra money and because of his connection with automobiles, Walsh had come into contact with Eddie Rickenbacker, a race car driver before World War I, a pilot during that war, and an automobile executive later. Walsh and the wartime ace also made money with Walsh ghosting Rickenbacker, the pilot, as the referee-in-chief of the

1919 Indianapolis 500 race; 37 papers bought the piece, and seven others asked for more of the same. It is said that he and the former driver split $874. For Rickenbacker's experience in the war, Walsh contributed a series of articles distributed by the United Press in June of 1919, earning about $9,000. We also know that Walsh was still regularly employed with Van Patten, Inc., a job that "ended dramatically on St. Patrick's Day in 1921."[6] Walsh himself claimed that he had signed up four well-known people before Ruth.

Thus it is clear that Christy Walsh had many jobs prior to seeing Ruth, that he was not young, and that he was not broke, not only employed in publicity but continuing to make money with Rickenbacker. To add to his own image, he made gaining access to Ruth an act of his own cleverness, posing as a beer delivery boy.

Another sign of his quick thinking was the contract Ruth signed with Walsh. A copy of the contract with the baseball star exists and is dated February 21, 1921, calling for a 50/50 split on "gross receipts."

A month after Walsh got Ruth's signature—March 19, 1921—another trade journal, the *Fourth Estate*, headlined, "Christy Walsh Starts New Feature Service. A news feature syndicate has been started by Christy Walsh, well-known journalist and cartoonist, known as the Christy Walsh Syndicate. This concern already has for its contributors" some 13 celebrities including D. W. Griffith, Eddie Rickenbacker, Jack Kearns—Jack Dempsey's manager—and historian D. Hendrick Van Loon. Ruth's name appeared twice a week as the author of articles in 1921. It seems most unlikely that Walsh could sign seven others in the space between signing with Ruth on February 21 and March 19, so the agent's genesis story is but one more tale told in the service of commerce and image building.

Walsh's arrangement with these celebrities began mostly with ghostwriting. Ruth was no stranger to ghosted stories, certainly as early as June of 1920. "He had already 'written' several articles (including 'Why I Hate to Walk' ghosted by Westbrook Pegler)."[7] Late in the summer of 1920, the New York City firm A. L. Burt Company rushed out a children's book, *The Home-Run King; or, How Pep Pindar Won His Title*, its author identified by libraries as "'Babe' Ruth (George H. Ruth)."

In an article from 2009, Michael K. Bohn, the author of *Heroes and Ballyhoo*, looked at what Walsh had accomplished. He created the paradigm for the sports marketing industry by seizing on the idea of "Selling the Brand." Bohn traces the phenomenon this way: "It started out as first-person accounts of the game, and it got bigger, as Ruth endorsed cigarettes and cars…. It was sort of a new science, because public relations and advertising came of age in the '20s." With Walsh's six years' experience in publicity and with Rickenbacker, "Advertisers had long sought athletes and celebrities to endorse their products. Walsh figured out how to maximize that and leverage it and get more money out of it."[8] The more positive the image, the brand, the more money to be made from that image. "Walsh made his client a national icon of mythic proportions…. Walsh helped mold Ruth's public image as benefactor of the downtrodden and friend of children."[9]

This was entrepreneurship seen in a new light. It did not matter, as Smelser says, that Walsh thought of "his ghosted stories merely as pleasant illusions, not deceits…. It did not matter that those old essays seem full of slangy, false heartiness and empty of content. It was business not probity that came into play and so Walsh's conscience was clear because he looked on newspaper feature articles as entertainment only."[10]

Anyone who believed these stories about Ruth, a story like Ruth being an orphan or the Johnny Sylvester whopper, was too ready to believe, too gullible, too hungry for sentimental nonsense. Walsh was in the merchandise profession, and "it was a wholesale business of buying professional prose and distributing it … under the names of famous sports figures." After all, "Walsh proved that he could sell hack prose by the yard [which eventually employed] thirty four baseball writers … four of them for Ruth."[11] Walsh's book tries repeatedly to justify ghostwriting or to portray it as benign. Walsh liked to say he never tried to fool the public, always seeing to it that Ruth was never photographed in front of a typewriter. Yet within a year of signing Ruth, Walsh photographed the player seated in front of a typewriter for the *Boston Advertiser*, *Seattle Post-Intelligencer*, and *Tacoma News Tribune.*

Jules Tygiel notes, "Walsh combined the proper blend of honesty and chicanery that characterizes the best publicity men."[12] Walsh was a job creator and saved Ruth from being hounded by all kinds of people. What was wrong with that? Walsh, like later commentators, found that, "The engine of publicity … once that machine is running in high … evokes a kind of circular intoxication in which the excitement about the object is made more furious by fresh excitement about the excitement itself."[13] Helped along by the public's new-found appetite for tidbits about the lives of the famous, "at a time when the editors of most newspapers were reluctant to publish even something as inoffensive as the notice of an impending birth for fear of crossing the boundaries of good taste," along came Walter Winchell and others who filled newspapers with anecdotes "of who was romancing whom, who was cavorting with gangsters, who was ill or dying, who was suffering financial difficulties, which spouses were having affairs, which couples were about to divorce, and dozens of other secrets. He suddenly and single-handedly expanded the purview of American journalism forever."[14]

Ruth apparently gave his agent much latitude. Eventually, Walsh let it be known that "Babe Ruth has frequently let me use his signature to endorse various things."[15] Endorsing something usually meant that Ruth did nothing at all, but just waited for the checks from Walsh to arrive.

Walsh, like Ruth, came along at the right time. "Cash and Carry" Pyle had briefly represented football star Red Grange. With Ruth's star status and with the change in the public's sense of taste, Walsh was able to go in new directions. For example, in May of 1931, the Christy Walsh All-American Sports Subjects, 26 short films, were distributed by Universal. Even without movies, Walsh Syndicate members were assigned to be ghosts for such lesser publicized baseball players such as the Meusel brothers, George Sisler, George Kelly, Bill McKechnie, Schoolboy Rowe, and Donie Bush.[16]

Walsh took command of all of Ruth's moneymaking activities, emerging, in Dan Parker's words, as "the man behind the Bam, the man who relieves Babe of his burden of thinking." Walsh's burden as Syndicate head seems to have ended at 1937, though still, "In an age of mass consumption, Walsh saw that stories of great deeds in sports were a commodity which he could mass produce."[17] And others saw how profitable it was to be a publicity man in sports. Walsh effectively retired in 1937, at age 51, going on to live until 1955, outliving many of his clients.

The prime era for the sport agent did not arrive until 40 years after Ruth left the Braves. The first of the two historical figures in the profession was named Mark McCormack, who began working with golfers beginning in 1960. Second is the best-known baseball agent, Scott Boras beginning in the early 1980s. In 1975, the Sports Lawyers Association, which included agents in their membership, was established.

Walsh's name does not appear in the list of pallbearers at Ruth's funeral, and he seems not to have attended the service at all. Someone else would have to concoct a way to make money from that, and to put the best light on it.

What Walsh began has become ordinary, as ordinary as a home run.

14

Free to Be a Cartel
(1922)

In December, though Landis suspended Ruth for the first six weeks of the 1922 season, "the Yankees had earned so much money the previous season that they were able to acquire a number of other valuable players, many from the Red Sox."[1] These four players moved from Boston to New York: pitcher Joe Bush (three years with the Yankees and 62 wins); pitcher Sad Sam Jones (five years on the team with a record of 67–56); shortstop Everett Scott (431 hits in four years) and Joe Dugan, who stayed on for seven years at third base, accumulating 871 hits.

In late February of 1922, Ruth left for Hot Springs for the well-publicized benefits of those waters. He was permitted to stay with his teammates before and during spring training. Though Ruth lost $20,000 or more to Commissioner Landis, he had made more than that on the stage in 1921. A kind of balm in its way, but not enough to soothe Ruth as 1922 would prove.

As for Landis, as Ruth was entraining for Arkansas, in Chicago the Judge's problems only mounted up. Opposition to Landis arose, as the owners and players had time to think about what their granting of power to the new Commissioner might bring about. The owners had given Landis absolute power over thousands of players and even over much of what the magnates themselves would decide to do. Had the decision to hire Landis turned out well? Why had he been hired at all, since the idea of a National Commission of three men had served Organized Baseball since 1903?

The reasons ranged from the very practical to the merely speculative. One source suggested that he was hired because he was a Cubs fan, since a minority owner of the Cubs first put forth Landis. Others thought of his appearance; that is, he looked like a stern judge. Many, many think that he was being rewarded—one writer said "bribed"— because from the bench he had delayed ("taken under advisement") the antitrust case against the two major leagues by Baltimore of the old Federal League, a case was being adjudicated by the Supreme Court even while he was hired and had not yet been settled.

What kind of judge was he, anyway? The owners had hired Landis even though he had a long history of having his decisions reversed by higher courts. Landis got the commissioner's job before the baseball antitrust case was decided. In 1908, "the Circuit Court of Appeals completely eviscerates the decision of Judge Landis" and "severely censures the trial judge."[2] After Landis' harsh sentences for more than 100 International Workers of the World, "The United States Supreme Court eventually reversed the decision and disqualified Landis for 'prejudicial conduct before the trial.'"[3] Victor Luhrs, writing in

1966, simply says: "Most of Judge Landis' decisions were reversed not through technicalities but for blatant disregard of common justice and common sense."[4]

People in baseball, and fans too, attacked Landis. Ten thousand fans petitioned Landis not to suspend Ruth in 1922, spurred on by the Christy Walsh Syndicate, which mailed postcards campaigning to get Ruth re-instated for the 1922 season. Other players supported Ruth.

> Several of the [Washington American League] Nationals ... claim that the rule is unfair and cite that Ty Cobb right now is playing in California at a reputed salary of $12,500 and that Rogers Hornsby and George Sisler are drawing down $10,000, whereas Ruth as a participant in the World Series only drew $3,362 with not a chance of picking up any more through his diamond prowess.... One of them said "It don't pay to be on a pennant winning team."[5]

In the spring of 1922, player militancy grew. A new union attempt—the fourth such try—called the National Baseball Players Association of the United States, sought new rights and benefits for players. Included were pensions for "disabled and indigent players." But Landis "all too often equated labor union militancy with foreign radicalism and un–Americanism," and like so many other attempts at unionization, the Association failed.[6]

The Sporting News reacted to all of this turmoil, while keeping in mind what it called "rebellious players" and the threat to start a new league, with Ruth as the league's linchpin. "The World's Series receipts [$900,000] and signs of players in rebellion" could "lead to another baseball war." One way to quiet the players would be to "amend or rescind the 'barnstorming' rule."

There was a more significant pressure on Landis. Money pressure. On February 21, 1921, the U.S. House Judiciary Committee voted, 24 to 1, to endorse a full investigation of Landis. Senator N. B. Dial, of South Carolina, demanded Landis' impeachment for taking money—a salary that amounted to seven times his judge's salary—from a source other than from his judgeship. In October 1921, the American Bar Association issued an "unqualified condemnation" of his conduct for not doing his job as a judge. On February 18, 1922, Landis resigned his federal judgeship, 15 months after baseball owners hired him.

"Judge Landis is paid $50,000 a year for keeping professional baseball clean."[7] Baseball made clean, for a few weeks, of Babe Ruth, who had polluted the sport by insulting Landis. Clean of the Black Sox, though a court had said they were not guilty.

So Babe Ruth had been so bad for baseball that he needed to be publicly, and financially, attacked. But if he was the visible sinner, there were others ignored or treated far more leniently by Landis. The gambler Arnold Rothstein, who "had been identified as the financier of the [Black Sox] fix by the state's star witness," was never indicted.[8] Did Landis punish Rothstein? The gambler had interesting ties to baseball, other than in fixing games. Rothstein had relationships: with John McGraw in a New York pool hall; with Braves owner Emil Fuchs, who was Rothstein's attorney. In partnership with McGraw and Giants owner Charles Stoneham, Rothstein had "purchased Oriental Park, a race track in Havana, Cuba, along with the Jockey Club, a casino on the track's premises."[9] Landis ordered those properties to be sold, but by 1923 they had not been. And "when Stoneham prominently displayed Rothstein as his guest in the Polo Grounds in 1921— after the scandal, after Landis had taken office—Landis issued a reprimand.... When [Stoneham] was indicted for perjury and mail fraud ... the owners added Stoneham to the league board of directors.... Owners and players are not held to the same standard."[10]

Julius Fleischmann of the Reds owned racing stables. Frank Navin, who owned the

Tigers, remained a frequent visitor at the betting windows. John McGraw might have owned five percent of the Cubs for acting as a purchasing agent for the sale of the team. "Several club owners were either professional gamblers or openly kept company with gamblers. Baseball was far less innocent than its fans knew."[11]

Author Fred Stein sees dishonesty years before the Black Sox, "The major league baseball establishment largely ignored gambling problems." Players associated freely with gamblers, and some team owners were active gamblers, [including] William "Big Bill" Devery and Frank Farrell, who sold the Yankees to Ruppert and Huston. "Devery was an infamous corrupt cop and Farrell was a well known gambler sometimes accused of swindles. In fact, Devery would get payoffs from Farrell's gambling dens."[12]

How much of this Ruth knew or paid attention to is not known. After Ruth signed on March 6, 1922, for his demanded $1,000 for each week of the year, co-owner Huston, in the *New York Times*, "proudly announced that Ruth now earned a salary 'worthy of a railroad president.'" The same paper, on its editorial page, noted, "Babe Ruth with his bat attracts more American citizens than Toscanini ever did…. Ruth's salary was minuscule, of course, compared with the sixty-seven persons who reported incomes of $1 million or more that year."[13] Other salaries on the Yankees shrank by contrast. Home Run Baker was at $16,000; pitcher Waite Hoyt, $10,000; Fred Hoffman, reserve catcher, $3,000. "A man could live in a big frame house, own an automobile, raise a family and live comfortably on $75 or $80 per week."[14] The Governor of New York State received $10,000. But if the baseball salaries seem very high, no team has ever gone broke. While the reported profits may not always be made every year by every team, the ledgers of 1920s baseball teams were not open books.

Though clearly the $52,000 a year seemed an astronomical figure in those days, the *New York Times*, pointed out that he was "head and shoulders over the rest" and worth whatever he was paid. His value was shown by the fact that the ball club insured Ruth for $300,000 for nearly a decade.[15] So on Ruth's salary, the team expected to make money, the insurance agent who wrote the policy made money, the insurance company made money from the premium with the additional value of saying that someone of Ruth's stature chose it to do business with. The return to the Yankees—from home and road receipts—on the 1919 cost of purchasing Ruth's contract reached 363 percent in 1921. It would average 283 percent return in the six available years for study of the Yankees ledgers now at the Baseball Hall of Fame. The Yankees pre-tax profit for 1921 reached $339,984. That was Colonel Ruppert's money.[16] "Babe Ruth's … earnings on the stage and in the movies and through the use of his name over columns of baseball chatter may bring the total to" about $30,000 or $40,000 more…. Ethel Barrymore went into vaudeville for a while at $2,500 a week and was said to have touched the high mark on the vaudeville stage."[17]

New York Giants manager "John McGraw receives some $60,000 for managing the Giants," contrasted with "the half million paid to such movie players as Mary Pickford, Charlie Chaplin and Douglas Fairbanks. Even Will Hays gets $150,000 as a moving picture manager."[18] "Norma Talmadge's … salary … at present is several hundred thousand dollars a year. In addition to this, she owns her own company; and her percentages from the plays swell her income to a million dollars a year."[19]

Some part of Ruth's income was threatened, sort of, by a candy bar case. The fact, according to records, "is that when the Curtiss Candy Company of Chicago introduced the [Baby Ruth] candy bar, in 1921, it denied having named the nutty confection bar for

Babe Ruth."[20] Ruth challenged it, but lost. He did not lose his celebrity, however. In March 1922, appearing in newspapers was a "Photo show[ing] Pretty Miss Emlee Haddone having a miniature picture of Babe Ruth painted on her skin."[21]

Another far more important court case was ended, one that went back to March 29, 1916, when the Baltimore Federal League club's owners sued Organized Baseball. This case is often referred to as the antitrust decision on May 22, 1922. Supreme Court Justice Holmes ruled that professional baseball might be run as a business, but it was not "trade or commerce in the commonly accepted use of those words."

Baseball, from now on, would rule itself. The power of the professional baseball cartel was absolute. No matter what each owner decided about the salary of players, the players were left with two choices: first, accept the terms of the owner for salary amount and contract length; or, second, do not play professional baseball. More than that, "The baseball cartel has enabled owners to engage in collusion, price and wage fixing, and various restraints of trade ... thus maximizing their profits. It has also protected each franchise within a league from competition because the number of franchises is controlled by the team owners; no franchise is allowed to locate in a given territory without approval of the owners."[22]

The cartel had its own newspaper, *The Sporting News*, a paper controlled by the owners that would always take the owners' side against a player or a player group. "In the best interests of the game," of course. *Baseball Magazine* wrote of its rival: "Without ever mentioning *The Sporting News* or any other publication, the magazine's editor wrote in the July 1915 edition: 'Certain scurrilous writers [are] subsidized by organized baseball.'"[23] More researchers comment. "*The Sporting News* received a subsidy by Major League Baseball."[24] John Shiffert points to the owner of the weekly, J. G. Taylor Spink, writing that the family got a subsidy from Organized Baseball."[25] Stuart Knee declared "*The Sporting News*, the organ of baseball, is subsidized by the club owners."[26]

Baseball team owners now, and for a long time afterwards, as one author called them, were rightly labeled "Lords of the Realm." Ruth was not an owner, and the owners knew they could handle him, something they would demonstrate often in 1922.

As for owner Ruppert, on May 5 he saw construction begin on Yankee Stadium on 161st Street, construction thought of as far back as March 18, 1915. So, as it will turn out, the stadium will not be simply the "House the Ruth Built." It will be the "House that Ruth Paid For." In addition, the team served as an advertisement for Ruppert's beer. The recent (1919) change in New York state law permitting Sunday paid baseball no doubt helped Ruppert decide to commit $3,000,000 to the purchase of the land and for the massive structure. At the same time Ruppert would have to pay the New York Giants $100,000 per year until the stadium was finished, he would be making about a dollar for every ticket sold, on average. But he would not take in any money on concessions, advertising, etc. That belonged to the Giants' owners. "Baseball was never simply a sentimental pursuit for Ruppert. Immediately he turned around and sold ten percent of the club to Barrow, his business manager, for $350,000... Ruppert made at least $50,000 in instant profit on the transaction."[27]

Thus Ruppert paid out $225,000 in 1914 for half of the team and then expended $1,250,000 in June of 1923 buying out owner former co-owner Huston, a total expended by Ruppert of $1,425,000. On the credit side, Ruppert received $300,000 from Barrow, so now his investment equaled $1,125,000 for 90 percent of the Yankees franchise, a corporation worth over three million dollars at the time.

No matter how much money Ruth might earn in salary over the years, the sum does not approach these kind of figures. But, with Christy Walsh now making deals for him, in 1922 he signed contracts for the following:

> Babe Ruth Caps from Hirschberg & Company, New York
> Babe Ruth sweaters
> Elite Chicago Coated Baseball Co. (ice cream)
> The Manhattan Knitting Mills offering to retailers a free, signed Babe Ruth baseball bat given away for each ten dozen sweaters sold
> Booklets "How Babe Ruth Learned to Swat" and "Homeruns of Babe Ruth"
> "The Babe Ruth Base Ball Scorer"

Ruth could count on checks from endorsements of home appliances, milk, and kennels. That a maker of kitchen equipment could think that putting Babe Ruth's name in an ad with a picture of his stove made good business sense remains a marvel. Clearly having Ruth's name so much before the public always helped, whether what he did was approved of by the magnates and Judge Landis or not. A Minneapolis newspaper had a contest that challenged readers to match their wits against Ruth. Ruth's agents would later create an all-star team, and readers were called upon to create their own. The three entries that came closest to Ruth's stated picks were ranked and were given prizes of $25, $15, and $10. "With his unforgettable grin, Ruth was also one of the first people to rake in millions for advertising endorsements."[28] Ruth's name alone, or with his signature inside a cap or in a photograph smoking a cigar or appearing in the newsreels of the day had cash value. Ruth, even more so than in 1921, had become an industry generating cash for himself and countless others. Ruth knew his commercial worth, had a pay telephone put in next to his locker at the Polo Grounds, and "had an answering service made up of the other twenty-four Yankees who raced to answer the phone. Half the calls were from businessmen trying to force money on Ruth. The others were from unknown women."[29]

The phone, of course, would not be installed until he came back to the team. Until he did, it seemed, Ruth stayed furious. He knew he was right about the barnstorming trip and that the rightness was never questioned. What was questioned was his obedience to Organized Baseball. His anger would not take long to show itself. The year 1922 turned out to be a year of turmoil, arguably so much turmoil that his anger never again would reach this year's level.

Would his anger abate if he were flattered enough? In March 1922, the *Spalding Guide* pronounced, "There is no one with whom he can be compared, including all ballplayers of all time." Paul Adomites adds, "Only the president of the United States had his name in print more than Babe Ruth."[30] Harry W. Trout wrote a song, a two-step called simply "Babe Ruth." During spring training, while the team visited San Antonio, Texas, Ruth was presented with a silver bat and ball. The U.S. surveyed, citizens were asked to name the 12 Greatest Living Americans; Ruth's name appeared among the 12.

On May 20, the day he came back to play, at home plate Ruth was given "a silver loving cup filled with dirt collected from the diamond at St. Mary's ... a floral horseshoe from the National Vaudeville Association, and a silver bat from Harry Weber, his vaudeville agent."[31] Ruth had given national prominence to St. Mary's and had earned money for his theater agent. He accepted these gifts, all of them, even something silly at times, with graciousness and cooperation, though sometimes he would give a grin that said "I know this is dumb." Doing so led to more publicly presented gifts, which only added to his celebrity, which only raised the dollar value of his fame. "The idea that the Babe was superhuman—[was] promoted in word, song, and home run measurements everywhere now."[32]

He was no superman earlier in the month, having his tonsils and adenoids removed. But he was fit for play on May 20 after missing 39 games. The $20,000 Landis may have cost him still seemed to burn in him. Ruth recognized this anger. In Allan Wood's book on the 1918 Red Sox, Ruth told Heinie Wagner, "Sometimes I think that if it wasn't for baseball I'd be in the penitentiary or the cemetery. I have the same violent temper as my father and his older brother."[33]

Five days after returning, he was suspended when he threw dirt into the face of umpire George Hildebrand and then attacked someone in the stands. He was suspended again less than a month later for five days for threats made to umpire Bill Dinneen. Ruth tried to amend his ways but 1922 only got worse for him. On August 13, 1922, he was operated on for an abscess on the calf of his left leg. In September 2, he had another run-in with a fan, and was suspended again. All these suspensions were presumably without pay.

After all the drama about barnstorming in 1921, the Associated Press revealed that on July 27, the "American League Club owners, meeting here today, voted to remove the ban prohibiting players from participating in post-season exhibition games, provided they obtained the consent of the club President and then gained the permission of K. M. Landis, Baseball Commissioner." Two weeks later came another change. Now World Series participants could barnstorm but no more than three on one team.

Toward the end of the season, on September 23, 1922, Ruth's wife Helen appeared at the Polo Grounds with a baby in her arms. The little girl, Dorothy, was said to be 16 months old. Ruth stated that the child was born in February 1921, wife Helen said June, the month that does add up to the child being her announced age. Many decades later, Dorothy said her birth mother was Juanita Jennings, a California woman who had an affair with Ruth in 1920, but at the time the baby's appearance seemed mysterious. Few sportswriters displayed curiosity about the baby.

Ruth had been out of baseball four times in 1922, had two operations, and became a parent. That he had been productive at all demonstrates, at the least, his love for playing baseball. He was even willing to pitch an exhibition game in Buffalo, New York, on September 25.

Some few then would ponder his statistics, certainly acceptable to most players—he hit .315, with 35 home runs while driving in 96 runs—but the numbers showed a drop of 24 in home runs and in batting average by 63 points. "But as long as he continued to hit home runs and the Yankees continued to win the American League title … brushes with propriety only heightened Ruth's stature with the fans."[34]

While Ruth was not in the lineup, says Ken Sobol, attendance dropped by more than 50 percent.[35] Though the Yankees' attendance dropped more than 204,000 from 1921, they still sold more than one million tickets. The American League drew almost one million more fans than the National. His Yankees team won the pennant again, though just by a game, the team's stout overall batting average was .287.

The fans could hear about Ruth facing McGraw's Giants again in the World Series in 1922 through the rising popular medium of radio. "The opening game of the world's series, play by play, direct from the Polo Grounds [was listened to] yesterday by great crowds throughout the Eastern section of the country, about 5 million people."[36]

Those millions and millions more in the United States heard Ruth's final humiliation of the year. With his team losing the Series four games to none (one game was a tie)— the team's Series batting average sank to .203 and they ended being outhit, 50 to 32— Ruth did not rise to the occasion. He made just two hits in the five games, with one run scored and one batted in. This failure to produce is rarely mentioned.

Conclusion? "Opinion was almost unanimous that Ruth had reached the lowest ebb of his career," reported the *New York Times*, probably after being fed information from Ed Barrow that Ruth "will be severely disciplined not only for his feeble showing in the World Series but also for the various offenses during the playing season."[37]

His World Series losers' share added up to $2,842. (Had the team finished in second place, their checks would have read $700.)

So two days after the Series ended, Ruth, accepting the authority of Landis, called on the commissioner for permission to barnstorm. The *New York Times* speculated that Ruth might take home $1,000 for each game, now permissible, that was not one year previously. Ruth had made some changes in his business dealings and logistics. His wife would travel with him, perhaps to demonstrate some stability in his life, some maturity. He hired a man for the 17 games—probably E. C. Allison of Kansas City—to be the "manager of the stars on their western tour." Other names would pop up—Mrs. Ruth, Christy Walsh, Marshall Hunt—and Ruth hired teammate "Long" Bob Meusel alone to travel with him, saving money on lodging and rail fares. From October 13 to October 30, Ruth hoped to collect over $15,000.

Ruth and Meusel boarded a train on October 11, 1922, for a game at Perry, Iowa, where the guarantee stood at $600 plus the first $2,000 collected at the gate. The 1,125-mile train trip ended in Des Moines, where the two were met by the local American Legion officers for the 50-mile trip to Perry by car.

Readers of the local *Chief* saw the opinion that "no person in the country whose name is mentioned in print more often than Babe Ruth's and he is the hero of every red blooded American lad in the nation." In addition, "Many of the stores will be closed [and] the superintendent of schools has announced that pupils who bring requests from their parents will be excused for the afternoon."

Before the game, Ruth and Meusel, in their Yankees road uniforms, were photographed as they shook hands with newspapermen, held babies, were surrounded by school kids, and batted. Ruth played with the Perry semipros and Meusel with the Pella semipros. Ruth struck out, singled and tripled twice. Meusel hit a grand slam and singled. Perry won, 12–4. The players were given a banquet by the Knights of Columbus after the game at the Hotel Pattee. The two Yankees left town having had to settle for $1,055.

After stops in Lincoln and Omaha in Nebraska, the best evidence available suggests that the next scheduled game would be in Minneapolis, a major city. But once that big city game was not viable, what money still might be made? October 16 remained open, and October 17 required the players to appear in Sioux Falls, South Dakota. What other game could be scheduled? One offer arrived, perhaps by telegram from Omaha, that looked possible, though the town making the proffer claimed only 2,500 residents. And who had heard of Sleepy Eye, Minnesota?

Once they searched the *Official Guide Standard Time of the Railways*, they could opt to board a train on the Chicago, St. Paul, Minneapolis and Omaha Railway, leaving Omaha at 9:05 p.m., and arrive in Mankato, Minnesota, at 6:55 in the morning, nine hours and 300 miles later. This number 2 train, *The Omaha Limited*, had sleeping

accommodations. The party was met at Mankato and driven the 45 miles to Sleepy Eye, halfway between Minneapolis and Sioux Falls.

The local newspaper in the town of 2,500 expressed its excitement and civic pride. Living up to its reputation as a real live, wide-awake, progressive city, Sleepy Eye "secured Mr. Ruth and his great fellow teammate Bob Meusel at great expense to stop off here.... To see the Bambino lean against an offering and smack the old pill over the gun club will be some sight.[38]

As the date for the game approached, optimism remained high. "The advance sale of tickets has been very brisk and indications point to at least a 10,000 crowd with any kind of honorable weather."[39] But the weather was not honorable. When Ruth and Meusel arrived at 9:30 in Sleepy Eye on October 16, they were told the temperature had reached only 27 degrees and they were greeted by the first snow of the year. When the group made its way to the Berg Hotel, they were played to by the local band.

With some very rare coverage of any barnstorming game, Wagenheim writes,

> Ruth and he were looking out the window, says Marshall Hunt traveling to this game with them, when the town band arrived to serenade the visiting hero. "It was hailing as hard as I ever saw. The tuba player lost his hat somewhere along the line and the hailstones were beating down on his bald head and filling up his tuba, too. So every once in a while he'd have to turn the tuba up¬side down and get the ice out. Then right back at it. He was a very dedicated tuba player."[40]

That band, "At 1:30 o'clock tried to warm things up by playing some peppy selections, but ... the valves [on the instruments] kept freezing." Ruth and Meusel were huddled in heavy sweaters. "The cold weather on the day of the game brought that number down to around 700."[41] That crowd of 700 "braved the elements" to see Ruth pitch the sixth and final inning and retire the side in order.[42]

The game was over by five o'clock, and Meusel and Ruth went back to the Hotel Berg to warm up and bathe. At 6:30, they appeared on the second floor auditorium of St. Mary's school for a Knights of Columbus banquet. This event was followed by a dance at the Standard Opera House, after which Ruth, Mrs. Ruth, Bob Meusel and the tour manager entrained for Sioux Falls, probably with newspaperman Marshall Hunt still in tow. This game marked the first mention of Mrs. Ruth.

Game ten, six games later, proved to be another game against a Negro Leagues opponent. Bill Jenkinson, at the site Babe Ruth Central, records that "Ruth didn't seem to care that he endangered himself by playing against Black ballplayers, then venturing into territory under the influence of the Ku Klux Klan." When the black Kansas City Monarchs beat the white Kansas City Blues in five of six games, the victory caused Thomas Hickey, commissioner of the American Association, to ban American Association teams from playing Negro National League teams.[43]

Coverage by the *Kansas City Times* began, "Babe Ruth is a grand entertainer," but when the games were about to begin, 2000 fans sat in the rain and watched a five-minute hitting exhibition in which Ruth hit four balls over the fence.

One reason that the 13th game was played in Drumright, Oklahoma, then a city of 6,500, was that it produced three percent of all the world's oil, with more than 1,000 producing wells.[44] For a game this long ago and so far from any major league baseball, this particular meeting of three major leaguers had produced a number of works.

The rival pitcher for Ruth was the hometown hero, Chief Moses Yellowhorse, a

Opposite: **Game time at Sleepy Eye, Minnesota, October 1922.**

Pirates pitcher in 1921 and 1922. The local newspaper, the *Derrick*, said, "when Babe fanned … you'd be sure he was the rottenest baseball player in the United States from the way the crowd hooted him. It was a downright shame." Drumright lost to Shamrock, 7–5.

For what turned out to be the last game, the 17th, the largest city, Denver, played host at Merchants Park to a game between the Carl Milliken Whiz-Bangs, with Ruth, and the Denver Bears, with Meusel. Coming to bat five times and making a hit each time, Ruth stole a base and hit two home runs.

After attending but one more local Knights of Columbus banquet, he and Mrs. Ruth returned to New York. An Albuquerque, New Mexico, game was never played although originally scheduled. Upon arrival in New York on November 1, "Ruth discoursed sadly on the perils of barnstorming. 'It's not everything it's cracked up to be,' the Babe ruminated…. 'However, the weather was good and we got enough money out of it to make the trip worth our while'…. The Babe was received as a conquering hero, and the crowds were big."[45]

After the touring that was labeled "financially disappointing" by Creamer, some calculations were made.[46] Smelser says that Ruth grossed $17,000, but it was more likely in the $15,000 to $16,000 range. Meusel probably pocketed more than $14,000. So for the year, the money that is known—from barnstorming, salary (minus the suspension), Series coverage for papers and his World Series losers' share, Ruth added to his bank account by about $75,000.

The money remained one of the achievements of the year. But his professional life had suffered. He performed less than his usual throughout the year, at least by his own measurements. His home runs dropped by 24 and his batting average by 63 points. In the World Series, with a tie-ending Game Two, he had been embarrassed not only as a team member—the New York Giants took the championship in four games—but individually as well, hitting just .118. He had been suspended many times in the year as well. Even so, newspapers knew that tales of Ruthian heroism, kindness and selfless behavior sold more papers than car crashes, fights with managers, and attacks on fans and umpires.

He knew that, with Walsh's help, he had to make amends and helped the process by throwing a dinner for the local sportswriters, at the New York Elks Club on November 15, 1922. Just before the dinner, Ruth suffered another setback when handed court papers. The complaint accused Ruth of fathering Dolores Dixon's expected child and asked for $50,000 and costs. What awaited him at the dinner was not what he expected.

Here, yet again, are many versions of the speech by Democratic state senator Jimmy Walker. Robert Weintraub's book records the words this way: "Babe, a kid just stopped me on the street and asked me for a dime. He wanted to make it to a quarter and buy a Babe Ruth cap. Don't you think you owe something to that kid and others like him? … Will you not for the kids of America solemnly mend your ways?"[47]

Bob Allen has the better-known phrase in his recounting: "Babe, are you once again going to let down those dirty-faced kids in the streets of America?"[48] Wagenheim and Montville have fuller versions: Walker said,

> These men, your friends, know what you have done, even if you don't. But worst of all, worst of all, you have let down the kids of America. You have let them down! Everywhere in America, on every vacant lot where kids play baseball, and in the hospitals too, where crippled children dream of movement forever denied their thin and warped little bodies, they think of you, their hero, they look up to you…. The kids have seen their idol shattered and their dreams broken.[49]

Some biographies have Ruth sobbing at Walker's words and promising to do better, to live a less hedonistic life.

Because of Ruth's decline in 1922, the press treated him roughly. Walsh knew that a hero created by newspapers could be destroyed by newspapers. Taken together, the sports pages made up a kind of kangaroo court. Walsh and Helen pressed Babe into publicly throwing himself on the mercy of that court. It worked. Unlike the classic poets, who could only report mythology, Walsh could make a myth on purpose and call it history.

Before very long, "Ruth's public remorse made him everybody's wayward boy and everybody forgave him." They forgave him his wealth at a time when the poverty level for a family of three ranged from no more than $1,750. Perhaps they would be even more forgiving had they known that Ruth's Yankees employer's receipts totaled more than $990,000.[50]

15

Celebrity and Hero

"Many heroes lived before Agamemnon, but they are all unmourned, and relegated to oblivion, because they had no bard to sing their praises" (Horace, Carmina, IV. 9. 25).

We attribute heroic qualities to some people. We forgive them their faults because their high merits please us so much. For the followers of baseball, forgiven and forgotten are the seven failures at bat while celebrated are the three successes. Ignored are the many, many strikeouts, while celebrated are the baseballs that land over a fence. And, over time, living in memory are not the failures. For the modern media, there are rarely any failures. In the age of the video clip, there are only successes—spectacular successes: the last-second field goal, the slam dunk, the "walkoff" home run.

The ideas of achievement, fame, and celebrity changed in Ruth's time. In biographical articles that appeared in the *Saturday Evening Post* and *Colliers* from 1901 to 1914, 74 percent of the subjects came from traditional fields such as politics, business, and the professions. But from 1922 until 1941, over half came from the world of entertainment: sports figures like Babe Ruth and Joe Louis, and movie stars like Gloria Swanson and Charlie Chaplin.[1]

The name of Ruth appears here not simply because he was an excellent baseball player. In 1928, John Kieran of the *New York Times*, as a beat reporter, concluded his story on the World Series that year by pointing out that "being in what might be called a form of the amusement business, it was lucky for Ruth that he was born a great showman…. In triumph he rushed off the field as the alien fans roared full-throated admiration of the great deeds of the greatest ball player of all time."[2]

Others, like F. C. Lane, who had no taste for the slugging form of baseball, wrote, "There is little substance for Babe Ruth the myth of popular imagination in Babe Ruth the reality…. When there is so much pure metal unalloyed at hand, why must the public, in the mold of its own distorted imagination, cast a heroic figure with feet of clay?" But Lane had no stake in promoting Ruth since the writer was not in Christy Walsh's stable.

A born showman, Ruth allowed himself to be displayed to a greater extent than many famous people before him. So long as there was a reporter with a note pad or a camera with film in it, he was known to wear any hat, put on any outfit, show up at any place, and sit on any animal, for he and his agent, Christy Walsh, knew there was money to be made. Ruth was not a reluctant celebrity. Amiable and accessible, Ruth knew he made good copy and because he did, the press looked after him. Ruth soon learned that no one was really interested in him personally. "Ruth … became America's first significant star commodity," a status that he seemingly accepted so long as that status give him what he wanted.[3]

True, once he was gone, writers might comment on his excesses. "Ruth's boyish charm and voracious appetite for booze, cigars, food, gambling, and women," Robert F. Lewis wrote in 2010, "gave him celebrity status far beyond the foul lines."[4] In his study of fame, Leo Braudy observed, "The test of performance in sports, as in show business, had become not merely doing your best so much as whether you could take immense focus on you while you were doing."[5]

Ruth learned quickly as well that on a given day, if he permitted others to put him in the spotlight, that bright light need not last very long. He discovered ways of escaping the need for a Ruth story.

Hero

Ruth's place as a hero in society did not negate to many the fact that he remained an employee for whoever hired him to do a job, whether it was an underwear manufacturer or a brewery owner. The rise to hero began with his ability to hit a baseball a longer distance than anyone before him and to continue to do that all over the country. These hitting feats were simple to understand and easily measureable. All a fan had to do was count them. If the number rose to an unexpected level, attention might be paid to you. If these feats made you a lot of money, that too was easily demonstrated.

His off-the-field behavior always fit the hero too. He had sex with a dozen women in one night yet never caught venereal disease, and he never had a hangover no matter how much he drank. No matter how much he ate, or how unwell he might feel, a glass of bicarbonate of soda in the clubhouse cured it completely. Though Ruth did nothing to earn those qualities in his constitution, he was still admired for them.

In addition, Ruth had the good fortune to have a face—almost always described as a "moon face"—that seemed open, and his smile always seemed genuine. He had the gift of looking a little foolish when being posed with something foolish, like with a chicken, so he appeared smart enough to know he was doing something foolish.

Did this lack of self-importance endear him to people? Yes. Did the fact that in public he mostly appeared to be genuinely happy to come to the smallest town, to have the smallest crowd grant him affection? Yes. No one has ever denied that Ruth was a true devotee of playing baseball. There remains even a sense of thankfulness from the public for Ruth, a gratitude for someone happy in their midst. Like comics and comedians, audiences tend to be beholden to anyone who can amuse them for 60 or 90 minutes. That idea may sound odd, but it is the truth. The notion may speak oceans to the general drift of many people's lives: that someone has come to me for the sole purpose of making me smile, and I know I can never hope to repay the happiness I have been brought.

Soon, Ruth became so much of an American hero for hitting a baseball that he even approached the fame of Charles Lindbergh, himself a hero for flying an airplane by himself from Long Island to Paris in 33 and a half hours. That a major impetus for the flight was the winning of the Orteig Prize of $25,000 quickly was forgotten.

Yet somehow the thought nags. Bertolt Brecht has Galileo comment, "Unhappy is the land that needs a hero."[6] Jacques Ellul understands the function of a hero in the modern world, certainly the baseball hero's relationship to the fan. "The individual who is prevented by circumstances from becoming a real person, who can no longer express himself through personal thought or action, who finds his aspirations frustrated, projects onto the hero all he would wish to be…. He lives vicariously and experiences the athletic or amorous or military exploits of the god with whom he lives in spiritual symbiosis."[7]

Raised to a level beyond the ordinary by a media eager to feed the public what is assumed the public desires, the media also discovered that pages can be produced, paychecks can be made, by building or destroying a hero. It does not matter to the media machinery either way.

It may be true that the writers operating the machinery that grinds out the hero understand that it truly is those rarest of persons who do not act in their own self-interest, and that the line between celebrity and hero is only a matter of point of view. Or as Norman Mailer once commented, whoever holds the microphone and the amplifying equipment whether print or electric, controls the perceptions.

Happy Is the Hero

There are those who envy the hero, those hungry to find someone outside of themselves to admire. The assumption resides as well that the hero loves the attention and the adoration, and has found a happy way to live. The modern world, through the growth and influence of media, has given us many, many manufactured heroes. Produced and packaged, often by corporations, the image becomes the reality. But those famous ones being mass-produced need not believe their own publicity. For one, "Babe Ruth managed to separate his public image from his private life."[8]

Part of that private life that became evident was, interestingly enough, a part that was ignored in favor of the packaged Ruth. There is one word that jars when Ruth is studied, yet that word refers back to his childhood all the way up to the end of his life. The word he used to describe his feelings is "bitter." For different writers, writing of different aspects in different times of Ruth's life, the Ruth of good fellowship, of bonhomie, disappears briefly. That it disappears in print does not mean it disappeared in Ruth. But except for his vulgarity and his wives, little is known about Ruth's life outside of baseball.

Of his childhood, as he neared death, a clearly ghostwritten article in *Guideposts* magazine, a periodical "dedicated to providing hope, encouragement, and inspiration to millions," Ruth's words were, "I hated most of the people who had control over me and could punish me." He went on to say that somehow religion "helped relieve me of bitterness and rancor."[9] "Relieve" here becomes an interesting word whose meaning is slippery. Does it mean "set free" from bitterness? In the context, does the word mean "lessen"?

The word appears again when he had been a major league star for more than 15 years. The genial, charming, and agreeable public Ruth had been denied very little in his professional career. Able to generate copy and money for so many people, Ruth had found he could have most things he wanted outside of baseball, and certainly all things that were for sale that he wanted could be his with money that came his way because of his celebrity and playing skills. Even when he had lots of money and people knew he had lots of money, they insisted on giving him valuable things: diamonds, bonds, etc. But then he wanted something he could not buy. He wanted something he was sure he had earned, like money he had earned, a job managing in the major leagues.

In 1934, another side to Ruth emerged in his expectation of giving him his version of justice, of what he had earned, what he had become accustomed to. After the trip to

Japan, Ruth and family visited Europe. "What really seared 'the sad heart of Ruth' when … he stood on the corner of the Rue Royale and the Rue Rivoli in Paris was that nobody knew him…. This was a bitter blow because the Babe is a fellow who dotes on being hailed in a friendly and admiring way by citizens by any city, village or hamlet through which he happens to be passing."[10]

At the end of Ruth's brief association with the National Leagues Braves, the *New York Times* showed its awareness of the rancor between Ruth and team owner Emil Fuchs. "Babe Ruth, breaking off his comeback with the Boston Braves amid an outburst of bitterness after only three months of his three-year contract had elapsed, last night found his major league baseball future in doubt, if not entirely behind him."[11]

Much later in life, Ruth vividly remembered what he considered to be an injustice directed at him. "I wanted to stay in baseball more than I ever wanted anything in my life, but in 1935 there was no job for me, and that embittered me."[12] Blevins agrees: "He was always bitter about not being able to manage in the major leagues, a job he felt he had earned by being one of the game's greatest stars."[13] And while it is true that he was later offered "a token job as a coach—fan magnet or a managerial gig in the minors," he found that those positions weren't "satisfying and he remained bitter."[14]

In 1946, with new owners of the Yankees, one being Larry MacPhail, who had hired Ruth with the Dodgers in 1938, Ruth asked for the job of managing the Yankees' minor league team in Newark. Turned down after weeks of waiting to hear back, "Babe was now bitter against organized baseball."[15]

When Ruth died, the *New York Times* obituary summed up his post-baseball life, saying that the star "retired to a life of golf, fishing, bowling and public appearances." But the piece did not forget what so ate at Ruth: "There was scarcely room for real bitterness in the expansive and warm Ruthian temperament, but the big fellow undoubtedly did feel at times a resentment against the owners in major league baseball because no place in it ever was found for him."[16] As Robert Frost wrote, at about the same time as Ruth's career ended, "No memory of having starred/Atones for later disregard/Or keeps the end from being hard."

A study by the University of Sheffield in Britain, which cataloged what it said was a complete list of about 250 baseball-related statues in the United States and Canada, reveals that 90 percent of the statues have been erected since 1990, and more than half of those are less than ten years old. A statue for Ruth giving him a "place in baseball"? While it is true that there are two statues of him in Japan, one of which is in a zoo, there are two statues of Ruth in America.

Fifty years after Ruth's death, a statue of him was erected in the northwest corner of Camden Yards. The price of a game ticket will get a fan access to that one. To see his statue in Cooperstown costs $23 for a look. There is none in any other place in New York, including the House that he Built.

The Yankees three-man syndicate—one of whom refused to hire Ruth as Newark manager—put up plaque in center field at Yankee Stadium for Ruth in 1949 that asserts that Ruth was "A Great Ball Player, a Great Man, a Great American." This caption was the group work of the Baseball Writers Association.

16

Yankees Win
(1923)

What about the Red Sox, Ruth's former team? Not many of his teammates remained with the Boston team. By season's end, four regulars and all but one of the most-used pitchers were bought from Frazee's roster and added to the roster of the Yankees. Starting in 1923, one of them, newly traded pitcher Herb Pennock, would win 162 games with the Yankees.

How had the Boston fans reacted? The year Ruth was traded, 1920, 402,445 showed up for Red Sox games; in 1921, 128,000 fewer. By the end of the 1922 season, just 242,352 had showed up, 3,457 on average for each home game, while the Yankees were averaging more than 13,000.

Owners, traditionally, cried poverty when assigning salaries, a cry supported by *The Sporting News* and many newspapers. (Frankly, the claim of poverty seems impossible since no one had seen the ledgers for the teams except each team's owner.) In July 1923, Red Sox owner Harry Frazee decided to sell the team and concentrate on theater. Newer research shows that he had paid $400,000 for the Red Sox in 1916, mostly through promissory notes. Now Frazee was paid the sum of $1,500,000 for the team ownership.

Inside the Yankees' clubhouse, plans were concocted all the time for after-game fun. The times, after all, were labeled in the popular press as "The Roaring Twenties." Ruth did not cavort alone, though the number of his companions was small. Joe Dugan and Waite Hoyt—names Ruth might bother to remember—regularly challenged Babe Ruth in the roistering. (Dugan was nicknamed "Jumpin' Joe" for his habit of simply walking away from losing ball clubs for days and later demanding to be traded. No doubt he and Ruth both understood the value of rebellion against owners over money.) Those New York Yankees were described as a "hard drinking bunch" by Wagenheim; so much so, that a spy named Kelly was hired to befriend the Yankees, spy on them, and report back, most likely to Edward Barrow.[1] Perhaps Ruth was beginning to understand how futile his anger at management might be. In the 1920s, "Management, whether in baseball or more broadly, utilized a wide array of tactics to restrain employee power and therefore the benefits derived from it. The methods ranged from antiunion employer associations, blacklistings, firings, on-the-job harassment, 'yellow-dog' contracts, injunctions, industrial espionage."[2]

Once more Ruth, though now a father of an adopted child, traveled to Hot Springs, Arkansas, without his wife and daughter as he later would repeatedly. We know that Ruth was in Hot Springs because Marshall Hunt had been assigned to cover everything Ruth did, including Hot Springs in February. Hunt was hired by the *New York Daily News* to write about Ruth—and only him—365 days a year.[3] "Hunt became his 'shadow,' following him about, suggesting visits to hospitals and orphanages, and inventing newsworthy situations that resulted in exclusive features for the *Daily News*."[4] He was news if he sat for a haircut, played a round of golf, or was met downtown for lunch.

This level of celebrity coverage suggested a sizable change in the press. Sports coverage in leading papers of typical towns of 1890 was about ⅟₂₅ of the news. By 1923 it was one-sixth.[5] And printing that one-sixth were 18 dailies in New York City—Hearst's *Evening Journal* alone had a circulation of 600,000. Yet each one of the reporters refused to print reports of Ruth being anything beyond naughty, like an impish child. He was invaluable to sportswriters because he continually provided copy for them. In his celebrity, anything about Ruth was fit to print, fit so long as it merely showed Ruth as enjoying his fame— no matter how—being kind to children and orphans, and being always ready to be photographed or talked to. Part of his amiability with reporters was the trust between them. They might know he often went to whorehouses, but they would not say so, or say directly. Arthur Mann at the time called these visits both an "unusual social program" as well as "entertainment and parties." Why would they be more specific and truthful? Ruth helped them do their job, which paid them money, and they helped him to maintain his fame and good reputation, which made him money. Christy Walsh saw to it that he too would earn even more money and for his syndicate, Walsh signed Ty Cobb, Giants manager John McGraw, Rogers Hornsby, Honus Wagner, Walter Johnson and, in 1923, Ruth's manager, Miller Huggins. In Walsh's work with Knute Rockne, telegrams and letters found in the University of Notre Dame's library archives reveal that articles about Rockne praised Ruth and other Walsh clients, and photographs of Rockne often were taken with Walsh being sure that Ruth and other clients appeared in the picture. This kind of togetherness is probably now called "synergy."

Then came the episode with Dolores Dixon, suing for $50,000—suing for what exactly seems unclear (paternity, breach of promise?). The *New York Times* thought something suspicious about the suit when it said, "Lawyer admits attempt to Settle." It became clear that the suit was an extortion attempt and by April 27, District Attorney Pecora refused to prosecute the suit. Fame, though, does cost money in lawyers alone.

Ruth had already signed a three-year contract in 1922, so he would be paid $52,000 again in 1923. Second in wages to Ruth on the New York Yankees in 1923 was Frank "Home Run" Baker, at $16,000. In Hollywood, Buster Keaton was earning $2,700 per week, and Jackie Coogan, age nine, made $1,250 per week. And on April 2, 1923, Coogan was signed to receive 60 percent of the net from each picture.[6]

The loud news in New York's sports was the opening of the Yankee Stadium. To build the park cost $2.5 million; to purchase the land, $565,000. Since Ruth had arrived in 1920, the Yankees' after-tax profit had been $821,456. Another aspect was this: in 1922 the team took in $993,828 and made an after-tax profit of $270,875. So their return was 27 percent on their revenue.[7]

The age seemed to demand outlays of money on sport. With big-time sports money invested with the thought of big-time returns on that investment, soon followed the construction of the third Madison Square Garden in 1925, Boston Garden in 1928, and Chicago Stadium in 1929. New York Yankees tickets cost between 55¢ and $2.20 when they were tenants of the Polo Grounds, and Ruppert was paying an annual rent for use of that facility of $100,000. Having to rent meant two things: first, the Yankees' corporation was limited by the seating capacity of the Giants' ballpark, a capacity which numbered 34,000; Yankee Stadium would have 58,000 seats. (The next largest park was Chicago's Comiskey at 35,000.) Second, they were not paying any rent. Concession money would belong to Ruppert and the concessionaire, not the Giants.

Even before the first game, from the same article about the opening of the first modern baseball building to be called a stadium—a place where games are played—it seemed that the stands came first, where the paying customer might want to come first, and then the ball field came after. Before this facility, stands were built around the field. It is also important to point out two other things. First, "'The House That Ruth Built' was in part a house built for Ruth. The Stadium, with its relatively close right-field bleachers just 281 feet away (and only 296 feet down the line in left) was built to help pull hitters."[8] Second, the impetus for the construction went back to January 1, 1915, if not earlier, at the time of Ruppert's negotiations for the purchase of the Yankees, a date even before Ruth had played his first full season with the Red Sox.

The year 1923 would prove to show beginnings for Ruth as well. This year marked the complete adoration of Ruth by all but a very few sportswriters. He would be given every heroic quality from now until his time with the Yankees was over 11 years in the future, except for a very brief period in 1925. The day after the first game at the stadium, the *New York Times* reported that "Before the game he said he would give a year of his life if he could hit a home run in the first game in the new stadium. When the blow was struck, Ruth circled the bases [as] the biggest crowd in baseball history rose to its feet and let loose the biggest shout in baseball history."

The statement "would give a year of his life" is now accepted as fact, without any citation. Neither is the statement taken as hyperbole. Ruth may have really said that. But the fact that no other writer heard him say what he is supposed to have said ought to make researchers suspicious; that the report is an unsigned *New York Times* piece ought to add to the suspicion; that it is not a direct quote even more.

This would not be the first time that words were put into Babe Ruth's mouth. Certainly, the idea often repeated, that Ruth rose to the occasion or that he had a flair for the dramatic, was true sportswriter language. The press had already chosen to forget Ruth's mediocre performances in the two previous World Series. They would forget many times in the future as well.

But the supposed remark has not been forgotten. Not that it doesn't fit the characterization of Ruth as the same kind of performer as an actor on opening night. It would be the chore of sportswriters to write first for a paycheck, second to dazzle or at least entertain—otherwise a small or no paycheck—and last to inform. Included in these were the over-inflated attendance of 74,217 for Opening Day, since the park held 60,000.

To lead off the unsigned article and the remarkable change that had come about in the narratives about games, the *New York Times* said, "Governors, generals, colonels, politicians and baseball officials gathered together solemnly yesterday to dedicate the biggest stadium in baseball, but it was a ball player who did the real dedicating. In the third inning, with two team mates on the base lines, Babe Ruth smashed a savage home run into the right field bleachers, and that was the real baptism of the new Yankee Stadium."

The language is revelatory. What significant event would bring so many of the powerful to a game? Why are they "solemn"? How is it that a first baseball game is being "dedicated?" Perhaps the answer to these questions is answered in the language choices that follow. The sentence highlight the words "smashed" and "savage" followed by a religious word "baptism." The word choice has been picked to impress, not to inform.

The Yankees' MLB.com website says that the new stadium's facade gave "Yankee Stadium an air of dignity that no other park possessed—before or since." Is this language to impress or inform?

With Barrow now in charge of the baseball operation, high above the playing field in Yankees offices; with Huggins secure in the dugout; with the new stadium open for business and christened with a Ruth homer, the first glory days of the New York Yankees were at hand. Ruth led the Yankees in 1923 as they tried to secure a league championship for the third straight year. One of the requirements for players included participation in in-season exhibition games. One such game in Paterson, NJ, on April 29 is typical and took place fewer than two weeks after the first league game. "Babe Ruth ... was the victim of a friendly mob. And all because he hit a home run in the first half of the ninth inning.... There were 12,000 persons present at the exhibition game between the Yankees and the Dougherty Silk Sox and Dougherty Oval is only big enough to accommodate about 6,000."

Generating large sums of money for Ruppert via in-season exhibition games was already the norm. Being mobbed would become common for Ruth in the years to come. On baseball diamonds he seemed to welcome it. However, that same fame caused him to stay away from the public except when he chose to be seen. He would travel in his own compartment on trains and have his own hotel suite at away games.

He was even permitted to choose his own mascot in the dugout, three-year-old Little Ray Kelly. "Hurtling down Riverside Drive one morning, the Babe had stopped at the sight of Little Ray, attired in a Yankees uniform, playing catch with his father. Three years old, the kid was good. The Babe recruited him on the spot to be his personal mascot at all home games. The arrangement would last for the next decade."[9]

"Asked in later years what his exact role was as Ruth's mascot, Kelly replied, 'I was just there to sit on the bench and look cute.'"[10]

Two events in May became important to Ruth. Professionally, on May 12, 1923, the Yankees slugger hit his 200th home run. No baseball player had ever—that is, in the 48 seasons of major league baseball—hit as many. Personally, in May 1923 he met Claire Merritt Hodgson at a game in Washington, D.C. Though legally named Clara, she was called Claire while she was on tour with a Broadway show, *Dew Drop Inn*. Her obituary in the *New York Times* in 1976 said that she came to New York City in 1920 after her first husband's death—she had married at age 15—and "sought work as a model and actress; she worked as a model for Howard Chandler Christie and later became a dancer in many Broadway musicals."[11] Claire was to become his "confidante and mentor," both workers in the entertainment industry.[12]

Though legally married to Helen, Ruth had long since not been a husband. A nominal Roman Catholic, Ruth knew the religion's stricture against divorce and obeyed it. If Ruth had rooms at the Concourse Plaza Hotel at Grand Concourse and 161st Street, a few blocks from Yankee Stadium, the rooms did not shelter Helen. Biographers guess she was back in Sudbury.

That hotel's bill might be paid for from Ruth's mounting endorsements. Walsh had plugged Ruth into the burgeoning advertising business, "a business that took in $793,893,469 in 1923."[13] In 1923, they brought money in from "Pinch Hit" brand chewing tobacco. Boys could have "a bat that is an exact junior size model of the one Babe Ruth has used … for selling … only one new yearly subscription for *Boys' Life* magazine." With Christy Walsh now under a full head of steam, Ruth's name, signature or photo appeared on ads for alligator shoes, pipes, baseball gloves, and automobiles.

> A commercial enterprise [may] … contact his manager, and be ready to pay an appropriate fee for … as little as $250, or as high as ten thousand dollars, but the one sure factor was that Walsh would squeeze out the last penny they could afford. He booked Babe into banquets, grand openings, smokers, founders' days, municipal picnics, country fairs, boxing and wrestling matches, celebrity golf tournaments—wherever there was money available.[14]

From 1915 to 1922, there had not been an official Most Valuable Player award. In 1922 and 1923, only one "baseball player who is of the greatest all-around service to his club" from all of baseball would be selected. Prior award winners were ineligible for the award. Ruth led his league, or tied, in most offensive categories, plus walks and strikeouts. He had played in every Yankees game, 152 of them in 1923, with the season ending on October 5. He almost hit .400, finishing at .393. Winning the award sent a clear signal that Ruth had indeed been forgiven for 1922.

Earlier, October 3, he had agreed to play in an exhibition game for John McGraw at the Polo Grounds, and four days later, the *Chicago Defender* of October 20, 1923, reported that "Babe Ruth was the honor [sic] guest at the Renaissance Casino Monday night October 7 at an entertainment for the benefit of Mother A. M. E. Zion Church at 140–148 West 137th Street in Harlem." Ruth auctioned off three signed baseballs, grossing $35.50, and Ruth donated $20 to the cause.

Walsh, keeping Ruth's name in front of the public, even told reporters that Ruth had sent a sympathy letter to Mrs. Harding upon the death of President Harding in 1923. In this way, Ruth seemed almost a friend of the late president. Ruth was news; the news was printed. Even songwriters found they could generate cash with Ruth, so in 1923 the song "Babe Ruth He's a Home Run Guy," with words and music by A. Atkins and Harry W. Trout, appeared for sale. So had "Batterin' Babe, Look at Him Now" and "Babe Ruth" in 1922.

The Yankees won the 1923 pennant by a near-record 16 games. The World Series began on October 10, and again the New York Giants were the opposition. Although baseball games were broadcast only at World Series time, the number of people listening to radio sets reached 3,000,000, 2,925,000 more than had listened in 1922. The radio audience now had access to 350 stations, and sales of radios and parts reached $358,000,000.[15]

Ruth's games in the Series seemed to underscore his recovery from his 1922 season and post-season performance. He helped his team to a four games to two Series win over the Giants, leading the Yankees in runs scored, home runs, and walks (eight in six games), placing second in batting average and in hits. He hit three of his team's five home runs. The Giants needed luck to keep him off the bases.

For both teams, playing in two large parks, the six games generated $1,063,815, making it the first million dollar Series, revenue that led to a paycheck of $6,160.46 for 26 Yankees. In some cases, these shares more than doubled what perhaps five of Ruth's teammates had earned for the entire season of 154 games. Ruth, along with his teammates, collected his 1923 World Series gold pocket watch to mark the first World Championship in franchise history. (The first World Series ring presented by the Yankees was in 1927.)

With the Series money, added to the $5,000 for having his name on a column commenting on the games, Ruth could add another $1,000 just for the time it took to play each game. At this moment in his life, he allowed Christy Walsh to talk him into buying an annuity policy from another baseball player, Harry Heilmann, a policy worth $50,000. When he received his World Series share, he bought $50,000 worth of life insurance from Heilmann. (And he paid $35,000 for an annuity in 1924.) The papers were signed on October 17, 1923, for the $50,000 annuity to come due in 1943. Though Huggins and Walsh urged him to buy, the decision was Ruth's. Looking to the future had not been the way Ruth had been portrayed for the most part in the press. The picture of Ruth as willful child played far more colorfully than as someone who, at age 28, would be purchasing an annuity.

The annuity premiums were to come from salary, and his "literary income" would continually add to the capital of the trust fund. Walsh expected the trust fund would grow to about $100,000 by 1929.[16]

Even though the World Series ended almost halfway through October, and even though he had put more than $11,000 extra dollars in his pocket, Ruth chose to barnstorm but also to stay close to New York City, with 15 games penciled in just in New York and Pennsylvania, with the most distant game in Oil City (350 miles).

After five games, the sixth was covered by the *Shamokin Dispatch* and the *Daily Herald*. "Although the Sheriff declared in newspaper advertisements that no 'kid' would be admitted until after school hours, hundreds lined up at the baseball park shortly after noon. They told the Sheriff they had been given a half holiday to see Babe. The *Oil City Derrick* described the game's end:

> Scranton Police Rescue Home Run Hitter When Cheering Admirers Pile on Him.... Babe Ruth narrowly escaped injury ... when more than six thousand wild, cheering youngsters brushed aside a squad of city and county police and bore down upon the Bambino.... Ruth tripped and fell. The boys, thinking it was a joke piled on top of him. Four husky policemen ... opened a lane through which the home-run hitter passed out of the park and into a waiting automobile in safety. "I'm sorry, kiddies," Ruth called back to the children as he doffed his cap and waved farewell.

Being mobbed by children ("kiddies" a common term then) would happen repeatedly over the years. Ruth spoke to a group as well. Smelser's clear eye helps here.

> While in Scranton Ruth also spoke to all the amateur ballplayers in a group. He made a speech for Sunday baseball in which he proved that he had learned civic poppycock and claptrap from the best masters (who were numerous and able in that decade). He took the position that Sunday baseball would distract the young from even worse pursuits. That's true—at least for the length of time it takes to play nine innings, and assuming they don't bet on the game itself.[17]

To some, this statement by Smelser might sound a little too cynical. But Ruth was a performer, had learned his lines, and had figured out that he could simply repeat and repeat what people liked to hear. Hadn't he done exactly the same on the vaudeville stage?

With games to his south now over, Ruth rested on November 2 and 3 while awaiting a big Sunday payday. Ruth again arrived at New York's Dexter Park (he had played there in 1920) by taxi an hour before game time to negotiate his fee with Bushwicks owner Max Rosner, who offered Ruth the choice between either a flat fee or a percentage of the gate. Ruth saw that the stands were empty. So the player chose a flat fee. What Max knew, and what Babe did not, was that the park did not usually fill until about 15 minutes before game time for the doubleheader.

After Ruth ate lunch, he returned to the park to give a batting demonstration, where he was greeted by a park filled to overflowing. In the years to come, Ruth would not make that same flat fee mistake again. The *Brooklyn Daily Eagle* reported that "Babe Ruth knocked a homer and his all-stars defeated and then tied the Bushwicks in the Dexter Park Stadium" when

> More than fourteen thousand persons turned out … [and] were packed in solidly on the playing field all the way around the outfield…. The Babe made three hits in four chances in the first game, but reached base only once in the second, as a result of a muff. He was so anxious to give the fans plenty of action that he … [made] two errors due to over-anxiety. He made a great dash from third and a beautiful slide to the plate.

Also covering the game, the *Washington Post* reported that a crush of children caught Ruth, making him "powerless in the throng. Just then, a mounted policeman came to his rescue but couldn't get away until he seized the horse's tail and the cop started … full tilt for the dressing rooms. Then the boys gave way and the Babe, hatless and almost uniformless, was dragged to safety."

Ever eager to play baseball, to add to his cash, and to hear the applause of the crowd, Ruth signed on for one more game in 1923. True, he was assured of another of his pleasures, that of traveling in a fine automobile, a pleasure increased by the Vanderbilt Parkway, a 45-mile, limited access road that ended in Ronkonkoma on Long Island. For the November 9 game, the *County Review*, a Riverhead paper, reported, "Babe Ruth Receives Ovation In Riverhead," saying also that "Babe Was Alright, But Attempted Ball Game was Only A Burlesque," praised Ruth both for his play and his willingness to autograph baseballs, but mostly derided the play of the other pros, although offering the cold weather conditions as an excuse.

That year, a list of the seven great Americans listed Ruth first, followed by names like Charlie Chaplin, Douglas Fairbanks, Henry Ford and Thomas Edison.[18] Greatness in 1923 was personified by a baseball player, topping actors and industrialists.

So the year 1923 can be marked as a good year for Ruth. He met his future wife, Claire, in 1923, found success on the field, and purchased an annuity as well. Yankees owner Jacob Ruppert succeeded too, posting profits from 1923 baseball adding up to $494,071.

All the barnstorming stops seemed to be surprised to find that Ruth was not arrogant and that he deferred to the wishes of the promoters and the fans, as much as he could. More than that, Ruth understood that he was likely to be received at barnstorming locales with admiration and respect. Who would not go to those places?

17

Advertising's Muscles

Advertisers know that to sell anything, you need to announce the product or service that will appeal to the largest possible audience. This means that to make known the product, a receptive audience of buyers will need to hear the announcement. The advertising processes cost money to the maker or provider and so are counted as debits. The product being successfully marketed and sold will bring money to the product maker or service provider.

Ruth quickly became a brand, according to many sources, because "he was also an ideal hero for the world of consumption. Americans enjoyed the Babe's excess; they took comfort in the life of apparently enormous pleasures that Ruth enjoyed."[1] The "voracious appetite for booze, cigars, food, gambling, and women gave him celebrity status far beyond the foul line…. He became America's first star commodity … establishing his personal national brand with product endorsements … including candy, cereal, cigarettes, soap, and even Babe Ruth All America Athletic Underwear."[2]

A "commodity" can be defined as "an article of trade or commerce…. Something useful that can be turned to commercial … advantage." In 1922, the Elite Chocolate Coated Ice Cream Baseball Co. in El Paso, Texas, after signing a contract with Ruth, decided on the production of "Babe Ruth Home Runs. Chocolate Coated Ice Cream Baseball." Elite set up a booth at the convention of ice cream manufacturers and "drew much attention … in and around the convention hall" with attendees "praising the Babe Ruth commodity."[3] Sixty-seven year later, in 1989, a case was argued stating that the "name and likeness of George Herman *Babe* Ruth is … a protectable *commodity*.[4]

The moment Ruth signed with Christy Walsh, he established himself as a brand, in that "A brand is a combination of attributes, communicated through a name, or a symbol, that influences a thought-process in the mind of an audience and creates value…. The value of a brand resides, for the audience, in the promise that the product or service will deliver."[5]

The true audience for the Ruth commodity early in his career, as reported by Edgar Wolfe in *The Sporting News*, could not be "restricted to the poor or to blue-collar workers. The middle class was the core of fan support … [and it was] estimated that 80 percent of the fans were business officials, office employees, and men of leisure. Only 20 percent came from the laboring classes."[6]

Ruth became a generator of income for many companies, so long as he could be used to sell products and services, particularly to a demographic with money, or to children, who possess no filtering mechanism about products. These two large audiences might be persuaded to buy a product or have it bought for them. The focus for the advertisers, no matter who the audience, was the reality that "what advertising advertises is … the value of a life centered around consumption."[7]

To generate the biggest income, needed were the biggest audience and the mechanism to create a big audience. An indication of the rapid growth of advertising was the proliferation—just during Ruth's major league career—of periodicals aimed directly at advertisers: *Printer's Ink Monthly*, "A journal of printed salesmanship" founded in 1919; *Specialty Salesman Magazine*, created in 1915; *Salesman's Opportunity Magazine*, begun in 1923.

To understand better the growth of a larger buying public, the routine for buying a specific product, butter, for example, went like this: before name brand butter, the shopper went to a neighborhood store, gave the grocer a list and came back for the gathered foods or had them delivered. One of the items might be three ounces of butter, a product that came out of one very large container of butter.

As Ruth became a resident of New York in 1920, a series of products were just becoming national brands, such as Coca-Cola, Juicy Fruit gum, and Quaker Oats. Advances in manufacturing technology and transportation helped to create these national items, advances like the production line and the use in factories of electric motors several times more efficient than the small steam engines of the 19th century. Ice boxes and the new electric refrigerators for consumers changed buying habits. Other products became available to a wide audience through chain stores and mail-order catalogs. For example, self-service food shopping began with Piggly Wiggly stores in 1916, where a shopper could buy brand name butter, such as Land O' Lakes, available only in one size, a one-pound package with a company-designed label.

To make known the availability of the product, advertisements would have to appear in various media. Land O' Lakes might pay an advertising company to write the copy, select the media, and sell the ad to newspapers or magazines. The newspaper might be part of a national chain like Hearst or Scripps-Howard. In 1922, the *Saturday Evening Post* bragged of a circulation of 2,187,024.[8] Radio too was beginning to garner its share of advertising money. On over more than 400 stations, 15,000,000 listeners could hear advertisements for Land O' Lakes. The idea was catching on that a national butter with a recognizable name, not a butter from a barrel, might be preferable, even superior, to its generic equivalent.

Now to the consumer. With a 94 percent literacy rate in 1920, with Americans living longer thanks to advances in medicine from 1923 to 1935 such as insulin being used to treat diabetes, a vast audience had developed of readers of newspapers and magazines. Markets further from farms grew in number in Ruth's time, even as more and more people left the farms for the cities. Medical advances and the dominance of mass production saw 30,214,832 Americans living in cities in 1900. By 1930, 69,160,599 were living in cities, as the percent of rural dwellers dropped from 60.4 percent to 43.9 percent. (The population of rural peoples dropped to just 15 percent.)

The advertisers stood ready, for just as demographics had shifted in the country, so had the numbers engaged in advertising. *Time* magazine in 1925 took note of the convention in Houston of the Associated Advertising Clubs of the World.

Ruth, of course, with Walsh's help, was always selling himself as a viable product. "Ruth had a warm human element that appealed to the public. He had totally mastered his business," wrote Richard Crepeau. As Arthur Miller pointed out years later, a salesman needs to be well-liked, "as the entrée to the growing consumer culture around him."[9] The culture was soon inflated by selling. Kyvig writes that "by 1920 $2.9 billion was being spent annually on commercial advertising."[10]

"Newly emerging national advertisers increased their advertising appropriations by geometric proportions," writes Roland Marchand. "Maxwell House Coffee, for example, expanded its magazine budget from $19,955 to $509,000 during the years from 1921 to 1927 alone."[11] The growth can be measured by the advertising revenue for newspapers—$800 million by 1929—and magazines—popular women's magazines generated more than $75 million in 1928.[12] The print medium and the radio medium had learned some lessons about advertising. "Sell them their dreams. Sell them what they longed for and hoped for and almost despaired of having.... Sell them this hope and you won't have to worry about selling them goods."[13]

Though "Cash and Carry" Pyle, agent just for football star Red Grange, "Walsh's first endorsement tries were successful enough that he decided to franchise the Ruth name.

Remington .22 caliber ammunition, endorsed by Ruth, 1938.

Ad for Babe Ruth's line of "athletic underwear."

Starting in 1922 and continuing over a span of several years, [there appeared] a series of Babe Ruth sweaters, caps, scoring aids, cheroots, dolls, socks, gloves, and uniforms."[14]

Walsh was greatly aided by Ruth's increasing celebrity in the early 1920s. "Only the president of the United States had his name in print more than Babe Ruth. With his unforgettable grin, Ruth was also one of the first people to rake in millions for advertising endorsements."[15] Part of Ruth's appeal is judged to be the "Consumers' desire to copy the Ruthian style and mode [which] meant that Babe Ruth endorsements could be used to sell not only baseball bats but also candy bars and other products unrelated to athletics."[16]

In addition to his skill with a bat, Roberta Newman notes, "Ruth was an accomplished pitchman," so much so that "Fees to use Babe Ruth as an endorser ranged from $500 for one-time, single market ads to $100,00 for a multimedia national campaign." It may not be possible to separate the influence of Ruth the merchandiser and Ruth the home run maker. In less than a year since signing with the Yankees, companies were twisting themselves into knots to use his brand, as in this ad titled "Two Sluggers Brought Together in Direct-Mail Advertising."

"Babe" Ruth is the man of the hour. He comes from Baltimore. Taking advantage of "Babe's" pre-eminence in the public eye, the American Hammered Piston Ring Co., also of Baltimore, has mailed to each of its distributors and wholesalers a little sales reminder card, upon which is glued a miniature replica of Ruth's game-wrecking bludgeon. The card contains this legend: "Babe" is from Baltimore—So are American Hammered Piston Rings. He hammers them out—we hammer them in. Better join our team and share in the championship profits.[17]

If the ad seems a stretch, nevertheless Ruth as a commodity to be sold meant "The Babe endorsed everything from baseballs and baseball caps to cigars and cars, pronouncing Packards, REOs, or Cadillacs the best car on the road, sometimes in the same issue of the same magazine."[18] People in the trade soon understood that using Ruth "sells the *celebrity* first and makes the product of secondary importance."[19]

18

The Usual Greatness
(1924)

For some, the year 1924 lies in the middle of "The Golden Age of Sports," an Eden of nostalgia for simpler times and simpler games. For some observers, like Proust, not so: "The only paradise is paradise lost." A certain amount of disillusion and cynicism arose around professional sports, which at that time meant just baseball. This appeared on August 28, 1924: "In the far-off, golden age of baseball.... Players were admired as athletes, but not yet envied as money-makers.... Today they are clever and extremely well paid professional entertainers."[1]

Some of that cynicism came via the owners. "A *Sporting News* writer in 1920 snickered that Ruppert and Huston, 'those excellent sportsmen,' were willing to show Ruth in certain cities for only 85 percent of the take and did not ask the mayor of each city to shine Ruth's shoes, nor did they demand the cotton crop for the privilege of their visit."[2]

Some of the cynicism arose from player salaries. Ruth, in the third year of a three-year contract at $52,000 was the highest-paid player in professional baseball. Others, George Sisler at $25,000 and Frankie Frisch at $12,000, still were being paid ten to 20 times more than the average salary. Not the salary of those who had reached the top of their professions, though.

As Ruth's money kept coming in, it kept going out too. "The Harvard vs. Yale game in 1923 may have been the one in which Ruth bet $5,000 on the wrong team."[3] In mid-February, Ruth again traveled to Hot Springs, and again his wife Helen and child were told to join him later. In mid-March, the group of players including Ruth left the Arkansas resort, headed to New Orleans, that year's site for Yankees spring training, where a headline gleefully announced, "Ruth Loses $1,000 Bill." (He had four of the bills, so he still had three remaining.) And yet it was news that Ruth lost a piece of currency.

During the training period, it was calculated that four full-time position players—Ruth, Dugan, Schang, Scott—and four pitchers—Jones, Pennock, Hoyt and Bush—on the 1924 New York Yankees had come from the Red Sox. In addition, from the Athletics had come pitcher Bob Shawkey. Those pitchers, whose contracts had been bought with Ruppert's money, started 143 of the 153 games in 1924 and were credited with 81 of the 89 wins for the Yankees. The team was not just Ruth, no matter how many headlines he might amass. There would be more headlines from two newly established New York papers, the *Daily Mirror*, a Hearst paper first published June 24, 1924, and the *New York Evening Graphic*, published in September of that year, a tabloid at which gossip would be king.

These additional papers added to all the others simply increased Ruth's notoriety. That celebrity had become so great that Ruth had found spots to go to for privacy and a good time in almost every city the team visited. When in New York City, he would go to Donahue's in Wayne, New Jersey, about 30 miles away. The reason a remote spot to relax at was necessary, given both his celebrity and his apparent willingness to please was exemplified in his advice to young teammate Lou Gehrig.

> "See, Lou, you've got to be careful who you talk to and what you say," Ruth said. "A guy sued me for damages in New York because he said I slapped him for crowding me as I came out of the baseball park. I don't even remember shaking hands with him. And another fellow threatened to sue me for damages because he was walking down the street when something flew out of the air and hit him on the head. Said I'd smacked a ball out of the park and beaned him. What hit him was an L rivet. You've got to be careful about some of these birds."[4]

However the price of fame added up, some fan and writer pessimism remained. The source for the distrust was all that money. The last World's Series, six games in all, drew gate receipts of more than a million dollars. It was inevitable that this jingle of coin should distract some attention from the game itself as an athletic sport. The players and the club owners were, and often are, too busy counting up their winnings and planning how to increase them to have much interest in the game as a trial of skill or as a means of recreation. "The crowds increase because of the modern man's feverish desire to be amused by someone else."[5] Part of the amusement can be viewed in even more self-promotion. On May 11, 1924, the *New York Times* headlined, "Yankees Will Celebrate Babe Ruth Day And Raise World's Title Flag..." during which this "special occasion ... the big fellow will get a diploma from President Ban Johnson and the degree of Master of Swat from the school of baseball."

The money paid to Walsh and Ruth came from all over, as soon as vendors discovered new ways of marketing Ruth's fame. A sporting goods store, looking to increase its sales for a large shipment of Babe Ruth bats, "secured the Pathe phonograph record giving Babe Ruth's account of how he makes home runs. A window display was worked out with the central feature of the bats.... The contest was also exploited by a newspaper advertisement and by the distribution of circulars."[6]

Certainly, stars like Ruth received the attention and endorsement cash. Somehow, there existed a world of difference between, for example, Frankie Frisch appearing in an ad for a baseball glove and the Yankees' home run hitter. Ruth became the first modern athlete to be sold to the public as much for his feats on the field as his "color, personality, [or] crowd appeal," said sportswriter Grantland Rice. Ruth's press agent, "Christy Walsh, developer of a syndicate of ghostwriters ... thus contributing to 'the ballyhoo,'" in the words of Warren Susman, "that promoted a professional athlete into a celebrity of ever exaggerated proportions."[7]

Reporters valued their association with the player so much so that this type of article was not the first: "My Friend Babe Ruth." It read, in part, "For some years I have had a peculiarly intimate friendship with Babe Ruth ... this modern Beowulf at bat." As Ruth's pal, Arthur Robinson said some extraordinary things about him. "Babe Ruth is a milestone in the progress of American life, yes even a vital economic and social force and factor."[8]

Ruth's performance of the field showed very few faults. By August 11, Ruth was hitting .405 with 38 home runs. By season's end, Ruth led the league average with .378 and home runs with 46, and the highest production in six every other categories. Still, his team finished two games behind Washington. It may have been the half-run per game advantage in earned run average that the Senators had over Yankees.

The *New York Times* headlined in its October 6, 1924, issue, "Babe Ruth a Reporter; This Year He Is Covering the Series from the Press Box." Christy Walsh had again secured a $5,000 fee for his name.

Leaving the Pacific Northwest for games in California, Ruth had time to read a syndicated story (or to have Walsh point it out to him) by Henry L. Farrell, the UP sports editor, who declared that while commissioner Landis "kept the While Sox crooks from being reinstated, baseball was saved in that crisis not as much by Landis as it was by Babe Ruth."[9] Chiming in on this and perhaps leading the support was *Herald Tribune* sportswriter Grantland Rice, a reporter described by the *New York Times,* as "spen[ding] most of his time covering up Ruth's many sexual and alcoholic peccadilloes 'for the good of baseball.'" So it was not unusual that Rice wrote "Baseball may well have gone down the drain of mediocrity," but Ruth "lifted baseball on his back and return it to the aura of respectability"[10] This viewpoint, Ruth as baseball's redeemer, would be repeated whenever Ruth became the topic of discussion. This kind of dramatic language "saved" baseball, and "in that crisis" plays well. But how do you measure the extent of the resuscitation and how do you measure the intensity of the calamity? What writers usually mean here is attendance, a supposedly reliable measure since it takes a customer some time, effort, and money to get to a game.

It is true that for a few years, attendance rose when Ruth's team came to most of the seven cities in the American League, and when the Yankees team was at home either in the Polo Grounds or the new Stadium.

Look at another case. About two decades later, in the period 1946–1948, attendance in the major leagues rose by 1,946 paid per team per year. Had the length of years measured been greater, then it is likely the numerical difference would also have been more striking. Does anyone claim that the leap should all be placed on the coming of Jackie Robinson into the major leagues? Certainly Robinson's entry stands just as startling as Ruth's home runs. Why not give Robinson the credit?

So let's look at Ruth's years. In 1918, a wartime year for the United States, each major league team of 16 averaged 3,055 fans per game. One year later, in 1919, the war had ended and the front-line players returned from service or from defense industry jobs. Looking just at the American league in 1918, an average of 3,388 fans came to each game; in 1919, 5,932 paid per game per team, a 57 percent increase. That was the year Ruth first broke the home run record. Of course, Ruth did not play in the National League. How did attendance do there?

In 1918, a National League average game drew 2,272 fans; in 1919, 4,672, a 106 percent increase. So the attendance rose in the National League with Ruth not playing a single game there. But the Black Sox scandal had not yet been felt, no confessions forthcoming until the very end of the 1920 season.

The next year, 1920, Ruth's home run total soared, and the major league average attendance again rose to 7,403 per game from 5,302. But in 1921, it decreased by 417 fans per game on average, some pointing to this being the year that the full impact of the scandal became most strongly felt. The number rose slightly in 1922 to 169 more fans, but decreased by 116 in 1923. The number rose once more in 1924 to 750 more fans than in 1923. A small decrease of 46 showed up in 1925, a small increase of 238 in 1926, and in 1927 an average increase of 73 fans per game. All of these number show no crisis, on average, for the baseball corporations from 1918 to 1927.

No matter how the numbers are calculated and interpreted, the logical fallacy called post hoc still applies. The rules of cause and effect are easy. Rule one, could there have been other possible causes? It is possible to point to economic changes happening in the country having an effect on the affordability of the price of a game and a hot dog. Rule two: when the cause is there, does the effect always follow? Did attendance always go up when Ruth was in uniform?

In its simplest form, attendance rises when a team starts winning and attendance drops when it loses, and particularly when it shows a losing record repeatedly.

So is there a causal relationship between Ruth playing baseball for one team of the 16 and major league attendance rising on average for all 16 in some years? Or for falling on average for all 16 in some years? If not, he did not save baseball. (A scholarly study from 2011 says in its abstract that "time factors[day/night; weekend/week, April/August weather], fan interest, city characteristics, team's performance, and fan's attendance behavior have strong influences on the game attendance."[11]

By now, Ruth has been selected, cynically or not, as the prime mover. Attendance increases? It's Ruth. Children in orphanages and hospitals have a half-hour of joy in an otherwise lonesome and dreary life? It's Ruth's visit. In just two years, Ruth would be given credit for curing someone who suffered from the same incurable disease "that carried off President Coolidge's son."

It may have been that Ruth's share for second place equaled only $992.69 that caused Walsh to line up a more ambitious barnstorming schedule for 1924 than in 1923. Walsh knew the amplification to use: "Babe Ruth's Pacific Coast Tour—America's Greatest Living Idol Moves Westward Immediately After World Series. Under Personal Direction Christy Walsh." Just three games on the East Coast were lined up, followed by two in the Midwest, with the remaining 15 games to be played on the West Coast. This scheduling meant fewer chances that weather would cancel a game, a payday, and travel miles would be held to a minimum after the few cross-country games.

There apparently was no hyperbole to Walsh's profits from Ruth. It will be remembered that the 1921 contract had Ruth and Walsh splitting the gross receipts. "As to Walsh's share, again, there are no specific figures available … under certain circumstances Christy's percentage went considerably higher than the normal ten percent. In cases when he himself was doing the actual promoting, such as the barnstorming tour of 1927, or in newspaper syndication work, in effect Ruth became his employee, rather than the reverse."[12]

Ruth never would barnstorm after the season to certain states, many of those because he had already played there in exhibitions before the season. Even so, a newspaper of April 1925 stated, "A visit from [Ruth] brought honor and fame to the most insignificant townships."[13] And loot for Ruth. It was the sports agent who negotiated prices for Ruth's appearance. In each new city, Walsh put Babe up for grabs to the highest bidder. On the tour, Ruth wore his New York Yankees road uniform and shared a room with barnstorming teammate Bob Meusel. Walsh came too.

For the fourth game, in Kansas City against Lavan's Leaguers, Ruth arrived by train at 8:30 a.m. with Bob Meusel and his bat bag, and was then taken to room 1015 in the Muehlebach Hotel. Once settled in, "two barbers were rushed to the Babe's suite where the home run king and his teammate, Bob Meusel, enjoyed their morning shave." [Ruth never shaved himself for fear of cutting himself and thereby damaging his income.] "It's a great day for the ball game," Ruth said, "I hope there's a capacity crowd for the sake of those crippled youngsters at Mercy Hospital. I always do more than my best for them. They deserve it."

Ruth's appearance schedule began at 9:30, first riding in a car and throwing balls to pedestrians; at 11, climbing to the roof of the sponsoring newspaper building and hitting balls to the crowd below. Then, at 11:30, "the idol of the youth of the land went to Mercy Hospital. There the Babe refused to be hurried. He tarried with the youngsters as long as he could, pressing each little hand, distributing gentle pats and smiles at random." It took about ten minutes to drive from the hospital to the ball field. So Ruth stayed about 40 minutes at the hospital to spend time with 50 children. The hospital's assumption is that all the children knew who Babe was and that they were wildly eager to see him.

Ruth reported to the playing field at 12:30 and performed a "long range hitting demonstration."

After the game, as their train moved west, newspapers nation-wide printed the selections of "Babe Ruth's All-American Baseball Team" for 1924. Smelser points out that beginning in 1924, "new literary income came immediately from the publication of Babe Ruth's All-American Baseball Team, picked by Walsh and his ghosts and sold nationally by Walsh's syndicate. Local papers gave prizes to readers who sent in lists most nearly identical with Ruth's selection. [It became] an annual feature."[14]

Clearly, Walsh knew his job. He negotiated endorsements as they arrived, he created ways to keep Ruth's name in front of the public, and he even created new ways for Ruth's name and photo to be associated with the notion of excellence.

For the sixth barnstorming game, October 17, 1924 (three days and 1,400 miles after the game at Minneapolis), Walsh had picked Spokane, Washington, already a city of 105,000. With Meusel and Ruth well rested, the day began with a local hospital visit in the morning. Soon, though, they moved to the site of the game. Another recreation area that began as a trolley park, Natatorium Park, named after its heated swimming pool.

Signaling that the game would turn out to be a relaxed affair, the large crowd of 10,000 would have things their way. The game's sponsors almost ran out of baseballs in order to please the customers. Simply stated, Ruth played first base and then pitched the ninth inning, and though the official box score might say that he hit three homers, "Their averages do not include a few clean singles and doubles they hit. The crowd insisted they were fouls…. After the third inning, the fans grew tired of watching common baseball players bat. 'Meusel's up' they would yell … or 'Ruth's up.' So Ruth and Meusel batted in every inning after that."

The local paper noticed the adoring children. The *Spokesman-Review* reported, "All kids grinned. There was the light of heaven in their face. They had seen Babe Ruth hit a homer." Ruth, here, was intended to be the source of divine joy in children. With such an idea being put forward, Ruth's status rises yet another level.

Spending the night in a Pullman, Ruth arrived at Union Station in Tacoma at 8:20 Saturday morning, October 18, after the 300-mile trip from Spokane. This visit would be a triumph for Walsh, Ruth and commerce. Before the game even started, Ruth, through Walsh, agreed to appear at 11 businesses in town, including two hospitals. Walsh, or the game's sponsors, had also contracted with 32 firms to sponsor an ad in either the scorecard or newspaper about his arrival.

Breakfast being consumed, at 9:15 he departed the hotel for the Cushman Veterans Hospital, visiting for more than a half-hour. The next hour ended at 11:45 at The Cave, where he was given a special box of candy made for Mrs. Ruth.

The official city reception took place at noon at the *Tacoma Ledger* office, where Ruth stood on a ledge, autographed balls, and tossed them into the crowd below in Ledger Square. Walsh knew how important it always was to show up at the local newspaper in every town you could. This ball-tossing stunt was followed by a 12:45 lunch at the Tacoma Hotel. One half-hour later, Ruth left for a visit to St. Ann's Children's Home, a Catholic orphanage for 22 children under the age of 17, after which Ruth needed to change and dress for the game. "While most players got two or three at-bats, the Babe was permitted to bat once an inning.... The box score noted: 'Game called when darkness approached and admirers stormed Babe Ruth and Bob Meusel ... there are baseballs autographed by The Babe still preserved on mantels around town.'"[15]

If Ruth's day wasn't busy and long enough, a story written in 1992 tells how Ruth was still at work, even with an airship. So "after the game. Babe was taken ... to a steel tower where the *Shenandoah* was approaching.... Ruth was seated on the platform with the mayor.... The master of ceremonies shouted, 'I'd like to introduce the one and only home run king of all time. Babe Ruth!' A spotlight, which had been scanning the skies for the *Shenandoah*, swept to Ruth, who had left the platform and was huddled below, urinating."[16]

On October 24, 1924, on what was supposed to be a day off, he met "with prominent

Ruth (left of center) with barnstormers in Tacoma, 1924. Fellow Yankee Bob Meusel sits to Ruth's right.

citizens" and visited Shriners' Hospital for Crippled Children. By now, a visit to a hospital for children or to an orphanage was recorded by the local paper, whether Ruth wanted the recognition or not. But Ruth knew his minute-to-minute movements were being followed—in New York papers. Whipple or Hunt, for example, traveled with him everywhere, so it seems disingenuous to say that publicizing the visits—long or brief—was unwanted. Ruth may not have thought much about it, as he was not one who self-examined particularly, but Walsh could see the value in those visits. The second of these activities seems clear enough. He was not meeting with newspapermen for fellowship.

That no game was played on October 30 suggests that Ruth took the time to play during the first day of the baseball players' golf tournament, a California event.

One of the most celebrated barnstorming games ever played took place in Brea, a part of which was called Olinda, where pitcher Walter Johnson grew up. Businesses in Brea began posting such signs as "This Store Closed Friday Afternoon, October 31, 1924, on Account of Walter Johnson–Babe Ruth Ball Game. Brea Bowl, Brea, California." The Brea Bowl, a natural amphitheater, held a ball field maintained by the Union Oil Company for its semipro baseball team. For that game, players included Rube Ellis from the Cardinals, Donie Bush, Jimmy Austin, and both Bob Meusel and his brother "Irish." Johnson's squad included a few chums from his Olinda days. Umpires hired for the game included Beans Reardon and Gavvy Cravath. In addition to Johnson, the lineups (and umpires) included Ken Williams, who beat out Ruth for the American League home run lead in 1922. That "Wahoo Sam" Crawford also played was just a bonus for the fans.

THIS STORE CLOSED
Friday Afternoon
October 31, 1924, on Account of
WALTER   BABE
JOHNSON-RUTH
BALL GAME
Brea Bowl, Brea, California   Auspices Anaheim Elk's 1345

Stores in towns where exhibitions were played held often shut down during the game.

The two starting pitchers were Johnson and Ruth. In his five innings, Johnson gave up eight runs, four of them homers, one by Sam Crawford. He did strike out six. In Ruth's complete game victory, he gave up just six hits. At bat, Ruth hit two home runs, one to center field estimated to travel 550 feet. Johnson admitted he may have put some pitches exactly where Ruth could hit them best.

Local writer Howe called the game "probably the greatest de luxe sand lot game Southern California has ever seen." All the players were invited to be the guests of honor of Anaheim businessmen at a Halloween party, thereby eating both lunch and dinner at someone else's expense.

Brea resident W. E. Griffith, who attended the game, years later recounted to the *Los Angeles Times* that Ruth "hit a foul ball that bounced off a car and hit a boy in the head. He started bawlin' and Ruth walked over to him, handed him a silver dollar and said: 'Don't cry, kid—here.'"[17] A charming story, but it seems unlikely, as many Ruth stories sound. Are we to believe that Ruth left the field because he heard a child crying? That he happened to have a silver dollar in his uniform pocket?

Walsh, summing up the 1924 tour, posted that Ruth "made twenty two scheduled speeches, headed four parades, refereed a boxing match, drove a golf ball 353 yards, visited eighteen hospitals and orphan asylums."[18] Two of his appearances happened in places under 5,000 in population; eight were under 100,000. He played from October 1–31 with ten days off in a row, traveling at a minimum 6,200 miles across the continent. Ruth did not return to the East Coast until December 6, because he had signed a contract for a week's appearances at the Grauman's Million-Dollar Theater.

"The greatest year that sports have ever known is about to pass into history. Never before have so many brilliant performances, shattered attendance records and important international events been crowded into a period of twelve months. Many of the sports individually enjoyed the most notable season their respective annals," the *New York Times,* at year's end, reported. For baseball, much of this "greatest year" can be measured in money. "In 1924 the majors took in $10 million at the turnstiles, made an estimated $4.6 million in profits, and paid out only $3 million in salaries."[19] Montville reports that Ruth claimed he made $66,215.34 that year.

But someone else was making money too. The *Altoona* (Pennsylvania) *Mirror* announced on October 3 that beginning with the 1924 Series, it would be "getting the baseball dope ... twelve or fifteen hours sooner than usual" and also that it would be printing an after the game edition, enabling the "fans [to] get today's news today" and enabling the paper to double its Series income. Under the headline "Babe Ruth's Price Is Topped At Last," the *Boston Daily Globe* reported that $100,000 was paid to the owner of pitcher Lefty Grove's contract, and his name was Jack Dunn, the same baseball man who had sold three contracts, including Ruth's, in 1914 to the Boston Red Sox for about 20 percent of the Grove price. Dunn had originally paid $3,100 to the Martinsville, West Virginia, team of the Blue Ridge League for Grove's contract.

Money was going out of Ruth's hands as well, but it was money used as an investment. He claimed a business deduction on his 1924 tax return of $9,000, "expended for the purpose of establishing and maintaining good will to the extent of entertaining sports writers, press agents and other similarly situated in order to constantly keep himself before the public."[20]

19

Barnstorming

Baseball barnstorming was one financial opportunity for many players. From Christy Mathewson to Willie Mays, there existed a 60-year span during which groups of players went out on what was called the Pumpkin Circuit in the early 20th century, since the games were autumnal. Part of the necessity arose from the fact that a player contract stipulated that he be paid only from Opening Day to closing day—about five and a half months. A month, typically March, would be given over to spring training, a time when there were no paydays for the players. So almost half of the year lay ahead of them without any income from baseball.

As Harold Seymour observed, "A sampling of winter occupations of many of the players which would include streetcar conductor, glassblower, interpreter, newspaper writer, undertaker, snow remover, policeman and printer.... Others engaged in more long-term enterprises which they sometimes invested their own capital as well as their services.... A good many players qualified as farmers."[1] But before they went off to the "winter occupations," many players signed on to join a barnstorming squad and play for a week or two, often in games not far from their team's home city.

Location, we're told, is very important in business, and Ruth's business choices often meant travel to smaller cities. For example, in his first year with the Yankees, he barnstormed in Bristol, Connecticut, and Medina, New York. Using the New York Central railroad route across New York State, he easily reached medium-sized cities: Syracuse, Rochester and Buffalo. The 1920 census noted that "urban places" of 100,000 or more constituted only about 25 percent of the U.S. population, with most of those cities in New York, Massachusetts and New Jersey in the Northeast, and Illinois and Michigan in the Midwest. The remaining large cities were found in California and Washington. Where had Ruth already played? An American League player visited seven cities and, before the season, as the teams traveled north from Florida or Louisiana, games were set up from Tennessee to Texas.

Most barnstormers in the first three decades of the century spent at most two weeks traveling short distances. Aware of the vagaries of weather and travel, they thought it best to be as efficient as possible in their tours. Perhaps piling into two cars, or taking interurbans and trolleys, the players came to a town early in the day, held a clinic for children, were fed lunch, played a game in less than two hours, were fed supper, and headed home, avoiding hotel bills. The opposition frequently was made up of semipro players. What did "semipro" mean? For some, a team was simply an advertising tool for a company or an individual. But in larger cities, the names of teams might be the names of neighborhoods.

Ruth, like everyone else, pursued what he found beneficial to him. What did he get out of barnstorming? It is important to keep in mind that Ruth was away from home in New York City, during the majority of his career, from February 1 until January 15. Before the season, he would often travel to Hot Springs, Arkansas, for the mineral baths and other pleasures. Then came spring training in the South. Then half of the season and more would be spent traveling to, and playing in, seven cities in the league. After the season, he would barnstorm and after that go on vaudeville tours, play golf, hunt, fish or make movies.

Without knowing it, many biographers have commented on the lure of barnstorming for Ruth. Smelser, in a summing up, stated, "What Ruth liked most was to play baseball. In second place came winning. Only then came money."[2] Barnstorming provided all three, and more. The barnstorming games took care of the baseball, the vast superiority of Ruth as player took care of the winning (or even any worry about winning), and he and his agent made sure of the profits. There was no pressure to win, just to perform, and for most of the time New York City writers were not in sight. Games often took fewer than 80 minutes to play.

Then too, as his teammate Waite Hoyt was convinced, "Ruth on the road was an incurable sight seer."[3] Jenkinson says Ruth "loved seeing new places and meeting new friends."[4] Wagenheim sums up this aspect, writing, "for Ruth life on the road was the best of all. Each city offered different adventures and delights. Everyone wanted to be around him—politicians, businessmen, gamblers. After the games, Ruth would retire to his hotel suite, change to a silk robe and light a big black cigar."[5]

Next was the show business aspect of Ruth's barnstorming. An Elmira, New York, reporter in 1928 understood that "Babe is everybody's friend apparently out for a good time and anxious that the public enjoy itself." In 1948, the ghosted Ruth memoir famously says, "Maybe it will sound a bit conceited but I always felt I had an obligation to my public."[6] Considering that there were very few years when he wasn't away from home most of the year, it seems clear that Ruth enjoyed the adulation, took it seriously and tried to do right by his fans. These trips were filled with the pleasures of being treated, as he was in many places, as the most important person ever to visit a town. For one biographer, "The small games on crabgrass fields … with local standouts brought together for a day of glory in the shadow of an exalted presence."[7]

Ruth loved to compete. It did not seem to make any difference if the opposition was unskilled or not. It did make a difference that barnstorming was one more way for Ruth to succeed and be seen to succeed. The end product of the barnstorming competition was more adulation, more money, and more new sights to see.

Ruth knew he did not have to deprive himself of pleasures just because he was away from larger cities. In fact, there were many pleasures beyond the big cities, pleasures of a different kind. He would step off a train, often one that made an unscheduled stop just for him, be greeted by excited and enthusiastic fans, and got the best room in the local hotel, where "he would pay the hotel barber a day's pay to come to his room" and shave him every morning.[8] Free of wife, free of worries about batting average, free for the most part of being mobbed by reporters and cameramen, Ruth knew he could ask for almost anything in these towns. Jenkinson can "imagine the reaction of a fan who saw Ruth just once in a lifetime."[9] Baseball enthusiasts who had never seen a baseball game except that played by teams staffed with their neighbors watched Ruth "hit the longest ball anyone had ever seen…. His best records weren't recorded in books; they were kept in individual memories of an astounding sight witnessed on a warm afternoon, the memories transferred by word of mouth."[10]

The games were exciting as well to other than fans. Local businessmen counted on Ruth's visit turning out to be a good payday. The town would fill up more than it ever had, and sales would increase. For Ruth and the merchants, these games were "hardly community service."[11]

In each new city Walsh [or Ruth or other tour managers] put Ruth up for grabs to the highest bidder, and if he happened to be plumping for a competitor of the product he had endorsed the day before somewhere else, well, who cared? If he spoke out in favor of Dr. Reed's Cushion Shoes in one town, it was only fair that he put in a good word for Crawford's Orthopedics in the next.[12]

The bids from towns and cities often arrived aboard the train as the tour moved on, frequently, if not always, included free lodging in addition to either a flat fee or a percentage of the gate receipts. Adjustments based on competing offers were made by using the *Official Guide of the Railways*. Available to travelers from 1900 to 1973 and clearly a comprehensive book of train timetables, this tool allowed a great deal of flexibility in scheduling games even as the train moved across the country. Walsh and others could hold an auction for Ruth's appearance in a town, as messages could arrive at any point along the way while on the train, at the local telegraph office, or telephoned to Ruth's hotel once he arrived.

These barnstorming trips provided Ruth with a chance to see new places, the opportunity to make new fans and to exhibit his skills and power, and the freedom of being on the move as much as possible. But they also increased his fame and thereby his celebrity. Walsh and Ruth knew how to transmute applause and celebrity into cash.

20

The Worst
(1925)

In early February 1925, Ruth and Marshall Hunt, his daily chronicler, left New York together for the Hot Springs resort once more. Hot Springs, in travel guides, has been described as "the land where golf, hiking, auction bridge and hot baths are the principal amusements of the residents." Ruth was clearly overweight, again, and though Helen once more stayed elsewhere, Claire met him in the Arkansas resort after some time. Helen arranged to meet him at St. Petersburg, where the Yankees trained in 1925, one month after Ruth's arrival in Hot Springs.

The Yankees, through Ed Barrow, looked for more ways to get back into the business of pennant winning. One pioneering strategy was to hire a pitching coach, in this case, George Wiltse, Giants left-hander of ten years before, who was signed by the Yankees.

Meanwhile, Commissioner Landis continued to worry about gambling by baseball players. A primary impetus for the prohibition may have been Rogers Hornsby, who flaunted his love of the race tracks' betting windows.

In 1925, 60 percent of Americans earned less than $2,000 per year. In major league baseball, the only man close to Ruth in salary was Ty Cobb, mostly because he also had the responsibilities of being a player and a manager. Debate continues to this day about whether Ruth's earnings allowed others to command the same level of money. Among baseball's employees, Umpire Bill McGowan, in his first major league year, was paid $4,700 plus $750 for expenses.[1] In California a lead baseball groundskeeper's wages amounted to $2,874. Publications in the year 1925 listed average wages at $1,250 a year. "[Red] Grange signed a movie contract for $300,000 and was paid $36,000 for one game. He also made $40,000 more in endorsements."[2] Ignoring the greater movie stars, all of whom sported income close to seven figures, working under contract at weekly salaries were actors Thomas Meighan, Dorothy Dalton and Alice Brady, whose pay reached $5,000 a week for their movie work. At age nine, Jackie Coogan was paid $500,000 in advance on his services for three years.[3]

Outside of show business, a physician might make $10,000 in a specialty, and a U.S. senator the same wages. Overall, "in 1925 there were 207 Americans whose income for the year was more than a million dollars apiece."[4]

Ruth would not get rich this year and neither would his team. Ruppert's and Barrow's Yankees would go on to lose more than $286,000 in 1925. No one was permitted to see Ruppert's ledgers, and if Ruth had it does not seem that he cared. He lived his own way, and his own way was to live in excess. "Once, in St. Louis, during a hot spell he wore twenty-two silk shirts in three days and left them for the hotel chambermaid when the team moved on to another city."[5] His excesses could be measured when he stepped on the scales and saw the dial reach 245 in early February of that year. His weight, it turned out, would be the least of his problems.

Through February and March, headlines shouted about Ruth's wrenched back, his chills and fever, and a broken finger. Other stories talked about the player being sued for unpaid bets on horse races. When the team played its way north, these early problems culminated at the railway station at Asheville, North Carolina. When Ruth was taken from the train and transported to St. Vincent's hospital, 170 West 12th Street, in New York City, newspapermen were left to guess—or fabricate—the true illness.

As days passed, the speculations for Ruth's poor health began to mount up: acute indigestion, a bump on the head, the flu, groin injury; grippe; nerves, convulsions, groin infection, fried potatoes for breakfast, attack of nerves. It seems odd now that the medical people were silent, though we may be able to see the hand of Christy Walsh in this circumstance. The accepted notion seemed to be that Ruth suffered from "the bellyache heard round the world." Five days after the collapse, the *New York Times* reported,

> Millions of anxious eyes have been straining for the bulletins from Babe Ruth's sick bed. It involves no disrespect to Calvin Coolidge or to Charles W. Eliot [Harvard President] to suggest that in the extent and immediacy of popularity the Home Run King is also the first citizen of the land ... yesterday it developed that the slugger's influenza and indigestion have developed an abscess and this morning he will be operated on at St. Vincent's Hospital.

Many observers are now willing to settle on "an intestinal abscess." While it is true that today's diagnostic tools, MRI for example, might be used for such a diagnosis, the recovery from having the pus drained from such an abscess would entail, again in today's medicine, the employment of antibiotics, but their early use remained a decade away. Rest and allowing Ruth's immune system to combat the infection must have been the only recommendation.

To further complicate Ruth's recovery, on April 24 wife Helen checked into St. Vincent's with a nervous condition. Contributors to her breakdown incorporated seeing her husband taken away with a life-threatening illness at Asheville and their own marriage breakup after a decade. They both may have used this time away from prying eyes to settle their affairs and make their break permanent.

Not ready to play for the first month and a half of the season, when Ruth returned to the lineup on June 1, he still showed weakness, some of his hits falling just short of the bleachers. After failing to deliver on June 23 with the bases full, he was taken from active playing and rested, some suggesting that he would be used rarely in 1925. Ruth, "Fearing his Right Ankle Bone Has Been Chipped ... goes for an X-Ray on June 28," but found it to be just a bruise. "Babe has joke with being pictured on verge of death," said the *New York Times*, mocking itself. Still trying hard, though clearly his ankle was damaged, Ruth hit two home runs on July 1 and slid home with the winning run on July 4.

In the meantime, Ruth was attempting to organize his personal life. After he put the Sudbury farm up for sale on June 18 for $50,000, Ruth and Helen moved ahead on the signing of a separation agreement. When the farm sold seven months later, Helen, given the money from the farm's sale and their child, disappeared from the newspapers. She apparently had been, and would continue to be, receiving checks from her husband via Christy Walsh with the aid of her lawyer.

By July's end, the papers counted 11 homers for Ruth and counted how far behind almost everyone else in the league the Yankees stood. One hopeful sign seemed to be the performance of the new first baseman, Lou Gehrig. But before long both Whitey Witt (who played only 63 games) and Joe Dugan (who missed 30 games) suffered serious injuries.

After their successes for three years and the near-win in 1924, the 1925 team found itself locked into next-to-last place, ahead of only the Red Sox. Ruth's season was declared a shambles by now, and the most powerful effect on him seemed to strike on August 25. That day, he went hitless, the only person without a hit on the team. His owner had threatened him with reduced wages, and he was taking abuse from many fans.

When he missed the team curfew in St. Louis, Ruppert, Barrow and Huggins were furious with him, the blame falling on Ruth's shoulders for the steep decline in team performance, for the loss of over 325,000 fans—one-third—from 1924—marking the first time in five years that attendance would not reached the one million mark. Ruth, they thought, was not only not earning his salary, he was somehow hurting the team by not being in his hotel bed when required. Manager Huggins decided to suspend Ruth and fine him $5,000 for missing the curfew. The whispers that he had burned himself out at age 31 began to surface.

The fact that adult men have a curfew in the first place was accepted as normal practice in professional baseball. As Smelser points out, "Owners liked to treat their players as children at best and as domestic animals at worst."[6] Ruth's history with Barrow went back to earlier fines, and "Ruppert and Barrow ruled skillfully, harshly and with disdain."[7]

Since the suspension was announced as "indefinite," Ruth began to look around for some help. He was furious, saying, "If Huggins Stays, I Quit," claiming the "Manager Is Trying to Make Him the 'Goat' for Yankees' Poor Showing" and "Calls Him Incompetent." Ruth found no backing, not from Barrow, an argumentative martinet as it was, nor from Ruppert, who still called him "Root." Ruth found that all in authority were arranged against him, including the American League president, Ban Johnson.

Teammate Waite Hoyt later wrote, "He was deep in debt. He was wrangling continuously with Miller Huggins. Besieged on all sides, Ruth met the situation the only way he knew; he fought with everyone, indulged in maudlin self-pity. And he blamed everyone but himself. It was the lowest point in Ruth's career."[8] The whispers that he had burned himself out at age 31 became even louder.

In an echo of the famous dressing down by Jimmie Walker in 1922, F. C. Lane—one of the few Ruth realists—of *Baseball Magazine* wrote that September,

> A popular idol fell with a crash to the dust when Babe Ruth was fined and suspended by Miller Huggins.... A haze of inaccurate, almost meaningless bunk endowed Ruth with virtues utterly alien to his nature, and softened or obliterated that coarse strain, those crude defects ... which made him an object rather of apology and of pity than of admiration to those who knew him best. Ruth's popularity has ... been exaggerated beyond all the bounds of sanity.... There is little substance for Babe Ruth the myth of popular imagination in Babe Ruth the reality ... a heroic figure with feet of clay.

Few paid attention to this piece.

After apologizing to Huggins, Ruth was in the lineup again on September 8, the same day that more trouble came his way when he was sued for a minor incident in Sudbury.

The 1925 season ended with the New York Yankees finding themselves in seventh place. In that Ruth played just 98 games of the 154, his production at bat had declined as well. He hit below .300 for the first time in eight years, not leading the league in any offensive category. He was even out-homered by Meusel, with 33 to his 25. But he still finished as the third best home run hitter in baseball.

Few, of course, can match Ruth's achievements in baseball competition. Few public figures can match his energy, his affable and genial dealings with ordinary people. He knew how to make money for himself and others and possessed a very efficient digestive system. Is it necessary to ask more of him? It is. But for many it is necessary to see him not as a model, an ego ideal, along with all the charming lies about him.

Later on, there came along writers willing to talk about aspects of Ruth that were less than heroic, less than attractive. Rubin, for example, says that Ruth "was largely unconcerned for anything but his own personal doings … [and] took almost no interest in the lives and activities of his teammates except as affecting him."[9] Carey, his driver, is labeled "his great friend" by Robert Creamer, and the chauffer said that he didn't think "the Babe really loved Claire…. I don't think he really loved anybody."[10] Creamer also quotes Waite Hoyt: "'Babe was not a sentimentalist and generally made no outward demonstration of affection either by word or action."[11] In fact, it is difficult to select anyone who was more willing to see Ruth straight on than Waite Hoyt, Ruth's teammate. To Hoyt, Ruth demonstrated "a childish desire to be over-virile, living up to credits given for his home run power" while possessing "a feverish desire to play baseball, perform, act and live a life he didn't and couldn't take time to understand."[12]

Perhaps out of necessity for his safety and peace, he spent a large portion of his time either by himself, or briefly in the midst of a crowd, at a hospital or at an orphanage. But he was always available to anyone who might bring him some money and spent his years after retiring in the company of his lawyers, accountants and other money men.

Still seeming unwell, Ruth left his seat at the 1925 World Series between Washington and Pittsburgh on October 8 after the first two games when rumor had it that he needed medical treatment back in New York. Apparently he was not too sick, since he left on a hunting trip to Maine on October 15. The train trip would allow him time to consider what he had told a *Collier's* writer before he left. It would be easy enough to tally up his money just in September: $5,000 fine; $3,000 lost in pay while suspended.

The October 31, 1925, *Collier's* article by Joe Winkworth certainly was titled aptly, "I Have Been a Babe and a Boob," in which Ruth claimed, "I have thrown more than a quarter of a million…. I am going to start all over."

Like Ruppert's ledgers, Ruth's financial losses might be set down:

—through gambling, horse playing, cards, and dice—$125,000 (some claim he lost $20,000 on jai alai)
—through failed business ventures—$100,000
—through fees to lawyers and detectives for contesting various suits like blackmail—$25,000
—through living as a libertine—$250,000

These totals mean that Ruth blew through $500,000. His announced income from 1915 to 1925, which included salaries, bonuses, World Series shares, World Series coverage fees, vaudeville and the movies, approximated a total of $448,854. If the spending total is accurate, a large clump of cash is not being included. We know, for example, that he loved to buy, and often wrecked, the largest and most expensive automobiles. He purchased and maintained the Sudbury farm while living in the finest hotel suites, principally in New York City. Money went out to his wife and child. He paid $35,000, that we know of, for an annuity in 1924. We do not know how much money he had on hand at the end of 1925.

We do not know his income from endorsements. Money totals from his barnstorming tours were kept vague. Ruth never claimed he was broke.

With the money damage added up first, Ruth began to consider changing the way he got ready for the season. He turned down $25,000 to tour Canada "as evidence of his latest reform."[13] Bill Jenkinson states, "Essentially Babe Ruth had ended the first half of his baseball life and was now starting the second."[14] The second half of his baseball life would demonstrate a lot more of Ruth's discipline and competitive spirit. It began in December 1925 at McGovern's gymnasium above Durland's Riding Academy at 5 West 66th Street, off Central Park West.

Artie McGovern had made a small name for himself among the rich and famous—bandleaders, athletes, magnates. In *The New Yorker* magazine profile of McGovern appearing on May 22, 1937, Ruth in that 1925 December was described as

> overweight at 254 pounds, with a high pulse, a bulging stomach, and flabby muscles ... even the slightest exertion left Ruth short of breath.... Babe Ruth, who had been on the verge of losing both his health and his baseball career, listened and followed this new regime. You can be sure that it was not easy for him. He was accustomed to doing whatever he wanted, whenever he wanted. In six weeks, his body's decline was halted and reversed, he lost 44 pounds.[15]

Ruth would spend time with Artie McGovern for some weeks every winter for the next few years. "To use a term that would not arrive until years later, he had a personal trainer."[16] It seemed that Ruth had finally faced the reality that his body was his fortune. Though he loved food, he loved playing baseball even more. The joy of the game, the money and the adulation that came from playing the game at last became something at which he must work very hard from now on. He grew to recognize his need for discipline. He needed to become less careless. He would work hard during that time.

Eventually, he also had a personal accountant at home. Claire took control of the checkbook and insisted that Ruth write checks for his needs $50 at a time. The household budget, described in *The Babe and I,* was $1,500 a month, no doubt much of it due to the size of their New York apartment.[17]

21

Newspapers and
Magazines Everywhere

Like radio, the print medium became part of the mass media through the perfection of machines and leaps forward in other technology. But first the raw materials. In 1899, only 569,000 tons of newsprint were produced, but by "1918 it had increased to 1,760,000 tons, approximately 200 percent, [while] the population of the United States had increased only approximately 70 percent." As production rose, the cost of the raw material dropped so that it was possible to say that "the low cost of newsprint made the cheap American newspaper possible."[1]

At a postwar high of 6.05 cents per pound when Ruth began his first spring training with the Yankees, the price dropped almost by half in January of 1927 to 3.25.[2] The coming of age of the half-tone process early in the twentieth century made easy the printing of photographs, rather than slowly made drawing and engravings; the photo quality increased too with the increased quality of newsprint.

As the raw materials became more available, new machines allowed for many changes: printing on both sides of the paper at once; the mass manufacturing of paper from wood pulp; a linotype machine that set an entire line of print rather than one letter at a time. As trains extended their reach across the country, new audiences for papers were found, and machines were purchased that printed and folded at the rate of 90,000 four-page papers an hour.

In the year 1914, when Ruth first came into professional baseball, the use of the teletype machine enabled the AP to transmit words by wire to newsroom printers everywhere.

The A.P., the Associated Press, was one of a growing group of press agencies, groups like the United Press International, the United Press Association, and the International News Service. These services sold their products to newspapers far from the source, so that even a smaller service like the Central Press Association might reach 400 newspapers. While more than two thousand daily and six thousand weekly newspapers … were being published throughout the 1920s, the bulk of the news came from relatively few sources.[3]

The "few sources" became known as "chains," and soon "55 chains [were] controlling 230 daily papers with a combined circulation of over 13,000,000."[4] The Hearst and Scripps-Howard systems' control over the news led one observer to write, "genuine public issues, about which the masses of the population could be induced to feel intensely, were few and far between."[5] Nevertheless, during the 1920s, "Americans possessed a seemingly insatiable appetite for news, [in] more than 2,000 dailies that in 1920, an estimated 27 million Americans regularly read newspapers; 10 years later, that number had climbed to almost 40 million."[6]

Not everyone thought the growth of newspapers was a laudable thing.

Distort the world until its news is all murder, divorce, crime, passion, and chicanery ... present ... witless millionaires ... contemptible yet glorious in their spending. Sentimentalize everything, with cynicism just beneath ... fill the mind with a phantasmagoria where easy wealth, sordid luxury, degeneracy and drunken folly whirl through the pages in an intoxicating vulgarity.[7]

Inside those papers, sports reporting had increased dramatically. "That year of 1923 the percentage of newsprint devoted to sports rose ... to 17 percent,"[8] partly because "in 1913 the Associated Press connected all the big-league parks with all the principal afternoon newspapers.... It was the broadest sports coverage ever, and more than is now available."[9]

It did not take long (1921) for trade papers to take notice of something unusual about Ruth and advertising. After all, Ruth was dominating baseball coverage, and coverage of him as a celebrity was constant as well.

The newspaper ink Ruth used up was not simply empty propaganda. Ruth's appeal was undeniable, and "Ruth was never politically or culturally controversial."[10] If the hyperbole and constant coverage became less than the high point of journalism, "sports pages remain among the best-read.... Editors learned ... that they increased circulation."[11] As circulation rose—the five-year-old *New York Daily News* was selling 750,000 papers per day in 1924—salaries of editors had a chance to rise, as did the salaries of writers. As circulation rose, the fee for advertisements rose, thereby making more profit through numbers of copies and numbers and prices of ads.

"By 1927, newspapers in New York had 10 columns of sports. The news tabloids often led their front pages with sports news and pictures. Even the *New York Times,* and *New York Herald-Tribune* were giving over more and more column space to sports."[12] As editors responded to the public's desire for sports coverage and coverage of Ruth in particular, the percentage of sports column inches rose dramatically. And as that rose, the New York City newspaper business changed with more and more papers—the *Daily Mirror* and *Evening Graphic* in New York City are strong examples—being started, causing even more coverage for Ruth and increasing his fame and celebrity even more.

In a book written in 1919, the author showed that he was aware of all of the changes in the newspaper business, the rapidity of transmitting information, and the interconnectedness of newspaper services and chains. "In less than a minute from the time 'Babe' Ruth swats the ball a primitive bang, sending it over the fence for a home run, the entire American people is aware of the fact."[13]

The print medium, with others, began to be very profitable enterprises. But not simply from the number of copies sold. Before Ruth was born, in one hard-headed observation, J. W. Keller said, "When the question of capital is considered, journalism becomes at once a business, pure and simple. Money is invested to make money. The fundamental principle of metropolitan journalism is to buy white paper at three cents a pound and sell it at ten cents a pound."

But more than the price of newsprint,

A reasonable estimate for 1928 places the annual expenditure for newspaper advertising at $800,000,000 and in periodicals of all kinds, including business and farm papers, at around $300,000,000, a total of $1,100,000,000. Adding an estimated $75,000,000 for outdoor advertising,

$20,000,000 for street-car advertising and $15,000,000 for broadcasting, we get a total of $11,115,095,000 as the estimated expenditure in leading mediums.[14]

With all that money being expended, was Ruth really being helped by the papers? Sportswriters, with few exceptions, favored Ruth enormously and celebrated him and his baseball achievements even as they were ignoring his vulgarity and crassness off the field. Baseball writers owned their allegiance to the newspaper, to the team they covered, who often paid their expenses, and to their paychecks.

But some other publications were not so upbeat about Ruth. A magazine for press people noted, "the publicity given to gigantic commercial enterprises such as professional baseball, boxing, wrestling, horse racing, etc., paraded around as sports has made it possible for the 'men behind' to accumulate millions."[15] Among sports publications, *Baseball Magazine* (1908 to 1957) was one that printed articles critical of Ruth and oftentimes critical of the baseball establishment.

Another sports journal was *Sporting Life*, a periodical that lasted from 1883 until April 28, 1917, and proclaimed itself "The Loyal Champion of Clean Sport." The paper's owner, Francis C. Richter, "was a financial backer of the 1884 Union Association and its Philadelphia team. He declared the new league 'the emancipator of enslaved players and the enemy of the reserve clause.'"[16] The magazine made a serious mistake by angering the baseball magnates who made up the major league owners.

The magnates did not take to this support by Richter of their business rivals and authority, even though they said welcomed competition. What owners really wanted was to crush the competition, and in the year Ruth began "to effectively compete, the owners lured eighty-one former Major League players (eighteen of which were active) and one-hundred forty Minor League players (twenty-five of which were active) into the Federal League Baseball Company, Inc."[17]

For a brief time, the owners of American and National league teams schemed to get rid of the new league, and "the Federals agreed to disband after the American and National Leagues both agreed to pay an enormous sum of $600,000 for distribution to owners, absorb two franchises (one American League and one National League) and recognize all former players as eligible picks at a Fed-controlled auction."[18] If players were to be hired as workers after an "auction," it may have sounded to many like slavery.

Not merely content with wiping out the Federal League, the magnates needed to wipe out any supporters of the league, which left *Sporting Life* as a target. "Following the United States' entry into the European war in 1917, Organized Baseball got its chance to get even with *Sporting Life* for its passive support of the Federal League. During the World War, Baseball gave financial assistance to *The Sporting News*, but refused to support *Sporting Life* [which] gave up its publication in 1917."[19]

How was this accomplished? A fellow owner, this time the owner of *The Sporting News*, "convinced the American League to purchase 150,000 copies of the newspaper every week at a discount and send them overseas to U.S. soldiers, boosting circulation and crushing competitors." So by supporting the owners, the owner-friendly *Sporting News*' "circulation rose from 50,986 in the aftermath of the scandal to 90,000 in 1924."[20]

And best of all, for Walsh and Ruth,

The free advertising that Babe Ruth has received through the sport columns of the newspapers ... is the greatest reason why Babe Ruth can pull down the salary he pulls down and draw the crowds he draws.... The big crowds are worked up chiefly that page after page of free advance advertising in the sports columns—sport propaganda of the most reckless kind—is the real force that brings the big

Ruth ad for *The Sporting News*, **1922.**

crowds.... Baseball clubs are organized for the coin just the same as motion picture producers or theatrical managers ... practically anything of normal human interest could be made just as popular as ... baseball ... if the newspapers of the country would give the free advance advertising ... given to sporting stars and sporting events.[21]

22

A Sign of Glory
(1926)

When his body, his instrument, had begun to show wear, doubts about Ruth began to appear. Ruth was alert to the fickleness of celebrity. To command a high salary during the season, to demand high fees for barnstorming, to be paid for the use of his name and image, he knew he must not only live differently, but, with the continued guidance from his business partner Christy Walsh, Ruth had to look more serious, while still not looking solemn.

Could it be Walsh's hand behind his New Year's resolutions listed in the *New York Graphic* on January 2, 1926? Sounding as if expressing his desire to live by the Boy Scouts oath, Ruth said he resolved to be temperate, obedient, and thrifty; he would try for more than 59 home runs, take part in every game, watch his diet, "conserve his health," and "share in bringing another pennant to New York." The Yankees, in the six seasons since Ruth arrived in New York, had amassed a record of 1–2 in World Series play, finished seventh once, and did not have a championship opportunity in three other years. No one seemed ready to point out the lack of success, only that Ruth could achieve wonders.

Walsh now had Ruth appearing at charity affairs, orphanages, and other events such as the Fordham Juvenile League and the Citizens' Military Training Camps.[1] The Walsh-led "campaign" (such remains the manly diction of advertising) may have been constructed so as to have Ruth admired for his pluck and his desire to reform.

Ruth waited until after the New York baseball writers' dinner on January 31, 1926, to leave for Florida. He hesitated until then partly because it had become Walsh's annual affair, but this year in particular he showed up because he knew he would be ridiculed by the writers, ridicule that would not be printed until much later. And so he was. "I wonder where my Babe Ruth is tonight?" sang some writers. "He may be drinking tea—or maybe gin…/I know he's with a dame."[2]

But Ruth and McGovern had the changes for Ruth to display. Smelser writes that pupil and teacher "were so pleased with their human sculpture that they gave a three-round boxing exhibition at the annual dinner … just to show off the limber Ruth bounding about in tights."[3]

Clearly, two major influences had toned down Ruth's careless behavior. Walsh supplied him with money and guidance about his money, and McGovern gave him a demanding physique, which might do him some physical good as well. Claire remained mostly in the background … for now.

Did Ruth create money for McGovern? Aside from McGovern's fee, Ruth also brought money into the industry of physical culture, as evidenced by the illustrated article (featuring photos of McGovern working with Ruth) in the *Physical Culture* magazine of August 1926, titled "Brought Back By Physical Culture." Since physical culture was getting itself a name, and since Mr. McGovern seemed to be the most prominent practitioner of the culture, then McGovern made much more money beyond his fee from Ruth. Ruth made him richer and perhaps added to the income to other practitioners of physical culture throughout the country.

Ruth left for the new Yankees' training site, St. Petersburg, Florida, for some golf for three weeks. Newspapers pointed to "the Babe, a new, slimmer, brisker Babe," during spring training. In Florida, Ruth found himself at the end of his five-year contract for $52,000, while pitcher Herb Pennock was paid $17,500. Those employees not at the top of their profession, not well educated, or not in high paying jobs, would average $1,310 for a year.

Other players in 1926 were very well paid, but the best pay went to seven playing managers. Other entertainers were doing well. Gloria Swanson made $20,000 per week in movies, and a football player was paid $4,000 to endorse Lucky Strikes cigarettes.

As Ruth was returning to his suite at the Ansonia Hotel at Broadway and 73rd Street, syndicated stories said, "The big question of the training belt has been: has Ruth passed the peak of his greatness?"[4] The commonly accepted truth about peak performance for a baseball player was at age 27 or 28, Ruth, who lived hard, was also, at 31, years past those accepted ages.

Can greatness be measured by how much someone will pay you for your services? According to Waite Hoyt, Ruth, as a kind of rented celebrity, was "paid the unprecedented sum of one thousand dollars an hour to stand next to a pile of underwear" in a Chicago department store."[5] He also found himself to be the owner of "a few apartment houses in Boston," thanks to Claire.[6] That same article claimed that Ruth's reformation earned him an additional $15,000 in salary. Virtue, it seemed, is not merely its only reward.

On August 6, the team won its sixteenth consecutive victory and reached its peak of an 11-game lead over second place Cleveland. Despite losing eight of ten games toward season's end, they held off Cleveland, when the Indians lost six of their last ten games. At season's end, Ruth had returned not simply to prominence but to dominance in major league baseball. He led the league in runs, home runs, runs batted in, and walks. Though he hit .372, he did not win the batting title. For contrast, his 47 home runs placed him 27 ahead of the second-most home runs in the majors; he also finished 26 ahead in RBI. The team hit 49 home runs more than anyone else in the league; Ruth hit more home runs than five teams in the American League and four teams in the National. More than one commentator thought Ruth had become "'submissive and sensible' and had learned that he wasn't bigger than baseball. Could being submissive pay off for him too? Yes. As Crepeau writes, "the reform of the sinner made great copy and was added to the Ruthian myth."[7]

The winning team in the 1926 National League was the St. Louis Cardinals, which featured five players who hit above .300. Their chief hitter, Rogers Hornsby, was paid $33,333 to manage as well, and during the season traded for pitcher Pete Alexander. At 39, the veteran had been a major leaguer since 1911. Hornsby oversaw an offense that scored the most runs in the league.

And it showed, with the Cardinals outscoring the Yankees, 31 to 21 in the seven-game World Series, which was a productive one for Ruth. In Game Four, he became the first player ever to hit three home runs in a single Series game. (He also tied a record for runs.) Ruth also walked 11 times, including a record four times In Game Seven.[8] The Cardinals may have scored nine unearned runs in the Series, but three games in the Series belonged to Alexander, who "pitched complete-game wins in Games 2 and 6" and in Game Seven, "entered the game to relieve … in the seventh inning…. He struck out Lazzeri, [and] held the lead, and the Cards were champs. Alexander … struck out 17 Yankees in 20⅓ innings."[9]

With two out and down by a run in the final game's ninth inning, perhaps it expressed Ruth's desire to be the difference, but he tried to surprise the Cardinals with a steal of second. When he was thrown out, the game and the Series ended with the Cardinals as champions. If that was a mistake, no one ever thought so, and reasons have been put forward. As Bill Jenkinson writes, "I have read over one hundred articles about Game Seven, but I have never encountered any contemporary pundits who faulted Babe Ruth. Since the game was a national event and thousands of different stories were published about it, there probably were some negative comments. I have just not personally encountered them."[10]

Ruth had become even more noticed for his Series at-bats, as the *New York Times* dutifully recorded. "Ruth Breaks Ten Records And Mark for Smashing Them." Baseball's ledger on the 1926 Series read that the seven games drew 326,051 fan and generated $1,207,864 in ticket sales. Other athletic contests were beginning to make their mark. The University of Notre Dame's football team grossed $1,400,000 in eight games that year.

More fame arrived for Ruth. The Series on the radio claimed to reach 15,000,000 listeners, while others kept watch on the Series via the telegraph, relayed perhaps to their local newspapers, which might post the results as they arrived on a chalkboard outside the paper's office or by using the large mechanical device called the Play-O-Graph.

Ruth dominated on movie screens as well that fall. By now, "almost all of America's 18,000 movie theaters showed a weekly newsreel."[11] "Running on average about 15 minutes in length…. A fashion or entertainment piece would round out the reel before ending with the sports segment."[12]

More loot for Ruth. In Game Four in St. Louis, "one of his home runs broke a plate glass window of an automobile showroom and bounced off the side of a Chevy coupe inside the showroom. The Bambino was presented with the coupe. The dealer was the Wells Motor Company and it quickly advertised the crack in the window with a large picture of Ruth with a large sign above explaining the break."[13]

And even more booty. "'Babe Ruth Is Awarded Automobile In Contest,'" once he was acclaimed as the most popular athlete in America today."[14] Did Ruth actually take possession of the cars? No one ever seems to have seen Ruth driving a Chevrolet. Did he simply take the worth in cash? If he donated them to orphanages and hospitals, there exists no record of the gifts.

So in addition to the value of the two cars, Ruth put in his bank account $52,000 salary, plus the $15,000 stipend; a World Series losers' payout of $3,417.75, and $5,000 for "covering" the Series.

Known endorsement deals for the years, but not the payment, included the Babe Ruth Health System, on sale for $12, $1 to get started. In 1926, "One of the most lucrative deals Walsh struck for Ruth was with McLoughlin Manufacturing Company … producer of men's underwear," and advertised itself as the "Home of Babe Ruth Union Suits."[15] Also

Bradley Beach, New Jersey, 1926. *Left to right*: **Waite Hoyt, Herb Hunter, Ruth, and Herb Pennock. Hunter would later arrange Ruth's visit to Hamaii.**

for sale in 1926 was Babe Ruth's Home Run Candy. Walsh and Ruth added another $100,000 for a 12-week tour on the Pantages vaudeville circuit, sending Ruth from Minneapolis to the West Coast. (Smelser thinks the amount was exaggerated by $35,000. If not, the money we know Ruth grossed added up to $175,417.75, about 2.3 million today.)

With another barnstorming tour lined up—13 games—from October 11–28, right after the Series, Ruth would have as his team before his trip to Montreal the Bay Ridge, New York Club, called by the *New York Times*, "Ruth's recruit team." This hiring marked the "first of Ruth's association with Nat Strong, a force in semipro and black baseball in the Northeastern United States" and a partner of Max Rosner in the Bushwicks team.[16] Gehrig would join him later.

Ruth began his 1926 tour on October 11, 1926, a tour from New Jersey north to Montreal and into Indiana, Iowa and Michigan. Bradley Beach, New Jersey, 60 miles away from Manhattan, was a Jersey shore resort town of 2,400. Ruth's so-called "recruit team" took the train to the town, but Ruth "had to make the trip in his new sport roadster."[17] Met "at Eatontown yesterday morning by two Bradley Beach motorcycle cops, a necessity since Ruth stopped to get gasoline and was mobbed by fans, he later stopped to see a boy named Johnny Sylvester in a town 11 miles away from his game site, who the press had written about in great and imaginative detail."[18]

His team was beaten by the Brooklyn Royal Colored Giants, 2 to 1. Even this minor game was covered on October 12 by the AP: "the game did not appear to be taken seriously by anyone. Ruth was obviously the attraction and he played his part well." There were signs that the players at least seemed to take playing seriously. Ruth stole a base; Cannonball Redding, now 36, struck out seven and walked but one.

Traveling 150 miles north and west brought Ruth into a familiar place, Wilkes-Barre, Pennsylvania. Gene Sullivan, "coal operator of Avoca," knew Ruth and persuaded him to make a stop in Wilkes-Barre. There came a sign that corporations were learning. One piece in the paper could laud the paper, a baker and the game itself. An ad in the *Wilkes-Barre Record* publicized "a chance for one thousand (1000) boys to see 'Babe' Ruth FREE at Artillery Park as guests of the Henry German Baking Co., maker of Luxury Bread."

Ruth did not himself understand the fascination with autographs. One book has him say, "Who the hell wants to collect that crap?"[19] Yet Inabinett quotes Grantland Rice, who wrote that Ruth "spent numerous hours going out of his way to ... take [youngsters] autographed baseballs, to help pay their doctors' bills."[20] Rice remains the only writer to claim that Ruth paid hospital bills for children or that a child immediately sold the ball to pay for a doctor.

Ruth arrived at 7 a.m. on Lehigh Valley train number 11 for game two. To get a sense of the effort Ruth was willing to expend to get to barnstorming games, the schedule for train number 11 showed that it could be boarded at 1:13 a.m. the morning after the Bradley Beach game for the almost six-hour trip northwest to Wilkes-Barre. Ruth had lunch at a meeting of the Wilkes-Barre Exchange Club at the Reddington Hotel.

At 2 p.m., Ruth and Gehrig went to Artillery Park, suiting up to play for the Hughestown Colts against the team from Larksville. "He waved to a few hundred youngsters and told the perplexed gate keeper, 'Aw, let them in.' And before order could be restored, at least 250 boys had 'crashed the gate' thanks to their idol." Gehrig was not their idol and so seemed to accept his role as the second banana.

Every time a ball rolled into the outfield, groups of boys would dash onto the field to get the ball, and the winner would run back to the bench where Ruth was sitting "and joined the line of others waiting" for a Ruth signature. The crowd was about 800 boys and 400 adults. Ruth's time at the park lasted from about 2 to about 5:30. With baseballs running out at the end of six innings and with Ruth not homering, Ruth asked pitcher Ernie Cockran to throw him some more balls, and Ruth hit a ball 200 feet beyond the outfield fence.

Though the home run at Wilkes-Barre did not receive much attention in the local press the day after the exhibition game, something unusual had happened, as evidenced by coverage of it by the Associated Press. "The ball cleared the right field fence 400 feet from the plate by more than 40 feet and was still ascending. The ball landed on the far side of the running track of a high school athletic field in Kirby Park. Officials estimated the length at 650 feet."

Many years later, a baseball historian began to study this home run by taking measurements of the field. Bill Jenkinson "firmly believes" that the home run "traveled well over 600 feet."[21]

The Perth Amboy, New Jersey, game, 130 miles away, received scant coverage for a number of reasons: the rain, the lack of a local daily in a city of 42,000, and an in-season exhibition by the Yankees played there in 1923, greeted by 12,000 fans, as were the Red Sox and Cubs in earlier years. In the Perth Amboy area, nearby Clifton bragged of its semipro team, the Doherty Silk Sox, and Ruth was to play that opposition on October 13, 1926.

After detraining, Ruth drove into town and was met by fans and police and taken

Ad from the Wilkes-Barre Records, promoting a Ruth appearance, sponsored by a local bakery.

first to city hall and then to lunch at the Majestic Restaurant. But rains came in the third inning at the Raritan Copper Works field, stopping the game. Since "the big attraction had done his stuff for the fans, his representatives contended he was entitled to more than the rain guarantee."[22]

Walsh and the game's promoter began to argue about Ruth's price for playing less than half of a game. Ruth had put on his usual batting practice show and hit many balls over the fence. The quarrel over full payment apparently forced Ruth to wait out the rain and play three more innings after the delay. Though he played first base, he went hitless for the game.

At game four's end in Olyphant, Pennsylvania, Ruth had to travel 500 miles, from the depot at Scranton on the Nickel Plate Road via Cleveland to Lima, Ohio. The trip would allow him time to sleep in his Pullman compartment. He would need it for the full day's activities that awaited him.

The visit by Ruth became a community-wide effort for Lima in Ohio, an occasion described in fine detail by the local historical society in 1995 in its publication the *Allen County Reporter.*

Local merchants advertised the giving away of shirts, shoes, watches, and even dental work for various feats achieved during the ballgame. Shortly after noon, Ruth and his siren-sounding escort arrived at the Allen County Children's Home (75 boys and girls), where he spoke to the children, gave out candy to the girls and gave autographed baseballs to the boys. Next Ruth drove to the Shawnee Centralized school and climbed on the running board so that the 500 cheering children could see him as he passed slowly along.

Ruth agreed to play for the Lima club against the team from Celina, in the "last of the three game inter-county championship series." During batting practice at the 900-seat park, "Ruth responded with eleven home runs in ten minutes." He also responded in the game, playing all positions except catcher and hitting two doubles and two home runs. The Lima team won, 11–7.

Then, quickly it was time for Ruth to go back east. "The Pennsylvania line being contacted, the Broadway Limited agreed to stop briefly at Lima."[23] Only the excellent trains and easy connections allowed him to keep up at this schedule, moving 600 miles by train back to New York City.

Having completed five games, traveling to New York City, Kingston, New York, Canada and New Jersey, he boarded the Pennsylvania Railroad to South Bend, Indiana, for 1926's games 10 and 11. The games had been carefully planned for a Saturday and Sunday when the Notre Dame football team would be playing an away game. With some major leaguers joining the squads, the best-known player was Freddie Fitzsimmons, who pitched for South Bend, his home in nearby Mishawaka.

Attendance for the South Bend games appeared to be in the 200–300 range, with "orphans in free compliments of the Babe." Ruth went three for four on Saturday, including a home run estimated at "600" feet by the *South Bend Tribune.* Of course it was the longest ball ever hit at the field and "one of the longest balls Babe ever hit in his career." The All-Stars beat the local South Bend Indians, 7–3, in a game called after six innings because of a late start.

The next day, Ruth pitched eight innings during which he gave up seven hits in a game that ended in a 3–3 tie. This game was called because of inclement weather, temperatures hovering in the mid–20s throughout the day with drizzling rain. He again went 3–4 with a double.

Of course, the publicity for Ruth rarely slowed down. By now, Walsh had arranged a high fee for Ruth to be a "guest editor" at local newspapers. He would go to the newsroom, be photographed there perhaps wearing an eyeshade. Someone would write an article using Ruth's byline. This was very typical on these barnstorming trips.

Now heading 420 miles west, closer to where he was obliged to start his time on the vaudeville stage, Ruth arrived in Des Moines on Wednesday, October 27, 1926, and went by train and car to Iron Mountain (146 miles) in Michigan's Upper peninsula. "Schools were dismissed early to permit children to see the game and employees of business houses were told they would be permitted time off to witness it. Barber shops of the city were closed for the event."[24] After he

Ad for All-Star game in South Bend, Indiana.

was given flowers by the local Knights of Columbus, Ruth once more hit some balls. Ruth making three outs in the game displeased the crowd "and so Babe was allowed to come to home plate and hit for fifteen minutes, which he did and hit many out of the park to the delight of the fans."

After the game, he sat down to dinner with the Lions Club, another fraternal group of businessmen. With money on someone's mind, Ruth was offered a mountain, Pine Mountain, for $100,000 "for the iron that's in it." Late in the evening, he motored 17 miles to Pembine to catch a train to Minneapolis (311 miles). This city appeared to be a taking-off point for a hunting trip in the North Woods for the weekend. Stories began to appear describing, yet again, how much money Ruth would be making in vaudeville. One source said $8,333 each week for 12 weeks, another estimated $6,000 a week for 15 weeks.

After a training season, a regular season of 154 games, a World Series, and 17 days of barnstorming, Ruth's energy seemed inexhaustible. It is true that in 1926, he played in 13 barnstorming games on 12 fields, but he also did not play for five days during that schedule of games.

And wherever he went, newspaper people followed. In Spokane from November 11–16 on tour, he arrived at 5:35 p.m. on the Northern Pacific, where he was met by boys and "the blare of bands" at the depot. That night he attended an Elks smoker. The next morning he went to the office of the *Spokane Press* at 8:14 a.m. "to read sportsmanship essays," for one more payday. Earlier, Westbrook's Pegler's "The Sporting Goods," of October 17, 1926, pondered Ruth's contributions to the wealth of team owners throughout the

American League, who "all fattened on the Babe's work." Pegler asserted that Ruth "went to their ballparks year after year … and packed the customers in because he was Babe Ruth."

Seeming to like the company of men in a relatively public-free setting, Ruth joined another fraternal group, this one the Goodfellows in Portland, Oregon. Signed to spend a week there, he breakfasted with writers at his hotel and drove golf balls off the ten-story roof of the *Oregonian*. While in Vancouver, it is likely that Christy Walsh sent a telegram to the local Auburn dealer saying that "I, Babe Ruth, prefer Auburns." The local dealer then offered the use of one of his Auburns to Ruth while in that Canadian city in late November 1926.

It is possible to trace his other activities on the West Coast. For example, Ruth went duck hunting with Linn Platner on Sweetwater Lake, east of Chula Vista in Bonita, California. Ballplayers have often claimed that walking through woods and up hilly terrain brought good physical result, particularly for their legs, though Ruth had not forgotten what changes Artie McGovern had helped him achieve.

The vaudeville work finished, Ruth and Walsh found another source of cash. Ruth signed a contract to film the movie *Babe Comes Home*, that brought him $50,000 to $75,000, depending on the source. The six-reeler was filmed in Venice, California, in early February and opened in May of 1927. No copies have survived of this movie. The *New York Times* review read, "it had no bigger fan than Babe Ruth himself, who later confessed to having sat through the 6-reeler ten times."

For the rest of 1926 and the beginning of 1927, it is known that Ruth was on vaudeville stages beginning on November 1 for a minimum of 12 weeks, followed by the filming of the movie, and that he arrived in New York City on March 2 from California. He left for Florida three days later. The break from his wife Helen now common knowledge, there is no mention of him ever seeing his daughter during all of 1926. It does not seem to fit the pattern of Ruth's coverage by the press nor of the press' fondness for stories about Ruth and the "kiddies," for Ruth not to have been covered visiting his own child even once.

But when he left on March 5 for the Yankees' training camp in Florida aboard the Seaboard Air Line train, children everywhere "Bid Farewell," said the *New York Times*. With money highlighted—"$210,000 Star Poses—" the headline continued as Ruth was captured as he "Autographs Baseballs for His Young Admirers at Penn Station." How long and how rancorous the negotiations with owner Ruppert may have been were not written about, but Ruth's three-year contract for $70,000 per year was sure to be noted.

23

Johnny Sylvester:
Seizing an Opportunity

A legend (some want to say myth) begins life as an attractive and harmless lie. Because it does no damage and because it caters to what we would like to believe is true, the lie flourishes, is repeated to let it become popular information, and hardens into history. Examples of such lies include Paul Revere being a sole rider and that Benjamin Franklin's kite helped him discover electricity. Attractive and harmless lies can sometimes be told about athletes, but, as time passes, they harden into myths.

In the fall of 1926, a boy in New Jersey asked his father for a favor. The father, Horace Clapp Sylvester, Jr., was a vice president at National City Bank and took the family for a vacation to Bay Head, New Jersey, part of the Jersey Shore's "Gold Coast." The boy, Johnny, not feeling well, asked if his father could get him an autographed ball from the teams playing in the World Series in 1926. Both St. Louis and New York sent baseballs to the boy.

Over the years, this story has been transformed into a miraculous occasion: the boy was healed of his terrible illness by Babe Ruth himself. The complication in the story lies in the problem of the various versions of this story from early October 1926 to the present day. Was Johnny ill? What was the illness? How serious was the Illness? How rapid was his recovery? What, if anything, did Ruth have to do with the recovery?

Here are a few versions over the decades, beginning with the boy's diagnosis:

1926—sinus trouble;
1926—same incurable disease "that carried off President Coolidge's son";
1927—thirty minutes to live at one point;
1931—in a coma;
1933—from a strange malady, a kind of melancholia;
1947—spinal infection;
1959—Johnny had been operated on and he was dying. His doctor asked the Babe to visit the boy. Medicine could do no more for him;
1987—his skull started deteriorating;
1990—serious infection of the forehead.

Years later, Ruth's *New York Times* obituary stated that Johnny asked for the ball and the next day Ruth, armed with bat, glove and half a dozen signed baseballs, made one of his frequent pilgrimages to a hospital. The boy, unexpectedly meeting his idol face to face, was so overjoyed that he was cured—almost miraculously.[1]

How did Ruth miraculously heal the boy? Some versions over the years:

1987—"Meet him he did. [Babe Ruth] dropped by little [Johnny Sylvester]'s hospital bed, shook his hand and asked him what he'd like. 'Hit a home run for me, Babe,' croaked Johnny. 'I will, in the opening game of the World Series,' came the reply."

2012—"He hit four home runs that Series/And every one for me/Thanks to those arcing wallops/My wretched body healed/Thanks to the greatest player/That ever took the field.../Before there was Paul Bunyan/Before old Honest Abe/Before there was John Henry, There always was The Babe."[2]

Best of all, five years after the 1926 World Series:

1931—"Boston *Post* sports columnist Bill Cunningham had seen Ruth kneel down before he batted. Cunningham speculated that when Ruth was taking practice swings, he was doing the sign of the cross. Cunningham speculated that Ruth had been praying and that he probably said, 'Please help me sock it just once more for that kid.'

"And then, Cunningham added, 'Some of the writers remarked that the Babe seemed a trifle blasé as he circled the paths and ducked into the dugout.... The truth of the matter just might reveal that the Babe didn't show them too much of his face—they might have seen something that looked dangerously like tears. For the Babe's just a kid after all.'"[3]

Two games of the 1926 World Series had been played in New York City on October 2 and October 3. October 4 was a day for the teams to travel to St. Louis for the next three games. On October 5, Horace Clapp Sylvester, Jr., through a friend, sent a telegram to Sportsman's Park in St. Louis, asking for an autographed ball for a sick child, home in bed. The very earliest this request could be honored was during a rain delay that day, when the two teams had time in the clubhouse to sign the balls. Or they might have signed after the October 5 game.

Next, to transport the baseballs, the fastest method would have been airmail. The balls, it seemed, were signed in the clubhouse around game time, three o'clock. Next, the balls had to be taken to the airport postal office. Charlie Poekel reports that the balls left on the 3:30 p.m. plane on October 5. By consulting a site devoted to airmail pioneers, a mode in its infancy, we can see that an average airmail plane's speed would reach about 150 miles per hour, without any stops. But the plane from St. Louis made stops in both Springfield and Peoria before landing in Chicago.[4] Thus, the 300-mile trip to Chicago might take about two and a half hours, enough time to finish the game on October 5.

Without knowing the layover time in Chicago, some time had to be used at least to refuel and add more mail to the cargo. The next legs would take the package to Hadley Field, New Brunswick, NJ, the Eastern terminus of the route, about 750 miles from Chicago. This would take another five hours, meaning it was likely that the earliest time the package could have arrived at the New Jersey airfield was about 11:30 the night of October 5. By then, Sylvester's father would have returned to Bay Head for the night. It is not known if the package was sent to the father's work address, to the Bay Head address or to the address of the friend of the father's. Certainly, no one would notify the father when the package would arrive. It would simply have to be waited for, there being no particular rush for its delivery.

Bay Head, New Jersey, lay 40 miles south, and by now Game Three of the Series, on October 5, was long over, and New York was shut out. (Not known for sure is the time when the package arrived in the boy's hands. His father, working in New York City and not knowing when or if the balls would arrive, would not stop at Hadley Field, and even if he did, the balls could not arrive until three hours after his work day.) Since the father wrote the request, or the friend, for the ball, it would likely be his work address to which the ball would be delivered.

On October 6, the day for Game Four in the Series, the second game in St. Louis, the Yankees, with the help of Ruth's three home runs, won the game. Once more author Charlie Poekel relates that the father received the package of balls and took them home at day's end on October 6. But the boy had not yet received the baseballs until the game was over, and there was no letter in the package, no note or encouragement. Just the two team-signed baseballs.

On October 7, the boy, the baseballs in his possession, but no note with a promise, may or may not have listened to the game on the radio which the Yankees managed to win, 3–2, to lead the Series by one game with two left to play. No home runs were hit by Ruth. October 8 was another travel day, this time east to New York City.

One day later, October 9, the opposing teams were ready to resume the World Series back in New York. On that October 9, "his parents left him at home and went to the game themselves."[5] If son Johnny was well enough to be left in the care of someone other than his mother and father, the odds are in favor that he had not been all that desperately ill in the first place.

Ruth wrote a letter, the first and only correspondence, dated Saturday, October 9, that said, "I will try to knock you another homer, maybe two today." Ruth did not hit a home run in a 10–2 Yankees loss on October 9. The next day, October 10, Ruth hit a home run in another loss for the Yankees to end the Series in favor of the Cardinals.

The letter from Ruth written on October 9, a Saturday, the one promising a home run, could not have been delivered until sometime Monday, October 11, a day after the Series ended. We do not even know if the letter was sent to the father's work address or to Bay Head. (It does seem to be true that some time afterwards, Johnny's father sat down to write to the two teams to thank them for the balls, saying that the balls had raised the boy's spirit.) Not the note, the balls.

That very day, October 11, the fabrications began, and on the front page of the *New York Times,* a story stated that the father dated the boy's recovery "since Babe Ruth wrote promising a home run" even though "Johnny has been taken ill with blood poisoning so powerfully so that doctors despaired of his life." But the boy did not get the letter with the promise until the World Series games were over. The *New York Times* claimed "the boy's improvement" dated from "Ruth … promising a home run" and then making "three in the following game."

The falsehood was repeated 66 years later, in Dave Anderson's column in 1992: "During his Yankee career, the Babe actually arrived at a New York hospital with an autographed ball for little Johnny Sylvester and promised to hit a home run. Which he did." (The ball mentioned sold on February 7, 2014, for $250,642.)

On October 11, with a barnstorming game scheduled nearby, "Christy Walsh … [to] generate even more publicity [had] Ruth, instead of going from New York City directly to Bradley Beach went with Walsh and a New York Daily News reporter to Johnny's home in Essex Fells, New Jersey."[6]

Did Ruth alert the reporter? He did not seem to forbid his presence at Sylvester's bedside. Others saw an excellent public relations opportunity as well: Rogers Hornsby also wrote a letter to the boy, and other sports people like tennis player Bill Tilden contacted the boy.

Clearly it was not enough that Ruth hit many home runs. He must approach legendary status. In Ruth's time, "Fact and myth and good PR, the new science, merged with marketing and America's great love for pathos."[7]

The country's "great love for pathos" and the magical powers of celebrities, were chronicled again in a story relayed by Charlie Poekel.

Sportswriter Fred Lieb wrote of one incident that occurred outside a spring training site in Phillips Field, Tampa, Florida, when Ruth walked by a boy who had not walked in two years. Lieb wrote that Ruth said, "Hi ya, kid!" and the boy jumped up to return the greeting. "Babe would later comment that 'I worked a miracle that spring in Tampa.'"[8]

As evidence of the miracle, Poekel added, "The story was confirmed by Leo Durocher, who was a rookie infielder at the time."[9] No one knows what prevented the boy from walking. No one seems to notice the disparity between jumping up—or bouncing on the seat—and walking. Or how long the miracle cure lasted.

The witness? Durocher's first few major league games were in 1925, his debut on October 2, for the New York Yankees. He could not have trained in 1925 with the Yankees since his minor league team for most of the year, the Hartford Senators, had no affiliation with the Yankees. The year 1928 was both his true rookie year and the only possible year for Durocher to be a rookie and in spring training with the Yankees. But the Yankees did not train in Tampa in those years; they trained in St. Petersburg.

Was there a game in which the Yankees visited Tampa during spring training? No. The Yankees played no games in Tampa in the spring of 1928, Durocher's rookie year. In Durocher's book, nothing is mentioned of the moment of healing. Bob Considine, writing Ruth's story in 1948, has Ruth confirm the version, saying, "I worked a miracle that spring in Tampa."

Nevertheless, Lieb thought, "They would try to touch Ruth and, when they did, seemed to feel they had been given something. It was like the woman who touched Jesus and was healed."[10]

In the next story, once more Ruth has the dramatic opportunity to display healing powers. Heroes must always appear in dramatic situations. An AP story reprinted in the *New York Times* had the headline, "Babe Ruth Fails to Save Dying Man" from November 1, 1928. "Babe Ruth made a futile attempt to revive Charles H. Tate a Sioux city salesman on a train … last night…. Tate was stricken with a hemorrhage and died despite an hour's attempt by Ruth to revive him." Ruth was on his way to Denver, a 600-mile trip. Although we do not know what methods Ruth may have used, or why Ruth may have been chosen to give medical aid, it does seem odd that no doctor could be found as the train rode through many places and miles in that hour.

It must be wondered that newspapermen would perpetuate so clearly a nonsensical story as the Johnny Sylvester healing. One, or a combination of three choices must be correct. First, limited resources or time forced them to repeat and embellish the story. Second, they actually believed that Ruth's effect on people contained powerful magic with healing properties. Third, the writers cynically believe readers would accept as truth any story appearing in a newspaper.

Finally, there are enough persons who say that it does not matter if the Sylvester story is true. "It just feels good," they say. Or it contains some startling aspect. For example, take the 1925 event witnessed by a private detective who then passed it on to Edward Barrow and thirdly to the writer Fred Lieb, who then wrote the story, a piece now 90 years old. The tale, supposedly an eyewitness story, had Ruth having sex with six women in one night. Montville, like others, accepts the story and is happy to retell it.[11]

And why not? It is a fine story. It has a great hero, it has sex, it has supposedly epic deeds. For so many it does not seem to be enough just for Ruth to be a skillful baseball player. If we are to have heroes, they must be selfless. If we are to have heroes, the heroes must be laudable in every aspect of their lives.

For a well-publicized hero like Ruth, he must be a sexual giant, he must consume vast amounts of cigars, food, and alcohol, and have god-like healing powers. It is almost as if heroes cannot simply be people of accomplishment in one field, but must be larger than life, larger than their limited skills in a limited field for a limited time in their youth.

24

A Prized Year
(1927)

During his Hollywood filming time, Ruth put himself under the regimen of his personal trainer, Artie McGovern, a regimen that included five-mile runs, followed by a rubdown by McGovern at his Hollywood Plaza Hotel. The Associated Press listed Ruth's morning diet as consisting of a glass of orange juice, cereal with skimmed milk, and a hot drink.

The workout and diet became well known enough, and the results so dramatic in the winter of 1925–1926, that Ruth and Walsh found they could use McGovern and his business as a lever in contract bargaining with Ruppert. By the end of January, from the movie studio, Ruth demanded that he be paid an even greater sum of money than before or he would not set one foot on the westbound train. "Babe Serious About Quitting" unless he signed for $100,000 a year, announced the February 11, 1927, *Times*, "Talks of a Gymnasium Chain" to bring him great wealth.

When he finally did travel to New York City, the benefits of McGovern's scheme were trumpeted in many newspapers. "Ruth now weighs 224 pounds, reduces waistline 9 inches." As long as he was asking for a large contract, he "also want[ed a] $7,700 refund" of fines paid to the team and threatened once more to "retire from baseball unless his terms are met." The fines still rankled. A letter to Ruppert was timed to arrive at about the same time Ruth did on a cross-country train. Though an admittedly short-term strategy by Walsh and Ruth at this point, threatening an autocrat like Ruppert might have repercussions in the long term. But right now, Ruth had bargaining power. Later, Ruppert would have it.

After the long trip from California, Babe Ruth arrived on the second day of March at Grand Central Station in Manhattan at 9:40 a.m., on the first section of the *Twentieth Century Limited*. That afternoon he met with Ruppert. Both men knew that Ty Cobb would be drawing $75,000 in 1927, and both men knew "it was widely commented, Ruth deserved $100,000."[1] One such source, the *Chicago Tribune,* had written, "Babe Ruth with his long hitting propensity is an invaluable asset to the Yankees at the turnstile. On the road Babe adds 25 percent at least at times."

Likewise, "The players support Ruth in all of his salary fights. 'We depend upon men like Ruth to increase our salaries all along the line,' one of his team-mates told me while the big Bambino was negotiating for his three-year contract."[2] Both men knew the February 22, 1927, letter written by Walsh stated, "If I were in any other business I would probably receive a new contract at higher salary without request," Ruth said in part. "Or rival employers would bid for my services. Baseball law forces me to work for the New York club or remain idle."

Ruppert, perhaps, did not think Ruth needed the money. The Yankees owner could read differing reports that in 1926 his player had made $180,000 or $200,000 or more. But even with Ruth's income in 1926, Ruppert could look in his ledger and see a 1926 pre-tax profit of $544,124. Ruth did not get to see the books, but he could look up at the stands and estimate. If Ty Cobb were worth $75,000, Ruppert might argue, that was what the owner of Cobb's contract thought he could afford—and besides, Cobb was also managing.

The image of Ruth as amiable and generous did not apply to contract dealings, as Claire Ruth remembered. "The Babe's salary battles with Colonel Ruppert were frequent, acrimonious…. There was a strong feeling that these battles were publicity stunts. They were anything but."[3] But the two settled quickly, and at the Ruppert Brewery Ruth "attach[ed] his signature to the three-year Yankee contract calling for $210,000 which he negotiated." His biweekly check for the 1927 season amounted to $6,595.38. The New York Yankees' median salary stood at $7,000, with at least one player making $13,000. Gehrig's 1927 salary was $8,000. Pennock was second on the club in salary at $17,500. Three others made five figures. Rookie pitcher Wilcy Moore signed for $2,500 for the year. Though a man might be a teammate, when Ruth was paid more in six days than Moore in an entire season, you were clearly not in his class either financially or as a player. If Ruth did not remember the names of teammates, if players told stories about Ruth that they had only heard, this gap in money and fame may have been the cause. A baseball clubhouse is made of cliques.

An aspect of Ruth the sportswriters found continually interesting was the cash that he pocketed from his contract with Walsh. The *New York Times* of March 6 reported that from six sources Ruth added $222,000. "He was a one man endorsement machine—for pure milk, appliances for the home, housing developments, different kinds of cars … like REO's, Auburns, Packards, Studebakers and Oldsmobiles. All told, it was estimated that the Sultan of Swat earned $250,000 in 1926 from playing baseball, movie work, barnstorming, endorsements and syndicated ghost written pieces."[4]

But Ruth had learned much about baseball money. One way of measuring for Robert Burk in *Much More* was to say that Ruth, for the Yankees, "generated at least an additional $200,000 a year in direct revenue."[5] Ruth's after-tax pay equaled $68,000. In February, with some of his cash, Ruth invested $33,000 in annuities, $1,000 for each of his years, and in August the player was able to deposit a check for $50,000 in the Bank of Manhattan in New York.

Ruppert decided to go for quantity in attendance in 1927, and lowered the price of admission on the 22,000 bleacher seats from 75 cents to 50 cents. Seats in the grandstands sold for $1.10. His pre-tax profits for 1927 would not be damaged, coming in at $601,351, $46,000 more than 1926.

In addition to the Ruth biographies—Smelser, Wagenheim, Creamer, Stewart, Hampton, Sobol and most recently Montville—five books have been written just on the New York Yankees of 1927, from 1974's *The Greatest of All: The 1927 New York Yankees* to 2007's *Murderers' Row: Babe Ruth, Lou Gehrig and the Greatest Team in Baseball, the 1927 New York Yankees*, the story of the season and of Ruth's home run hitting has been covered in great detail. Some of these books have issued later editions as well. There is now also a "graphic novel" published in 2011 just about Ruth in 1927.

Loyalty and sentimentality do not apply in professional baseball. As in any other business, only success matters. Since 1921, every team member except these five had been sent away: Huggins, Ruth, Shawkey, Hoyt and Meusel. Those who looked elsewhere noticed that Ruth, second baseman Tony Lazzeri (age 22) and first baseman Lou Gehrig finished in the top ten for home runs in 1926. Others noticed in 1926 that manager Miller Huggins decided to change his shortstop and second baseman for two young men, Mark Koenig at shortstop and Tony Lazzeri at second base. Writers noticed Earle Combs now in center field and Pat Collins catching most of the games. Except for most of the pitchers, Ruth at 32 became the oldest starter. And while the team won the pennant in 1926, the contrast remains remarkable with the 1927 squad, which tallied 128 more runs and allowed 114 fewer runs.

Ruth hit his 400th home run that year and, famously, he hit 60 home runs, breaking his own record. The day of home run number 60, he made three hits in three at-bats and drove in two runs in a 4–2 Yankees win. By comparison, the entire Boston Red Sox team hit 28 home runs, and the Cleveland Indians hit 26. By comparison, the National League leader hit 30 home runs. Ruth hit 60 of the 439 home runs in the American League that year—14 percent. The year Roger Maris hit 61 home runs, he would have had to hit 214 to match Ruth's 14 percent; the year Barry Bonds hit 73 home runs, he needed to hit 413 to match Ruth's 14 percent.

With a very strong team, the Yankees won 110 games, a winning percentage of .714, finishing 19 games ahead of Connie Mack's Philadelphia Athletics.

Ruth's celebrity grew even more to match his income. Being paid $5,000–7,000 for covering the series for U.S. papers, he was also signed to cover the series by the Japanese newspaper, the *Manichi* in Osaka. His fame grew too with the growth of radio listeners, now approaching 20,000,000 to 35,000,000 people. His celebrity grew as the sportswriters looked for grander analogies, like this: "And now the populace had its homer and it stood up and gave the glad, joyous howl that must have rang out in the Roman arenas of old" (Harrison). Sportswriters began to refer to the team with the words "wonderful," "savage," "invincible," and "glittering."

In the four-game World Series, the Pittsburgh Pirates managed just ten runs while the Yankees scored 23. American League president Ban Johnson wired the owners of the Yankees, saying "four straight victories will have a wholesome effect upon the public mind and strengthen the position of professional ball."[6] When the Series was over, Ruth held nine records for all of World Series play since 1903, two of which broke his own records. If average game attendance at the games set a new mark—and therefore the players' share—some would like to attach credit to Ruth. Ignored in these plaudits remains the calculation that the home field of the Pirates seated nine percent more than the home field of the 1926 Cardinals. That the Yankees team mascot was voted $700 of the money may be telling about the size of the team payday.

Ruth himself added another $5,782 for his share of the World Series money.

Three days after the Series ended, he began his travel once more. Ruth was quoted as saying in Hoyt's book that "I can get twenty-five hundred a game in exhibition work."[7]

Other barnstormers that year included an Athletics squad who would travel from Baltimore to California. But that tour did not have Christy Walsh, and Walsh had come to terms with the two best home run hitters in baseball, Ruth with 60 and Gehrig with 47. Walsh's press notice on his letterhead read, "After the season closes! After the World Series ended! The battle for the home run title continues. Ruth Vs. Gehrig! A series of

Pre-tour photo from the 1927 barnstorming tour. *Left to right*: **Gehrig, Christy Walsh and Ruth.**

post season games from New York to California. Christy Walsh Management 570 Fifth Avenue-New York." In addition,

> Walsh cleverly capitalized on the [regular season] home run race by offering a "Copper Cup" trophy to the one with the most home runs at the tour's end. It was a small reward, but it kept things interesting during the journey across the continent.[8]

For the trip, Walsh ordered trunks labeled "Home Run Tour" to hold special uniforms for the two teams at each stop. One set was colored black with white lettering reading

Custom Home Run Tour luggage, 1927 (Baseball Hall of Fame).

Bustin' Babes. The caps were white sporting "BB" on it in black letters. For Gehrig's team, each player's uniform was white, with black lettering reading "Larrupin' Lous," and the black cap had white lettering that read "LL." For both sets, on the left sleeve was a patch that looked like an oversized baseball with the word "Spalding" in its center, that sporting goods firm the supplier for the trip. So Ruth, Gehrig and the teams were wearing advertisements on their sleeves. Walsh traveled with the two players. The intense promotion of the tour had a little to do with the competition for the entertainment dollar in the fall. The football season was underway. In addition to high school and college games, for example, the New York Football Giants played in Pottsville, PA, on October 9, and defeated the Pottsville Maroons in an early National Professional League game.

After a rained out doubleheader, Ruth, Gehrig and Walsh moved 200 miles north to Kinsley Park in Providence, Rhode Island. "At times, both men were surrounded by half a hundred fans often while playing their position in the field…. Everything that would take an autograph was pressed into use. School books, pocket books, diaries, handkerchiefs, order slips, collars and cuffs, scraps of paper—anything and everything except checks were signed by the king and prince of swat with greatest good nature…. Nobody who had a scrap of paper was denied."

The game ended early this way: both Ruth and Gehrig were scheduled to pitch the last three innings. In the seventh, Ruth allowed Gehrig to drive the ball to right center. In the eighth, "Gehrig stuck Ruth out three times and walked him at least once … and then on the 25th or 26th pitch the Babe hit a single and kids stormed the field."

Once back in New York, said the *Trenton Times*, Gehrig, on his radio show the Sunday night before, publicized a game in Trenton. Gehrig and Ruth initially had been scheduled for a game in Portland, Maine, but then the Trenton promoters outbid Portland. Around the same time, Walsh took advantage of the newer technology and had the Perfect Company make a recording of patter by Ruth and Gehrig.

That Tuesday, Ruth and Gehrig traveled 250 miles to Trenton. "The high cost of home runs is indicated in the announced price which George Giasco and Joseph Plumeri are guaranteeing Babe Ruth and his companion in crime Lou Gehrig to appear in Trenton." But not without the help of Nat Strong. For one, Strong owned the opposition team, the Brooklyn Royal Colored Giants. Showing Ruth's appeal to the public, "On 48 hours notice, Ruth packed the High School Field."

The *Trenton State Gazette* described how "the coming of Busting Babe and Larrupin' Lou turned Trenton upside down." But then, "Ruth refused to play until he cashed in on his share of $2,500 which delayed the start of the contest. Before the game started an attachment of $468 was placed against the promoter William Turby."[9] An attachment, in most dictionaries, is considered "a very harsh remedy" because it "to coerces a defendant into appearing in court and answering the plaintiff's [Walsh's] claim. The legal part being completed, at the Knights of Columbus home on East State Street "they donned their playing uniforms" and left for the game.

Once at the playing grounds, "they were imposing figures on the field…. Neither loafed … and participated in every form of the warm-up drill," according to William R. Clark in the *Trenton Times*. Attendance was listed as 3,500 paid. But it was estimated by the *Trenton Evening Times* that 3,000 children climbed over or under the fences. Ruth homered to right field in the first inning. "As soon as the ball cleared the fence, he was mobbed by screaming children who burst from the stands. The Babe waddled around the bases with children wrapped around his legs and clawing at his arms. In the third inning, he homered again. Again, he was mobbed."[10]

The Associated Press, too, covered the game, writing, about the boys at game's end, "With hundreds of boys pounding him, slapping his back, climbing all over him and pushing and shoving just to touch him…. Carried off his feet, shaken by the wonderful demonstration, Ruth still had a word for a kid whose adoration wouldn't increase the Ruthian bankroll one cent. Baseball is Ruth's business; small boys his love."

Some of these barnstorming exhibitions became a sort of festival, not a baseball game. A story is told by Negro Leagues historian John B. Holway about this game.

> Trenton promoter George Glasco recalls that he took the Cannonball [Redding] aside before the game: "You know these people … are out here to see Ruth hit home runs, right?"
>
> "Right."
>
> "Now when the Babe comes to bat no fancy stuff."
>
> "Got ya," Redding winked, "Right down the pike."[11]

Bill Jenkinson argued differently, having had access to Negro Leagues star Judy Johnson, who over time, "offered many unsolicited remarks about his admiration and affection for Babe Ruth."

Jenkinson recalled one of Johnson's observations: "Occasionally, I saw isolated incidents where opposing pitchers 'grooved' balls for Babe.... However, I never encountered a single instance when a local player ... was asked by the organizers or the Babe to 'lay down' for him ... the consensus was that these guys tried even harder against Ruth than anyone else."[12]

For game three, on October 12, 1927, Ruth and Walsh again did business with Nat Strong in order to play against the Bushwicks at Dexter Park. Strong controlled, was a partner in, or owned all or part of many of the baseball grounds as well as the important semipro teams of the Eastern United States, including three black teams: the Brooklyn Royal Giants, the Cuban Stars of New York City, and the Philadelphia Giants. That game, which took place on the Brooklyn and Queens border, paid the Ruth and Gehrig duo $1,900, from which Ruth received 75 percent and Gehrig 25 percent. This may mean that the pair were paid ten percent of the gate. Gehrig may have had a great year, but Ruth had a better one. Besides, Gehrig was not known to complain or to seek attention.

Thomas Holmes of the *Brooklyn Daily Eagle* covered the game, said to be watched by either 20,000 (or 22,000 or 24,000). Holmes stuck with 22,000, as "five or six thousand" of them "lined the outskirts of the outfield. The standees and sitees on the greensward were given to occasional sorties beyond the limit prescribed by the gallant but insufficient police."

Though this was a barnstorming game, the box score appeared in the *New York Times,* and accounts of the 72-minute game also found their way into other papers like the *Chicago Tribune*, which reported that "two fans were slightly injured and several others are sporting black eyes as the result of a boisterous riot which followed the last out of the exhibition."

That night, it was announced that Lou Gehrig had won the Most Valuable Player Award in the American League. The next day, they traveled back to the Jersey shore, 60 miles to Asbury Park. The racial arrangements stayed the same, as they always did in that era. Though it was true that in some games Ruth would play for one team and Gehrig another, when facing a black team, there would be no "race mixing." Still, it was likely to be a fine payday for the Brooklyn Royal Giants again.

Ruth and his agent understood all too well that he was playing for the Asbury Park money as well as for other reasons. "For more than an hour ... 7,000 people fidgeted in the stands the Babe was comfortably ensconced in an armchair in the Berkeley Carteret Hotel while Surrogate Joseph R. Donahey taxied around Asbury Park in an effort to get a cashier's check for $2,500.... Ruth refused to go on with his show until he got the entire sum due him."

Eig writes, "Walsh always demanded upfront money, with paydays ranging from $1,000 to $2,500 depending on the size of the town and the expected crowd."[13]

At the end of the 700 miles and after game five in Lima, Ohio, lay Muehlebach Field in Kansas City. While in that city, Ruth "visited the Guardian Angel Home For Negroes.... There is a delightful photo from that event showing a beaming Ruth holding a black infant in his arms. In addition, he personally hosted fifty orphans from that institution during the exhibition game on that same date."[14] He also visited Mercy Hospital "and gladdened the day ... for a number of crippled youngsters."[15]

SOUVENIR PROGRAM

BABE RUTH AND LOU GEHRIG

BROWN PARK MERCHANTS
OMAHA SUNDAY CMAMPIONS
(WITH RUTH)

vs

OMAHA PRINTING CO.
OMAHA SATURDAY CHAMPIONS
(WITH GEHRIG)

Western League Park, October 16, 1927

AUSPICES OMAHA POST No. 1,
THE AMERICAN LEGION

Babe Ruth

Lou Gehrig

NOTE: Ruth and Gehrig will participate only in the first game of the double-header.—The second game, in which the teams will use ONLY their regular players, will be the final game for the city championship of Omaha.

Ad for a Ruth-Gehrig exhibition double-header in Omaha, October 1927.

Gladdened too must have been Christy Walsh, for the number of paid approached 10,000 for the October 15 game. Both Ruth and Gehrig homered that day, with 19 runs tallied.

It must have been quite a sight to see these two players arrive at a ballpark. Taller and broader than anyone else, Gehrig, at 24, weighed 200 pounds and stood six feet tall. Ruth stood two inches taller and 20 pounds heavier. Ruth's head seemed so big that a teammate sometimes called him "two head." So both men measured four to six inches more in height and 40 to 70 pounds more in weight than the average American male.

For a Sunday game, the tour's seventh, Walsh had agreed to terms with money men in Omaha, Nebraska, one of the larger cities booked, with 192,000 residents. Eager to show their celebrity guests the best that Omaha had to offer, with great civic pride the local paper announced that, "The Loftis Brothers Jewelry company will present a diamond stickpin to Ruth and to Gehrig." With equal pride, Ruth was presented with an unusual gift: the "171st consecutive egg laid by Lady Norfolk—the 'Babe Ruth' of hen layers—who had shattered a poultry record." Then, two days later, in Sioux City, a local meat packing company gave a ham with his name spelled out in cloves. The newspaper photo caption read, "So Now Babe Ruth Can Have Ham and Eggs."[16]

This item was found in the annals of the Nebraska State Historical Society: "A notable feature was the zest and spirit with which the two Yankee stars entered the contest, side by side with the amateurs, several of whom showed signs of nervousness and stage fright at appearing in the same lineup with the big boys. The batting behemoths kept up a lively

LOU, BABE &
LADY AMCO.

Gehrig and Ruth with champion egg layer Lady Amco, Omaha, 1927.

chatter throughout the game, encouraging the hurlers and keeping up the pep of the contest."

With 4,500 miles behind them, Walsh had accepted offers for another dozen games after the tenth game in Colorado. But these would average about 100 miles of travel each, all in California. Bookings for that state would ensure few if any cancellations, the weather being ideal even in late October. In addition, for decades it had been an established place for baseball due to the presence of the Pacific Coast League, as well as the California Winter League, that league becoming even more popular in 1927.

As the train rolled on 1,300 miles west, Ruth and Gehrig could relax after the ten games played, knowing they would not be called on until after lunch on the 21st, almost 48 hours.

A San Francisco columnist identified as E. R. H. recounted that, "Babe said Lou get a tremendous kick out of some real Indians he saw in Denver." And "Christy Walsh, who is in charge of the tour, says it has been a tremendous success. He says they have played to more than 100,000 already and he expects to play to 100,000 more in California." Walsh's use of "play to" helps it be seen that this was show business.

The San Francisco and Oakland games would have rosters that featured players out of the majors or not yet in the majors and now in the PCL. The second of the three weekend games was played across the Bay, at the Oakland Oaks Park in Emeryville, where 13,000 paid their way in. "Gehrig again outshone his Yankee rival by knocking in four runs with a homer, triple and a double, leading his team to a 6–3 win. Ruth, meanwhile, popped up repeatedly." Abe Kemp of the *Chronicle,* seeing Ruth at his most eager to entertain, said, "Ruth tried everything to please. Failing to hit … to satisfy the customers he jumped into the stand and led the band … the crowd was so anxious to get a close up look at him that they refused to let him bat in the ninth inning and the game had to be called."

Ruth understood he was a performer in show business.

Afterwards, John J. Peri reported in the Stockton paper, "a local chiropractor worked on Ruth's back for more than an hour trying to smooth out the knotted muscles, while Gehrig tried to relieve some of his soreness with warm baths and other applications." Harry B. Smith of the *San Francisco Chronicle* wrote, "aside from the handsome emoluments, it is not all peaches and cream…. Hardly a moment of their waking hours can be claimed by Ruth and Gehrig for themselves…. The hands of each are so swollen … they can hardly grip the bat handles. In addition, Babe has a 'crick' in his back and has taken to wearing plasters…. Truly the boys are paying for their pin money."

On the morning of October 24, 1927, they arose early—for a 10 a.m. game—and were driven 90 miles from Stockton to Marysville, a town of 5,600. The *Appeal-Democrat, a* local paper, said, "Marysville businessmen today put up a guarantee of $1,000 in the First National Bank of Marysville to insure the appearance here of Babe Ruth and Lou Gehrig." The city's Mayor declared an official holiday between 9:30 a.m. and 12:30 p.m. and recommended that schools be closed at the same times.

Arriving in town, Ruth was described as "immaculate in a blue suit, cravat and with dark wavy hair" but showing an expression of "tolerant boredom" since he has had "several years experience with banquets and endless rounds of social affairs." At the small morning reception, the toastmaster "presented to Ruth a large square cake. The top, made to represent a telegram, read: 'Babe Ruth, Lou Gehrig, Hotel Marysville. Welcome may your visit to Marysville be most enjoyable. Ideal Bakery.'" The cake represented a wonderful combination of generosity and business shrewdness. After all, Ruth and Gehrig were neither going to eat the cake nor take it with them when they left. Ruth and Gehrig were allowed to go up to their rooms and rest until they reported to the ballpark at 9:20.

Ed Burt of the *Marysville Appeal-Democrat* wrote to end his piece that "At the game's conclusion the pair were again lost in a swarm of kids who escorted them bodily to the sedan which rushed them back to the hotel where they made a quick change of clothing and departed for Sacramento," 45 miles away for an afternoon game that same day.[17]

Total gate receipts were $1,413.25 minus $1,100 for Ruth, Gehrig and Walsh (either 77 percent or an agreed-on flat rate); minus $275 for expenses; so $38.25 went to the Christmas fund, a total that equals 2.7 percent of the gate. It may be that the small city's merchants showed increased profits with an increase of people coming into the city for the game. Some concession, scorecard or parking money may have been generated by the game.

With people waiting in San Jose, Gehrig and Ruth arrived at noon and spoke briefly at both Rotary and Lions lunches. The 18th game of the tour turned out to be a relaxed affair, having "to be halted for 10 minutes in the fifth inning when hundreds of kiddies in attendance literally mobbed Babe and Lou.... Lefty O'Doul ... almost stole the show ... with his clowning."[18]

Ruth and Gehrig spent the rest of the day at Stanford and were the dinner guests of coach Pop Warner at night. Warner had signed on with Walsh's syndicate some years earlier. The *San Jose News* calculations came out for the local orphanage, "Profits amounted to $128.88," with that 65 percent of the gross receipts to Ruth and Gehrig [and Walsh]. "Another fairly sizeable item was money spent for labor and material to strengthen the stands to accommodate the exceptionally large crowd. As many as 3,400 youngsters saw the game."[19] By the time the money was totaled, Ruth, Gehrig and Walsh would be long gone.

After three more games, back to Los Angeles—the named charity being the American Legion disabled—"if the two teams of stars don't prove enough of an attraction to draw out the fans of their own accord, the Legionnaires are willing to suffer a loss and let it go as a bad guess." The Hollywood American Legion Band was hired by Joe Patrick, Angels president, to entertain. With usual seat prices listed, it fell to Patrick to see to supplying the up-front money for the ballpark use, umpires, ushers, scoreboard workers, someone to line up players, police, ticket takers, etc.

"Before the game, Ruth and Gehrig put on a batting exhibition, both sluggers hammering half a dozen home over the fence. After the contest, Ruth tossed 100 [autographed] baseballs to several hundred kids who had gathered on the field to receive them."[20] Though the city's Wrigley Field could generate enough money if all 22,000 seats were filled, the game exceeded everyone's expectations when 25,000 appeared. Chet Thomas, who caught Ruth with the Red Sox in 1916, caught Ruth again for two innings. Beans Reardon umpired while Charlie Root, Cubs pitcher, worked six innings and Red Oldham finished up for Gehrig's team. (Oldham was Ruth's teammate in Providence in 1914.) "The game itself was a thriller," said the *Los Angeles Times*, with "numerous spectacular catches" during the 70-minute game. Ruth did not homer, but Gehrig hit two.

The last game, number 22, was cancelled on October 31, 1927, because "one of the heaviest October rains in recent seasons" prevented the game at Long Beach's Shell Field from being played.

Over the tour, which covered 8,000 miles and was played before 220,000 persons attending 21 games, 13 of those completed, in 20 cities and in nine states. A modern researcher, Rick Cabral, who has extensively studied the 1927 barnstorming journey, substantiates an aggregate attendance number of 149,830. Many writers claim Ruth earned $10,500 from the Wrigley game, the one that counted 25,000 paid.

Opposite: **Poster for a 1927 exhibition in California.**

Sportswriters and biographers then and since have made estimates:

1. Ruth earned a reported $25,000–$30,000 for the tour.[21]

2. "the grueling one-month tour … grossed approximately $220,000. Ruth reportedly made $70,000."[22]

3. Walsh, according to *The Babe*, earned $40,000.[23] According to Rick Cabral "Walsh's $40,000+ was sourced in the Sacramento *Union*, October 26, 1927, in a column by sports editor Rudy Hickey in which he stated, 'Five more games are booked before the barnstorming tour is complete and Ruth said here it will pay his manager, Christy Walsh, over $40,000 for the tour.'"

4. *Sports Collectors Digest* in 1999 asserted that Ruth made $30,000.

5. "Here is what Babe Ruth earned since this time a year ago: World Series and post-season exhibitions, $20,000."[24]

6. November 10, 1927, *World-Telegram*—Ford Frick wrote that Ruth made $180,000 this way—$70,000 salary; $50,000 for *Babe Comes Home*; $25,000 "syndicated articles"; and $30,000 from barnstorming plus World Series share.

Still, the money came rolling in, the AP reported, and Ruth made $3,000 for "posing in a new patent pair of overalls."[25] Another observer wrote that by the time 1927 and early 1928 were past,

> Ruth was thirty-three thousand dollars ahead. He was at the time thirty-three years old…. Walsh convinced [his player] that it would be a great publicity feat if the Babe announced that, because of his misdemeanors and wild spending, he was fining himself one thousand dollars for each year of his life. To make it look real, the Babe was photographed signing the thirty-three thousand dollars over into an untouchable trust fund.[26]

As another sign of the artificiality Walsh had constructed for the image of Ruth, a year after Walsh had seen to it that another "great publicity feat"—Ruth miraculously healing the near-death Johnny Sylvester—this sometimes told story of Ruth took place.

> A year later an elderly man accosted the Babe in a hotel lobby and, after receiving the customary whole-hearted greeting of "Hello, doc," said: "Babe, I don't know whether you remember me, but I'm Johnny Sylvester's uncle and I want to tell you the family will never forget what you did for us. Johnny is getting along fine."
> "That's great," replied the Babe. "Sure, I remember you. Glad to hear Johnny is doing so well. Bring him around some time." After a few more words they parted and no sooner had the man removed himself from earshot than the Babe turned to a baseball writer at his elbow and asked: "Now, who the devil was Johnny Sylvester?"[27]

If one example of Ruth's consumption of hot dogs became a picture of Ruth every day, then this story, if true, suggests any number of things. First, it suggests that Ruth was asked so often, every day on his barnstorming tours, to cheer up children who were ill or were orphans, that the whole business became mechanical and of little interest to him, other than receiving the kind of affection that only children can give, affection with few demands except to allow them to love you. Next, it suggests that Ruth understood exactly what Walsh had been doing with him since 1921. Third, it suggests that Ruth had learned not to make too many social gaffes over the years, by not saying anything to the uncle.

According to baseball-reference.com and Smelser, the payroll for Barrow, Huggins and all the players totaled $316,250. If you subtract Ruth's salary of $70,000 from the team payroll in 1927, the total labor cost was $246,250 for 25 batters, ten pitchers, one business manager and one field manager, an average salary of $6,655.40. The Yankees' after-tax profit for 1927 was the highest in the team's history—$567,664, the equivalent of $7,500,000 today.

Ruth knew that "Ball players today are businessmen, first, last, and always."[28]

25

Radio and Newsreels
and Play-O-Graph

It may be difficult for some to understand in 2018 the slower pace that existed prior to radio for the general public to receive information. While newspapers had access to teletype machines since 1914, instant news was not relayed directly to the public except by unusual means. A photo caption from September 26, 1921, before the World Series was played that year, also demonstrated the level of enthusiasm in the city that season, while indicating the limited means to rapidly transmit information: "So intense was the interest in the Yankees-Cleveland series Charles Farbizo, a resident of the [East Side took], a flock of carrier pigeons to the games and sent back the score by innings via the winged messengers. The photo shows Babe Ruth releasing one of the pigeons at the game. He will use the pigeons for the same purpose during the World Series."[1]

The success of radio as a cash creator depended on three things: the necessary technology, proper organizing, and attractive content. The technology became necessary to radio stations because of the first problem of generating enough power to sufficiently amplify the sound coming out of the stations, a problem solved by Lee DeForest and later improved on. Next, radio receivers—radios in the home—were improved thanks to the work of Major Edwin Howard Armstrong, in 1918, in the invention of the super-heterodyne that raised the amplification of the radio signal in the home receiver.[2]

Organizing the young industry began in early 1923, a need that existed simply because each listener could hear only one isolated station. What was needed was a station that could work with other stations. In stepped the AT&T Corporation, which "began tests using telephone circuits to connect radio stations…. By the late 1920s there were over 500 broadcasting stations operating throughout the United States, although few were located in the vast spaces of the rural interior."[3] The first radio network, NBC, began operating in November 1926, and CBS followed. By 1928, "Radio receiving sets in use in the United States … reached the record total of 7,500,000 and the radio audience is estimated at 35,000,000 persons."[4] From 75,000 radio sets in 1922, advances in technology and organization had made radio grow a thousand times over in just six years.

Once the radio industry discovered how to make money through advertising in 1922, and as the sales of radio sets grew to $842,500,000 in 1929, it became clear that "network radio changed the ad industry, giving it greater reach an impact than the industry had known previously."[5]

One boxing match in 1921, the Dempsey vs. Carpentier bout, drew 300,000 listeners. So eager for a description of the fight were fans that seats could be sold in theaters where the radio signal was boosted through a loudspeaker system. There was money to be made.

In 1928, radio was calculated to be a $500 million advertising industry "and the contributor of an estimated $18 million annually to newspaper and magazine advertising."[6] The commercial system brought about the "new and vastly important phenomenon of radio broadcasting, which on occasion could link together a multitude of firesides to hear the story of a World's Series game or a Lindbergh welcome. The national mind had become as never before an instrument upon which a few men could play. And these men were learning to play upon it in a new way—to concentrate upon one tune at a time."[7]

Ruth made money for himself and for companies through radio as well. Since Yankees home games would not be broadcast until 1939, Ruth's exploits and those of his team as they happened could be heard on the radio for half of the regular season. But as radio grew in scope, the team appeared in the World Series six times, and for those few games radio did provide coverage. With limited stations broadcasting the games in 1921 and 1922, some by re-creations, in 1923 the reach of stations extended from the South in Washington, D.C., to the North in Massachusetts, including games directly from the ballpark itself. In 1925, for example, a Denver newspaper would receive reports from the United Press and quickly repeat the action over their radio station. Also in 1925, the World Series was recreated for Newark, New Jersey's WJZ from ticker tape reports. Radio stations themselves grew from five in 1921 to 681 in 1927, the first year that the World Series was broadcast from coast to coast.

There does not seem to be much doubt that "The presentation of the World Series helped advance the regular coverage of baseball by radio."[8] Even with baseball in its beginnings, the focus of radio manufacturers was "simply as a way to sell radios. Over its first three years of selling radios, RCA's revenues amounted to $83,500,000. The sale of radios and parts amounted to $650,000,000 in 1927."[9] Quickly, by 1930, "nine out of ten broadcasting stations were selling advertising time."[10] And "radio, as it turned out, was the best advertising the game ever had, carrying the sport to countless people who otherwise might never have fallen under its spell."[11]

So there existed a beneficial relationship between the two. Radio helped popularize baseball, and baseball helped to sell radios and parts. As radio's popularity grew, construction costs for its newer and higher towers became necessary, and there were paychecks for the workers, for the designers and makers of the towers, and for the men who erected the towers.

Radio helped Ruth as well since it "helped baseball capitalize on ... [baseball's] larger- than-life superhero," Ruth.[12] The player's World Series performances would be heard by millions, increasing his celebrity, which in turn increased his opportunities for endorsements as well as help to encourage barnstorming game promoters to hire Ruth.

Ruth would have his own shows later on, but as a far-reaching example, it is now possible to buy from Amazon.com "Babe Ruth Radio Call (ca. 1927)" for 99 cents. That his batting was celebrated through the breathless newness of radio broadcasts helped him to be paid for endorsing such products as Wheaties, Home Run Candy, Puffed Wheat Cereal, Red Rock Cola, Old Gold Cigarettes, Pinch Hit Tobacco, Esso Oil, Babe Ruth Boys Club, Sinclair Oil, Murphy-Rich Co. Soap, Girl Scout Cookies and Mrs. Sherlock's Bread.

Radio served Ruth well. Expanding his fame was a kind of tease to those who had never seen him play. Being denied the pleasure of seeing him play would make the impetus to hire him as a barnstormer even greater.

Play-O-Graph

Before the coast-to-coast radio broadcast in 1927 became a reality, and even after as well, there was another way to reach millions of people during the World Series and for important college football games, a way that extended even before Ruth's Red Sox days and well into the 1930s. Though it was true that by the late 1920s, there were over 500 broadcasting stations operating throughout the United States, rural areas had to depend on newspapers.

In rural areas, as well as large cities, new communication devices are sometimes valued by those who have a wager on an baseball game. One such early use, according to a piece on the web by Mark Schubin, referring to the book, *A Game of Inches*, "'the prototype of the sports bar' might have been Massey's billiard hall in St. Louis, where, in 1875, telegraphed bulletins, pro-

Bambino tobacco tin, ca. 1923.

vided every half inning by Western Union, were posted on a blackboard." Schubin goes on to delineate other ways including, in 1884, a large painted poster of three men who "painted a ball field onto a large poster, which they placed in a theater. Using the telegraph "cards with the players' names [were moved] around the poster."

Two years later, instead of cards, "young boys, dressed in the uniforms of the players ... ran around a ball field on the stage, recreating the plays." These sorts of recreations were embraced by the sporting public and "the audience ... was wrought up to a very high pitch of enthusiasm ... when ... there came a storm of applause, just such as is heard on a veritable ball field."[13] Also in the nineteenth century, "Joseph Pulitzer's *The World* in New York ... erected a ball-field diagram with holes for colored, numbered pins representing the players. It quickly attracted a crowd estimated at about 6,000 people ... blocking traffic on the nearby Brooklyn Bridge."[14] Joseph Pultizer used this diagram to advertise his paper, since the name of the paper was blazoned at the top of the Play-O-Graph device and attached to the side of the building where the paper was made. There was no direct payment for the expense of erecting and manning the machine.

By 1909, a clear example of cash exchanging hands "via the Rodier Electric Baseball Game Reproducer ["which set Atlantic City wild," quotes Schubin] ... admission prices of 25 and 50 cents" were charged at a time "when ... the admission price for a typical movie theater was just five cents." This practice, so profitable, was seized on, as in Washington, D.C., in 1914, where viewers could "attend" different baseball games inside theaters named Bijou, Columbia, Cosmos, Gayety, Keith's, National, and Poli's, and, if one of those was busy with a play, the equipment was moved into an armory. In New York, the Coleman Life-Like Scoreboard was also set up in an armory, as well as in Madison Square Garden.[15]

The Rodier and the Coleman machines seemed to have a short life. The machine that dominated these public game representations was the invention made by the Baseball Play-O-Graph Company of Stamford, Connecticut, a mechanism that "used a ball affixed to an invisible cord that emulated the course of the ball while white footprints illuminated the path of the baserunners." This company became dominant in this specialized field and apparently manufactured these displays from 1907 to 1939. A Connecticut history site describes the machine, the operators of which received details via the telegraph: "In 1913 Western Union paid each Major League Baseball team $17,000 per year over five years for the telegraph rights to the games."[16]

Play-O-Graphs resembled large billboards, often standing about nine feet high. Making up either side of the Play-O-Graph was the vertical listing of the lineups for each team. In the middle of the Play-O-Graph was a reproduction of a baseball diamond, along with places for Play-O-Graph operators to indicate balls, strikes, outs, and runs in real time."[17]

Eager baseball fans, and nervous bettors too, formed large crowds from 1911–1913 in Herald Square in New York where the *New York Evening Telegram* had mounted a Play-O-Graph. Even though 80–90 policemen had been put on duty in 1913 to try to control the 30,000 to 40,000 jamming the area, Shaw's Jewelry Shop at 1341 Broadway sued for $729.59. Shaw's complaint stated that the crowding around the device prevented customers getting to his shop. Shaw won his case in February of that year but lost on appeal in December, when the court said the Play-O-Graph display was a public service being performed.

With these size crowds, those who might put up a Play-O-Graph saw the advertising value of the machines, measuring 15 by 20 feet. In large cities, the Play-O-Graphs drew large crowds. One was erected on the superstructure of the elevated "el" tracks that make up Chicago's Loop. New York City saw three: one at on the facade of the St. James building at 26th and Broadway, one at the *New York Times,* building on 43rd Street, and one more at Madison Square Garden at 26th and Madison. But there were also Play-O-Graphs in Galesburg, Illinois; Waynesburg, Pennsylvania; Vincennes, Indiana; and Laramie, Wyoming. One was erected on the Cornell campus during the 1932 World Series. For the comfort of the viewers, in some places bleachers were set up; in others, a fee of 25 cents was expected.

Play-O-Graph's acceptance and success brought about competition. "At least 44 U.S. patents that would be issued by 1927 for remote baseball viewing systems (and some of the most popular weren't even patented)."[18] Foremost among the competitors was a company which placed this advertisement in 1919 which claimed that

> the invention transports the spectator in a moment of time from the farthest point of the Pacific slope to the very heart of the Polo Grounds. The Hartford *Times* which will reproduce the series this year, the sixth year in succession, says that the Star Ball Player is valuable to any newspaper eager to win friends by the swiftest and most attractive method. Leased by Star Ballplayer Company, 24 Van Cortlandt Street, New York City.[19]

The Star Ball Player Company, with patents back to 1913, sued its main competition. "This case," wrote one court, "concerns the baseball display boards used by newspaper offices, department stores, and others to visualize baseball games." A continuing legal battle began based on patent infringement by Star, a company that had signed on with 20 locations such as Dayton, Ohio, and Erie, Pennsylvania. For that company, besides the cost of manufacturing the devices, was the loss of leases in a range of $200–300 each. Play-O-Graph, on the other hand, was taking in $7,645.20 from 26 leases, an average of $294 each. The court ruled in favor of Play-O-Graph in 1929. But the court also wrote, "The device [is]less valu[abl]e since the broadcasting of national series games by radio."[20]

Consigned now to history, the Play-O-Graph, though useful in its time, was soon superseded by radio and bi-weekly short films.[21]

Newsreels and Movies

In Ruth's time, while the World Series was imaginatively followed on the radio and through the use of Play-o-graphs, the only two ways to see a baseball game were to go to the park or see brief highlights of games in a movie theater.

By Ruth's most famous year, 1927, silent newsreels had been shown in theaters, in some instances for more than 15 years, and of those eight- or nine-minute films, Jules Tygiel tells us that 25 percent was sports.[22] Paying your money for a ticket would be sure to include a newsreel, since the Pathe and Hearst movie corporations produced material covering baseball stars and games during the regular season and of course World Series highlights as well, beginning in 1910. With movie attendance approaching 80 million paying customers each week, three other companies—Paramount, Fox and Universal— quickly joined the makers of newsreels. It was true that "a News Reel producer employs very few cameramen on salary. Only in the big cities does he have to keep them on salary."[23] Since, again by 1927, Ruth had played in eight World Series, and since he had dominated the Series both by his pitching and his hitting, it would be expected that Ruth would figure prominently in these newsreels, with the big cities of Boston and New York having the most cameramen.

The fact that two different newsreels were delivered to theaters each week contributed to Ruth's fame. That people, not fans, who attended movies for the entire experience—trailers, 10–20-minute short, cartoon, newsreel and two movies—could not miss but view Babe Ruth in action, putting Ruth into the same category of fame as Lindbergh, beauty queens, and treasury agents raiding speakeasies, a status that only helped to bolster his standing as a brand, a commodity.

Again, referring to 1927, it may be true to say that Ruth and Walsh did not need newsreels to contribute to the player's celebrity. After all, "the 1927 Yankees … drew 25 percent of all American League attending fans," more than 5,000 more customers per game than the second-place Detroit Tigers.[24] But the many hundreds of millions who watched Babe Ruth on movie theater screens vastly outnumbered the two million or so who saw him at the ballpark.

26

Another Sweep
(1928)

While the Yankees averaged more than 12,000 paid customers per game on the road in 1927, the St. Louis Browns averaged 3,219 for home games, and even that St. Louis figure is skewed because when Ruth and the Yankees came to town, attendance would greatly increase for those 11 of the 77 home games. Owner Ruppert kept his profits invested. Michael Haupert and Kenneth Winter show those profits as, rounded, $77,000 in 1926 and $544,000 in 1927. According to ballparks.com, "The Yankees' sixth season at Yankee Stadium opens with the left-field stands enlarged to three decks, with a capacity of 82,000, up from the 1923 level of 53,000 seats."

In salary, Ruth again made $70,000 in 1928, while Gehrig's salary was increased from $8,000 to $25,000. The effect on baseball of Ruth's power hitting began to be felt. For example, slugging percentage, a measure of how many bases were being accumulated per at bat, rose out of the .480-.580 level, where it had stayed for more than four decades, into the .750 (and higher) level. That is, more players were producing more bases per at-bat than ever before. Before the 1920s, American League sacrifice bunt leaders averaged around 38; after Ruth retired, the decade averaged 25. The era of the single and the bunt seemed to be largely over. At year's end, Connie Mack manager of the Philadelphia Athletics said, "[I] won't bother with players who haven't the driving power of Babe Ruth." The White Sox, searching for a star player, paid the Portland Beavers of the PCL "$75,000 to $100,000 in cash and two players as well ... valued at $48,000."[1]

On May 22, 1927, Charles Lindbergh had landed in Paris after the first solo transatlantic airplane flight. The magnitude of the feat, and the fact that it was done by the pilot alone, made Lindbergh instantly famous as demonstrated by his ticker tape parade watched by four million people. Lindbergh appeared to be so strongly against being treated as a celebrity that "Lindbergh's chief rivals as the most popular male were dismissed as greedy, cynical and undignified. Compared to a real hero, they were products of hype and ballyhoo."[2] Montville admits, "Unknown when he took off, the aviator was bigger than kings and presidents, actors and great thinkers, bigger than Babe Ruth."[3]

Not that Ruth was being ignored. That year he was awarded a medal from the Boy Scouts. A fountain pen given to him by the same group was lost, or discarded. "Ruth's Gift From Boy Scouts Dug Up in Obscure Coal Pile.... Babe Ruth's fountain pen, given to him by Boy Scouts of Burlington, Iowa, was picked from the coal pile of Gus Dittmore today" in Menominee, Michigan.[4] Was this more "crap" to Ruth?

Ruth had just finished a season during which he had hit 60 home runs and his team became the first team ever to sweep—win all four games in a row from—the National League in a World Series. The fact that the Yankees had won but two World Series in their history was forgotten, even as within living memory the Red Sox had won five championships. But Ruth was the story, the supplier of copy. Sportswriters now elevated Ruth beyond the status of Ty Cobb, Sisler, or Hornsby, or, for that matter, any pitcher.

Cobb, 41, was old news. George Sisler had made 257 hits in 1920, but 171 of them were singles, and Sisler played in far-away St. Louis, for a team that finished most years well below first place. Rogers Hornsby, who averaged a .400 batting average over a five-year span, was the opposite of Ruth when it came to traits of amiability and charm. Bill James, in his *New Historical Baseball Abstract*, says plainly, "Hornsby ... might be called creatively rude. He invented ways to offend people and seemed to take pride in his ability to do so."[5] In addition, 64 percent of his hits were singles. Sportswriters covering Ruth would not flock to Hornsby. Hornsby, in the National League, would never be on the same field with Ruth.

The press was now willing to accept that Ruth, after disastrous years in 1922 and 1925, and at age 32, had resurrected himself and reached a new level of excellence for a baseball player. In April 1928, in the *New York Evening World*, fans could find out about "The New Babe Ruth" when they read, "Two years ago Babe Ruth was a fallen idol. Today he has regained his pedestal and more than that. He has become an institution of this country."[6] Even while keeping in mind the urge in sportswriters for hyperbole, this seems excessive.

And so the writers did their best to erase Ruth's early boorishness and vulgarity. Without saying so, they knew he was in a stable relationship with Claire. They knew too how much the game of baseball, the game the writers counted on for a paycheck, depended on Ruth. Simply put by Ralph Davis, Ruth was "the biggest factor in the financial success of the entire American League." Davis saw that "Ruppert knows ... that for every dollar he pays Ruth, he pays five more back."[7] The word maturity was seldom used to describe Ruth, yet "he displays a sane attitude toward both work and play."[8] The new attitude Ruth showed in 1928 was influenced by his understanding of his celebrity and his position on the American marketplace. Mann continues, "Finance and big business revolve around Babe Ruth," and he knew it. He knew, too, the price for that. While Mann is praising Ruth, calling him an institution, he sees the weight of being an institution.

How puzzling it might be to Ruth, living in his own skin, all this insistence by sportswriters that he be treated like a secular saint. Mann concludes his piece by describing Ruth's effect on the public. "Millions of boys accept him as the ultimate in sports achievement. Grown men look upon him as they themselves might have been or dreamed they could be. Women regard him as the personification of ideal strength in man." Ruth knows he is no saint, and he understands that the image or reputation carved out for him by Christy Walsh and American corporations feels a burden to him. Mann understands that Ruth "has no friends" and that being a brand, a product, "Babe Ruth has become hardened almost to everything and that is the chief reason for the impenetrable shell by which he is encrusted." Furthermore, "Babe been shorn of all outward sentiment. There is no place for it in his life." There would be plenty of room in his life for the press.

It is the contention of biographer Kal Wagenheim that real changes had come into Ruth's life. The Yankees' trainer "spent half of his time" signing baseballs with Ruth's signature, and the famous man used "a secret exit" from the ballpark to get to his car, now guarded by policemen.[9]

Walsh continued to cash in for Ruth and himself at every opportunity, but sometimes failed. The premier case of this failure had to do with the Curtiss Candy Company, which filed an appeal with the Examiner of Interferences in the office of Commissioner of Patents when Curtiss felt interfered with by the George H. Ruth Candy Company, Inc., purveyor of "Ruth's Home Run Candy," a treat which included baseball cards, one of which read, "Knocked out 60 home runs in 1927. His candy helped him." In a trade journal, Ruth was named as "vice-president, in addition to being guaranteed a royalty on sales." Ruth's company lost its attempt, and Curtiss was able to wiggle and win its suit by claiming it had not meant Babe Ruth but President Cleveland's dead daughter Ruth, although Curtiss made their candy in 1921 and the daughter had died in 1909.

But others came calling. Product makers saw to it that Ruth was connected to the "Babe Ruth Yankees 1928 Home Run King Pennant" and "Babe Ruth Chewing Gum." He became the pitchman for White Owl cigars, as well as both Raleigh and Old Gold cigarettes, Pinch Hit chewing tobacco, and Kaywoodie pipes. Even manager Huggins found a way to cash in on Ruth's fame. "In the dressing room at Navin Field in Detroit," the ad copy read, "Babe Ruth and Lou Gehrig gave the blindfold cigarette test to Manager Miller Huggins, the famous Yankee pilot."[10] Ruth appeared many times in the comic strip "Smitty" in July and August.

Babe Ruth supposedly wrote an autobiography in 1928. It was titled, "Babe Ruth's Own Book on Baseball." It was Ford Frick's own book. Walsh often employed Frick as Ruth's ghostwriter, and so successful was Walsh's syndicating business model that soon another syndicate of writers appeared. The North American Newspaper Alliance (NANA), a large newspaper syndicate, flourished between 1922 and 1980. Founded by John Neville Wheeler, NANA employed some of the most noted writing talents of its time, including Grantland Rice, Joseph Alsop, Dorothy Thompson, F. Scott Fitzgerald, and Ernest Hemingway.[11]

Ruth appeared on movie screens in something other than newsreels. Comedian Harold Lloyd hired him to play the role of Babe Ruth in *Speedy,* a silent comedy released on April 7, 1928. There flooded in so many requests for autographs, though he could seem to refuse, trainer Doc Woods was now signing most of the balls for Ruth. Perhaps by now it was not only the number of requests, but Ruth's disdain for anyone who wanted the signature.

Continuing to be interested in the dollar signs for Ruth, the *New York Times,* of February 7, 1928, could say that the 34-year-old player in "the past year saved $70,000 … and his bank accounts now boast the figure of $120,000 [equal to $1,680,000 in the year 2018]. All of Ruth's savings were so tied up that neither Ruth, lawsuits, investments, whatsoever will be able to cut into the principal. The trust fund, it will pay him better than 5 percent per annum for the rest of his days."

Some large part of that fortune, with Walsh's help, rested in the hands of New York City sportswriters, photographed at the Yankees spring training camp, St. Petersburg, Florida, March 1928. In that photo are displayed 13 writers representing ten New York City papers: the *Telegram, Evening World, Sun, American, Journal, Herald Tribune, Times, Post, Daily News,* and *Mirror.* Also covering the Yankees were the AP and the International News Service. One newspaper, continuing the elevation of Ruth's character, making smooth the less publicly desirable of Ruth's appetites, wrote that "the bad boy of baseball" had gotten all of the badness out of his system. Accompanying cartoons showed Ruth yelling at a horse at a race track, and betting on a hand of cards.[12] The very forgivable badness was lessened when another paper, in February 1928, pointed out that professional baseball counted just one dozen players who possessed "personal drawing power," Ruth clearly drawing the most money into a ballpark.

The 1928 Yankees, a well-acknowledged team playing at a high level, won fewer games than in 1927 not because they seemed to be a weaker team, but because another team, the Athletics, were beginning to show their strength in the league even in 1928. Though not yet champions, the Athletics stayed with the Yankees almost all year, the Yankees finishing just 2½ games ahead of them after the 154-game schedule.

Contributing greatly to the team's performance, Ruth scored 54 times on his home runs, scored 109 more runs with help, and drove in 146 runs. He led the league in home runs for the ninth time, even as Al Simmons, and Jimmie Foxx, for example, were just beginning to produce home runs. Seeing teams sending out more than 100 home runs in a season was becoming commonplace.

The era continued to increase its entertainment possibilities as it expanded over the country. Radio again broadcast the World Series, with Ruth once more homering three times in one game, and even finishing the games off by catching "a foul fly on the edge of the boxes in one hand and ran home, openly bearing the ball in his outstretched palm that all might see it was the third out."[13] Ruth batted .625 for the Series, and Gehrig batted .545 with nine RBI. Four of Gehrig's six hits were home runs.

The victorious Yankees walked away with $5,813.20 each.

But whatever the dollars, the amount did not satisfy. "Ruth, Gehrig … are going to dabble in the barnstorming racket in the next few weeks," noted *The Sporting News.* "They are allowed to exhibit themselves … until November 1" so that they "can harvest extra dollars and hero worshipping."[14] Ruth's extensive touring began in 1919, making 1928 his tenth year. No matter that he won the Most Valuable Player Award, Gehrig again, in the reports by local papers, remained almost completely absent in each game's story.

This second Ruth-Gehrig trip, set to travel not further west than Denver, played almost all of the first half of the 19-game schedule in New York and Pennsylvania. Partly because in 1927 the pair traveled 5,900 miles, the majority of the other games would only demand average travel of 100 miles. Again wearing the 1927 Bustin' Babes and Larrupin' Lous "team" uniforms, they planned to tour of 4,600 miles in 1928.

By beginning in New York City, the two and Walsh were assured of extensive publicity, demonstrated by the coverage in both the *New York Times,* and the *Brooklyn Eagle.* Once more at the Bushwicks' Dexter Park, in pre-game publicity Ruth and Gehrig appeared in cowboy outfits complete with chaps. Photographers arranged with Ruth to sit on the hood of a car as if it were a horse, or a steer, since horns were mounted in the front of the vehicle. This stunt was to publicize a "World Series rodeo" that would start shortly in Madison Square Garden. There is no doubt that Ruth picked up an additional check for that stunt. As for the game, Ruth and Gehrig made $3,600 together, with Ruth getting $2,600 (two years' pay for a typical American worker) and Gehrig $1,000. The Bushwicks management, headed by Max Rosner, would gross a minimum of $10,000 for ticket sales and additional sums from their extensive food, drink and scorecard sales. As semipros, the Bushwicks players would be paid, and players with Ruth would too. Still, when an owner can triple his money, there will be no grumbling.

After playing first base like Gehrig, says Tommy Holmes of the *Brooklyn Daily Eagle,*

the Babe was the life of the party, making a lot of good natured noise and bantering with the other players and spectators alike…. It was joke ball game. The famous busting twins were permitted to bat

Bushwicks Rodeo promotion, 1928 (Baseball Hall of Fame).

out of turn no less than twice in the ninth inning and given all manner of swings until they connected. By actual calculation, the count on Ruth was six strikes and five balls when he smashed a hard grounder down to the first baseman for the final out of the game.

With games behind them in Canada and upstate New York, Trenton, New Jersey, became the October 18 site of game five. During the game, "some 3,000 kids yesterday … shed tears of genuine anguish at not being able to catch a glimpse of the mighty Babe." Ruth played first base for his team, the Young Italian-Americans, and Gehrig played right field for the same team against the Trenton A.A., for which the pair was guaranteed $1,500 "rain or shine." The game was called in the first half of the ninth inning after 65 minutes when the kids came onto the field.

With no game scheduled for October 19, Ruth returned to New York City, where he was signed up to speak "over station WJZ and a nation-wide network" at 10:30 at night in support of the Democratic ticket, headed by Al Smith. Previously, "Franklin D. Roosevelt asked Babe Ruth to endorse Al Smith for President. Ruth agreed, signed a hearty letter about poor boys, like himself, rising from humble beginnings (very likely written by someone in Smith's headquarters), and accepted a nominal place on an Al Smith for President Committee."[15]

Being "for" someone did not mean Ruth voted. He did not. At the time, there appeared no indication that Ruth's support of a candidate who was against Prohibition and a Roman Catholic was going to hurt the star player. But it certainly would not hurt Ruth's reputation when as a "companion speaker" listed was John W. Davis, unsuccessful Democratic candidate for President in 1924.

Moving west after two more games in upstate New York, Ruth could read about the death of Jack Dunn, who had signed Ruth to his first professional baseball contract. The AP wrote that Ruth "expressed regret 'at the loss of a fine fellow and a good sportsman.'" The words sound like manufactured copy from Walsh's office. Thus, we do not know Ruth's feeling, if any, about the death. This cold boilerplate response shows no emotion.

When the Columbus, Ohio, game, the tenth, on October 23 was over, the *Columbus Citizen* saw no need to write more than a 150-word report. The 1,300 attendees (just 1,400 the day before in Dayton) saw Ruth go two-for four and Gehrig two-for-six, with the Babes winning, 7–4, in yet another game in which the rules were lightly tossed aside. "The Babe pitched the last inning and Lou Gehrig batted twice in the last frame in an attempt to loft the ball out of the park."

With game 13 contracted for, the tour moved to Flint, Michigan, where the "home run twins" would perform at Athletic Park on a Friday afternoon. Ruth seemed to know the impossibility of hitting a home run to his strength—right field—since this park's right field fence stood 482 feet away. He hit a double to left field and walked in a game that ended in a 5–5 tie. But 8,000 paid, and Ruth knew there was an added bonus for him. "We came a long way out of our route to hit this country. I did it because I was told that an automobile concern in Flint wanted to give me an automobile…. Then I was told that the gift of the automobile was a ticket-selling proposition and all the tickets hadn't been sold. Somehow the Packard Company got ahold of what was going on. I've got eight Packards now, but the Packard Company must have, in 15 minutes, made a decision and gave me a Packard."[16]

If the reporting from Flint remains skimpy, the report from the home of Kellogg cereals provided a series of reports of the business dealings of the 1928 barnstorming trio. Thanks to the *Battle Creek Moon-Journal,* more specific details were made known of typical demands on a Ruth barnstorming tour. For their $1,500, Mr. Bowen and Mr. Weickgenant of Battle Creek insisted that the players adhere to the following itinerary:

1. Arrive five hours before game time and appear in Battle Creek the morning of the game
2. In mid-morning go to Kalamazoo (30 miles) to meet a delegation of business men
3. Travel back to Battle Creek and appear in a parade
4. Go to the Kellogg plant for luncheon
5. Show up for a radio broadcast
6. Address a welcome to the crowd over public address system
7. Conduct a batting demonstration
8. Play the game
9. Appear at dinner in Post Tavern

As a further condition, pitchers were not allowed to walk either player. Tickets were put on sale at the Main Cigar Store, Oppenheimer's, Central, and Ye Old Mission Billiard Hall. Profits were to be turned over to the Welfare Fund and police relief association. The city's mayor bought 200 tickets to give to boys, because, he said, saying not much of anything, "Babe Ruth and Lou Gehrig are heroes of the average boy and that they have inspired and stimulated much interest in the minds and hearts of the boys of today." If the players were thought of with admiration by children, the reporter repeated the idea that Ruth himself was less than a mature adult. "The ball game itself was more or less of a travesty, but to the hundreds of kids gathered at Kellogg Park, the appearance of the two home run kings was a treat. Babe in reality is just a big kid himself and his interest in every youngster is not forced or done for publicity; it's genuine."

That being said, "The appearance of the stars in Battle Creek was a financial flop." Gehrig and Christy Walsh had checked in to the Post Tavern, where they were scheduled to attend a 5:30 p.m. banquet. After the game, both Ruth and Gehrig were handed summonses for two suits, one for failure to live up to the contract and the other for failure to pay back expense money spent in their behalf in "recent games" by Jack Mickie Bowen. Walsh refused the $400 tendered to his group as 60 percent of the gate receipts ($665 total) "holding that the telegram guaranteeing $1,500 and signed by Mr. Bowen and Mr. Weickgenant constituted a contract that he had accepted and fulfilled." Walsh already knew and had accounted for bad weather—rain, cold, etc.—that might affect attendance and therefore receipts. Walsh seemed to have insisted that in such cases insurance was to be in place to cover the payments for Ruth, Gehrig and Walsh. The promoters apparently either neglected or refused to buy that insurance. So, Walsh, Ruth, and Gehrig took not a nickel out of Battle Creek and caught the 5:57 Michigan Central train west.

After the 250-mile trip for a game played in Milwaukee, *The Sporting News*, ever the friend of the owners, reminded the barnstormers that the end of October must be the end of the tour. "This is the last day on which the two stars will be permitted to perform under the laws of organized baseball." Those laws remained the incontestable decisions of Commissioner Landis. Meanwhile, Ruth spoke of how eager he was to go hunting for birds after the tour.

Two Iowa games followed, the first covering 375 miles from Milwaukee in Des Moines, where Ruth had visited in 1926. The "demon swatsmiths" had to arrive early in the morning and sit down to breakfast with F. Lee Keyser, who "was later known as the

'Father of Night Baseball'" for being "among those to introduce night baseball games at the Des Moines facility [on May 2, 1930], the first night professional baseball game, played under permanent lights."[17]

Local reporter Rec Taylor wrote very disparagingly about the game, saying first that the weather was "too chilly for baseball and dismal." He also remarked that "Batting practice, Ruth's showcase, was curtailed" and that "the pitchers were so wild" no one could hit. He called the contest a match between "two teams of alleged ball players." And though the reporter thought it unseemly to have the two stars batting out of turn several times, the reporter was not like the fans, 500 of them who had come for entertainment. They got to see Ruth pitch four innings, hit a home run over the left field fence, and saw, in total, 19 runs scored in the game. "In 1928 Bob Feller [then ten] received an autographed base-ball from Babe Ruth when Ruth and Lou Gehrig barnstormed through Des Moines on a cross country trip.... To get the ball, Feller trapped gophers ... around Van Meter. Each pair of gopher claws brought Feller 10 cents. After trapping $5.00 worth of gophers, Feller was able to purchase the ball."[18]

Feller is quoted as saying, "'Baseballs with autographs were sold for five dollars from a bushel basket.'"[19] Thus it becomes clear that not all of the signed baseballs were given freely to children.

In Sioux City on October 30, 2,000 fans (in a ballpark that seated 7,500) watched Ruth hit two homers, a triple and a double, while playing for the Ryal Miller team. Gehrig made one double and two singles for the Kari-Keen club. Ryal Miller won, 9–2. Because the temperature registered very low, the game was called after six innings. Both mainly played first base, but also pitched toward the end of the game. They then visited both St. Anthony's orphanage and the Boys and Girls Home. They left the same night for Denver.

When snow and rain made playing that last scheduled game impossible, the tour headed back to New York. Barnstorming close to 1928's magnitude, 18 games, would not be attempted again by Ruth until 1931.

The press, in this case the *Milwaukee Journal*, claimed that Ruth amassed $150,000 in 1928. Once again, as if to justify Ruth's fabulous earnings, the *New York Times*, of October 14, 1928, announced, "when the confidence of the fans was shaken by the revelation of the 'Black Sox' scandal, it was the hitting of Babe Ruth that kept the fans flocking through." This idea keep being insisted on though fans in Cincinnati or Pittsburgh never saw Ruth.

That same year, Gene Tunney took home $500,000 for his bout against Tom Heeney of New Zealand. The previous year, he collected a purse of more than $990,000. He retired from boxing with two million dollars in the bank at age 30 in 1928 after 83 bouts.

As further indication of the money now possible through professional sports, on October 27, 1928, the *New York Times* reported "that the Yankee stadium In New York is to be enlarged to seat 125,000 patrons." Some of that plan may have been influenced by the September 27 game that year, a game that could stand as a tribute to Ruth. It supposedly drew 85,265 paid to Yankee Stadium. The box office report on the doubleheader says that they took in $115,000 that day, or $1.34 per customer.

27

Male Clubs and Masculinity

After 15 years as a professional athlete, and after eight years of having his public personality shaped and defined by the Christy Walsh Syndicate, and through Ruth's own behavior among the public, one attribute, though not named directly, comes to the fore. Of all of Ruth's traits, it seems to be the one most natural to him, and, at the same time, the one that remained understated. That trait was his manliness.

"Baseball became one of the central mechanisms by which masculinity was reconstituted at the turn of the [20th] century.... Sports were a place where manhood was earned."[1] How did baseball and Ruth, its biggest star, become the mechanisms for reaching a rekindled maleness? And why, in Ruth's era, did masculinity need to be "reconstituted"? It was the times. Ruth's sport, baseball, "became popular at a moment in U.S. history," Carroll writes, "when white middle-class men felt that their manhood was being threatened."[2]

Manifest in this crisis, and primary, appeared to be the growth of the influence and accomplishments of women, either by themselves or in groups. Women were entering into the areas of men, advocating to change the very male habits and practices. Alone, women became well known athletes: Babe Zaharias and Gertrude Ederle. They won prizes only men had won: Marie Curie. They showed they could do jobs supposedly the sole province of men: Amelia Earhart and Aimee Semple McPherson.

The authority of women was partly exemplified by the more than 300,000 women who belonged to the Women's Christian Temperance Union (W.C.T.U.), a group who battled against the use of tobacco and alcohol. The image of men, like Ruth, with a cigar in one hand and a drink in the other remained as a dominant picture of males for a long time. Partly because of the W.C.T.U. as well as other women's groups interested in expanding their influence, within two years both the Prohibition amendment and the right of women to vote became federal law.

Men's primacy began to wane. Men no longer provided all the income for all families, and so lost control of the their discretionary income as well. With women rallying against the barroom and the cigar store, men wouldn't need the money anyway. As their dominance diminished, men looked for other ways to feel in control. With the American frontier marked as closed, a man's role as a hunter, or a mountain man—or a cowboy—faded.

As a class, women had taken enough jobs in the work force that "by 1920 the[ir] percentage had risen to 28.3 percent."[3] Women began to leave their marriages behind through divorce, a social change made possible by women working outside of the home and that work's corresponding economic independence.

Of course, not every workplace had men working with women. But social scientists observed the change in the mix of workers and the corresponding revolution because of the newer ways of accomplishing tasks. When Ruth was a child, close to 50 percent of the U.S. population lived in rural areas. The year 1920 marks the decline of rural peoples and the rise of urban. (Rural population in 2015 was less than half of what it was in 1900.) The downturn in rural numbers is due in no small measure to the rise in machines that did the work of men in farms and other work-intensive areas. So workers came to the cities and began to build machines or work at the machines that did the work they had done just a decade before. Working on a factory line, that is, in a job in which he was not autonomous, differed greatly from the mass of rural work, the kind that had been the hard, physical labor of men working by themselves as the sole provider, or men working exclusively with other men.

The cities still saw masculine sorts of jobs: steering a taxi around busier city streets, even while men were still shoveling manure to keep streets manageable. But for white, Christian, native males, their factory and office co-workers had changed. Foreign-born people sought out the cities, and by 1920 the "Great Black Migration from the South" brought 800,000 potential workers to Northern industrial cities.[4]

Where might be solace for the white, Christian, native male in this new compounding of life? Looking to heroes might be one way. The new American Irish, one group, could point with pride to their boxing champions Jim Fitzsimmons, Jack Dempsey and Gene Tunney. But for all American males, baseball had been identified as a truly American game in its origins. With so many major league players, each nationality could claim its heroes. After Cobb's period of dominance of the game, after the time of the famous pitchers, came Ruth's time. As the work force changed, as women's roles began to change, Ruth's years were the times of the slugger, the long ball, the quick run.

Ruth was both exemplar of maleness in the country's most popular sport as well as someone who demonstrated that he preferred the fraternity of men off the field. As for his women, he had a wife but stashed her away, and the sex that he had was the type without any commitment. He took what he wanted, or rather he paid for it. Even after he was painted to be the reformed family man with Claire, we now know he was not.

Like men for millennia, Ruth was a hunter and was often photographed with the animals he had killed. He ate what he pleased; he drank and smoked in amounts, so it was written, that never failed to astound; he traveled as he pleased. In all meanings of the word, he was "undomesticated." To outsiders, Ruth seemed to work two hours a day (baseballreference.com says games in 1928 took, on average, 1:23 to complete) and spend all of his time in the company of men. In addition to all of Ruth's nicknames like the Sultan of Swat, some writers dropped the regal titles and replaced them with labels such as "the Caveman of Baseball, a big baboon, and an ape."[5] For F. C. Lane, in a July 1921 piece in *Baseball Magazine* by the contrarian, Ruth's "dominant quality" among all the others was plainly stated: "brute force."

Ruth's maleness made it into public consciousness as his home run numbers increased. In addition, he seemed to be eminently likeable, without pretension, a man born with gifts that needed no polishing, only harnessing. In addition, you could not fail to see Ruth in a group picture, his size alone making him stand out. Even in the company of other physical men, he was large, measuring six inches more in height and 70 pounds more in weight than the average American male. Jerome Charyn calls Ruth "our national exaggeration," and part of that hyperbole was his maleness.[6] It was true that in his career he had worked his way up using his own strength.

This "crisis" of manhood during which "masculinity was reconstituted" affected the ways of not just adult males. Boys might be raised according to attitudes established decades before the 1920s. In the century of Ruth's birth, what was valued was "a game that exhausted boys before they could fall victims to vice and idleness, instilled … manly virtues … an activity that would distract boys from vice and idleness that was closely associated to the two unmentionables of the Victorian period: masturbation and homosexuality."[7] The notion became popular that the consequences of taking part in athletic games extended beyond the playing fields. "Baseball and other sports tended to correct or alleviate physical defects and mental aberrations in boys and young men until the danger period is past."[8] A 1924 sportswriter, noting the repugnance at the Chicago murder case, wrote, "had Leopold and Loeb been more interested in 'clean and manly sport,' such a crime would not have been committed." In popular American thought, to be a man after all required American men—if they wished to be accepted as true men among their fellows—to know about, to praise and to celebrate those very masculine celebrities like Ruth.

Fathers, and their sons, could turn to Ruth for a model of a life lived manly, free of the demands of women and free to spend 90 percent of the year in the company of men. The fathers could choose for their children Puffed Wheat, Ruth's favorite cereal, or for schoolwork a Big Giant writing tablet with Ruth's picture on the cover, and for a treat buy the boy a bottle of pop called Red Rock, sponsor of Ruth on the radio.

As Ruth's standing as a celebrity and as a commodity began to increase in America, another great solace for men were male fraternal groups. By the turn of the 20th century, there were over 300 different fraternal organizations in America, with six million members. For example, by 1912, the order of the Moose had grown from 247 members to nearly 500,000; the Lions Club by 1927 counted a paying membership of 60,000 in 1,183 clubs; the Rotary grew to 150,000 in 1930. At the National Convention of Elks in July of 1929, 100,000 members attended. In fact, more than half of all Americans participated in clubs, fraternities, militias, and mutual benefit societies."[9] For most of these clubs, membership requirements included being white and Christian.

The Catholic fraternal group The Knights of Columbus loved to brag about Ruth, a boy raised by priests in a Catholic reformatory. Their public giving of gifts to him, such as the presentation of $600 in treasury savings certificates and a traveling bag in 1919, was not limited to Ruth's first meeting place, the Pere Marquette Council 271 in South Boston. Ruth spent many hours in the lodges and temples of fraternal groups. On October 22, 1924, he was selected to be a lifetime member of the Lions. These two memberships were added to by his joining the Goodfellows in 1926 and the Elks on February 12, 1928. One of the reasons these groups were eager to have Ruth on their rolls was that Ruth "gave males everywhere a masculine ideal and national pride."[10]

Michael Kimmel's judgment is that the cause for forming these male groups in the early twentieth century was the "crisis of whether or not the traditional white, middle class version of masculinity would continue to prevail over both women and nonwhite men."[11] Discussion arose over whether men ought to have just two prevailing traits: power and aggression, the kind of traits that a cowboy hero, defunct except in movies, might have, the kind of traits that Clark Gable often played and that were so clearly irresistible to his female co-stars even if they pretended otherwise. Those men who were not aggressive were considered female, or at least non-male. One attitude that connected Ruth and fraternal societies was the absence of women. Being the anointed savior of baseball from the treachery of the Black Sox and the sport's biggest and most recognizable star made him, for many men and women, the ideal of masculinity in the 1920s.

The combination of masculinity and nativist esteem became another way to understand Ruth's ubiquity and therefore his popularity among the buying public. That there were Goodfellows and Elks buildings all over the country was a plus to the inveterate traveler that Ruth was. For Ruth, whether barnstorming or on a vaudeville tour, he knew he would be welcomed at those meeting places. Simply, the presence of Ruth at these fraternal groups validated their very existence and increased their attractiveness.

Many photographs of Ruth picture him and the other men in the group as delighted to be together. As good company as Ruth seemed to be, it must not be forgotten that a celebrity of his status visiting a small group—Watertown, New York, or Dunsmuir, California—caused excitement and pleasure among the membership; it would be a day they would remember and brag about. For Ruth, these lodges had the additional unspoken idea that there would be no lasting friendships. He would be in all of those places simply someone who might be a visitor of a day or a few days' duration. While Ruth may not had a thought of doing business while he visited fraternal groups halls all over the country, he could have a legal drink because the meeting hall was not a saloon, though it often served as one for the membership during those prohibition years.

Ruth, who endorsed so many products, was a fraternal brother to many of these men and so it would be almost a duty to sell the products that Ruth endorsed when given a choice of similar goods to choose from. Then too, in their own private lives they might pick a product aligning themselves with the masculine Ruth. They might select, for example, Chesterfield cigarettes, or Old Gold, both brands with which Ruth's picture and statement appeared. Why not pick the aftershave Ruth seemed to approve of, drive the car that the big man drove? After all, had not they themselves, or their fellows, sat down with Ruth in their very own meeting hall?

28

Many Deaths, One Marriage
(1929)

In December 1928, as Montville describes it, Helen Ruth and her sister, Nora Wood-food, met with Walsh and Ruth in New York City, and the two women proposed a payment of $100,000 to cover a trip to Reno for a divorce, for the care of Dorothy, the adopted daughter, and for her support. "'I'm not going," said Ruth, "to give you another cent."[1] No one knows how much money, but it seems likely that the sale of the Sudbury property, at least, went to Helen.

Meanwhile, Dorothy was in a convent boarding school in Massachusetts, registered under the name of Kinder. No one has ever suggested that Ruth's visits to orphanages compensated for being so far distant from his daughter. "That arrangement seems to have been Helen's idea of what was best for Dorothy … [Ruth] didn't see much of them after 1925."[2] To further complicate all of these relationships, Helen's will called Dorothy her "ward and charge" and even stated that Dorothy was "one time known as Marie Harrington."[3]

On January 14, 1929, news arrived that Helen had died in a fire in Watertown, Massachusetts, where she had been living with dentist William Kinder. "After Helen's death, two nuns roused Dorothy from her sleep, informed her of the accident, and whisked her away from her boarding school, taking her to a New York hospital where she, once more, was abandoned."[4] Grantland Rice's version claims, "Ruth and Helen's daughter, who was living in a parochial school under an assumed name, was not told about … her mother's death until months later."[5]

The *New York Times* has called Dorothy's birth "mysterious." Odd that the man's activities were followed so closely, yet the birth of his only child remains a mystery. No one has yet noticed that the permanent address for Dorothy, the address named in Helen's will—175 East 68th Street—was the address of the New York Foundling Hospital. That is, the true home for Dorothy was not Babe Ruth's address, 345 West 88th Street in New York, nor Helen's address in Massachusetts, but an orphanage. Ruth waited five months to "finally claim his daughter" despite his well-publicized loved for all children."[6] The word "claim" remains unclear.

Not until October 30, 1930, did Ruth sign papers to adopt his "ward," Dorothy—almost 600 days—and Julia, the daughter of his new wife, Claire. It remains unclear why Dorothy was said to be under Ruth's "protection" up until she was adopted—or why as his daughter she needed to be adopted. "He loved Dorothy" wrote Hoyt, "but he just didn't have the time to allot to her the role of loving father."[7]

Jacob Ruppert continued to hope someday to be able to pack thousands more into an expanded stadium. There were changes going on for the team. For example, the third baseman for eight years, Joe Dugan, had been selected off waivers by the Boston Braves, so with Dugan gone, the infield remained unsettled except for Gehrig at first base. By the end of March, the pitching too remained uncertain.

The team's spring training trip north made stops in Houston, Ft. Worth, Waco, Dallas, Oklahoma City, Tulsa, Little Rock, and Charlotte, in states Ruth, for the most part, never scheduled when constructing his barnstorming stops. When the team arrived back in New York, Ruth and Claire made arrangements to be married. If anyone thought the marriage came too soon after Helen's death, they were silent about making that judgment. "It was his intention to be married secretly … but as an appreciation of the consideration that has always been shown him by newspaper writers and photographers…. Ruth decided to announce the upcoming ceremony."[8] It cannot be seen as anything but certain that Ruth understood his debt to the writers.

Living with Claire on West 79th Street at the time of her marriage were her daughter, mother, maid, and two brothers, Eugene and Hubert. There appeared no news of when Dorothy might be arriving at the 11-room apartment at 345 West 88th Street in Manhattan. One writer thinks that with a new wife, "he steadfastly remained the same Babe, more serious-minded, but as cordial and affable as ever."[9] Moving out of the Ansonia Hotel, it must be wondered what had happened to all those gifts to Ruth, like the Copper Cup. All those stickpins and fountain pens and hen eggs. All those things not cash. Whatever happened to them? Given away, thrown away as soon as received, sold?

In place now were the threefold influences: Walsh, for money, McGovern, for physical fitness, and Claire, for companionship at home and management of Ruth's $70,000 salary. Claire's control was often described as firm and kind. Financially secure, married, at last, to the woman who had been his companion since 1923, Ruth's roistering that characterized his life disappeared only to reappear, almost with longing, in the full-blown wishes and lies of sportswriters, those sometimes referred to as myth.

What was not mythical were the increasing sources of money for the new husband. For example, in place by 1929 was a network of radio stations, a system which connected 60 broadcasting stations by wire, 16 hours a day every day in the year, and which carried the best radio talent to 50,000,000 persons or more in every part of the country.[10] Advertisers, who spent "$3.4 billion in 1929," now spent a portion of that money on radio ads.[11] More specifically for Ruth, "customers spent $66 million for spectator sports, mostly for baseball and college football" tickets.[12]

"The New York Yankees' payroll in 1929 equaled $365,741."[13] Subtract Ruth's $70,000 and Gehrig's $25,000, and the team average was $11,000. To contrast those salaries, the Brookings Institute reported that "$2,000 a year was the minimum family requirement to purchase the basic necessities and 60 percent of American families were below that figure."[14]

Ruth had some accomplishments in that year to savor, however. When he hit his 500th home run on August 11, nearest to him was Cy Williams with 237. The *New York World* called the feat "a symbol of greatness."[15] Just as sportswriters' acclaim of Ruth's power reached new heights, the Athletics, a few days later, began to extend permanent stands for use in the World Series, with more than a month to play.

The *Evening World* saw Yankee Stadium as a monument to Ruth's achievements. The stadium had the "austere dignity" of a bank and for the same reason: "Money speaks there in the low, modulated voice that is more eloquent than the shouts of a mob storming the Bastille. Yankee Stadium a bank, built by the home runs of Babe Ruth! What higher compliment could be offered to the Babe in the United States of the late Twenties?"[16]

For the Yankees' pennant chances, a powerful team from Philadelphia, one that would match the 1927 Ruth and Gehrig Yankees in fame and dominance, came to the fore so quickly in 1929 and so completely that by July 6 the Yankees could see they were nine and a half games back of Connie Mack's Athletics.

The nadir of the Yankees' season came on September 25, when manager Miller Huggins died. Some current biographers seem to be ascribing Huggins' early death to Ruth, as if he could bring death to someone he disliked, so great were Ruth's powers. They like this quote: "'Babe Ruth took five years off my brother's life,' Huggins's sister, Mildred, told one reporter."[17] Huggins died at age 50 from what the *New York Times* called "blood poisoning."

Now with Art Fletcher as their interim manager, the season drew to an end. Although the Yankees scored but two fewer runs than the Philadelphia team over the course of the season, the Yankees' pitching gave up 157 more runs than the Athletics. Ruth and Gehrig had fine seasons, driving in 279 runs between them.

During the Series, Ruth made some money with stories with his bylines. "Seven ballplayers, seven ghosts, and Walsh split $43,252" for covering the 1929 World Series.[18]

Not long after the end of the season, rumors appeared like this one by William Ritt in the *Berkeley Daily Gazette*. "Babe Ruth may be the next manager of the New York Yankees. Babe Ruth! Big. blundering Babe Ruth, the careless, carefree playboy." Ruth's thinking seemed to be tied to the idea that in the years before (and after) 1929 there were many successful first-time managers—that is, player-mangers who had no managing experience in the minor leagues or major leagues. Keeping in mind that in the chronicle of major league baseball, there were 47 player-managers, in Ruth's time alone the following were successful: John McGraw, Fred Clarke, Frank Chance, Bill Carrigan, Rogers Hornsby, Tris Speaker, and Bucky Harris. Ruth could see the end of his career on the horizon and very much wanted to be a big league manager. He had correctly pointed out earlier that, "During the Winter season I book my own exhibition games and without support from other professional players."[19]

Also to Ruth's credit, he had enough discipline and self-control to perform at a very high level from 1915 until the present day. At the age of 34 in 1929, Ruth played in 143 games, with 46 home runs, 154 runs batted in, and a .345 batting average.

For those paying attention, and balancing the younger Ruth's behavior with the Ruth since 1926, the story that they could read was the popular American story of redemption. From wastrel to family man; from, as the story keeps being told even now, orphan to wealthy man; from street urchin to celebrity. But the magnates did not see that story, or did not want to see that story. The management of the team had an objection to Ruth that they spoke out loud. Managing might very well damage his performance as a player, was one spoken opinion.

Sportswriter Fred Lieb summed up the popular wisdom: "Babe was headstrong, easily provoked, and never could accept managerial discipline."[20] The Ruth reputation of his earlier years would not die. So much so that a statement has been attributed to owner Ruppert that he never made. Likewise, Ruppert did not say it in the various years that he has supposed to have said it. The quote is this: "You can't manage yourself. How can you manage others?" Besides the two sentences being a model of elegant writing, not the unlettered utterings of Ruth, the words were never spoken by Ruppert and did not appear until four years later, and only then in the October 1933 column of an accomplished writer.

"Ruppert pretended to take the Babe's request seriously and told him he would think it over and call him in a couple of days. A week later, Ruth picked up a paper and read the headline that Bob Shawkey, another of the Yankees' coaches, was selected as manager, a way for 'Carrying Out Wish of the Late Miller Huggins.'"[21] Ruth knew he must formally announce that he "would not manage the Yankees next season ... as long as I can deliver the goods as a player, it would not be wise for me to take on the trouble and worries of a manager."[22]

So the team signed Shawkey to a one-year contract at a salary of $15,000. Perhaps to soften the blow for Ruth, Ruppert refunded the 1925 fine of $5,000 assessed by Huggins. But the extra $5,000 did not satisfy Ruth. To play some more baseball, to be applauded, and to pick up some quick cash after the World Series, Ruth and Gehrig played two post-season games. The first needed only a quick drive through the Holland Tunnel and a few miles north to Miller Stadium in West New York, New Jersey, and a win by 5–4.

For the thousands who crowded into Cameron Field at 5 Mead St. South Orange, New Jersey (again a short drive), a memorable game was witnessed on October 27, 1929. More than 70 years later, a post by L. Craig Schoonmaker described the game. "The South Orange team, with help from Ruth and Gehrig, played for a crowd of some 12,000 including about two dozen Major Leaguers. Spectators paid one dollar each to sit in the grandstand and watched South Orange best New Brunswick."[23] The *New York Times* wrote a few words on the game, describing how "Babe Gets Homer and Mate Hits Three." During Ruth's 5–5 show, "six dozen baseballs were used ... the crowd ... keeping the balls when they were knocked into it."

The year 1929 ended with a roll call of the dead. Besides Huggins, a number of people important to Ruth, for good or not, had died. Helen, his wife, dead. Jack Dunn, his first manager, died just the previous year on October 22, 1928, Dunn's success was calculated in dollars. "In 1926 ... the *Baltimore Sun* reported that Dunn had sold 29 players to major league teams and received a total of $404,100 in cash from these transactions."[24] Joe Lannin, Red Sox owner who bought Ruth's contract from Dunn in 1914, died on May 15, 1928. Earlier that year Harry Frazee, who bought the Red Sox from Lannin, died at the age of age 48. In his obituary, the *New York Times*, remembered, "For years, he seemed to possess the golden touch, but recently, it was reported among his associates that his fortune had dwindled. His more recent ventures were less fortunate and he always was a generous spender." Urban Shocker, a teammate for three years and a barnstorming companion at Ruth's 1926 game in Montreal, died on September 9, 1928, at 37. Luckily, the Yankees were scheduled to play in the city of his burial, St. Louis, on the day of the funeral. Ruth was not chosen as one of the official pallbearers.

As the 1920s ended, was Ruth's slugging reputation safe? It appeared harder for a Ruth to stand out from the rest of the sluggers. Now Ott, Hornsby, Foxx and Simmons, in addition to Gehrig, challenged him for the lead in home runs. Even newer names: Klein, Wilson, O'Doul and Hurst. Ruth fell more than 12 percent behind in total bases, and did not rank in the top ten in runs scored. His competition, for example Gehrig, had just turned 26, Ruth eight years his senior.

The effects of the stock market crash on October 24, 1929, would be truly felt for some time. In the long run, Ruth's annuity protected his future income.

29

Ruth and Children

"Just a few weeks before Yankee Stadium opened, Ruth was in Vicksburg, Mississippi when he learned there was a sick boy in town who was praying to get better in order to see Ruth play. Ruth immediately summoned an automobile and journeyed seven miles into the country and ended up spending an hour with the boy."[1]

That Ruth genuinely liked to be in the company of children, that he would go to some lengths to bring them some cheer, seems undeniable. Some writers think Ruth himself was childlike and so would seek out their company. Most observers are convinced that it was Ruth's St. Mary's childhood—that he grew up in a dorm with other children and that upon awakening there was no parent—that motivated Ruth to seek out children in general and institutionalized children in particular. They think the lack of compassion for Ruth as a child perhaps influenced the generous present of his time. Many credit this willingness as a saving grace for Ruth, a counterpoint to the hedonism, coarseness, and vulgarity of his earlier years in baseball.

But to say that a complicated affection has one cause does not tell the truth. Ruth's experiences must be looked at to produce a more complete answer. "Baseball writers believed that there was a special relationship between baseball and the youth of America. As the leading figure in base-ball, Babe Ruth therefore had to demonstrate this relationship."[2] From Organized Baseball came some pressure as well. The National Agreement in baseball, published in 1921, included an advisory council which wrote, "If any special responsibility rests upon the ball player it is a responsibility to young America. The boy in the bleachers is in school, even if he doesn't realize it. The heroes of the diamond are his teachers." The new baseball commissioner, Judge Landis, also backed the idea. The baseball establishment accepted the relationship between the American boy and baseball as a kind of sacred trust. Judge Landis, for example, often said in his public speeches: "Nearly every boy builds a shrine to some baseball hero."[3]

After entering the demands of the corporate world, Ruth learned from Christy Walsh what behavior might do him some good—that is, make him more attractive to endorsements—and what would not. Ruth, of course, followed Walsh's counsel only sometimes, but he did know about it. While it is true that "Ruth appeared at hospitals and orphanages willingly and often without fanfare," certainly those appearances did him no harm.[4] Years later, in honor of Ruth's 50th birthday, Arthur Daley of the *New York Times*, would write: "The joy this good-natured man brought to sick or crippled children never adequately can be computed. Occasionally word leaked out of some of his expeditions to hospitals or homes but the Babe never did anything of that sort for publicity purposes. He did it because he wanted to."

Were those appearances appealing to him? That he traveled to hospitals and orphanages, or even just to one child often over a distance of many miles, does indicate he received pleasure from the visits. Humans work at what pleases them. That Ruth liked to be on the move, to travel, only helped him to make the visits. That he did not linger at the hospitals, nor spend very much time with each orphan, remains true simply because it was impossible to do so. Too many children, all strangers, too little time. How many photographs appeared with Ruth surrounded by many, many children? Sometimes he simply tossed baseballs from a moving car. "He is ever ready to speak with anyone, even if only to utter his celebrated 'Hello, kid!' and shamble on," Arthur Mann wrote. Ruth had learned over the years that all he need do was say a few words, acknowledge a person, or even a group, or just give a wave in passing by.

So it is possible to understand Ruth acting in the same fashion as a grandfather. That is to say, he had no true responsibility for the child, he may be allowed to do nothing but please the child, he is not expected to spend very much time with the child, and it costs him no money to spend time with the child. How could he? There were so many children, many of them isolated in hospitals, orphanages or just in a sick bed, eager for anything to break up the tedium of confinement in an institution or sick room. There were so many children at a barnstorming game eager for an autograph or a touch, a touch maybe not of Babe Ruth, but a touch of someone famous. So many that Ruth could have only the briefest time with each and all. It must be pointed out that Ruth may have preferred to have his time with children in that briefest of fashions.

It also needs to be said that much of the material written about Ruth and children sounds a great deal like noblesse oblige. If Queen Elizabeth waves to the crowd when she passes by or stands on a balcony, does that provide a thrill for some onlookers? Perhaps. Does it have any lasting and positive effect on the onlooker? Should we assign praise to the Queen for her wave? Probably not. And yet Ruth was repeatedly blessed for his time with a child or children.

His history with his own child, Dorothy, does not speak very well of his devotion to her as a father. It has been documented that he and Helen rarely spent any time together, meaning that neither did father and daughter. As the *New York Times,* on October 30, 1930, remembered, lawyers had decided that "she was not the child of Ruth and his wife either by birth or adoption" from her birth on June 7, 1921. Never officially his child but only Helen's "ward and charge," she became his "adopted" daughter in October of 1929.

The reaction from the "kiddies," as they were called in Ruth's time, seemed to be universally enthusiastic. Ruth could witness how excited the children were to see him, how happy. Who would not want to go to a place where you would be greeted with smiles? Certainly that reaction made the visits attractive to Ruth. The children only wanted to show their affection for him. They were not trying to sell him something, not trying to talk him into anything, not asking for anything but to have him nearby, if only for a little while. Time spent with the kiddies appeared pressure-free, a kind of haven.

Ruth's life, a mostly solitary life, and his relationship with teammates or people outside of baseball, look shallow today. Simply stated, Ruth "has no friends."[5] And children were different from adults. "He will sign anything for a youngster, but only baseballs for grown-ups. Through a base trick in which someone once tried extortion with his autograph on a program," Ruth had learned that "only the kids can be trusted."[6]

Now it is necessary to understand that Ruth may be separate from his business partner, Christy Walsh, and that the ballplayer would frequently go his own way and leave the cash flow to Walsh: "Babe Ruth has frequently let me use his signature to endorse various things."[7] With Ruth constantly on the move, business decisions were left to Walsh, who knew where the money was. Walsh also knew that Ruth simply did not care about how the money was made. If Ruth went to visit with orphans without publicity, he could certainly do that. But "Walsh guaranteed that these visits would not be forgotten, cementing the saintly side of Ruth's persona."[8]

But even before his contract with Walsh, Ruth was publicized from sales emphasizing children. A shoe company needed to liquidate its stock in the summer of 1920. "The exploitation men" decided "to present to Babe Ruth a pair of shoes for every home run hit" and then Ruth

> generously donated them to some fifty orphan children right at the sale in Grand Central Palace, a dozen motion picture cameras being trained on him and Mrs. Ruth during this presentation, and a like number of photographers taking stills. The photographs were shown in theatres throughout the country, not merely locally, and syndicated throughout the country. Pictures of the Colossus of Swat donating the shoes were shaped into human interest copy."[9]

Forgotten, again, conveniently for Ruth's image, remains the fact that it was unlikely that Ruth needed fifty pairs of shoes. He owned them but had no use for them. Could he sell them? To whom should he give them then? Something had to be done with them.

This seeming kind of generosity to "orphan children" only increased as Christy Walsh applied his expertise to delivering pathos. Some of the people who wanted to use Ruth to hawk their products either made things children would buy or made things that children would buy once they matured. Walsh was shrewd about his celebrities, but corporate America was shrewder still, even in the beginning times of market research. In fact, "innovative mass merchandisers played a vital role in promoting children's goods and nurturing children's consumer appetites and identities ... during the late nineteenth century."[10]

In Ruth's first year in New York, a trade journal, *Printers' Ink*, ran an article that insisted "First of all, you want to get clearly into your head the fact that a boy is more or less a primitive creature."[11] Designed specifically for the primitive creature were four magazines. Two were *The Youth's Companion*, begun in 1827, and *Boy's Life*, aimed at Boy Scouts, begun in 1911. "*St. Nicholas* [begun 1900] and *American Boy* [1899–1929], in particular, waged extended campaigns in the advertising trade press to promote the virtues of child consumers.[12]

Boy's Life often featured ads that had products named after Ruth or showed him endorsing a product such as this one: "Designed by Babe Ruth, made by Reach. 'I sure am glad to have the Reach outfit put my personal signature on every glove in the Babe Ruth line. I'm mighty proud of these gloves, for the Reach people did a swell job of carrying out my ideas and I recommend every glove.'"[13]

An ad for Kodak was "courting middle-class white boys [was] ... especially important because advertisers assumed that such boys could sway the consumer loyalties not just of family members but of other children as well.... Kodak, for example, ran special advertising contests in Boys' Life ... on the grounds that Boy Scouts were 'the best and liveliest boys in town' and as such sure to set enviable examples for others."[14] In 1928, Ruth was given a medal by the Boy Scouts.

If girls are left out of all this appeal, there was a reason, as Lisa Jacobson explains. She says, "Advertisers also concentrated primarily on boys and boy culture because they

thought girls were far more flexible and boys far more rigid in their gender identification." As advertising authority Evalyn Grumbine observed, "Girls admire and enjoy boys' books and many boys' activities. Boys, however, do not reciprocate in their feelings about girls' activities."[15]

Babe Ruth and boys were a fine selling match. If Ruth "led a life he didn't and couldn't take time to understand," the intricacies of juvenile advertising would not be of importance to the ballplayer. Walsh did not need Ruth's okay. A check still arrived at Ruth's address, as did a check at Walsh's, a check to *Boy's Life*, sales for Reach, and sales for Kodak.

According to Fred Lieb, at least one writer confronted Ruth, saying "You're smart enough to know that your visits to sick and maimed kinds square you with the club and the public for some of the rotten things you've done." Lieb, as devoted of a Ruth fan as Grantland Rice, himself was willing to write, "I believe Ruth cared for the boys he visited."[16] What benefit to the children is indefinite, just as the depth of Ruth's interest is unknown. To ask of Ruth—surrounded by children, in a ward full of children—to have any but the briefest of contact and the briefest of effect on a child was probably asking the impossible.

Stories about Ruth and children almost completely disappeared after his marriage to Clare in 1929, and even more so once Ruth and Walsh retired. The visits, or at least the publicity of the visits, slowed to less than one a year. By then, presumably, he had children of his own and might be able to show how much he cared for them. After baseball, any contact he had with children came mostly through signing things that children might win as prizes from one of the companies he endorsed. He may have even actually signed some of them himself.

In a book years later, daughter Dorothy consistently portrays herself as being continually reminded that Julia was Claire's favorite and that Dorothy was not a real daughter of Claire's. Dorothy Pirone specifically points out instances where she was treated badly by Claire.

Ruth did not seem to get any pleasure from being a settled married man with two children after his playing days. Ms. Pirone's book, which blames wife Claire's harassment of her husband for Ruth's absences, mentions Christmas time, when Ruth would be "out visiting the sick in hospitals and not return until late at night exhausted."[17] She lists daily excursions for her father: "Every morning Babe left the apartment at 7:30 a.m." not to return for 12 hours. She names a female companion for Ruth named Loretta, a comrade for almost two decades, who even hunted with him. From about 1938 on, Ruth enjoyed traveling to the resort village of Greenwood Lake, New York, almost always by himself. Lake Oscawana was nearby, and Ruth had visited there many times, since Christy Walsh owned a cottage on the lake.

Ms. Pirone forgives Ruth while lamenting, "Babe was a good father, given the circumstances…. I know he loved me very much. He was just uncomfortable saying it." Later, with Dorothy's children, "Dad took great pride in his grandchildren, so it was a shame he was unable to spend more time with them."[18]

Opposite: **A 1928 ad with Ruth endorsing ice cream cones, touting their wholesomeness and "youth units."**

30

The $80,000 Year
(1930)

Though "his yearly income tax for the next two years will be $10,246, as the Associated Press figures it," his true "Final Determination of Tax Liability" amounted to $21,184.97 for 1929. Ruth's income for the year 1929, when the tax rate was at a maximum of 24 percent—and for the future—rose from many sources.[1] Once more, many advertisers remained eager to pay Walsh and Ruth for the rights to his image, words, and appearances. The best estimate for Ruth's income puts him in the top 8.67 percent of Americans.

The largest chunk of income for the year came from his salary of $80,000. Did Ruth take any pleasure from realizing that his salary now stood at $15,000 more than Commissioner Landis'? With some of that cash, Ruth continued to be required, like the other players, to put down a deposit of $104.46 for uniforms. Yankees General Manager Ed Barrow speculated, and probably hoped, that "No one in baseball will ever be paid more than Ruth." With a salary that high, was Ruth abusing the team, the corporation? "Ruppert privately told Grantland Rice he could pay Ruth two hundred thousand dollars a year without overpaying him."[2] Why was that so? The Ruppert Yankees took in $979,624.85 in 1929. Though the team's profits were down, they still stood at $229,919. Was he paid too much? For the decade, team profit equaled $3,202,678. The *Literary Digest* in 1930 added Ruth's total baseball salaries, which brought "the Babe's total to $739,397."

Was he paid too much? "With the Yankee Stadium and the Yankee team, including the great Babe Ruth, Col. Jacob Ruppert would not value his baseball holdings at anything less than $5,000,000, current coin of the realm," said the *Saturday Evening Post* that year.

It has often been repeated that when told he was being paid more than President Hoover, Ruth said, from the depths of his political wisdom, "I had a better year than he did." If he said this, it was a secret, since it was never "recorded"—not even printed—for almost two decades. In some books, it is Coolidge who was the President in question. The first mention in the *New York Times* of this statement appeared on December 16, 1947.

Even non-league games paid off for Ruth and the Yankees. "For the first time, a team financed its spring training from the tickets sold for exhibition games.... Before Ruth, there would have been a loss, on average, of roughly $20,000 per year. The 1929 exhibition games income added $17,535.50 to Ruppert.[3]"

Thrift and Ruth had become friends. As Will Wedge wrote in the *New York Sun*: "Ruth is believed secretly elated over his new salary.... But.... He has thrown no party for his mates.... Mrs. Ruth has said that their one extravagance will be her accompanying

AGREEMENT AS TO FINAL DETERMINATION OF TAX LIABILITY

This Agreement, made in duplicate under and in pursuance of Section 606 of the Revenue Act of 1928, by and between

George Herman Ruth

570 Seventh Avenue

New York, N.Y.

a taxpayer located at

RECEIVED

DEC 14 1929

INT. REV. AGT. IN CHARGE
NEW YORK

and the Commissioner of Internal Revenue;

WHEREAS, there has been a determination of the tax liability of said taxpayer in respect of

Income Tax
(Character of tax)

for the year 1927
(Period covered)

in the principal sum of **Twenty One Thousand One Hundred Eighty Four Dollars**

and Ninety Seven cents ($21,184.97), exclusive of any penalty or interest properly applicable thereto as provided by law;

Now, THIS AGREEMENT WITNESSETH, that said taxpayer and said Commissioner of Internal Revenue hereby mutually agree that the principal amount of such liability so determined shall be final and conclusive if this agreement is approved by the Secretary of the Treasury, or the Undersecretary, within six months from the date this agreement is signed by the taxpayer.

IN WITNESS WHEREOF, the above parties have subscribed their names to these presents in duplicate.

[If the taxpayer is
a corporation affix
its seal here.]

Signed this 13 day of December 1929

George Herman Ruth x
Taxpayer.

The above agreement has been approved by the Secretary of the Treasury, or the Undersecretary, in accordance with the provisions of Section 606 of the Revenue Act of 1928, the approval being specifically enumerated on—

By

Signed MAR 12 1930 , 192
(Date)

Wm H Lucas
Commissioner of Internal Revenue.

Schedule No. 1101

Dated MAR 12 1930

By

WAIVER OF RESTRICTIONS ON ASSESSMENT AND COLLECTION OF DEFICIENCY

Irrespective of the execution or approval of the foregoing instrument, the undersigned taxpayer hereby waives the restrictions provided in Section 274 (a) or 308 (a) of the Revenue Act of 1926 or Section 272 (a) of the Revenue Act of 1928 on the assessment and collection of any deficiency in tax included in the principal sum of the tax liability as set forth in the said instrument, together with any penalty or interest properly applicable thereto as provided by law.

[If the taxpayer is
a corporation affix
its seal here.]

George Herman Ruth x
Taxpayer.

By

(See Instructions on Reverse Side)   2—14698

Ruth's income tax bill, 1929.

the Babe on all trips this year." For the future, for his new dependents, Claire, Dorothy and Julia, Ruth was heard to have banked $120,000 in a trust fund that would yield $500 per month for life, an amount that would soon double.

And why wouldn't the money increase? One of Christy Walsh's ways to keep Ruth's name in front of the public, and at the same time to appoint Ruth the reigning expert for the game, was the creation of "Babe Ruth's The All-America Board of Baseball." (All Americans in football went back to 1889.) Ruth would claim that "The committee and members of the All-American Board of Baseball worked with me in the selection" of honorees, the best players at each position in both major leagues, and then presented awards to their winners. Each winner received a certificate signed by Ruth, who was called "Chairman" on the certificate. In place since the mid 1920s, this process would continue until 1938.

Walsh saw to it that for endorsing a brand of cigarettes, $5,000 was collected.[4] Walsh, notifying the *New York Times*, also knew how to create a media event by having Ruth himself show up. That summer, Walsh's client appeared at the opening of Babe Ruth's Shop for Men, a haberdashery at the corner of Broadway and 52nd Street, to which he'd lent his name for a fee. More than 600 persons cheered as Ruth alighted from his auto accompanied by Knute Rockne, Bob Shawkey, and Gehrig. Graham McNamee announced the event through a loudspeaker setup. It must be noted again that the celebrities showing up for Ruth were all members of Walsh's syndicate. The next year, Ruth's feelings about the store changed, a legal document claiming the store was so bad that it was in fact "designed to bring the name 'Babe Ruth' into disrepute."[5]

Walsh similarly created the Christy Walsh Syndicate Cosmopolitan Book Corporation and published the book *How to Play Baseball*, with the author's name listed as Babe Ruth. Woods in Nowlin claims, "With exhibition game receipts, movie shorts, personal appearances, and endorsements, Ruth probably earned close to $200,000 in 1930."[6] Ruth happened to be in the midst of the growing advertising industry and of radio's burgeoning influence. Radio commercials, for example, generated $60,000,000 in revenue, and Will Rogers was paid $72,000 for 14 radio talks of 20 minutes each.

Ruth understood very young that baseball was not simply a pastime.

> It isn't right to call me or any ballplayer an ingrate because we ask for more money. Sure, I want more, all I'm entitled to. The time of a ballplayer is short. He must get his money in a few years or lose out. Listen, a man who works for another man is not going to be paid any more than he's worth. You can bet on that. A man ought to get all he can earn. A man who knows he's making money for other people ought to get some of the profit he brings in. Don't make any difference if it's baseball or a bank or a vaudeville show. It's business, I tell you. There ain't no sentiment to it. Forget that stuff.[7]

This quote first appeared in the March 10, 1922, edition of the *Sandusky* (Ohio) *Register*, a copyrighted story by Douglass Hotchkiss, editor of the *Hot Springs Record*, and appeared with the story title, "Babe Ruth is a Business Man!" In the piece, Hotchkiss said: "Ruth was asked by the writer if he thought other ball players were worth salaries approximating his own." The 125-word answer remains the most complete statement of Ruth's ideas about money from his labor. Ruth had reached the age of 27 at the time. From this statement, particularly clear are Ruth's feelings about the subject early in his career.

There are factual statements built into the quote, such as this one from 1930: "An average player of today, lasting eight years in the majors, ought to earn around $65,000 and perhaps twelve to fifteen thousand more during his declining years in the minors.[8]"

Some of those average Yankees players left the team in 1930. Ruth's barnstorming partner, Bob Meusel, had his contract sold to the Reds. After a full season in Cincinnati, Meusel finished his pro baseball career with two years in the minor leagues. (Playing at AA level, he was paid about $300 a month. In 1928 with the Yankees, he earned about $2,400 per month.) Gone after 21 games with the team in 1930, infielder Mark Koenig was traded, playing seven of his 13 years with other major league clubs. Traded as well was pitcher Waite Hoyt, who went on to play eight more years after his Yankees time.

"The Babe ... in the closing years of his baseball activities trained as faithfully to fulfill what he considered his obligation to his public as it was humanly possible."[9] How can it be an "obligation"? What about all those biographies of Ruth claiming it all to be relentless fun?

In 1930, another championship year for the Athletics, he hit .359 with 49 home runs and 153 RBI, missing just nine games and piling up 518 at-bats. Others were catching on to the home run swing. Players seeing Ruth's salary began to move their hands down the barrel of the bat to increase the leverage of the swing. No more moving your hands up the bat for better control, as had been the practice for so many years in the past. Bunting frequency, for example, began its decline in 1924, and the number was halved by 1932. Hack Wilson of the Cubs learned and hit 56 home runs in the National League.

Though the Yankees added catcher Bill Dickey, 1930 marked their worst year ever for runs allowed. The Yankees dropped to third in the league but still led in attendance with 1,169,230 paid. It did the team no good that Gehrig broke his pinky finger in 1930 (he played three weeks of the season with a small cast) and still showed signs of the unrepaired bone chips in his elbow from 1928.

The year 1930, a decade marker, attracted some writers to look back at the Ruth money-making phenomenon. A biography of Ruth, *The Great Gate God*, by Dan Daniel, was serialized in 1930 in the *New York Telegram*. This is what the writer said of Ruth's contribution to the game: "What the New York club really thinks of Babe Ruth, in so far as his box-office value is concerned, is indicated by the fact that it has carried a life-insurance policy on him for $300,000 for nearly a decade.... In 1928, on September 9 ... 82,000 fans were jammed into the big arena in the Bronx. They paid close to $170,000."

Daniel realized that the Yankees' success—six pennants from 1921 to 1928—had to be called an organizational effort. "The Babe hasn't done it all alone. Colonel Ruppert's lavish policy has afforded the Babe a stellar supporting cast.... The Great God of the Gate certainly has done his share and then some."

Ruth had lined up three games to play with Gehrig that year, as in 1929, all of them close to New York City. Apparently, Gehrig's ailing elbow would still permit him to play briefly before he entered the hospital. The first baseman knew how much money Ruth's presence could generate in a post-season game.

Dexter Park on the Queens and Brooklyn border the day after Columbus Day, matched a team with Ruth and Gehrig against the semipro Bushwicks once more. Before a cold weather crowd of 6,000, or 12,000 depending on whom you believe, Ruth played first base and pitched, and Gehrig played left field and first base; it was probably the two men's old teammate, Joe Dugan, who was stationed in right field. Gehrig homered in the eighth inning and Ruth homered in the ninth, when he also pitched, helping the team to an 8–5 win over the Bushwicks. There were never any bending of the rules at Dexter Park when Ruth played there.

The next game, on the following Saturday, October 18, 1930, was played on a cold, windy day at the Meridale Baseball Park in Lindenhurst, Long Island. "Bundled up in blankets and overcoats, none of the 4,000 fans seemed to mind that the local team got beat by Ruth and his cohorts by a score of 10–4.[10] Ruth played first base, tripled and scored on a Gehrig single, and pitched two hitless innings against Addie Klein's Lindenhurst Nine, an amateur baseball club."[11]

Eight days later, another crowd-drawing day, a Sunday, the two men again played against the Bushwicks at Dexter Park, Ruth and Gehrig both on the Springfield squad, which won, 4–3. Ruth pitched the last three innings against former major leaguer Stanley Baumgartner.

Gehrig's elbow was operated on October 30 at St. Vincent's Hospital, and he recuperated there. During that hospitalization, Ruppert was working through the process of getting rid of manager Bob Shawkey and replacing him with another man who was not Babe Ruth. John McMurray's piece on Joe McCarthy said, "Whatever the heat or coolness of the relationship between Ruth and his new manager, money was not affected."[12]

McCarthy succeeded in managing Babe Ruth. According to his SABR biography, "No matter what his thoughts might have been, Joe ran the rest of his club and left Babe to his own devices. Ruth never bothered Joe much either. He did just about as he pleased, just showed up for the games and gave McCarthy four pretty good seasons. It was hard to tell what he thought of the manager."[13]

What Ruth thought of his own strong need to be a manager would be told repeatedly over the next decade.

31

Ruth's Confederates, the Sportswriters

A sportswriter is entombed in a prolonged boyhood.—Jimmy Cannon, sportswriter

The odd sportswriter (or World Series broadcaster) might say something unflattering about Babe Ruth. But it was one voice among the many. Paul Gallico, three years after Ruth retired, might refer to Ruth as less than a god, and Roger Kahn too would write unflatteringly about Ruth, but 30 years after Ruth's death.

For more than a decade during Ruth's era, in New York City's 15 newspapers, and their syndicated columns that appeared throughout the entire country, most of the writers understood that they were all working for Babe Ruth. By praising Ruth in the breathless hyperbole of Ruth's time—of the same breathless yet loud hyperbole of most people who cover sports now—the writers understood that they were one part of a process that delivered money into whosoever's hands took part in the process. (Should anyone think that the hyperbole has gone away, see the *New York Times,* five years ago, on its front page, to find baseball games described as "a spellbinding frenzy" and "simply riotous" and ones which "rip everything apart." Or count the superlatives like "great" and "tremendous" directed at a commonplace play in just one televised football game.)

The commercial enterprise called Babe Ruth, the commodity who hit home runs, became spread out among some areas in American society (though not really affecting either women or black people in any appreciable way). Those in the service of protecting and embellishing the narrative of Ruth—some choose to call it the myth—made Babe Ruth Incorporated a well-oiled cash machine. How broad was the effect of those in charge of the narrative?

It could be argued that the lumberjacks who felled the trees to make the newsprint might be the furthest from the ball field. Closer were the workers who supplied the materials to produce, for instance, Babe Ruth All America Athletic Underwear. Workers in the companies who made the underwear banked paychecks, as did everyone involved in creating the advertisements for the underwear in the newspapers and magazines. With Ruth endorsing automobiles, cigars and cola, the print media increased revenue by charging for the placement of the ads. The people who wrote the ads and their companies profited as well. Those employed in the printing and distribution of the media also benefited.

As for the readers of the sports pages, true then and truer now, "the people wanted heroes, and the average reader of sports pages was 'as sentimental as a seminary girl.'"[1] Raising Ruth to legend for the readers chiefly lay with the writers. It must be said that very few cash customers sitting in the stands saw Ruth perform in those moments for which he became known. It must be said that only the writers would see Ruth over a space of time. Other people may have gotten a wave or an autograph or been in a crowd surrounding Ruth. But it was the writers who manufactured the product, who sold the Ruth commodity. At the time, "newspapers all over the country carried a feature entitled 'What Babe Ruth Did Today,' and that did mean every single day, not just from February to October."[2] For years, the writer of those pieces was Marshall Hunt, who worked for the fledgling *Daily News* in New York City, just one of the newspapers which had many editions each day so that all day long, updated papers would appear on newsstands.

The sportswriters for these papers included those whose names later became familiar outside of the sports pages, writers such as Paul Gallico, Ring Lardner and Damon Runyan. There were many others less familiar now that many newspapers and Ruth are long gone. But while they lived, the chief example for Ruth was Ford C. Frick, who wrote for the *Evening Journal*. Susman says of Frick's contemporaries, "They invented along the way an often brilliantly different and always special kind of rhetoric and style. Their unique prose delighted readers, sold more copies, appealed to more advertising agencies with products to sell—which was done through buying space in publications or time on the radio."[3] Writers then and now seemed to believe in "the matchless magnetic power of the home run drive."[4] If reporters overdramatized a person or event, "no [one] … challenged their embellished stories."[5] It was patently true that "writers served as both reporters and publicists."[6] Mark Starr explains, "during the first half of the century, only a tiny percentage of the fans actually saw their heroes in action…. Accounts of their feats were left to sportswriters and … these guys were true mythmakers…. These were great athletes and, by extension, great men…. Baseball was … truly ruled by Babe Ruth … the first of many baseball heroes served by New York's newspaper wars."[7]

It should not be forgotten that, "During this time, sportswriters had developed close relationships with baseball owners and players. This was due to the fact that such relationships were mutually advantageous because it created a profitable partnership."[8] The working friendships with players came about during all those times off the field, at meals, on long train trips to the west and back, in card games and even at other sporting events like boxing matches. The working relationships with team owners showed the tightness of all of those involved in enhancing the reputation of the baseball entertainment industry, whose chief exponent and most visible representative was Ruth.

There are many roads to cashing in on newspaper writing, and especially in writing about sports. There are facts to be stated, such as the score; there are colorful versions of the facts, by the use of comparisons such as the one from 1919 describing a Ruth home run: "like a shell fired from a field piece"; well beyond exaggeration, writing so often repeated, so often slanted, in favor of someone like Ruth, that any truth disappears or is transmuted into legend. Thus a writer in 1921 can call Ruth a "colossus of wonderment and veneration."

Likewise, the baseball businessmen worked at making certain that the sport was properly viewed and people were willing to pay for it. The publishing family of *The Sporting News,* the "Spinks, were getting a subsidy from major league baseball."[9] For the sportswriters, some cash came directly from the owners. "Initially the clubs paid all their expenses, and as late as the 1940s some newspapers still had not assumed all their reporters' travel costs."[10] Sportswriters of the period have written of the pleasures of their work: "I had the dream assignment, traveling the country for five decades with both Chicago's big league clubs. We had the best seat in the house, stayed at the finest hotels, all expenses paid."[11] But it cannot be ignored that when teams paid travel expenses for their baseball writers, the payments caused the writers to be "somewhat beholden to them."[12] Some of the writers rationalized that they saved money for their newspaper and were beneficial to the team, keeping it in the news.

Clearly the newspaper benefited by avoiding all the travel, meal, and lodging costs they did not have to pay, but the writer became very much like an employee of the team. The writer understood, as all journalists must understand, that if you want access to a source, a player or manager, the team owner can deny you that access, or the player can avoid you, if he is displeased with you.

One reason why sportswriters wrote reams about Ruth as hero, as the orphan who rose to wealth, as the healer of children, may be because they chose not to write about his vulgarity, his excesses, and his dangerous carelessness. "Hell, I could have written a story every day on the Babe," Richards Vidmer said in Montville's book. Montville himself acknowledges that, "An unwritten, sometimes-spoken code existed not only with him but with virtually everybody in public life."[13]

Ruth welcomed access—"he was a wild and extravagant figure who never failed to give sports writers and gossip columnists material and lively quotes."[14] As far as one writer, Dan Daniel, was concerned, "Without the Babe there wasn't an awful lot to write about."[15] Because he was such good copy, making their jobs easier, writers helped him out.

The writers helped Ruth, Ruth helped the writers, and the team owners helped the writers. The owners helped the sporting paper, and the paper supported the owners. The help for the writers, in another form of extra money, came from being hired to work as publicists for a team. Clearly this was commerce at its most efficient. Certainly these business secrets, these clandestine arrangements, did not make it into public knowledge.

The writers were helped by another source too. This was the commercial enterprise of Christy Walsh. If pleased with their treatment of his clients, Walsh, through his syndicate, would hire the sportswriters to produce pieces for him. Soon, more than 30 writers were employed for year-round ghostwriting work, and in 1924 Walsh could brag that his syndicate produced "one million words in eight days." Walsh went on to provide copy for many athletes and coaches, such as Ty Cobb and Knute Rockne, and even for another writer, historian Hendrik Willem van Loon.

The writer Westbrook "Pegler still delivered him to various private functions in need of a celebrity and then pocketed most of the fee. Many sportswriters arranged appearances for him."[16] No wonder Ruth spent so much energy on, and time with, writers. They made him sound important, they made him look almost saintly, they even granted him the power to heal. They made him money. There was no radio, no television, not even long lenses for their cameras. There were only the writers.

An affiliation with Ruth could be beneficial in large ways as well. Ford Frick, a New York City sportswriter at age 28, moved on to radio, broadcasting from the New York City station WOR. When the National League asked him to, Frick took on the job of head of publicity by being named the first director of the league's Service Bureau, a position that led to his employment as the chief of all publicity for Major League Baseball. From there, he moved on to President of the National League, and finally became

Commissioner of baseball. In that last job, he saw to it to question the record 61 home runs of Roger Maris, trying unsuccessfully to keep his old friend Ruth as the top home run hitter.

For a clear-eyed look at sportswriters from one of its own, Paul Gallico, when he left sports in the late 1930s, wrote,

> The sportswriter has few if any heroes. We create many because it is our business to do so, but we do not believe in them. We know them too well. We are concerned as often, sometimes, with keeping them and their weaknesses and peccadilloes out of the paper as we are with putting them in.... We sing of their muscles, their courage, their gameness and skill because it seems to amuse readers and sells papers, but we rarely consider them as people and strictly speaking, leave their characters alone because that is dangerous ground.[17]

32

The Last Tour
(1931)

In the year 1930, it became very clear how much the leagues of professional North American baseball presented a different sort of game from a decade before. The strategy of power, of the big inning, won games, and not the tactic of moving runners up a base at a time with bunts and steals. Babe Ruth, not Ty Cobb, won games. To give a sense of how the game had changed—to a great extent because of Ruth, in the 1911–1919 period—Cobb's time—there were 3,613 home runs tallied; from 1920 to 1930—Ruth's time—the home runs now totaled 11,459 an increase of 310 percent over the 1911–1919 total.

And the year just passed, 1930, really showed it. The entire National League batted over .300, while setting a record for home runs with 892. In contrast, the National League of 1920 had hit 261. The increase in production in the National League was influenced by the production of American League power hitters such as Gehrig, Ruth, Foxx and Simmons. Some said the ball was different—higher quality yarn was wound around the ball. Some say that the National League ordered up baseballs for 1930 with lower stitching, making it harder for their pitchers to throw sharp-breaking curves. (The ball ordered for 1931 in the National League went back to the older design for stitching, and the numbers showed a sharp decrease.)

But 1930 made a deep impression on some baseball observers, the most striking of which appeared in the *New Yorker* with the title "Sport and The Showoff." Perhaps as a reaction to the 1930 season, Morris Markey wrote that "Babe Ruth has made it as a circus performer.... During the last decade or two" baseball had seen "such enormous gates it became necessary to produce a pageant that the most dumb witted could understand ... rules were passed forbidding pitchers to be too good.... Obviously it is a poorer game, but equally obvious it is a better show for the great crowds ... the transformation from a good game to a good show for the boobs."[1]

The arguments about the superiority of the one-run-at-a-time game versus the power game continue to this day, expressed then as Ruth versus Cobb. After all, Ty Cobb in 24 years was credited with 117 home runs, a total Ruth reached after three years of full-time play. Clearly, the era of the modest seemed to have died with Lindbergh's flight, but contempt for the power game had not.

Cobb was paid $80,000 for the 1927 season, playing for the Philadelphia Athletics. In the *Literary Digest*, Ruth bragged, "If I don't save over $100,000 out of the $160,000 that I will earn the next two years [1930 and 1931], I want someone to shove me into Tampa Bay." Ruth would pay $10,512 in income taxes in 1931, while Chick Hafey of the

Cardinals would agree to a salary of $10,400 for the year, $112 less than Ruth surrendered to the IRS. Another way to see Ruth's pay is to view it from an average salary for the year. Some list the average as about $1,800, while a poverty level, at least in Colorado, for a family of four equaled $1,767.[2]

It is true that the multiplier to be applied for money in all of Ruth's baseball years remains the Consumer Price Index, or CPI. Since in 2018, the CPI stands at 14 times larger than it was in 1931, Ruth's 1931 salary is equivalent to a salary today of over one million dollars. (However that amount lies some 3.5 million dollars below the current average major league average salary.)

Ruth signed a movie contract with Universal Studios on February 11, 1931, which stipulated he would do promotional advertisements for the studio, as well as make some short movies for them. He also wrangled a deal with Ruppert that for each Yankees exhibition, he would be paid $2,500 plus 15 percent of the gate. It is hard to know if the payments were for pre-season and/or in-season exhibitions. The pay here reflected once more the true worth of Ruth to the club. "No one has ever compared with Ruth as a box-office attraction. He is one of the things to be seen in New York, like the Woolworth Building and the Aquarium."[3]

In 1931 the team scheduled six in-season exhibitions, with one game each in April and July and two each in August and September. Over the years, sportswriters often paid tribute to Ruth's devotion to his fans when he ignored illness and injury to play in exhibitions; they seldom mentioned the fact that he might have other motives as well."[4] Yankees ledgers for the year show that the team took in more than $12,000 in 1930 for exhibition games, but they also reveal one of the lowest amounts in years. Even so, before Ruth's first year with the team, a typical amount generated by exhibitions equaled $2,000 to $3,000. In Ruth's first years with the team, Colonel Ruppert saw that amount jump to $21,972.77 and then to $35,259.18.[5]

More books with Ruth's byline kept appearing throughout the 1930s some published by Christy Walsh's Cosmopolitan Book Corporation and some tied to the Quaker Oats Company, perhaps as giveaways. Titles included pamphlet-sized publications such as "How to Play Baseball."

Ruth reached another personal milestone on August 21, 1931, when he hit his 600th career home run. No Major Leaguer was close to that number. (For some perspective, 38 years would pass before Willie Mays hit his 600th, and fewer than two years later Henry Aaron would hit his number 600. Beginning in 2002, in a nine-year span, four more players would reach 600.)

By season's end, the impact of the Great Depression was felt almost everywhere. Colonel Ruppert did not feel it, however. Unemployment in the United States reached 24.1 percent. According to baseballlibrary.com, late in September the three New York teams, including Ruth, agreed to a round-robin playoff, which added $48,000 to a fund for the unemployed. The year before, Will Wedge in the *New York Sun* wrote, "But he will not donate any of his salary raise to the battle funds of the unemployed." He was a self-made man, after all.

As for Ruth, at age 36, in 1931 he tied with Gehrig for the league lead in home runs with 46 while hitting .373—second in that category, as he was in runs batted in and runs scored. Again, for the third straight year, there was no World Series play, or share, as the season ended for the Yankees on September 27, 1931, 13½ games back of the Athletics, even though the team set a Major League record for runs scored in a season with 1,067.[6]

No matter how much sports hyperbole made it into the media about Ruth, after 12 seasons with the New York team, they had won three World Series. But the gap between teams in runs scored and runs allowed was not that great. Finishing second added up to little difference in the money brought in for Ruppert. With Yankees attendance at 912,437, first in the league, the team that finished first, Mack's Philadelphia Athletics, came in second in seats sold at 627,464, almost a third less than the New York team.

At World Series time, Babe Ruth sat in the working press section, most likely for a minimum of $5,000, to demonstrate that he actually was at the games, since the column with his byline appeared for syndication after each game. For a while, Ruth's record batting average of .625 for a World Series seemed likely to be broken as Pepper Martin's average jumped to .667. (It ended at .500. Ruth's record Series batting average lasted until 1990.)

Ruth would return to California in 1931—he hadn't played there since the wearisome 1927 series of games—but this time he would appear there after just a few games east of the state. Thirty-six years old now, he would take nine days off between the first and second games and five days off between a Denver stop and California. Once in the state, between October 18 and 31, little more than 500 miles would be traveled during those nine California games, allowing him more time to rest, with a total of 4,200 miles planned.

Ruth and Gehrig played on rival teams in West New York, NJ, again as in 1929 at West New York Stadium. For this first game on October 4, Gehrig wore a New York Yankees road uniform, while Ruth was fitted out with new apparel from a movie studio, a "Babe Ruth's Universal Stars" uniform. The movie uniform was decorated in maroon and white, with an "S." Across the chest appeared the words "Babe Ruth's Universal Stars." The right sleeve said "Universal Pictures"—more part of his deal to advertise the studio—and on the left a patch in the shape of a baseball that said "Spalding." He was a walking advertisement for the studio, for the Spalding sporting goods corporation, and for himself as a brand.

The director of parks and playgrounds for West New York arranged for "Ruth to toss autographed baseballs to the youngsters and to mingle with them which the big-hearted Babe did." Three thousand kids with more than 5,000 paying adults watched as Gehrig and Ruth took turns playing first base. The *New York Times* described the game in fewer than 100 words, simply listing the inning-by-inning score, a 7–4 West New York win. From the 5,200 paid admissions, receipts totaled $4,345, an average of 83 cents per seat. Of that, Ruth got $1,500 (34.5 percent) Gehrig $500 (11.5 percent) and Walsh $177.50 (4 percent), leaving $2,167.50, half of the gate, for expenses and profits. Ruth watched the remainder of the World Series that year until he was ready to depart for his first date in the West, Gehrig going his own way.

The long train ride with Walsh over, the October 14 Colorado game, number two, matched Goalstone Brothers Jewelers (dressed in Ruth's Universal uniforms) and McVittie's Restaurant. For Ruth's fourth visit to the city, admission was set at 75¢, with another 25¢ for a box seat; children 50¢. Arriving that afternoon at one o'clock, Ruth played first base for the first four innings and pitched the last five. When he made his only hit in the ninth inning, it drove in the game-winning run, making him the winning pitcher.

Charles Parsons of the *Denver Post* remarked of Ruth, "he still autographs baseballs as graciously as ever" and recorded that "after the contest ... Babe still had time for a call at the hospital. Joe Cahill, Jr. ... has been ill at St. Luke's and the lad nearly jumped out of the bed when Ruth came into the room. Ruth's visit, no doubt, will act as a tonic to the boy."

Babe Ruth's Universal Stars, West New York, New Jersey, 1931. Center back row: Ruth, Walsh and Gehrig.

How long lasting or how potent a "tonic" was not bothered with. It is impossible to know if the sportswriter truly believed such things.

That stop being completed, Ruth left on the 6 p.m. train. He had spent five hours in Denver. Between the West New York game and the upcoming game in Los Angeles, 13 days would pass. They were putting miles behind them, but the plans were to jump to Los Angeles, where two weeks of games had been set up. Or, perhaps, the games were a way to have his travel paid for a while on his way to make even more money for a series of short films produced by Christy Walsh. The games seemed to serve as a way to make some money on the way to make even more money. It is likely that the death of Knute Rockne, another in the newspaper syndicate, earlier in 1931, had a marked effect on Walsh's income.

Meanwhile, Lou Gehrig had his own all-star barnstorming squad in California, including Al Simmons, Mickey Cochrane, and Frankie Frisch, in preparation for games in Hawaii and Japan. And Claire Ruth left New York to meet her husband in California.

At about the same time her husband and Christy Walsh arrived in Los Angeles, so did Mrs. Ruth. The city's leading newspaper declared, "Babe Ruth, baseball's one and only Bambino, swipes the spotlight from football in Los Angeles," at a time when the University of Southern California's team was rated a powerhouse in national rankings.[7]

Moving 125 miles to San Diego for game four, a novel night game, Ted Steinman of the local newspaper quoted Ruth saying, "'I don't know how this night stuff is going to affect me…. I haven't even seen a night game, let alone played in one.'" With a crowd of 3,300 paid, "Last night at Navy Field, the home run king of baseball led his Babe Ruth All-Stars to a 4 to 1 victory over the White Kings Soaps of Los Angeles."

Ruth and Gehrig with a young fan, West New York, New Jersey, 1931.

Since cash could be paid to Ruth in many odd places, money more easily garnered by the presence of Walsh, Ruth delivered a short talk to the California Hotel Greeter's Association convention, a talk followed by another night game. With Ruth back in Los Angeles for that October 20 game and the net profits going to the Marion Davies Clinic, the *Evening Herald* reported that the star "was to pay a visit to the Marion Davies Clinic for the children of World War veterans." Billed as a game between the Babe Ruth Universal Stars and the Major-Coast League Stars, led by ex-major league first baseman George Burns, 4,000 fans showed up. Playing first base, Ruth had a homer and two doubles in the 5–4 loss played in 110 minutes. He was credited with being paid $10,500 for the game by Sobol[8] and $10,000 by Wagenheim.[9] (Both books appeared in 1974.) Currently, difficulty exists in finding the source for this amount. If 4,000 attended and if the Clinic were to get their piece of the admissions, and if so far the admission to Ruth's games had only reached 75 cents, this stated amount seems very unlikely.

The remaining games, except for one, had been slotted for either San Francisco or Oakland, so Ruth headquartered at the Whitcomb Hotel at 1231 Market Street in San Francisco. By now, Ruth had tired of the barnstorming grind. "'I'll certainly be glad when this barnstorming tour is over,'" Ruth told the *Sacramento Bee.*

Thursday night, October 22, at Seals Stadium, Ruth's team was constituted as usual of former and future major leaguers. For these games, the lineups included Frankie Crosetti, Babe Pinelli, Frenchy Uhalt, Augie Galan, and Art Garibaldi. Ruth's team took the 8–4 win in a game that only took 75 minutes to complete.

At 2:45 the next afternoon in the same park, Ruth hit seven homers and another against the center field fence (400 feet) in batting practice, but went hitless against the Coast All-Stars in a 10–6 loss before a small crowd in a 22,900-seat park. The game ended after 82 minutes, but "the crowd called for more. Ruth obliged by stepping to the plate and rapping one of the Wee Willie Ludolph's offerings over the right field fence and then another to right center." Completing his third game in 24 hours, this contest in the Oakland ball park across the bay, as he had in 1927, Ruth homered in the bottom of the ninth to win, 8–4, over Pinelli's team.

The next game required a journey of 90 miles to Sacramento for an afternoon game with ticket sales very low, perhaps due to the date also being a football Saturday, so a decision was made to change the game to 8 p.m. (Maybe, too, the low sales were because this was Ruth's third visit to Sacramento.) The delay made no difference in sales. At the 10,000-seat field, only 500 seats were filled. Even the reporting on the game was small, and since there was no Sunday paper, the Monday edition read, "Babe Ruth hit a home run, single and fly out in three times at the bat in a game here at Moreing Field. Ruth played in a game in which the sides were made up of mostly semipro players who showed a lack of practice under the lights."

The reporting by the *San Francisco Chronicle* of October 28, 1931, showed a more realistic picture of both the strain of barnstorming and the effect of Ruth's age. Ruth's continuing opposition, Babe Pinelli's team, won, 8–7. "With Christy Walsh riding hard on him, the Babe is straining a hamstring to hit balls over the fences … but even Babe, the greatest showman since Barnum, can't hit home runs to order." Jimmy Zinn walked a man on purpose just to bring up Ruth with the bases loaded. Ruth singled instead, in another game that clocked in under 90 minutes.

Newspaper coverage, like Ruth, began to show a weariness for these games. The accounts became more terse and spent more time pointing out Ruth's struggle to be productive. How many games had he already played that year? The number was approaching 190. Ruth was 36.

For the 12th game on the tour, played on October 27, 1931, at Oakland, the game's account read, "Babe Ruth's all-stars took a 7 to 0 victory from the all-stars…. Bambino walloped out one home run and two singles in 5 trips." In game 13, on Wednesday night,

Babe Ruth's Baseball Book, 1932.

October 28, 1931, at Seals' Stadium, Ruth made four hits and scored two runs in an 11–6 win over Pinelli's team. "In the ninth inning Ruth was thrown out, short to second, to end the game, but Babe was given half a dozen more chances to get that homer … [and] when Babe finally called it quits he was tired out from gripping the bat."

The October 29 game and the tour ended with an epitaph written by Homer Johnson of the *Long Beach Press-Telegram* that Ruth and Walsh would have approved: "The faithful came away with hearts aglow and the skeptical departed believing."

The barnstorming tour over, the pocketed receipts added to more money from the "Universal–Christy Walsh All America Sports Series," five baseball comedy shorts for Universal Pictures, which Walsh co-produced."[10] The movie poster read, "Christy Walsh All America Sports Reels, the only baseball reels officially sanctioned by the All American Board Of Baseball," a board invented by Walsh. According to Smelser, Walsh also manufactured a book of stills from these nine to ten-minute shorts, perhaps the 32-page publication, *Babe Ruth's Baseball Book.*[11]

Ruth had chosen not to go to Japan with, among others, Gehrig, Lefty Grove, and Lefty O'Doul. Money there would have to be divided among lots of players, coaches and executives.

"The home run king, is believing he is paying a heavy price for glory" said the *Hartford Courant.* The *Lewiston Daily Sun* read far wittier: "According to Babe Ruth the paths of glory lead strictly into the myths of virtue." There appeared then a series of laments of the 36-year-old for the things he couldn't do, but would like to: swim, gamble, fly on an airplane, read a book on a train. "I can't enjoy a round of golf because I'm followed from tee to tee by persons seeking my autograph. Hang it all, I can't do anything. Not just yet."

Not right away, but "Babe Ruth Wants To Be Manager In Two Years" said the *Norwalk Hour* of October 14, 1931. Well, really longer. Two days earlier, the *Ottawa Citizen* had reported "Ruppert Rewards Joe McCarthy With New Three-year Contract."

Ruth had reached an age where being both player and manager was unlikely. He also announced that this 1931 trip would be his last barnstorming trip. He came in fifth in MVP voting in 1931.

33

Last Times
(1932–1935)

1932

On December 10, 1931, the major leagues announced adjustments that would have to be made in recognition of the serious economic realities of the time. Baseball attendance dropped 1.4 million from 1930 to 1931, a figure averaging close to 88,000 paid per team. Owners foresaw that they needed to plan for yet another year with a drop in revenue. They were right. Attendance numbers—the principal and virtually sole source of income—would drop again in 1932 almost as much as they had dropped in 1931, making the decrease from 1930 through 1932 to be almost a third. The St. Louis Browns would fill about 1,500 seats per game on average in 1932, leaving 32,500 seats empty. The magnates reduced major league rosters by two players and called for a ten percent payroll cut. According to a story titled "What the Leagues Did" in December 1931, a measure passed that said the leagues would contribute $7,500 to needy baseball veterans. There is no way to know from this story if this meant that each of the 16 teams was asked for $468.75, but that is the way it seems. Even for the bankrupt Browns, that amount would total about one-third of attendance money for one game.

Ruth's contract for 1932 shows a $5,000 pay cut, and Gehrig's salary dropped from $25,000 to $23,000. No matter what their production had been in 1931, the Depression was stronger. But with Yankees attendance at 912,437, first in the league, Ruth was supposed to have said, "I don't see much of a depression with the Yankees."[1] This sentence does match Ruth's continual insistence on being paid what he was worth, and it does match his cynicism about the way owners treated employees.

Ruppert was able to offer Ruth a deal the player had seen before—25 percent of exhibition profits. Professor Michael Haupert notes that Ruth's exhibition bonus payments for 1932 were $2,969.82.[2] One of those games was played on June 5 against the Grand Rapids Ramonas.

One commentator calculated that Ruth was worth an additional $280,000 per season to the Yankees. A contemporary writer took out his abacus and stated, "Ruth [has] earned $3,500,000 for Colonel Ruppert in the last twelve years … over and above what the club would have taken in without him…. Another averred that the money Ruth brought in from exhibition games (regular and preseason) alone had been enough to pay his salary every year since 1927."[3]

The two writers above, Paul Adomites and Saul Wisnia, write about money but, like so many others, fail to cite neither the "commentator" nor "writer" nor "another." Many writers had to guess at money for a number of reasons. First, the club's ledgers were closed books. The money from barnstorming was only mentioned occasionally in local papers, but no pattern stands out. Public information about salaries appeared widely for a brief time in *Baseball Magazine* in 1918 and then in limited fashion from Congressional hearings in 1951.

The Ruth and Walsh movie shorts from Universal came out early in 1932. They ran from eight to ten minutes each. Ruth had already deposited the check for this work.

Now 37, Ruth left some games early and took sick for part of September. Still, he had 457 at-bats in 133 games. Pitchers still did their best to avoid him, as he led the league yet again in walks and finished among the top ten in most offensive categories. But his 41 home runs fell 17 below the league leader, Jimmie Foxx, who hit 58. Hitters were learning the kind of uppercut swing needed for home runs.

Foxx's team, the defending champions Athletics, scored plenty of runs that year, but it was their second-line pitching that failed. Grove won 25 games, but George Earnshaw and Rube Walberg (Connie Mack's only two other reliable starters) slipped to ERAs approaching five. The Yankees won 107 games and took home the pennant by 13 games.

In the World Series against the Chicago Cubs, the Yankees outscored their opponents, 37–19, in a four-game sweep. Ruth homered twice, Gehrig three times. This was the Series in which Ruth was given credit by many for "calling his shot" in the third game. Bill Jenkinson's research on the topic lists various primary sources, some who agreed that he pointed, some who did not even mention the pointing. The pitcher said that if Ruth had pointed, he would have been thrown at.

As time passed, sportswriters have made much of this "called shot," but after all these years there does not seem to be agreement about Ruth's gesture, or lack of it, in Game Three of the 1932 series. Where there exists no agreement, there is no certainty. None, unless we take Ruth at his word.

> Aw, everybody knows that game, the day I hit the homer off ole Charlie Root there in Wrigley Field, the day October first, the third game of that thirty-two World Series. But right now I want to settle all arguments. I didn't exactly point to any spot, like the flagpole. Anyway, I didn't mean to, I just sorta waved at the whole fence, but that was foolish enough. All I wanted to do was give that thing a ride … outta the park … anywhere.[4]

If Ruth himself refused to take credit, why should anyone else give him that? And yet they do. It was a better story for the writers if he did. It still is.

Ruth, with his teammates, received a check for $5,231.77 from his share of the $717,000 the Series took in at the box office. By now, Ruth was drifting toward the end of his active days in his profession. Soon estranged from Lou Gehrig, his other two teammates of some length were the quiet Tony Lazzeri, eight years his junior, and Herb Pennock, one year his senior at age 38. Consciously or not, he was choosing his after-baseball circle, and as Sobol writes, "Babe and Claire's close friends were all from outside baseball.… Perhaps coincidentally, they were all men who solicitously fronted for Babe in one way or another—as financial or legal advisors, ghostwriters, social guides, and general image protectors. Babe felt comfortable with them."[5]

1933

Per capita income in the United States in 1933 had dropped by 28 percent from 1929 levels, the highest decrease during the era. As many as 4,000 banks closed. Using his powers as president, Franklin Roosevelt thought the country's economic situation daunting enough to push through the National Recovery Act, urging employers to sign more than 2.3 million agreements, covering work week length and minimum salaries for 16.3 million employees. In baseball, by 1933 the major leagues were filling 40 to 45 percent fewer seats than in 1930. Team owners suffered a collective loss margin of 23.9 percent.[6]

Ruth's salary of $52,000 kept him as the highest paid player in baseball. His exhibition bonus payments for 1933, a deal not publicized, were $2,681.37; with Ruppert taking in 75 percent from exhibitions, that means the owner had collected $10,725.48 just for in-season games. This money arrived via eight games, including one contest against the Wheeling Stogies. That year, Will Rogers was signed by Gulf Oil to star for seven-weeks in a half-hour radio show for $50,000. Four years into the Depression, some workers had not yet felt its force. Greta Garbo, according to *Movie Mirror*, drew a weekly salary of $7,500 from MGM. Kay Francis earned $4,000 each week of work.

Ruth began a quarrel with Lou Gehrig over a relatively petty matter—the wrong words said at the wrong time, resulting in a coolness between the two. This separation from Gehrig became but one more sign of Ruth's slowly dissolving relationship with the Yankees. He and manager McCarthy had never gotten along, a coolness there as well.

Though he was not named to the all-star team published in *The Sporting News* that year, Ruth was picked as a starter in the first baseball All-Star Game, played in 1933 in Chicago. Five of his teammates accompanied him on that roster, but it was Ruth who hit the first All-Star Game home run.

On August 17, 1933, Lou Gehrig set a record for consecutive games played with 1,308, breaking former Yankee Everett Scott's record. Gehrig clearly had become the star of the team now, and at season's end the first baseman finished third in the American League hitting at .334 and in homers with 32. He also ended second in RBI with 140, and first in runs with 138.

But it was not Yankees hitting that prevailed that year in the pennant race. Washington's pitching, mainly General Crowder with 24 wins and Earl Whitehill with 22 wins, led the Senators of Joe Cronin, with his three future Hall of Fame teammates: Heinie Manush, Sam Rice, and Goose Goslin. At season's end, they topped the Yankees by seven games.

Ruth clearly struggled to reach the benchmarks for excellence in hitting with an average of .301 and RBIs adding up to 103. His 34 home runs put him second behind the league MVP, Jimmie Foxx. His writers still liked him. "As the end approached there was a considerable amount of myth-enhancing and image polishing by the sportswriters as they prepared for the inevitable canonization of this man."[7]

For some time, Ruth intended to keep his promise made at the end of 1931 not to barnstorm any more. But Christy Walsh had heard from Herb Hunter, who became "a baseball tour impresario of sorts, leading a group of major leaguers to play baseball in Japan, eventually becoming known as Baseball's Ambassador to the Orient and leading numerous tours to the Land of the Rising Sun."[8] Gehrig had agreed to one of Hunter's tours in 1931. The organizer told Walsh that Ruth could travel to Hawaii, play two or three games, and pick up five figures. Ruth, seeing how this offer might combine three of his favorite things—sightseeing, baseball, and money—agreed to go.

But as Ruth prepared to take the trip, he was contacted by Frank Navin, the owner of the Tigers, who was thinking of hiring Ruth as his manager and "wanted the Bambino to come to Detroit to talk terms."[9] Navin could read his own ledgers and saw that his team's attendance had sunk for the fourth straight year, partly because of the team's second division finishes. The team had not won a pennant since 1909, and had never won a World Series. Navin needed to revitalize the team, and Ruth always was able to fill seats. In 1933 the Tigers drew 320,972, averaging just over 4,100 paid for the home games in a park named for Navin that seated 30,000.

Ruth said he'd like to come to Detroit, "but he had a commitment in Hawaii that would take a couple of weeks. The Babe said he would call Navin when he got back" (Montville, 323). When Ruth reached San Francisco, where he would board ship, Navin again called. Ruth again said he must honor his commitment to Hunter and Walsh. Some might think that Ruth would be respected for honoring his obligations. It's what a good businessman would do. Navin seemed to be put off by Ruth not rushing to see him. (Navin hired Mickey Cochrane on December 12, 1933.)

Ruth, Yankees uniform in his trunk, boarded the Matson liner *Lurline*, and as it approached the islands, John Snell, in the *Honolulu Advertiser* of October 16, 1933, insisted that Ruth would never be anything but an overgrown kid: "a genial giant in stature, but as tender and considerate as a woman with the fun-loving good-natured mind of an unspoiled child.... Idol of the nation, equal only, perhaps in its great affection for Colonel Lindbergh." Ruth was 38 years old, but the idea that all athletes are really children remains a popular idea.

As fully delineated in *The National Pastime* article by Frank Ardolino called "Babe's Banyan Tree Grows in Hawaii," Ruth, Claire and a daughter arrived in Honolulu on October 19.

He played with an all-star team from the Hawaii Baseball League, who played against the league champion Wanderers. Before the game, "female admirers filled his neck with ilima and ginger leis, which he wore through most of the game. Ruth's team won the game, 5–2, in part because of a Ruthian homer over the right field fence."[10]

On October 23, another game was played just for the 3,000 children who paid 25 cents admission and the 1,000 who were allowed in free. Ruth felt "dead on his feet from a long trip to the Boys' Industrial School at Waialee" 40 miles north of the big island. The game took 1:25 for a seven-inning game, all Ruth could tolerate. When Herb Hunter counted up his receipts, he found himself in the red and talked Ruth into one more game, this one in Hilo where, on the 29th, "he again played for the local all-stars, pitted against the Ka'u League champions. He went 3 for 5 with two long home runs, in an exciting 7–6 game, which his team lost."[11]

In addition, Ruth played many rounds of golf, visited an orphanage and an industrial school, and was asked to plant a banyan tree, something that other visiting celebrities like Cecil B. DeMille had also agreed to.

Is there yet more money to be made from—not by—Babe Ruth? If you now visit the website of etsy.com, you will have the chance to buy both a "Quality and unique wood pen made from the trimmings of the Banyan tree Babe Ruth personally planted in Hilo, Hawaii" and "two wooden jumbo hairsticks in Banyan Wood ... that comes from the trimmings of the Banyan Tree planted by Babe Ruth on Banyan Drive in Hawaii."

With the offer from Navin now off the table, Ruth's return to the mainland may have been filled with more thoughts of a manager's job in the big leagues. At work here is the past practice of big league stars who were appointed as major league managers without having minor league experience. Those men included Max Carey, Rogers Hornsby, George Sisler, George Burns, and Frankie Frisch. Ruth himself pointed out that

Ty Cobb and Tris Speaker spent no time in the minors, and Joe Cronin in Washington was hired at age 26.

Though Ruth chose not to, others *had* taken minor league jobs. Players as well known as Tris Speaker and Walter Johnson were willing to at least start in the minors. But when, on November 23, 1933, Ruth was offered the job as manager of Newark of the International League, "Ruth's wife and business manager both advised against going to the minor leagues, and he told the writers that going to Newark would be the same 'as to ask Colonel Ruppert, one of the foremost brewers in the country, to run a soda fountain.'"[12]

Is it possible that Ruth had dreams of being paid an even higher salary as manager than as a player? One writer took up Ruth's cause, at least he looked carefully at the possibility in his October 22, 1933, *New York Times*, column titled "Mr. Ruth, the Manager." At one point, phrasing the question rhetorically, knowing that some critics of Ruth would think this, John Kieran wrote, "If he didn't know how to take care of himself, how could he take care of a ball club?" (This was to become the well-known "If you can't manage yourself, how can you manage others.") But as part of a longer column, Kieran was seriously listing both Ruth's flaws as a managerial candidate and his strengths. Arguing first that Ruth has become "a different chap from the careless, boisterous, swaggering and unruly Playboy of the Western World of ten years ago," Kieran cited Ruth's experience in the American League, that he could "call off the batting preferences of any of the good hitters" and "can tell any bystander what the regular pitchers on other clubs throw and when they throw it." Of the players he might be placed in charge of, Kieran's opinion was that "they have always looked up to him as the grand master of their own trade." Kieran concluded his argument by calling Ruth "a worthy candidate" for a managerial position. "On the evidence that is known and the record as submitted, he might make a good manager."

Kieran looked at the situation with as reasonable an eye as he could. But it seems likely that a wealthy man like Ruppert, a man accustomed to being in charge, to not having his decisions questioned, would grow to see Ruth as an antagonist. Certainly, Ruppert would be angered by Ruth's threats over the years to quit the team. Is it possible that Ruppert told other team owners about Ruth's threats? These magnates, as we know, ruled their fiefdoms with virtually no interference. Why should anyone be an exception to their power? Perhaps it is accurate to say that the owners might derive some pleasure from denying Ruth what he wanted, what he said he wanted over and over. Many owners, in every industry, have demonstrated that team loyalty or fairness means little when the opportunity comes to demonstrate their power and authority over their workers.

1934

While the career average is not available directly, the Baseball Data Bank has the necessary raw data. Of the 3,343 players who debuted between 1910 and 1935, the median length of a major league career was two seasons. Only 30 percent of the players had careers of five or more seasons. About 13 percent of the players had careers of ten or more seasons.[13]

In 1934, at age 39, Ruth would be playing in his 20th full season. That year, he signed with Ruppert for $35,000, his lowest salary since 1921, but even that amount kept him the highest paid player. Again he would collect 25 percent of exhibition profits; in 1934, they totaled $1,696.81. Montville's summation: "The parties were basically locked together for one last fractious year."[14] This is not exaggeration. Almost every new contract found Ruth (and Walsh) quarreling in the press about Ruppert's salary offers.

Of the 1927 team, in 1934 just Ruth, Gehrig, Earle Combs and Lazzeri remained. Not one pitcher was the same. That seven-year turnover was a repeat as the year 1927 contrasted with 1921, or 1923 for that matter. Ruppert and Barrow did not hesitate to rid themselves of unproductive, or decliningly productive, employees. Businessman Ruppert knew very well that newer and younger employees would work more cheaply.

Ruppert had "given Admiral Richard Byrd a quarter of a million dollars to go to the South Pole (Byrd named his flagship *Jacob Ruppert*) and let Ruth help underwrite the exploration with a seventeen-thousand-dollar pay cut."[15] The year did not hold much sentiment for the Yankees corporation. The team's star, Lou Gehrig, signed for $23,000, the same as 1933, and Adomites and Wisnia's judgment reads, "all things considered, though, Lou was making about half Ruth's salary ... [he] was now twice the ballplayer."[16]

But had Ruth lost his value to Ruppert's corporation? "Ruth Is Besieged By Crowd At Camp: Proves He Is Still Idol of the Fans" headlined the *New York Times* in mid–March. "In 1934 the Browns had over 25 percent of their total home attendance from games with the Yankees."[17] Money also arrived from Standard Oil. The Esso-Babe Ruth News of January 1934 describes the Babe Ruth Boys Club and continues building Ruth's fame by saying, "The Home Run King always gets a lot of letters from his young admirers, but they have simply overwhelmed him since the club was formed. And Babe enjoys reading them." Ruth was not well known for his love of reading.

On July 13, 20 years since his first game, the *New York Times*, wrote, "the incomparable Babe Ruth reached his goal today with his 700th home run, a wallop that helped in sending the Yankees back into the lead in the American League pennant race." One week later, the AP described 1934 as Ruth's "fading career as a home run collector" (July 19). Fading he might have been and yet at the time "only Gehrig and Hornsby [age 38] had as many as 300 home runs."[18] At Detroit the next day, he received walk number 2,000. And by that game, he had driven in more than 2,100 runs.

Often repeated is the story that some of Ruth's teammates went to their boss and demanded that Ruth be sat down. If this sounds like a manufactured story, consider that though the contrast between what Gehrig produced and what Ruth produced seems unambiguous, it remains true nevertheless that of the 1934 Yankees, Ruth finished second in home runs, third in RBI, fourth in runs, and second in walks, more than Hall of Fame teammates Dickey, Lazzeri and Combs. Only Gehrig was on base more than Ruth.

Ruth was still attractive to advertisers. *On the Air: The Encyclopedia of Old-Time Radio*, by John Dunning, reveals that he appeared on two different 15-minute radio programs in 1934, from April 16 to July 13 on the old Blue Network three times a week, and from May 14 to July 9 on CBS twice a week.[19] One program was often called, "The Adventures of Babe Ruth." These radio tales were conceived to "portray Babe's good sportsmanship, generosity, and compassion." Like so much of the Ruth legend, these 15-minute tales are fiction and include titles like "Ruth Kidnapped." Likewise the narrator of the stories turns out to be a creation named Steve Martin, described in the show's introduction as "the sports writer who knew [Ruth] so well, Ruth's pal," because Ruth "saved my life and my future."[20] In addition to his radio checks, money came from his share in the Yankees' second place money, $763.09 for 1934.

What about Ruth's very powerful ambition to be appointed as a major league manager? How many of those jobs had he been passed over for? Whether his doing or not, whether influenced by wife Claire or business partner Walsh, he had not secured a job. But just since December 1933, he had not been offered the vacant manager's jobs for the following teams: Pittsburgh, Brooklyn, the Chicago White Sox and the Philadelphia Phillies. Rumors about jobs persisted. He would take over for Walter Johnson in Cleveland. Joe Cronin, age 28, moved from Washington to Boston to manage the Red Sox in 1935, so that D.C. job had been open, but the corporation hired Bucky Harris, age 38. Seven of the 16 major league teams had hired new field managers for 1934 and 1935. None of them hired Babe Ruth. "I think I'm entitled to a manager's job or a try at it anyhow," said Ruth to the AP on February 21, 1935.

There are many pieces of speculation about why Ruth did not get his wish. A few biographers believe that since Ruth would demand such an oversized salary, the amount would anger the team's players. More speculation about a manager's job came when, in late October 1934, Ruth joined a group of players and their wives on a two-month tour of the Orient, which would include exhibition games in Honolulu, Japan, Shanghai, and Manila. This tour has been thoroughly covered by Robert K. Fitts in his *Banzai Babe Ruth: Baseball, Espionage, & Assassination During the 1934 Tour.*

As far as the *New York Times* of October 12, 1934, is concerned, initial tour interest centered on "Babe Ruth … sa[ying] he would like to be the manager … of the touring American Leaguers" and that he would serve as the field manager.

Claire and Julia, but not Dorothy, went with him—he had been offered more than $25,000 to go—and even before the ship left the Vancouver port, on October 25 the *New York Daily News* was reporting that "Babe Ruth Is slated to become manager of the Philadelphia Athletics next and that Connie Mack will retire." On the tour, "Ruth will learn Mack's system of diamond strategy."[21] Mack was 71 and had managed for 39 years.

The trip was judged a great success, and many commentators have written of Ruth's popularity in Japan. But not so afterwards in Europe. In Paris, he walked streets unrecognized. "Babe Ruth Anxious To Get Back Home; Stranger In Paris," noted the *Lewiston Daily Sun* of January 19, 1935. "What galled him most was a tiny notice in the 'unclaimed mail' section of the Paris Herald Tribune … asking a George H Ruth to pick up his correspondence."[22] After being in both Switzerland and London as well, Ruth arrived back in New York on February 21, 1935, having been away from home four months. "The Babe said it seemed strange to walk all day in a city without anyone recognizing him."[23]

As for the job managing the Athletics, Connie Mack was quoted by reporter Joe Williams as saying, "I couldn't have made Babe manager. His wife would have been running the club in a month."[24]

1935

No owner seemed interested that no one had shown loyalty to baseball and to its fans as Ruth had. But no owner saw any significance to Ruth's contribution not just to their attendance money, but even to their very survival. "It's true," John Kieran wrote, "that the magnates made much more money by the Babe's effort than Ruth made for himself."[25] No one in baseball, or few, seemed interested in his "contributions to the game," that he had achieved "legendary" status; that many accept as true that he had saved baseball from the Black Sox scandal; that he had helped bring the Yankees their first pennant and had contributed to his boss being able to fund and build a mammoth new stadium; that he had played hard, even in exhibitions.

Jonathan Eig, in his book on Gehrig, judges that "Ruth had been valuable to him [Ruppert], despite his faults, so long as he'd been able to hit home runs and bring in fans. Now the Babe played neither well nor often enough to justify his price tag."[26] Like any other used-up worker, Ruth's time was up.

It was clear that Ruth's playing days were over. His 1935 Yankees contract, for one dollar, went unsigned. Ruppert needed to be rid of Ruth without much noise made about it. Other players were homering on other teams, not on Ruppert's Yankees. Since the 1928 championship, the Yankees had won but once.

Smelser comments, "Babe Ruth's unwillingness to quit was discomfiting to Jacob Ruppert. How do you get rid of a demigod who won't go quietly?"[27] For the *New York Times*, James P. Dawson related, "'Last September,' Ruppert said early in 1935, 'Ruth told me he would not sign another player contract, that he would sign only as a player-manager. Reports were circulated regarding Ruth's future, but of these, I knew nothing officially. All I knew was that Ruth was determined to sign only as a player-manager, and in this capacity, our lists were closed to him.'"[28]

Would any loyal worker want to hear the cold language "our lists were closed to him"? Of course not. His value to the club as product was gone. His body no longer trim, his output diminished, his feats were no longer so scarce or extraordinary that his ability as a money generator had diminished, reduced so much that a player replacing him could be paid at $6,000 or less. And besides, Ruth had been in New York since 1920. He was old news.

By February 26, he was, in baseball language, "released" by "Ruppert who ... more than ever wished to see Babe gone from the Yankees without a lot of commotion and unfavorable press."[29] That is, he was fired in such a way as to not damage Ruppert's corporation. Ruth's uniform number 3 was given to George Selkirk. The clubhouse man at the Yankees' training camp, evidently not a sentimental soul, filled Babe Ruth's old locker with kindling wood.[30] All the press clippings, all the photographs of Ruth with children, all the product endorsements meant nothing now. Ruppert was conducting a business transaction, nothing more. Had Ruth been a bit more aware, as he claimed to be, about his own business dealings, his delusion might not have been so great.

At the same time he was handed his "release," he stood in the Yankees office with Ruppert and they were joined by "Judge" Emil Fuchs, the owner of the Boston Braves. Fuchs had seen some worth in signing Ruth. Newspapermen were offered the chance to ask Ruth about his duties as "Vice President" of the Braves. Ruth, unsure how to answer, allowed Fuchs to say, "Advisory Capacity." Ruppert made sure to say—twice—"I don't get a cent" from the deal with Fuchs. Ruth's salary with his new club from the National League was $25,000.

Later, the agreement with Fuchs, in language as vague as possible, appeared to say that Ruth would act as vice president and assistant manager. The job title "assistant manager" was invented by Fuchs, a title with no real meaning. It may have seemed to Ruth that once he had some experience at the major league level as an assistant manager, he could become manager, maybe as early as 1936. The current manager, Bill McKechnie, in his post since 1930 with the Braves, had finished as high as fourth. Fuchs' letter to Ruth of February 23, 1935, read in part: "if it was determined after your affiliation with the ball club for you to take up the active management on the field, there would be absolutely no handicap in having you so appointed.... It may be that ... you would rather have someone else, accustomed to the hardships and drudgery of managing a ball club." What did Fuchs expect of Ruth? Ruth would soon learn that he would be used as he had always been used: as a generator of revenue.

Resentment burned in some of Ruth's colleagues. Rogers Hornsby stated, "Babe Ruth was driven out of the American League by self-protecting [team] business managers. Ruth would be a great manager in my opinion and would be the boss."[31] This is to say the Red Sox might have signed Ruth for the $25,000 he signed for with the Braves.

Ruth hurried to Florida. Soon, "making his debut in the uniform of the Boston Braves, he filled Waterfront Park in St. Petersburg with some 3,000 spectators [that number equaled nearly one percent of the paid admissions for all of the 1934 season for the Braves]."[32] By March 22, the Associated Press could report that, "Ruth has drawn 20,000 at gate for Braves; 150,000 total seen; more money received in eight games so far than in entire 1934 training season with 19 contests to come, club expects Spring profit for first time." Team owner Fuchs was pleased. He needed the money. He needed to cover expenses. Had Ruth already paid his own salary? Did Ruth know about Fuchs' background? That in 1929 Fuchs had "pled no contest to spending money illegally to influence the legislation of Sunday baseball in Boston?"

Clearly delighted to be in front of his fans again, Ruth imagined himself in a good bargaining position for the managerial job. However, not much time would pass before he pushed the corporation. The corporation pushed back. Before many days had passed, a vice president of the Braves, Charles Francis Adams, said that Ruth "needs to prove himself to be a good soldier if he is not that already, and he must gain the loyalty of his team-mates."[33] Adams, on March 1, also said, "We can hardly consider him managerial material now." Apparently a good soldier is one who brings his team more money than they pay him. Ruth did not know whom he was dealing with.

Fuchs not only knew how to be paid; he had been known to pay people, notably in the same year when Arnold Rothstein fixed the World Series. Fuchs was Rothstein's lawyer. In the summer of 1921, in the midst of the Black Sox troubles, "Powerful New York gambler Arnold Rothstein, deeply implicated in the scandal as the man who gave the go-ahead, greatly helped the owners' strategy by arranging for the theft of the players' confessions from the Chicago district attorney's office.... The prosecution was doomed."[34]

In another case, after Fuchs had been given bribe money by gambler Rothstein, Fuchs passed on the money to a New York City assistant District Attorney and the judge who would preside over a Rothstein trial in the shooting of three detectives.[35] The trial of baseball player Benny Kauff lay also in Fuchs' colorful past. After that trial, sportswriter Fred Lieb summarized Kauff's acquittal as "smell[ing] to high heaven."[36]

About a month into the baseball season—May 7, 1935—newspapers could summarize the situation very clearly. "Ruth Pondering Over Problem Of 'To Play or Not to Play'; If He Can Continue as Regular, Braves Will Prosper, Fuchs Will Keep Control and McK-echnie Will Stay—Otherwise Adams Will Get Club and Make Babe Manager."

The next day, Fuchs said that if the other team executives—Adams and Bruce Wet-more—brought the club from him, Ruth would probably manage, but if he—Fuchs—controlled the team, McKechnie would remain as manager and Ruth as a player. It is Creamer's opinion that "The Babe was angry and chagrined—he felt like a sucker—because Fuchs, far from paying him as much or more than he had earned with the Yankees, had asked him to invest $50,000 in the club.... His duties as vice-president seemed to be confined to attending store openings."[37] The possibility of the cash infusion from Ruth's presence was perhaps the Judge's true reason for hiring Ruth in the first place.

Decades later, there would be those who claimed that Fuchs' interest in the Braves was cash. "Some observers thought the judge had only invested $35,000 of his own while withdrawing $300,000 in salary and expenses."[38]

By late May, Ruth knew he would exit the team very soon. But he had one achievement left in him. In Pittsburgh on May 25, he had a perfect day at bat, four hits in four at-bats. Three of them were home runs, the last being judged to be the "longest drive ever made at Forbes Field." He also drove in six runs. As he rounded the bases for his last home run, coming in to pitch was Waite Hoyt, his teammate with both the Red Sox and the Yankees for over 12 years.

Ruth played one more game, and then the team moved east. "But Fuchs, who chose to use Ruth as a scapegoat for his team's poor play, suddenly released him as a player and assistant coach and fired him."[39] Ruth did not go quietly, saying in a statement, "Yes, I have received my unconditional release from the Braves and am mighty glad of it.... No, I am not going on the retired list.... I hope to stay in baseball for all of my life."

Fuchs, like Frazee before him, tried to put the blame for the action on Ruth. The owner forced his manager, "Deacon" McKechnie, to say that "Ruth was undermining the morale of the club and that was the reason for all their losses."[40] Ruth counterclaimed, "Fuchs wanted me out because he couldn't pay me the salary he agreed to ... but he didn't know how to go about it so I quit."[41]

Fuchs himself didn't exactly quit. On July 31, he "forfeited his majority stock holdings." Manager McKechnie and new president Adams led the 1935 team to 38 wins out of 153 games. At the end of 1935, Adams had the team effectively taken away from him by Commissioner Landis because Adams owned Suffolk Downs racetrack, and that old fear of gambling had not departed. McKechnie lasted two more years. The team business showed a loss of $48,025 for the year, averaging just over 3,103 paid per game. Finishing 61.5 games back, the poor performance could not help attendance.

Ruth knew by now that no real job offer for managing in the majors would be forthcoming for some time, if ever. But more crowds wanted to see him, and so he would have a few more chances to play nine innings before he was through.

It may have been that Ruth had counted on the money from the Braves for a full season. No one doubts that he truly loved to play baseball. And it may also have been his desire to be applauded by a crowd. So he would go on to appear in a half-dozen more games in his last year as a player, if not at the major league level. Two months after leaving the Braves, he accepted an invitation for a game to be played on September 1, an offer perhaps made by Donie Bush, then manager of American Association Minneapolis Millers. Bush had played in the 1924 Brea Bowl game with Ruth, played against him for 16 years in the American league, and managed against him in the 1927 World Series.

The crowd that showed up for the game surely surpassed any numbers that might have showed up for the game between the Minneapolis and St. Paul police teams. Bettering by many years a local attendance record for a baseball game, Ruth drew 13,000 customers and "gave the fans an idea of how he can hit a baseball by walloping a dozen or so out of the park in a batting exhibition that preceded the actual contest," though he only doubled and walked in the game itself.[42]

With everyone in baseball seeing Ruth's minor and major league career now over, and with little likelihood of his managing, "Babe Ruth today cherishes a lifetime pass for all National League baseball games … forwarded to the Babe by President Ford C. Frick…. Ruth declared it a 'touch of sentiment and appreciation that will never be forgotten.'"[43] The president of the American League, William Harridge, made no such offer. Rumors persist that the Yankees insisted that Ruth pay for his tickets to the ballpark, and it may have been the Yankees who blocked the league from offering Ruth the same kind of life-time pass.

For $3,000 and acclaim, on September 29, 1935, Ruth played first base during the first game of a doubleheader against Alex Pompez' New York Cubans, a team starring Martin Dihigo and Alejandro Oms, with Luis Tiant, Sr., pitching. Pitching for the Ruth All-Stars was 39-year old Clyde Barfoot, and probably John O'Flaherty, minor leaguer, was catching. The games were played at Dyckman Oval at Manhattan's West 204th St., in a park that held 4,600 seats. To see the games and Ruth came a crowd of 10,000 (the *Pittsburgh Courier* said 12,000). Joe Bostic of the *New York Amsterdam News* wrote, "Ruth hit a few over the fence between games." During the game Ruth hit a double, walked and make three outs. Afterwards came "the collection of his share of the day's take."

Seated above the crush of fans, one lone reporter, Tom Meany of the *New York Telegram*, chose to write of the pathos he interpreted. "The spectators seemed to sense they were watching something pathetic…. There were neither newsreel nor still cameras in evidence and no telegraph keys clattered brassily in the press box, which had less than half a dozen occupants. No civic dignitaries, not even an alderman, could be observed in the crowd."

With this game, Ruth had one again extended the idea of baseball beyond major league and all-white professional baseball. In Minneapolis he had played for an amateur team. At Dyckman Oval, he met a squad of Negro Leaguers and dark-skinned Cubans, and these next two Dexter Park games marked contests with semipros. These semipros, the home team Bushwicks, had already played 84 games in 1935, winning 64 of them against a variety of semipro and Negro Leagues teams. Their great local rival at the time was another New York City team named the Bay Parkways, and the games against each other in October had often become a kind of semipro World Series. Ruth, then 40 years old, played first base for the Bay Parkways on October 13, with Dazzy Vance, 44 years old, pitching for the Bushwicks. This were games seven and eight in 1935 against the Bay Parkways, and this doubleheader drew 15,000 fans, who saw the Bushwicks win game one and tie game two.

The *Long Island Daily Press* story of course concentrated on Ruth.

> In two previous times at bat he had gone hitless. The crowd was razzing the Babe good-naturedly as he picked up his war-club and he turned to the stands. "Hell," he shouted jovially, "I'm tryin' to get a hit." The Dazzler grinned as Ruth entered the batter's box, and waved the outfielders to come in…. His grin widened as the Babe missed a fast one straight down the middle. On the next pitch Ruth swung and the stands rose as a man as the ball whistled like a bullet on its way over the right field fence. And the Babe minced around the bases, his broad face wreathed in smiles.

It was Ruth again the next Sunday but this time, before the game of October 20, 1935, Bushwicks owner Max Rosner had Vance and Ruth autograph 25 baseballs. Then each ball was assigned a number matching coupons that were given out at the gate. Reporting the October 20 game was left in the hands of the *Brooklyn Daily Eagle*.

> Babe Ruth delivered a little speech over the amplifying system at Dexter Park yesterday that brought tears to the eyes of even hardened fans that were included in the crowd of 15,000. It was Babe saying

farewell to the game that skyrocketed him to fame and fortune. The adieu was delivered after he had played first base for the Springfields, who beat the Bushwicks 6 to 5 in the opening game of a triangular doubleheader. After game one, Babe was sad as he told the fans this was the last time they would see him as a player.[44]

Ruth went one-for-three with eight putouts at first base. It was Ruth's last barnstorming game, the last time he would play nine innings, his last as a team member, the end of competitive baseball for him. He would exhibit himself at bat in other circumstances, but nothing was on the line in those situations.

Ruth could not know it yet, but the last game he played with the Braves, May 30, 1935, marked an end not just to his time in the major leagues. It served as an end to his high level of celebrity. Look for him in the newspapers if you might, but you would be hard-pressed to find him. What he had left was his reputation in baseball. The 15 seasons with New York were finished. The constant appearances in public—pre-season exhibitions, the regular season, barnstorming games and vaudeville—appearances that lasted 11 months of most of those years, had vanished.

For some this might betoken a sadness on Ruth's part. But like all effects, his reaction to his absences tend to be complicated. For years he had searched out places like golf courses and small taverns, where he did not feel the pressure to act the roles assigned to him. He had played the wastrel, he had played the good guy, he had played the star. At 40, the pressure was gone. Rather than a sadness, he may have felt a lifting of a burden.

He tried hard not to leave baseball. Ruth had spent just 20 weeks in the minors in a career that lasted from 1914 to 1935. He had spent more than 20 years as a major leaguer. What he thought he deserved now was a chance to be a big league manager.

Early in 1935 he told the *New York Times*, "I have played baseball a long time and the urge is still there…. I don't want to leave baseball. I'd be lost without it."[45] And later that year, "I still think I am entitled to the chance to make good as a manager."

Why did he think he was "entitled"? From Ruth's point of view, he had been a loyal worker and had "always kept faith with the baseball fans and my employers."[46] But keeping faith—that is, loyalty—never has mattered to an employer though the boss may mouth how vital it is. A player always was to most magnates a piece of property. Without Ruth, baseball continued to do business as it had always done. "In 1935 the IRS ruled that baseball teams could depreciate the value of their player contracts. This is an anomaly since labor is not a depreciating asset."[47]

The off the field reputation that Ruth built from 1915–1925 remained set in concrete. Because Ruth made so much money for so many people and companies, because part of his reputation was his well-known amiability, few ever said "no" to him. Why would he then not think that everyone approved of him and, in fact, were always glad to see him? Why would anyone not want to be Ruth's pal?

In the retelling by his wife, Ruth waited for the call to come, the call offering him the job of big league manager. It did not. His time was taken up with golf and time spent with a few sportswriters. More often, social occasions were spent with persons who were not famous, not ballplayers, but, for the most part, persons he employed. True there was a songwriter and his wife, a Broadway character (Toots Shor), but most of the rest were Ruth's lawyers, accountants and a chauffeur.

On the last day of 1935, a photo was printed with the caption, "ACME: Babe Ruth looking over the collection of photographs and cartoons on the wall of the den in his

New York City apartment. The former home run king seems to be the forgotten man of baseball and will go south this year as a private citizen; no spring training camp for him this year."

Ruth would be remembered again in 2013, when a 1935 Babe Ruth game-used Boston Braves cap sold at auction for $120,000.

34

An Entertainer
(1936 and After)

During the winter months of 1936, 226 National Baseball Hall of Fame ballots arrived from players and writers, ballots that were intended to select the first group of players who "should be represented in the game's memorial hall at Cooperstown, New York" when its official opening took place in 1939. Just five players received enough votes on January 29, 1936, for inclusion. Ruth came in second to Ty Cobb. The voting was not unanimous: four did not include Cobb, and Ruth was left off 11 ballots.

The Baseball Hall of Fame was from the first a business investment, a venture to bolster the village of Cooperstown's tourist income and, in the midst of the Great Depression, to boost baseball's reputation, as well as its patriotic origins. The project, begun in 1934, was to be the centerpiece of the celebration of the so-called centennial of the invention of baseball by Abner Doubleday. Backed with $100,000 from the office of the President of the National League, Ford Frick, the idea was to designate a place at which the game's stars, traditions and distinctly American beginnings could be celebrated. Part of the plan was to refurbish the village's old baseball field, and to that end New York State and the village contributed another $40,000 to the scheme. The Clark Foundation contributed $43,000 to the project. The close to $200,000 worth of support for the Cooperstown Hall of Fame marked its seriousness.

The year 1936 could be thought of as the time Ruth accepted and maybe even appreciated the fact that his celebrity had moderated greatly, particularly in the sense of being called on to appear at events. His daughter Dorothy, in her book, indicates that the year may have been the time when Ruth fully resented the controlling ways of wife Claire while disliking her growing alcoholic dependency. For example, the *New York Times* reported on March 9, 1936, that "The Reds offered Babe Ruth a chance to return to baseball, but Mrs. Ruth put her foot down and the former home-run king decided today to remain in retirement." As a result, Ruth found that he needed someplace nearby where he could distance himself from the family, and from where, not that long ago, he had been sought after, praised and celebrated.

Leaving New York City behind, Ruth crossed the Hudson at some point and drove north and west to an area with its southern point around West Milford, New Jersey, and its northern point at the end of Greenwood Lake, New York. Various conflicting sources indicate that it may have been Ruth's interest in hunting and fishing after he found a teammate with the same interests. The pitcher, Russ Van Atta, was born in Augusta, New Jersey—18 miles from Greenwood Lake—and spent most of his life there, so he knew the hilly areas and many lakes that Ruth might want to be taken to. A teammate beginning in 1933, Van Atta ran for sheriff in 1940, and his hunting pal Ruth campaigned for him.

In the area where Van Atta lived, called now the Highlands region of New York (highest point at 1,664 feet) or the New Jersey Skylands (1,803 feet), Ruth found a small cabin in Hewitt, New Jersey, on the southwest side of Greenwood Lake, a spot handy for its general store and post office. That Ruth had mail sent to him in Hewitt speaks to how long his stays lasted. It is not known how long each stay continued, but a decade would pass with Ruth in the area in all seasons, having plenty of time to do what he had done only for brief periods: hunt, fish, and play golf.

Greenwood Lake itself is nine miles long, half in New York and half in New Jersey, and about 17 miles in circumference. That village, population 232, had become known early in the century as a destination for motoring trips from the city. The Erie Railroad had a division of its line that stopped at the village station. Well-known people had and would spend some time there, including Greta Garbo and Cecil B. DeMille; boxers Sugar Ray Robinson and Bob Fitzsimmons, Jr., used the hamlet to set up their training camps. Many years later, Derek Jeter lived here.

When the name of Ruth appeared again 15 months later in the spring of 1937, descriptions of well-attended golf matches were the usual stories. He remained a money generator. Warner's Vitaphone paid him to make a short in 1937 called "Home Run on the Keys," in which he joined two others in song.

But then, in June of 1938, an offer to come back to baseball arrived from Larry MacPhail, new president of the Brooklyn Dodgers. Ruth chose to take the offer to coach in the most optimistic of lights: that he soon would be manager of the Dodgers. The Dodgers had drawn about half of what their National League competitors, the Giants, had drawn in 1937, and the team had not finished higher than fifth since 1933.

Called to MacPhail's apartment, with Christy Walsh there as well, the odd man out that day seemed to be the Dodgers' shortstop, Leo Durocher, burning with ambition to be the next Dodgers manager, Burleigh Grimes holding that job in 1938. The team paid Ruth a $15,000 yearly salary, but since he worked just 68 percent of the season probably not that much, probably closer to $10,000. In 1937 the team averaged 6,265 fans for their home games, but when "28,000 Turned Out For Babe Ruth's Debut As Coach Of Brooklyn," the team moved well on its way to getting the maximum value out of Ruth.

In addition, because of Ruth, the Dodgers scheduled ten extra exhibition games during the remainder of the season, during which they grossed nearly enough to pay his entire $15,000 salary."[1] Ruth drew 11,724 in Albany, 6,000 in Buffalo, and 3,200 in Dayton. The July 5, 1938, a UPI notice said, "Ebbets Field critics estimate he has drawn an extra 20,000 fans to games since his June 18, 1938, signing. Large crowds were predicted for both Syracuse and Elmira on successive days in July."

But also in mid–July, Gayle Talbot in an AP story wrote, "MacPhail simply paid $15,000 … for the privilege of exhibiting the great Bambino for the remainder of the season in the same spirit that P. T. Barnum once intrigued the public with the 'missing link.'" True, Ruth weighed 240 pounds, but Talbot was 18 when Ruth joined the Yankees and he certainly knew what Ruth had accomplished in baseball. In mid–August, William Harridge, president of the American League, was quoted as saying that his league would give the fans "high grade baseball" without any of "the side show or hoopla stuff," stuff that included "ballyhoo men for coaches." MacPhail spoke up in the same article, saying

"I resent the thinly veiled remarks about Babe Ruth our coach … who has made a valuable contribution to the spirit and morale of our club."[2]

Did it matter to Ruth if the mocking of his reputation might lead to the managing job? Ruth may, or may not have been positioned at third base by manager Burleigh Grimes, and he may or may not, have missed one sign, or a few, to flash. Most sources, for instance, say he coached only at first base, not third, and so did not relay any signs. The truth did not matter to the ambitious Durocher, famous for his lack of sentiment toward non-producing team members (except himself, a lifetime .247 hitter), and famous for his lack of sentiment to anyone who might be in his way for the manager's job he desired. Durocher was not at all silent about his disdain for Ruth, noisy to newsmen and to the team owner, MacPhail. Smelser quotes Durocher saying, "He's a while elephant … out here to drag in customers … nothing more."[3] The quarrel eventually led to a shoving match in the locker room.

Meanwhile, the Dodgers increased attendance by 200,000 paid in 1938, despite winning just 69 games and finishing next to last in the league. Signed as the new manager of the Dodgers, on October 12, 1938, was Leo Durocher. (In 2008, Ruth's 1938 Dodgers road uniform brought $310,500 at auction.)

Paul Mickelson of the AP wrote on October 13, 1938, "Babe now has about as many friends among big league magnates as Yankee hitters among pitchers." So neither a full season with the Braves, nor a full season with the Dodgers, nor rehired by either. Ruth was mystified and did not seem to understand that much of his history in baseball was a repetition of defying owners and its commissioner. Did Ruth not remember the phrase "mutinous defiance" from Landis in 1921? Had he considered the situation deeply, he may have recognized the struggle between money and power that he had taken part in all these years. Soon Ruth signed contracts to be heard by an invisible audience on the radio once more.

The deaths of a number of people he knew took place in the late 1930s and early 1940s. Sportswriter Heywood Broun died at age 51 in 1939, a year after Colonel Huston. The other Yankees executive, Jacob Ruppert, in early 1939, despite his millions and the loosening of his hand on the tiller, was still drawing an annual "salary of $25,000 from the Yankees, as club president."[4] The New York Times knew that "the Ruppert Holding Corporation was the owner and holder of the majority of shares of the capital stock of the American League Baseball Club of New York, Inc … the colonel's stock … is tentatively valued at $2,400,000." In addition, "he maintained the Ruppert Stables for many years and they are said to have realized $50,000 annually." When he died in 1939, Ruppert held $30,000,000 just in real estate; his entire estate was judged to be in the range of $40 to 45 million.[5]

Ruppert died rich enough to be able to leave his mistress $300,000. Not long after he died, a curious piece of journalism appeared. The New York Daily News of January 14, 1939, painted a death bed scene right out of Dickens, but this scene starred Ruth and his former employer. The newspaper reporters clearly were not in the room with Ruth and Ruppert.

> Old Ruppert was stirring, trying to sit up, trying to form words, trying to say something. "Babe," he murmured, and that was all he could manage. The Colonel was a blunt fellow, the sort of barking Bavarian who routinely, all his days, addressed his men by nothing but their last names. Never once before in his life had he ever called Babe Ruth "Babe." Bam went down the elevator bawling like a kid. Jacob Ruppert was dead the next morning.

The *New York Times'* version: "The colonel smiled faintly but could not talk. Ruth turned away and started to leave the room, but the colonel summoned up his strength and called him to the bedside … and murmured the one word 'Babe.' 'It was the only time in his life he ever called me Babe to my face,' Ruth said. 'I couldn't help crying when I went out.'" It remains difficult to tell whether this is the sentiment of old men or the sentimental claptrap demanded by newspaper editors. Perhaps it was simply a human response to the death of a work friend, even if the work friend fired you when you cost him too much money.

Also in 1939 came the news that Lou Gehrig was dying. Ruth and Gehrig had quarreled for some years. In the judgment of the *New York Times,* though Ruth famously threw his arms around Gehrig at a July 4, 1939, ceremony, the one of Gehrig's famous speech, "it appeared that the disaffection between them may have eased. But in the last two years of Lou's life, Ruth paid little heed to his dying ex-teammate."[6] Ruth did not go to Gehrig's funeral mass. This may not in itself be unusual. Once no longer teammates, players go their own ways.

Over the years, up until 1946, there would appear stories about possible managing jobs with the Reds, the Dodgers and the St. Louis Browns, as well as minor league teams: the Albany Senators, Oakland Oaks, Manchester New Hampshire Nine and Seattle Rainers. In May of 1946, after being greeted by 15,000 fans in Mexico City, there seemed to be a chance that Ruth might serve as a peace emissary between American baseball and Mexican baseball.

Most writers about Ruth see a positive, calming effect brought about by his marriage to Claire Ruth. One observer, Wayne Stewart, writes a number of paragraphs about the changes in Ruth's life with Claire. She would accompany him on road trips, traveling in the same compartment, living in the hotel suite. She curbed his spending to $50 checks at a time. She forbid him the use of hard liquor during the season and established a "curfew for guests."[7]

Another version of life with Claire, according to daughter Dorothy's book, shows Claire adopting a domineering attitude toward Ruth. Throughout his life, Ruth pushed back against limitations on his pleasures, and Dorothy writes that Ruth chafed under Claire's mothering. But there is no clear agreement about Claire's behavior, as a writer emphasized in a 1995 article about daughter Julia, married to a man named Stevens. "Some of Ruth's friends resented Claire's tightfisted control over the Babe. But Stevens says her father never did."[8]

Over the years, too, there would be other job offers. Someone wanted Ruth, but not for baseball. The *Milwaukee Journal* reported, "The Babe has a $75,000 bid for his services as a circus performer with an option of 30 percent of the gross receipts with the '101 Ranch Show.'"[9] Ray Doan, Muscatine, Iowa, sports promoter and manager of the House of David barnstorming baseball team, offered Ruth $35,000 a year to play.[10]

By October 1938, almost a quarter century after Ruth began living perhaps beyond the first-hand experience of many sportswriters,

Increasingly, the writers waxed sentimental over him and his generosity to the kids. (Ruth himself may have begun to believe the new image the writers had projected of him; he even began to color his days at St. Mary's in terms of kindnesses done him by some of the brothers.) Increasingly, the press transformed him into an older, less boyish "idol of the American boy." They began to forget the excesses and the crudities.[11]

But the Ruth of the 1930s and 1940s—the sentimentalized and reformed "idol" of American youth—was not the hero of the 1920s. Ruth built his reputation as a player, and when he "continued life as a celebrity ... it was rather hollow. As Joe Garner wrote, 'he seemed lost, a man in search of a purpose.' ... Ruth ... languished at home."[12] When the playing stopped, the spotlight moved to others, and his reputation moderated. Charles Lindbergh, not unlike Ruth, stood as a rival for fame and renown in the 1920s and yet "[b]y the time American entered World War II his reputation was at an all-time low and to that generation of Americans it never really recovered."[13] Before Pearl Harbor was attacked, U.S. Secretary of the Interior Ickes was branding Lindbergh a "Nazi tool" in the *New York Times*.

Still in contact with Walsh, Ruth appeared at the New York City World's Fair in 1940, and as an instructor at a baseball school at Palatka, Florida. He is reported in Creamer as not going to many ballgames, and in 1941 saw three games and two World Series games.[14]

But perhaps Ruth had had enough of the pressure of celebrity, and once more retreated to Greenwood Lake—driving his "Morincraft" speedboat, with nights at the Hi-Spot and Greck's Maplewood Inn. For Ruth, in that area of New York and New Jersey, we can think he felt few demands on him, few people asking something from him, no one telling him what to do. The strain of meeting schedules, the strain of always being the center of attention, seems to have mostly dissipated. He was remembered in the small village as a friendly guy, but now his public had shrunk to the tiny towns in the New York Highlands. Ruth, during the war years, appeared at many functions, mostly raising money for bond drives. He was pictured, according to Greenwood Lake historian Steve Gross, at one such bond drive in Greenwood Lake. He continued to seek out opportunities to be in front of the public, although the newspapers paid little attention to him. Ruth was no longer hitting a baseball, showing his strength, producing, as the newspaper had called them, thrills, excitement, and wins. In 1941, he took on a new label: grandfather. What he did not have was baseball.

When he returned to his apartment in New York, he could once more see 11 by 14 photographs and cartoons of himself displayed on the walls of his apartment. This display made some writers conclude that he oftentimes needed to be reminded of the glories and renown that had come to him though baseball.

Ruth was briefly taken to a hospital in 1942, when rumors of suicidal depression began to circulate. We do not know the many causes of that depression, if the rumors are true. Sportswriters and fans are prone to jump to the conclusion that lack of baseball alone can cause despair. Wikipedia counts 70 baseball suicides out of about 20,000 major league players.

In the early 1940s, when "Babe Ruth's health began to deteriorate and doctors cautioned him to take better care of himself. He grudgingly limited his drinking and travel, but still continued to make regular trips to his usual haunts in Sussex County" in northernmost New Jersey and Greenwood Lake.[15] In that lake resort, most years with a population of 483, he was now part of the village's everyday life. There are reports of Ruth's minor generosity to village causes and his continuing relaxed ways with children in town. His photo could be found in places like Demarest's Lodge, Gertrude and Herbert's, the Old Heidelberg, and the New Continental. A 1974 special edition of the *Greenwood Lake News* named Anton's On The Lake for Ruth's boat dock.

Not far away south was one of his drinking places, "Gyp's tavern on the shores of

Raleigh cigarettes, endorsed by Ruth and medical science, 1945.

Lake Kittatinny" in the township of Sandyston, NJ. The entire 43-square-mile township listed only 651 people in 1940. Likewise, Ruth had played for years on that state's many golf courses—in 1920, for instance, in Leonia, New Jersey, at the Englewood Country Club. In the company of the wealthy in 1936, he took part the New York Stock Exchange event at the Echo Lake Country Club in Westfield. The Wall Street Golf Association invited him to the Upper Montclair Country Club in Clifton. Years later, he played in West Orange at the Crestmont.

In 1942, "*The Sporting News* conducted a survey of more than 100 former Major League players and officials, asking them to name the 'best player ever.' More than 60 percent voted for Ty Cobb, who far outdistanced runner-up Babe Ruth."[16]

By 1945, a decade after his last game, just as the final wartime season was about to begin, the *New York Times* printed the headline, "Forgotten by Baseball, Ruth Becomes Referee" in Boston, where he began in 1914. "It's the lure of the crowds that is bringing back Babe Ruth to the sports stage as a wrestling referee." A photo appeared dated April 2, 1945, from Portland, Maine. Wrestling remained an entertainment that might draw an audience, but, except for a paid advertisement, it would take a bribe from a promoter for a newspaper to print anything about the matches.

But did Ruth seem content as the baseball season began in 1945? "I haven't had much chance to keep in touch with the crowds." Ruth, "the old warrior [bowled] by himself at the lanes of the Riverside Plaza Hotel on 73rd Street."[17] Pathos also makes attractive copy.

As a revenue generator outside of baseball itself, money still came to him because of what he had been and what authority his name still had. From 1939 to 1947, income flowed to him from three sources: advertisements, radio and the movies. First, for example, were White Owl Cigars and Raleigh cigarettes, the latter claiming, "No other leading cigarette is safer to smoke!" Combining product endorsement and radio work, NBC radio and Red Rock Bottlers paid $9,250 to Ruth to appear on broadcasts and in magazine ads in 1939.

In 1943 and 1944, the retired player was heard on Saturdays, hosting a "Baseball Quiz" show. A contract exists saying Ruth signed for $750 per episode. Through arrangements with Hollywood in 1942, "Ruth refuses to confirm or deny the report that he is getting $25,000" to portray himself in "Pride of the Yankees."[18]

Babe Ruth Day was held at Yankee Stadium (and every other major league park) in April 1947. A crowd of 58,339 was there (or 49,641). If the former number is correct, Ruth brought in 27,000 more fans than the average for a home Yankees game, one last time making money flow into the company's till. The total amounted to enough money to pay the entire year's salary for outfielder Tommy Henrich and catcher Yogi Berra, both starting players.

The book, *The Babe Ruth Story,* reviewed on May 2, was listed as having Babe Ruth as the author "as told to Bob Considine," And here, out of yet one more fiction, comes this truth: "sports writer, Fred Lieb, who worked for the *New York Telegram* newspaper, became the real ghostwriter for the book."[19] (By June 6, Martin Weldon had produced *Babe Ruth*, another biography.)

Ruth's fee to lend his name to the May 2 book amounted to $1,926. For the movie of his own life, biographer Wagenheim says Ruth was paid $150,000.[20] Ruth attended the opening of the movie but left before it was over. Apparently the movie critics wished that they could have also left before the film ended. Even *The Sporting News* objected, summarizing, "the film had to be ... turned into a sermon for Young America." In the *New York Times*, Ruth was "depicted herein is a childish, misunderstood oaf." Reviewer Bosley Crowther called the picture "sloppy sentiment.... Ruth ... is made to seem just a big, mawkish clown whose chief personality is a friendly feeling for pathetic little boys."

An ad written and photographed in connection with the movie showed how Ruth, even near death, could make money for others. A baseball collectibles site on the internet now reads:

Opposite: **Quaker cereal comic strip ad featuring Ruth, 1936.**

This is an original 1948 Louisville Slugger Advertisement Poster/Sign. Advertising the Genuine Babe Ruth Louisville slugger Bat, also used, and donated to the movie "The Babe Ruth Story." This sign would be distributed to dealers that carry Louisville Slugger baseball bats for display. The ad Reads; "This 'on Location' Shot shows the Great Babe Ruth giving the screen Babe (Bill Bendix) pointers on how he gripped his Louisville Slugger Bat."

The ad also features the Western Union Telegram supposedly sent to Louisville Slugger in thanks for their contribution to the production of the movie.[21] So the advertisement at the time was able to publicize six different entities: Ruth, the movie, the actor William Bendix, the Western Union Corporation, and the Louisville Slugger Bat Company, as well as the dealers who sold the bats.

In the spring of 1948, the Ford Motor Company hired him to promote youth baseball, to serve as a consultant, and it gave him a new Lincoln Continental in 1948 "as a measure of its appreciation for his tireless devotion to Little Leaguers and baseball." Another odd statement, since the Little League organization had only existed for two years.

On July 26, 1948, the *New York Times* said, "It's Babe Ruth Day Here by Official Proclamation of Mayor O'Dwyer," but part of the visit by O'Dwyer included being presented with an invitation to the Ruth bio movie in order to promote both the movie and the Babe Ruth Foundation. It was a noisy day in Ruth's hospital room with reporters, photographers and newsreel men.

Once Ruth entered Sloan Kettering Memorial Hospital on June 24, 1948, he would never leave alive.

Ruth's funeral took place on August 19, three days after his death. Of the *New York Times'* obituary, one commentator describes the piece as "a traditional and detailed obituary, rich in sentiment of recalled moments of sorrow and joy as well as prosaic biographical fact."[22] This official obituary featured the words "star," "idol," "dramatic," and "bizarre." Not long after, as *Life* magazine noted, "Manhattan newspapers printed 490 eulogistic columns. The mourning was unquestionably sincere, even though written sentiments were incredibly mawkish."[23] Public expressions of sadness often seem cold and hollow. It is common for a "moment of silence" for a recently dead person to last fewer than ten seconds. One of Ruth's pallbearers, Waite Hoyt, according to Creamer, was of the opinion that "'Babe was not a sentimentalist and generally made no outward demonstration of affection either by word or action," adding, "I have no maudlin sorrow for Ruth's passing. I believed he lived a rich, full, complete life."[24] It must be said that had Ruth either lived longer or had he died suddenly, the sentimentality would have had less time to build. Ruth died at age 53, at a time when the life expectancy for someone born in 1895 rose to about 48 years.

Perhaps indicative of the important people in his public life, Ruth's honorary pallbearers were listed as being 13 sportswriters and nine others.

The funeral service was presided over by Francis Cardinal Spellman, who was assisted by 44 Roman Catholic priests and 12 altar boys. (Spellman, not at all averse to having his name mentioned with celebrities and in fact himself a celebrity, had also presided over the 1946 funeral of Major Bowes, producer of the radio show the *Original Amateur Hour*, the radio predecessor of *American Idol*.) The funeral, said to be for the benefit of his many fans, was held in St. Patrick's Cathedral. It was fitting that a man who toiled in the entertainment industry for most of his life and who married a woman who was also in that trade would have a funeral mass that required extras. It was fitting that this baseball entertainer—and radio and movie entertainer—would go to his grave with a large audience watching. Two days before the mass, Ruth's body in his coffin was viewed by an estimated 75,000 to 100,000 people at Yankee Stadium. With 6,000 inside the church, another 75,000 lined the street to see the funeral procession move out of the city toward Westchester. A Babe Ruth memorial pin was hawked on the streets outside St. Patrick's on the day of Ruth's funeral.

Cardinal Spellman's speech that day held hope that Ruth would "continue to inspire the young to live chaste, sober and heroic lives" and pleaded with God to "bless Thou with especial love him who we honor thus today."

Spellman found his way onto Ruth's gravestone as well. On the right side of Ruth's tombstone, divided into three parts, is carved his name and birth and death dates. In the middle is a depiction of Jesus holding the hand of a small child. On the left side is a quote from Cardinal Spellman, stating that Ruth was "animated … to win the crucial game of life" by "the divine spirit," and Spellman hoped that same "divine spirit" will "inspire the youth of America."

That, figuratively, the "House that Ruth Built" was never even considered to be changed to Babe Ruth Stadium demonstrates, as with modern day ballparks, that it is the corporation that exercises its authority when it comes to truly important matters in baseball.

Soon after Ruth's death, the City Council voted to turn an area outside the stadium into Babe Ruth Plaza, rather than rename River Avenue in his honor. "Ruth Tosetti called the plaza terrible, saying, 'It was just a bunch of bricks.'"[25]

Three months later, around the time the body was moved from a receiving vault at the cemetery to the burial site, barnstormers including future Baseball Hall of Fame players Jackie Robinson, Roy Campanella, Al "Red" Schoendienst, and Yogi Berra of the Yankees barnstormed in front of crowds in Canada, Louisiana, and in places where Ruth too had played in the post-season: Maine, New Hampshire, Pennsylvania and California. A barnstorming team starring Rex Barney of the Dodgers, Johnny Hopp of the Pirates, and Richie Ashburn of the Phillies played in Omaha, almost 26 years to the day when, in Omaha, Ruth played first base for the Woodsmen of the World before 4,000 enthusiastic Nebraskans.

In 2008, Heritage Sports Collectibles Auction #710 offered for sale a "Babe Ruth Game-Worn Bustin' Babes Barnstorming hat." The asking price was $50,000. That year, it sold for $110,000. Five years later, the cap sold for $130,000.

35

Collecting Baseball Objects

Before Ruth's time in baseball, certainly in the 19th century, the collecting of important autographs, according to the magazine *The Collector*, was limited to a letter, other document, or a book signed by its author. The signer was almost always a king, a president, or a general. One president, Woodrow Wilson, signed a baseball in 1917 which, when auctioned, brought in $151 for an army regiment.

In Ruth's second year with the Yankees, *The Collector* wrote, "There is the baseball autographed by Babe Ruth, or by some high official like the President. This is filed away with other bric-a-brac."[1] *Total Baseball* notes the difference in eras. "For the longest time, baseball autographs were something to be personally treasured but not necessarily valued. No one, for instance, put a value on a Babe Ruth autograph even twenty years after the Babe's death."[2] Dorothy Seymour Mills observes, "At first … autographs were collected simply to look at and share with others, as proof that the collector had actually seen the hero up close and exchanged a word or two with him."[3]

To begin with, picture Ruth standing next to someone and writing "Babe Ruth" on a ball or a piece of paper. One step removed, Ruth signs a baseball and tosses that ball from atop a hotel or newspaper building to a crowd below. Two steps removed, Ruth, having sat in a hotel room or office or clubhouse, puts his signature on a ball and then the ball is won in a contest. Three steps removed, someone is assigned by Ruth to inscribe his signature on a ball. The proximity to the signer seems to matter. That such proximity can be delineated speaks loudly.

Ruth signed many, many baseballs. For example, in 1927 in Los Angeles, Ruth tossed 100 autographed baseballs to several hundred kids who had gathered on the field to receive them. In 1931 in San Diego, the line of youngsters before the game was more than enough to use up the 200 autographed baseballs Ruth gave away. Linda Ruth Tosetti estimated, "If they lined up all the bats and balls he signed, I think it would reach to Australia." The production of these autographed items became a kind of assembly line, as the granddaughter of Ruth remembers from 1926 or 1927 in an interview with *Autograph* magazine. Ruth "used to sign baseballs and bats all winter and store them in the barn. Mom's job was to make sure the ink was dry, wrap them in paper, and put them in boxes. That way, when he'd see kids, all he had to do was grab the bats and balls and give them out."[4]

This memory, if accurate, shows two things: first is Ruth's generosity. He paid for the bats and balls; he spent the time signing them. Secondly, it shows how little he valued them. He is the one who said, "Who the hell wants to collect that crap?"[5] By 1928, the *New York Times* was making no secret that the Yankees trainer, Doc Woods, signed "the vast majority" of baseballs "for autograph hounds have always been the bane of Ruth's existence." If trapped by autograph seekers, he would sign only if the seeker had a baseball and a pen.[6]

It does seem that he signed at least 100 baseballs at every barnstorming stop, making the signed total from those games alone to be more than 20,000. During those games, the total signed on a scrap of paper, for example, can't be reckoned nor can it be counted for 20 years and more, of being asked for an autograph. What must have Ruth thought, during his vaudeville tours, as he signed balls atop a hotel or newspaper building and blindly tossed them into a crowd below, not unlike tossing a balled-up piece of paper into a scrap basket.

A mania began to develop for something that Ruth had touched. It seemed to be the same idea about a religious relic. "They were checks—one hundred and forty god-damned checks, anywhere from one dollar to five dollars. They were for his autograph. The fans figured he'd be sure to endorse something that meant money, and then they'd have his autograph."[7] Ruth's daughter Julia tells the story of a young man named Matthew who wrote her father, requesting a lock of his hair. Ruth, not willing to turn down a request from a kid, dutifully sent the boy some of his hair with a letter telling him: "'I don't know what you're going to do with it, but I hope you enjoy it.'"[8]

In 1936, Goodrich shoes offered as first prize two tickets to a World Series game, as advertised in *Boys Life*, or, "A chance to win … a bat autographed by the players on the Championship World Series team of 1936." *Life* magazine in May 3, 1937, featured an ad that read, "Sinclair is giving away every week absolutely free in its Babe Ruth Baseball Contest 'additional weekly prizes' of '500 Spalding National League baseballs, Babe Ruth autographed.'"[9]

But Creamer, writing later, sees that

> Babe Ruth once said of autographs, "Hell, who wants to collect that crap?" But the Babe signed willingly, even happily, and Jocko Conlan, the 82-year-old former umpire, thinks Ruth began the sports-autograph craze. "I started in baseball in 1920," says Conlan, "and Babe Ruth hit 54 home runs that year, the first ever to pass the 50 mark. I think I'm right when I say that he was the only one anyone wanted an autograph [of] from then [on]."[10]

Clearly, collecting baseball items grew in popularity, but really not until 25 years after Ruth's death did the industry begin to flower. Before then, modest pitches were made. In 1950, an ad featured a "pencil sharpener, mounted on display card in the form of a baseball glove, that sells for 19 cents. The baseball-shaped sharpener with base for standing on table or desk is autographed by Jackie Robinson, the baseball star."[11]

In 1948, Ruth's book noted a difference. "At the start of my baseball career kids weren't autograph hunters to the degree they are now."[12] In addition to the market value, some expert had to authenticate its condition, the rules for grading now reaching 3,270 words. Value and condition noted, accessories to store and protect the autograph had to be manufactured, and publications listing prices had to be published. "Before autographs became a commodity, in the sixties and seventies, a lot of great stars simply signed whatever was put in their hands or sent to them in the mail. Babe Ruth was famous for promiscuous signing (even through the actual work was done by a clubhouse man or an accommodating sportswriter)."[13]

But like many things associated with Babe Ruth, Incorporated, money began to flow. It reached the hands of those who had kept their Ruth-signed baseballs. It reached the appraisers, the certifiers, and the auctioneers.

The first *New York Times* piece on memorabilia appeared in February of 1974. This dating matches the rise in baseball nostalgia in all of its forms—books, movies, uniforms, caps, even stadia. For autographs, *Total Baseball* places the date more exactly, writing, "the first meaningful hobby publication and price guide devoted to autographs was probably the *1982 Sport Americana Baseball Memorabilia and Autograph Price Guide.* Once baseball card companies, like Topps, choose to label their products as part of the "collectible picture card market," buyers ought to have been alerted.

Just as autographs like Ruth's began to be priced, there came a similar frenzy for anything baseball connected. *Sports Collectors Digest's* first issue appeared in 1981. When the baseball objects took off in popularity, the first *Beckett Baseball Card Monthly*, a pricing guide, was published in November 1984, with a 10,000-copy print run. It quickly became *the* reference source for card collectors, and in 2010 recorded a paid circulation of more than 725,000. Beckett.com offers collectors instant access to more than 27 million sports memorabilia items from close to 140 hobby shops worldwide, with a Beckett online baseball price guide 12-month subscription costing $81.00.

At the height of the card frenzy, as Dave Jamieson recounts, a card dealer was murdered for his wares and a major league umpire, Bob Engel, stole 4,180 baseball cards, a 1990 theft that cost him his job when he pleaded no contest.[14] With a Ruth baseball ball selling in 1998 for $126,500, Ruth's collecting value would reach seven figures. (The sale was conducted by one auction house and the purchase was by another auction house. There are now no fewer than 13 major auction companies selling sport-related items.) In 1999, the most famous of all sports collections went to auction, Barry Halper's, and there a lock of Babe Ruth's hair was sold for $38,187.50. After that sale, the auctioning of any Babe Ruth items—and the profits from the sale—should not have been surprising.

These baseball-connected objects have become so "collectible" that offered for sale are mud, grass and broken bats. Now, of course, you can buy the mud used to rub new baseballs. For sale is "Yankee Grass" sold by the company that installs the sod, though not actually sod from the field. By 1982, Gaylord Perry changed baseball caps each inning while pitching his 300th career victory and later autographed and sold each cap. The Smithsonian shop will sell you a Demolished Ballparks Tie for $45.00.

Baseball fans, or collecting fans, even like to boast of the number of baseball parks they have paid their way into. Baseballs hit into the stands in those stadia have become so valuable that more than once, a father with his baby in his arms has reached up to catch a ball. "Buying a game-used, broken bat with Pete Rose's name on it almost ensures that it is a bat that Pete actually used."[15]

To demonstrate the financial aspect of collecting, the 33rd annual National Sports Collectors Convention was held in 2012 and played "host to over 600 dealers and distributors, 50 Corporate Displays in 350,000+ square feet of convention show floor exhibit space at the Baltimore Convention Center." First organized in 1980, the show often hires tens of athletes who will be paid to attend and sell items that they sign. "The *Baltimore Business Journal* ranked The National as the show with the highest economic impact for the city in 2010. The estimated impact of $15.48 million surpassed the second-ranked convention by nearly $4 million."[16] By 2014, more than 43,000 people attended.

Though collecting baseball memorabilia is still flourishing, baseball card collecting is not. Greed killed it. "In the 1980s, the mainstream financial press—like the *Wall Street Journal* and the *New York Times*—started hyping baseball cards, comparing them to stocks and bonds." Seeing cards as an investment, people began buying cards by the case, not by the pack. Card companies, "at the height of their popularity in the early 1990s, produced an estimated 81 billion baseball cards a year."[17] Diminished by the overproduction, the industry survived even through its 1994 crash, a year when 350 sets were manufactured. One company, Donruss, for example, trying new approaches, included swatches of the 1925 Babe Ruth uniform in one of its 2004 baseball card sets. The company had purchased the jersey for $264,000. There is no information on who profited from this, other than Donruss, the seller and his agent.

But Donruss and the others except Topps are no longer sanctioned by Major League Baseball. Nevertheless, some baseball card collectors can look back and forward at the same time. One blogger wrote, "I chronicled the rise of baseball cards from advertising tools—for a sporting goods company, for tobacco products and for bubble gum—to a billion dollar industry that crashed in the mid-nineties…. The baseball card takes me back to the fifties, an age of innocence…. Baseball cards will always hold … memories."[18]

The irresistibility of baseball nostalgia makes one wonder how much might be asked for the gladioli stolen from the flowers on Ruth's coffin as it was taken into the cemetery vault in Westchester on August 19, 1948.

Afterword:
The Selling of Nostalgia

Baseball nostalgicists assume there was a period in baseball history ... when baseball players played for ... almost anything except for money, when owners owned franchises for ... almost anything except financial profit, when spectators could ... count on teams staying in their city decade after decade.[1]

In one of Babe Ruth's last public appearances, certainly his last one in a ballpark, "Nostalgia dripped all over Yankee Stadium.... In impressively sentimental ceremonies ... eyes grew moist and.... There was a reverent hush when the Bambino ... strode hesitatingly to the microphone."[2]

The reverent hush was soon followed by the sound of moving vans taking teams out of the cities they had occupied for half a century. It is undeniable that five years after Ruth's death, major league baseball began to go through a series of changes that have lasted to the present day. Teams left behind empty stadia in St. Louis, Philadelphia, and Boston. In New York, both the Dodgers and the Giants left. Before long, the demolition began of the parks in those four cities and in Cincinnati and Pittsburgh as well. In another ten years, four more teams were added, and in 1969, both leagues split into two divisions and the League Championship was created. Major League Baseball's expansion of 1977 had ownership groups paying as much as $7 million ($15.7 million in 1991 dollars) to join, but the 1991 winners had to pay $95 million. The pitcher coming to bat in the American League vanished. The grass on a baseball field was disappearing, with plastic Astro-Turf installed at the Astrodome.

Clearly, since Ruth's death, his game of baseball had faded in American life. Where there were more than 400 minor league teams, there are now 180. Fewer and fewer children are enrolled in Little League. Ruth's name had faded too, home runs by then being so common in the sport. There had been stars, of course, since Ruth in baseball, but no one had been able to match his star power, his fame, or his marketability and therefore his ubiquity.

Selling power always depends on the product itself and how an item or service is marketed. If an advertiser can merely suggest that the purchase of his goods will evoke in the consumer a feeling or a set of feelings, the product is likely to succeed in the marketplace. History can be sold, though an abstract, if attached in some way to an object. Commemorative coins, plates, class rings, plaques and the like are examples.

But history with nostalgia attached? Then you can put up for sale many things, because nostalgia, for many, is irresistible. You might be able to sell dirt, cloth, and pasteboard. You can even convince customers to come to a building just because the building has been in the same place for a long time. Likewise, you can convince customers to come to a new building if the new building looks like an old building. A person cannot reminisce about, and long for, events during a time when he was not alive. But much of nostalgia is an imagined, and positive, past anyway, and it allows you to feel that if you had been alive back then, why you surely would have gone to that particular game or watched that particular player at his job. When buyers are devoted to the objects of the past, it suggests a kind of religious feeling.

Much like the words of Arthur Daley on Ruth's last day ("Nostalgia dripped all over Yankee Stadium"), the religion of baseball nostalgia is best articulated through the words of the James Earl Jones character in *Field of Dreams*, the character who promises that through baseball "the memories will be so thick, they'll have to brush them away from their faces." All those memories will be happy ones, the kind of imagined history that is declared to be "a part of our past, Ray. It reminds us of all that once was good, and it could be again." This idea is called "nostalgia," the belief that only in the some glorious part of the past lies the key to making another golden age in the present. The remembered past becomes the past unconsciously stripped of cynicism, greed, and voraciousness. In the dreamlike book for *Field of Dreams*, a novel (not a polemic) called *Shoeless Joe*, W. P. Kinsella has the J.D. Salinger character call the feeling a "longing for the gentility of the past."

In the rules of logic, such a false belief has been named an appeal to tradition. Tradition is an argument from authority that proposes that the world (or a car or a game) was beautiful once, and if we revive that splendor by repeating those beautiful moments, by possessing once more all those marvelous things, or their reproductions, we can remake in our time those earlier times so often labeled a golden age. One way, then, to recreate the time is to imagine that at least one part of the golden age can come again. For *Field of Dreams*, we ought to begin with baseball, a game so wonderful that even greedy and crooked men loved the game, and broken families reunite with an unhurried and graceful game of catch. The 112th Congress had faith: "Baseball has mirrored our Nation's history since the Civil War, and is now an integral part of our Nation's heritage."

But how does that work? The past lies golden, its grandeur just out of reach, yet ways might be found to possess some part of it, wiping out for a time the ugliness of the present. You would be willing to spend a little money for that loveliness, wouldn't you?

Books about baseball, starting with 1966's *The Glory of their Times*, took readers back as far as 1899. That book was followed by the first of the scholarly baseball books by Harold Seymour. *Baseball: The Early Years,* published in 1970, discussed baseball from even decades earlier than the 1966 book. Lastly in this non-fiction progression was baseball from the sport from 30 to 50 years before 1970 with its nostalgic title, *Baseball When the Grass Was Real.* Others would soon follow.

These books sold well, and the sound of the cash register was heard throughout the land of baseball. Other writers picked up the notion, and within the space of a few years the country was reading *Shoeless Joe* and lining up to watch its movie version, *Field of Dreams*. Movies about much earlier baseball proliferated—*The Natural,* with a Babe Ruth figure in it, *Bull Durham*, and movies with children playing baseball such as the *Sandlot* franchise and the *Bad News Bears* franchises.

Something was afoot. It was not history; it was history as it ought to have been. It was nostalgia. History does not sell, but nostalgia does. So began the commodification of this feeling of longing, and soon scholarly papers appeared, "investigating the history of nostalgia from the origin of the concept to its contemporary use as a buying motive in consumption behavior."[3] It took some time for the various baseball corporations at the team and national level to understand the phenomenon, but they soon cashed in.

The selling of nostalgia in baseball began with baseball cards, first as a way to remember a fan's favorite players and then changed to a way to strike it rich. A man in middle age might seek out baseball cards from his youth. Influential to the examination of nostalgia is a 1979 book by Fred Davis titled *Yearning for Yesterday: A Sociology of Nostalgia*. Its appearance coincided with the rise of interest in profits to be made from baseball memorabilia.

Within five years of Davis' book, three publications marked what presumably began as a hobby. *Sports Collectors Digest* was first issued in 1981, followed by 1982's *Sport Americana Baseball Memorabilia and Autograph Price Guide*. As the baseball objects took off in popularity, the first *Beckett Baseball Card Monthly*, a pricing guide, was published in November 1984. Prices were beginning to be calculated. Before very long, there would be baseball card shows in shopping malls, a small-time and inefficient way of doing business.

Early in this process, 1980, a group of collectors organized the First National Sports Collectors Convention, an assemblage that in 2014 was predicted to draw 40,000 to 50,000 attendees over five days. At this convention, players from earlier eras were hired to sit at a table and, for a fee, sign objects—bats, balls, baseball cards, piece of paper—brought to them. In the *New York Times* story from 1989, we learn that

> Through appearances at trading-card and memorabilia shows to sign autographs, an activity that earns them from $3,500 to $15,000 an afternoon.... The nostalgia craze has helped revive the market in such past players as Harmon Killebrew and Brooks Robinson, who do about 25 memorabilia shows a year for about $2,500 apiece, more money by far than they earned when their careers started in the 1950s.[4]

This model of efficiency precluded waiting outside a ballpark or writing to a player, as it had been done. The efficiency level reached one billion dollars for the sale of memorabilia in 1989.

This model for the signed signatures, it was presumed, could be sold at a profit back in your hometown shop, sales not counted in the one billion. Bob Feller, a pitcher, who as a boy bought an autographed ball of Babe Ruth's, "believes this increased interest in the artifacts of the National Pastime" is "part of a national phenomenon. Cars and farm equipment and antiques. Maybe it's an island of security."[5]

Of course the signatures and other items had to be protected, so the manufacture of items made to contain and protect sports memorabilia had to be on display at the show as well. Companies began to act as rating services, giving each card a score, for a fee, based on its condition. Baseball cards supposedly had a profit built in because there were so few of them produced in the period from 1950 to 1985, and earlier.

In that period began what might be called predictive nostalgia. Here, a few players still in the majors who had performed at high levels might provide ways to earn cash. The purchase in 1990 of the rookie card of that player from, for example, 1980, could produce high profits, it was thought. The card would serve as an investment for future capital. Likewise, it became common in baseball card stores to see a ten-year-old spend $20 for a number of baseball card packs. On the spot, the cards would be searched through for a rookie card of a highly rated player who just might be a great success in the majors.

If found, the card would be immediately transferred to a protective plastic sleeve and inserted into a hard body plastic holder. The rest of the cards would be immediately trashed. But people began buying boxes of cards, then an entire set, and soon cards by the cases.

Soon there were 14 brands of cards. Each of the 14 was producing so many cards in each set that the industry refused to disclose how many they printed. There were even reprints of earlier baseball cards with a price assigned to each. One company produced more than 700 cards in 1990.

With all the cards manufactured after 1985, the prices dropped, and hundreds of people with thousands and thousands of cards all sleeved and wrapped had nowhere to sell them. Anyway, the price in a Beckett guide only meant that the price quoted would be the very best price you could expect to receive for you card, and likely you might get half if you could find a buyer. Just as history can be twisted into nostalgia for sale, a hobby can be twisted into an investment.

A person's affection for baseball, their good kind of baseball, can be displayed. Baseball caps have been produced by the New Era company for major league teams since 1934, but for fans an official on-field cap of a major league baseball team could be bought only at the stadium the team played in or at a single store in Cooperstown, New York, called Wood's. Not until 1978—a time again during the rise in baseball nostalgia—could you buy them elsewhere. You can now buy Negro Leagues caps with team logos from the 1930s, you can buy uniform shirts for $200–300 dollars, and jackets for $100 and more. For sale are officially licensed uniforms from earlier years; to make sure the money flowed freely, the Milwaukee team wore ten different jerseys during the 2013 season. Looking for a profit, "A uniform collector ... bought the Atlanta Braves' entire collection of 1987 home and road uniforms ... because they contained a new logo—a tomahawk, which had been missing since the team moved from Milwaukee in 1966."[6]

The caps, the jerseys and the jackets need licenses through a company founded just before the rush of nostalgia, a company founded in 1966 named Major League Baseball Promotion Corporation, a company clearly established right on time. Now named Major League Baseball Properties, Inc. it is the owner of the licenses for all aspects of anything that uses the logo of that corporation, which own the rights to call the clothing official. In a lawsuit named "John Chen, et al., v. Major League Baseball, et al" from 2013, the corporation was shown to amass annual revenues of about $7 billion.

While you may be able purchase an "official" 1934 St. Louis Cardinals baseball cap, what about seeing former players play the game as they had in the past, sort of? The Cracker Jack Company, seeing the nostalgia movement as it gained speed, sponsored the Old-Timers' Classic Game, played from 1982–1985, the kind of game which would appear, and had appeared before only with the Yankees, in other places "during an era in which the marketing of sports memories has become a growth industry."[7]

But those games were once a year and happened rarely. A former player invented a way to play with former players, an idea now called a fantasy camp. In 1981, retired major league catcher Randy Hundley put a camp together with cash customers, but before long major league teams were running them. By now, every team has one, and each league has a Dominican Republic All-Star Fantasy Camp. The Yankees have three scheduled fantasy camps in either November or January, lasting one week for the price of $4,950. There are also camps for women and one for fathers and sons together. The camps are responsible for bringing in close to $20 million.

Is there yet another technique to attract business by playing the nostalgia card? Certain ballparks have put up statues from their past: Baltimore has six, San Francisco four, the Pirates five, Minnesota seven, with the total is above 70. There is also a "Walk of Fame" and/or a "Ring of Honor" in many ball parks. The park for the Texas Rangers had principles for its Hall of Fame: a minimum of four years in a Texas Rangers uniform.

If major league baseball seemed somehow spoiled after cocaine problems in the 1980s, you could turn your back on the modern game and take part in Town Ball. Town Ball was a United States game from the early 1800s. "Often referred to as 'The Massachusetts Game,' it is still played by the Leatherstocking Base Ball Club every Sunday in Cooperstown, New York since at least 1992."[8] Town Ball is considered a stepping stone towards modern baseball. Playing the sport as it was contested in 1845 is a group formed in 1996 named The National Vintage Base Ball Association, which demands not only that the rules of 1845 apply but so do the uniforms.

Again, in the same time period as the cocaine scandal among Pittsburgh players, another book appeared: *Green Cathedrals*, in 1986. Published by a baseball statistical group, the book described itself as a book of "all things ballparks," including facts and factoids, dimensions and capacities, locations, occupants, names and nicknames." Interest arose in the older baseball parks, now rubble. At the same time, ballparks being used were showing their age. Could nostalgia, and the growing interest in all things baseball, be used by team owners and the city of South Bend? The Midwest minor League sought new cities, and the Indiana locality applied. Winning a place in the league, it was decided to hire HOK architects to build Stanley Coveleski Regional Stadium in 1987 for $11 million. The place, renamed now, is judged to be "an early rendition of the standard template that has been used by nearly every new ballpark built since 1990."

Again in the middle 1980s, the movie *The Natural* was looking for a park to film its playing scenes, scenes set in the 1930s. They chose Buffalo, New York's War Memorial Stadium, since it had been erected between 1935 and 1937. Studies have been completed concerning the effect of attendance on a new stadium, and it was found that "the attendance 'honeymoon' effect of a new stadium … increases attendance by 32 percent to 37 percent the opening year of a new stadium, [but remains high] 6 to 10 seasons at newer ballparks."[9]

The Buffalo Bisons came to town when Buffalo ownership interests purchased the Jersey City A's of the Double-A Eastern League and moved the team. They commissioned a ballpark both revolutionary (for its time) and nostalgic. Revolutionary because baseball parks had moved to the suburbs, to customers with cash. But for opening day 1988, what opened was a rendition of what is now called a "retro" ballpark, that is one that resembles a park from the past through the use of red brick and exposed steel as the look of the park, while setting the location in the middle of downtown. A light rail system, not unlike the trolley lines that brought fans to the parks in the first four decades of the twentieth century, brought fans in Buffalo to the new field. The field itself earned raves. The stadium included a full-menu restaurant, from which batting practice and the game might be viewed, a team store, and inside, specialty concessions and what was then a massive, modern scoreboard. To underscore the nostalgia, 19,500 paid to be at Pilot Field on June 21, 1988, to see the National Old Timers Baseball Classic.

Did a nostalgic attitude toward the sport pay off? Even before the season ended, Buffalo's park passed the all-time minor league baseball record for tickets sold. By season's end, they outdrew three major league teams.

In addition, the field sold its naming rights to a corporation, to Pilot Air Freight. All of these decisions about the park found the Buffalo franchise valued at $26 million, with a revenue of $7.5 million. The building craze began. In the next 11 years, 55 stadiums or arenas were remolded or built in the United States: total cost, $8.7 billion. The adage, "You have to spend money to make money," seems to be in play here. But the costs were spread around.

Of the $8.7 billion in direct costs, about 57 percent—around $5 billion—was financed with taxpayer money. Between $14 billion and $16 billion is expected to be spent on these post–1999 stadiums and arenas, with somewhere between $9 billion and $11 billion of this amount coming from public coffers."[10]

At least seven major league parks have been built in the retro style, as well as 23 new minor league facilities. Localities have insisted that there be separate football and baseball fields. For purity? Well, so long as taxpayers are putting up a majority of the money.

The earliest retro park in the major leagues was Camden Yards in Baltimore. Built with money from the Maryland Stadium Authority, from 1992 through 2009 the Orioles' average rent was about $4.5 million. What does Baltimore, what does Maryland, get from the building of this stadium? Steve Kilar's report states,

> Rent for the park equals 7 percent of net admissions revenues plus $5,000 for each special ... played at Camden Yards. On top of this base is added: less than 10 percent of concessions, 50 percent of the Orioles' parking receipts, 25 percent of the advertising revenues and 7-to-10 percent of suite and club-level admissions. Who gets the rest? The Baltimore Orioles. Ah, nostalgia.[11]

But more than anything else, the center of baseball nostalgia that generated so much income for so many—with Ruth's items at the very top of the list—has been the Baseball Hall of Fame, a "tourist destination" that helped create and capitalize on the way baseball is thought about. As with many other aspects of the baseball game, the Hall is not a mere museum. How can it be? It believes, "Baseball was, and is, an inseparable part of America, the American identity, and the American spirit is undeniable."[12] The Hall prides itself on "housing the stories honoring the greats of baseball's past." The past remains the focus of the Hall, and its version of the past uses words such as referring to ballparks as "America's cathedrals" and claims that visitors on a "pilgrimage" come to Cooperstown to "pay homage" to "America's Pastime" in an "unspoiled" place in upstate New York. There are only two-lane roads that lead to Cooperstown, and if you want a Big Mac, you'll have to leave the streets of the village itself and drive four and a half miles, where you can also find a Best Western motel.

The Hall of Fame lately has continued its focus on nostalgia with an event called the Hall of Fame Classic (since 2009) funded by assistance from Major League Baseball.

A carefully crafted message, as you might expect, the Hall by and large shows limited interest in the negative aspects of the history of baseball. That approach has worked well—revenue reached more than $20 million in 2007. The National Baseball Hall of Fame and Museum at Cooperstown, New York, still draws visitors to celebrate the past as it is sold to them within the walls of the building, sold in the stores surrounding Doubleday Field, sold in the many memorabilia shops, sold even in the way the village steadfastly remains a hamlet. But "Unlike any other sport, its core appeal is sentimental—and strong enough to withstand labor disputes, the designated hitter, or even years of steroid revelations."[13] In place of ugliness, or veracity, the Hall sells the idyllic past that nostalgia has always stood for. Here the past is "sacred" because for the Hall, a big part of the holiness is the hallowed relationship formed between fathers and sons, a bond that baseball alone can sustain down the generations. As the book *Cooperstown to Dyersville: a Geography of Baseball Nostalgia*, observes, during that period when nostalgia first began to take hold in America, the Hall "explicitly attempt[ed] ... to sell the museum and shrine as the experiential locus of masculine emotionality and family relationships."[14]

To gauge the power of Cooperstown for some people, the baseball park in the village, a facility amateur teams book for games, is still called Doubleday Field. (Booking the field can bring the village as much as a quarter of a million dollars in fees each year.) It is partly the job of the manager of the field to see to it that after the games, players do not succeed in their attempts to scoop up dirt from the field into jars to take home.

And this idea brings us back to *Shoeless Joe* and *Field of Dreams*. Why will people come to a baseball field? In the novel, the Salinger character says, "I don't have to tell you that the one constant through all the years has been baseball." Setting aside the clearly nonsensical statement, it is a premise that begins with the familiar "Everybody knows" argument. You cannot dispute the premise because no proof is offered: it is true because I say so.

Moreover, the movie does not just end with a father and a son reuniting and connecting. As that pitch and catch game goes on, we are shown the masses of headlights of cars driving on a narrow country road in a beautiful dusk toward that corn field in Iowa. (In the same way, cars must drive on two-lane roads past dairy farms and lakes to Cooperstown to "pay homage" to "America's Pastime" in an "unspoiled" place of memories and dreams.)

And as the movie camera pulls up to show how many cars there are, we remember that each person in each car that will have to pay $20 to get to the field.

Appendix I:
Marketing Ruth

So durable is Ruth's celebrity, a celebrity with "powerful, mythic and mischievous appeal," that at the 100th anniversary of his birth and up to the present day, companies that manage the Ruth name and companies that attach Ruth's name, image or autograph to any number of objects or advertisements continue to believe that Ruth can make them money, or at least draw attention to them.

Ruth the brand continues to make money for others to this very day, when his items go up for auction. Clearly the seller will profit from the sale, since the prices paid for Ruth pieces keep rising. But then too, the auction house takes a percent from the seller to process the piece and a fee from the buyer to cover the transaction and advertising. Someone places the advertising, someone prints the catalog of items to be sold, and someone is paid to prepare the item for display at auction time or to be photographed.

It seems that Ruth has also continued to provide income for his relatives through licensing agreements. Since Ruth's second wife, Claire, lived for 28 years after Ruth, the arithmetic looks to show that much of Ruth's estate was gone long before the value of Ruth's name, image and memorabilia began to rise.

Ruth's daughters registered the words Babe Ruth as a trademark with the Curtis Management Group—"the worldwide leader in intellectual property rights management"—which took care of the trademark through, some years ago, deals with more than 90 companies, and so Ruth became a kind of salesman for Coca-Cola, Delta Airlines, and Owens-Corning. CMG was not very forthcoming about their business, but apparently they required a 60 percent commission from their end. It is also known that in 2003, more than 200 firms sold Ruth-associated products ranging from ceramic beer steins to iced tea that generated $50 million in annual sales. Over the years, these products have included the Official Babe Ruth Wrist Watch, packed in a plastic baseball, a commemorative medal, a die cast truck, a bottle of Red Rock Cola, a "100th anniversary two pin set," a gold shirt, a director's chair, and a "classic collector's tankard."

Apparently, now the Luminary Group of Indianapolis is the business representative for the family of Babe Ruth and the Babe Ruth League, to work with companies who wish to use the name or likeness of Babe Ruth in any commercial fashion. His name, image, words, signature, and voice are protectable property rights owned by the family and the league. Luminary writes that "Any use of the above, without express written consent of the Babe Ruth family and the Babe Ruth League is strictly prohibited."

How much money goes to the Babe Ruth League is unclear. How large a percentage of sales will go to them when the last daughter dies is also unknown.

The makers of these Ruth-themed items are clearly not concerned with Ruth's stature, only his money-making possibilities. There was even something for academics at "a two-day conference ... to study Ruth's impact on everything from law and poetry to the women's movement and international relations—along with baseball, of course."

The conference would, of course, make a profit for Hofstra University, the meeting's site, by renting out the spaces for the talks and the "26 panel discussions" in addition to whatever popular and scholarly credit might accrue to the university. Then too, like any other gathering of faculty, these days would add to the academics' reputation, speed their movement toward promotion and corresponding raises. It was also a chance for authors to publicize and sell their books, for publishers to display their Ruth-related wares, and for booksellers and video sellers to ring up some sales.

Appendix II:
Sales of Various Ruth Relics,
1929 to Present

The Ruth family, on his death in 1948, donated "his collection of baseball mementoes and trophies valued at $1,175" to the Baseball Hall of Fame.

July 5, 1929—$50—Ball signed by Ruth and other members of the Yankees

July 13, 1934—$20—baseball when Babe Ruth hit his 700th home run, on July 13, 1934

July 31, 1978—$300—A baseball signed by Babe Ruth and Lou Gehrig

August 16, 1981—$400—signed photographs of Babe Ruth

Four-figure sales—first amount asked; second dollar amount is price paid:

1915 Boston Red Sox "Photographic" Scorecard with Babe Ruth $200.00 $1,066.50

1915 Boston Red Sox World Series Program $500.00 $2,251.50

1915 Boston Red Sox World Champions Leather $500.00 $1,185.00

1922 Neilson's Chocolate Canada Collection Including Babe Ruth $2,000.00 $6,517.50

1924 Babe Ruth Barnstorming Photo $300.00 $1,659.00

1928 George Ruth Candy Co. Near-Complete Set $300.00 $2,666.25

1929 Rogers Peet #48 Babe Ruth NYC Clothing store $300.00 $1,185.00

1932 R328 U.S. Caramel #32 Babe Ruth $300.00 $2,251.50

1933 Babe Ruth Feen-A-Mint (Laxative gum) $1,000.00 $2,370.00

1933 Worch Cigar Babe Ruth SGC EX 60 $1,000.00 $3,555.00

1938 Babe Ruth Signed Check $1,000.00 $3,555.00

1947 Babe Ruth autographed song sheet for the Song "Babe" $1,000.00 $6,517.50

1934 Babe Ruth Spalding "Home Run Special" Ball $300.00 $1,540.50

1988 Babe Ruth's brass locker tag from Yankee Stadium $7,150

2018 Babe Ruth's Personal Monogrammed Hand Mirror $300.00 $2,370.00

Five to seven-figure sales:

May 4, 1992—$200,000—60th home run baseball

April 1994—$63,000—56th home run in 1921

September 22, 1996—$14,930—ink handprint of Babe Ruth

June 15, 1997—$35,000—Ruth cap bought by Yankees pitcher David Wells

December 9, 1998—$110,000—ball Babe Ruth hit in the first Yankee Stadium home run

2005—$771,000—complete uniform worn by Babe Ruth in a 1934 Japan barnstorming tour

June 2005—Ruth's "called shot" jersey, from the Yankees' World Series against the Cubs, was sold for $940,000

July 14, 2008—$327,750—hat Ruth wore

July 14, 2008—$195,500—signed bat from 1924

November 22, 2008—Topps—Babe Ruth's and Lou Gehrig's uniforms were bought at auction—"Mr. Ruth's pants cost $90,000 and Mr. Gehrig's $60,000—and will be sliced into tiny pieces and embedded into cards."

November 13, 2010—$996,000—1919 Babe Ruth 1919 Contract with Red Sox

November 14, 1998—$1,265,000—1923 Babe Ruth Bat from First Yankee Stadium Home Run November 11, 2012—$253,000—1924 Babe Ruth autographed professional model baseball bat

December 2, 2004—$537,278—1934 David Wells' 1934 Babe Ruth Cap

December 2, 2004—$1,265,000—Historic Babe Ruth Bat For A Record

June 10, 2005—$996,000—contract sending Ruth from Red Sox to Yankees

July 13, 2008—$38,000—the hair of Babe Ruth

October 6, 2009—$537,750—1918 Babe Ruth 1918 World Series Bat

November 13, 2010—$264,500—home run number 702

May 20, 2012—$591,007—1924-1928 Babe Ruth vault marked bat sold for $591,007

May 20, 2012—$4,415,658–1920 Babe Ruth Jersey

May 21, 2012—$491,007—1927–1928 Ruth bat

November 11, 2012—$253,000—a 1924 Babe Ruth autographed professional model baseball bat

December 27, 2012—$415,000—A bat believed to be ordered by Babe Ruth in July of 1920

November 29, 2013—$517,000–1914 Babe Ruth Baseball Card

June 21, 2013—$130,350—Babe Ruth Rookie asked was $10,000

2013—$26,662.50—1915 Boston Red Sox Real-Photo Team Postcard

February 8, 2014—$250,000—the baseball Ruth signed for Johnny Sylvester

February 23, 2014—$717,000—Babe Ruth's 1923 World Series pocket watch

May 18, 2014—$650,108—Ruth's pocket watch from the 25th anniversary celebration

July 7, 2014—$90,000—Babe Ruth's Game-Used Pants

July 14, 2014—$$1,020,000—Babe Ruth's contract with the Boston Red Sox in 1918

July 14, 2014—$215,000—bat from his early career

July 14, 2014—$96,000—a signed ball

July 21, 2014—$151,250, one of the original three promissory notes given to Frazee in payment for Babe Ruth's contract, "Note of $25,000, due November 1st, 1921, made by the American League Base Ball Club of New York in favor of the Boston American League Base Ball Club."

November 2014—Babe Ruth's 1934 contract for $278,300, and a Ruth game-used bat for $181,500

December 19, 2014—a 1914 Babe Ruth rookie baseball card for $695,000.

2015—$204,000–1916 Babe Ruth baseball card

January 9, 2016—from the official Lelands' website: "The formidable Hillerich and Bradsby model weighs in at nearly 40 ounces (39.7 to be exact) and is 35 inches long. From later in The Bambino's unprecedented career circa 1930 and '31 when he was in his mid–30s, the bat is accentuated by the "George 'Babe' Ruth" branded on the barrel in script lettering. The final price realized in the auction? A cool $70,443.67."

Appendix III:
Ruth's Complete Barnstorming Stops in the Continental U.S. and Canada

The sources for these, with very few exceptions, are the newspapers from the places he visited. Very few of these games had to be shortened or canceled. In some cases, Ruth came back later in the same year to play the rainouts. There are notable instances when Ruth stole bases, including home.

Date	City	Population
Oct. 17, 1915	Baltimore, MD	
Oct. 24, 1915	Baltimore, MD	735,000
Oct. 15, 1916	New Haven, CT	160,000
Oct. 17, 1916	Laconia, NH	10,000
Oct. 4, 1917	Fenway Park, MA	
Oct. 7, 1917	Woonsocket, RI	44,000
Sept. 14, 1918	New Haven, CT	160,000
Sept. 15, 1918	Hartford, CT	138,000
Sept. 22, 1918	Springfield, MA	128,000
Sept. 23, 1918	Hartford, CT	138,000
Sept. 28, 1918	Lebanon, PA	25,000
Sept. 30, 1918	Reading, PA	110,000
Nov. 10, 1918	Baltimore, MD	735,000
Sept. 28, 1919	Hartford, CT	138,000
Sept. 29, 1919	Baltimore, MD	735,000
Sept. 30, 1919	Portland, ME	70,000
Oct. 1, 1919	Sanford, ME	
Oct. 3, 1919	Lynn, MA	100,000
Oct. 4, 1919	Attleboro, MA	20,000
Oct. 5, 1919	Rutland, VT	15,000
Oct. 10, 1919	Beverly, MA	22,000
Oct. 11, 1919	Troy, NY	73,000
Oct. 13, 1919	Ebbets Field, NY	
Oct. 17, 1919	Scranton, PA	140,000
Nov. 1, 1919	Los Angeles, CA	580,000
Nov. 2, 1919	Los Angeles, CA	580,000

Date	City	Population
Nov. 8, 1919	San Francisco, CA	510,000
Nov. 9, 1919	Oakland, CA (a.m.)	220,000
Nov. 9, 1919	San Francisco (p.m.)	510,000
Nov. 11, 1919	Sacramento, CA	70,000
Dec. 21, 1919	Los Angeles, CA	577,000
Dec. 28, 1919	San Diego, CA	74,000
Jan. 18, 1920	San Diego, CA	74,000
Oct. 1, 1920	Springfield, MA	128,000
Oct. 2, 1920	Bristol, CT	20,000
Oct. 3, 1920	Bronx, NY	732,000
Oct. 4, 1920	Bacharach Giants, NY	
Oct. 5, 1920	Dover, DE	4,000
Oct. 7, 1920	Philadelphia, PA	1,824,000
Oct. 8, 1920	Philadelphia, PA	1,824,000
Oct. 10, 1920	Bronx, NY	732,000
Oct. 13, 1920	Buffalo, NY	510,000
Oct. 14, 1920	Rochester, NY	300,000
Oct. 15, 1920	Oneonta, NY	12,000
Oct. 16, 1920	Jersey City, NJ	300,000
Oct. 17, 1920	Bronx, NY	732,000
Oct. 18, 1920	Medina, NY	6,000
Oct. 19, 1920	Syracuse, NY	130
Oct. 22, 1920	Johnson City, NY	8,500
Oct. 24, 1920	Buffalo, NY	507,000
Oct. 26, 1920	Dover, NJ	10,000
Oct. 20, 1920	Trenton, NJ	120,000
Oct. 17?, 1920	Rochester, NY	300,000
Oct. 30, 1920	Havana, Cuba	720,000
Oct. 16, 1921	Buffalo, NY	510,000
Oct. 17, 1921	Elmira, NY	46,000
Oct. 18, 1921	Jamestown, NY	35,000
Oct. 19, 1921	Warren, PA	15,000
Oct. 20, 1921	Hornell, NY	16,000
Oct. 21, 1921	Scranton, PA	140,000
Oct. 13, 1922	Perry, IA	57,000
Oct. 14, 1922	Lincoln, NE	56,000
Oct. 15, 1922	Omaha, NE	192,000
Oct. 16, 1922	Sleepy Eye, MN	2,500
Oct. 16, 1922	Sioux Falls, SD	26,000
Oct. 17, 1922	Denver, CO	257,000
Oct. 18, 1922	Sioux City, IA	73,000
Oct. 19, 1922	Deadwood, SD	2,500
Oct. 20, 1922	Scottsbluff, NE	7,000
Oct. 21, 1922	Tarkio, MO	1,500
Oct. 22, 1922	Kansas City, MO	325,000
Oct. 23, 1922	Leavenworth, KS	17,000
Oct. 24, 1922	Bartlesville, OK	15,000
Oct. 25, 1922	Drumright, OK	6,500
Oct. 26, 1922	Fort Scott, KS	11,000
Oct. 27, 1922	Pratt, KS	52,000
Oct. 28, 1922	Pueblo, CO	43,000

Date	City	Population
Oct. 29, 1922	Denver, CO	257,000
Oct. 30, 1922	Albuquerque, NM	450
Oct. 18, 1923	Hornell, NY	15,000
Oct. 19, 1923	Elmira, NY	46,000
Oct. 20, 1923	Olean, NY	21,000
Oct. 21, 1923	Brooklyn's Saints, NY	
Oct. 22, 1923	Hazleton, PA	33,000
Oct. 23, 1923	Shenandoah, PA (cancelled; rain)	30,000
Oct. 23, 1923	Polo Grounds, NY	
Oct. 24, 1923	Shamokin, PA (cancelled; rain)	21,000
Oct. 25, 1923	Scranton, PA	140,000
Oct. 26, 1923	Mahanoy City, PA	16,000
Oct. 27?, 1923	Oil City, PA	22,000
Oct. 28, 1923	Erie, PA	95,000
Oct. 29, 1923	Larksville, PA	9,000
Oct. 31, 1923	Williamsport, PA	38,000
Nov. 1, 1923	Shamokin, PA	22,000
Nov. 4, 1923	Ruth at Bushwicks, NY	
Nov. 9, 1923	Riverhead, NY	
Oct. 1, 1924	Springfield, MA	129,000
Oct. 2, 1924	Hartford, CT	138,000
Oct. 3, 1924	Altoona, PA	62,000
Oct. 13, 1924	Kansas City, MO	325,000
Oct. 14, 1924	Minneapolis, MN	400,000
Oct. 17, 1924	Spokane, WA	105,000
Oct. 18, 1924	Tacoma, WA	98,000
Oct. 19, 1924	Seattle, WA	317,000
Oct. 21, 1924	Portland, OR	260,000
Oct. 22, 1924	Dunsmuir, CA	2,600
Oct. 23, 1924	Stockton, CA	42,000
Oct. 25, 1924	San Francisco, CA	510,000
Oct. 26, 1924	Oakland, CA	220,000
Oct. 26, 1924	San Francisco, CA	510,000
Oct. 27, 1924	Los Angeles, CA	580,000
Oct. 28, 1924	Santa Barbara, CA	20,000
Oct. 29, 1924	San Diego, CA	75,000
Oct. 29, 1924	Los Angeles, CA	580,000
Oct. 30, 1924	San Diego, CA	75,000
Oct. 31, 1924	Brea (Fullerton), CA	5,000
Oct. 5, 1925	Queens, NY	732,000
Oct. 11? 12, 1926	Bradley Beach, NJ	2,400
Oct. 12, 1926	Wilkes-Barre, PA	75,000
Oct. 13, 1926	Perth Amboy, NJ	42,000
Oct. 14, 1926	Olyphant, PA	10,000
Oct. 15, 1926	Lima, OH	42,000
Oct. 16, 1926	In Kingston, NY	27,000
Oct. 17, 1926	Montreal, QU	
Oct. 19, 1926	Portland, ME	75,000
Oct. 21, 1926	Atlantic Highlands, NJ	

Date	City	Population
Oct. 23, 1926	South Bend, IN	72,000
Oct. 24, 1926	South Bend, IN	72,000
Oct. 27, 1926	Des Moines, IA	128,000
Oct. 28, 1926	Iron Mountain, MI	8,500
Oct. 10, 1927	Providence, RI	250,000
Oct. 11, 1927	Trenton, NJ	120,000
Oct. 12, 1927	Dexter Park, NY	
Oct. 13, 1927	Asbury Park, NJ	13,000
Oct. 14, 1927	Lima, OH	42,000
Oct. 15, 1927	Kansas City, MO	325,000
Oct. 16, 1927	Omaha, NE	192,000
Oct. 17, 1927	Des Moines, IA	128,000
Oct. 18, 1927	Sioux City, IA	73,000
Oct. 19, 1927	Denver, CO	258,000
Oct. 22, 1927	San Francisco, CA	510,000
Oct. 23, 1927	Oakland, CA	220,000
Oct. 23, 1927	Oakland (Sun 9:30) & San Francisco, CA	730,000
Oct. 24, 1927	Stockton, CA (p.m.)	42,000
Oct. 25, 1927	Marysville, CA (a.m.)	5600
Oct. 25, 1927	Sacramento, CA	70,000
Oct. 26, 1927	San Jose, CA	70,000
Oct. 27, 1927	Santa Barbara, CA	20,000
Oct. 28, 1927	San Diego, CA	75,000
Oct. 29, 1927	Fresno, CA	46,000
Oct. 30, 1927	Los Angeles, CA	580,000
Oct. 31, 1927	Long Beach, CA (cancelled, rain)	57,000
Oct. 12, 1928	Bushwick, NY	
Oct. 13, 1928	Syracuse, NY (cancelled; rain)	172,000
Oct. 14, 1928	Montreal, QU	
Oct. 15, 1928	Hull, QU	10,000
Oct. 16, 1928	Buffalo, NY	510,000
Oct. 17, 1928	Elmira, NY	46,000
Oct. 18, 1928	Trenton, NJ	120,000
Oct. 20, 1928	Reading, PA	110,000
Oct. 21, 1928	Syracuse, NY	172,000
Oct. 22, 1928	Watertown, NY	32,000
Oct. 23, 1928	Columbus, OH	
Oct. 24, 1928	Louisville, KY	237,000
Oct. 25, 1928	Dayton, OH	154,000
Oct. 26, 1928	Flint, MI	92,000
Oct. 27, 1928	Battle Creek, MI	37,000
Oct. 28, 1928	Milwaukee, WI	458,000
Oct. 29, 1928	Des Moines, IA	128,000
Oct. 30, 1928	Sioux City, IA	73,000
Oct. 31, 1928	Denver, CO	258,000
Oct. 20, 1929	West New York, NJ	30,000
Oct. 27, 1929	South Orange, NJ	7,000
Oct. 13, 1930	Bushwicks, NY	

Date	City	Population
Oct. 18, 1930	Lindenhurst, NY	
Oct. 26, 1930	Bushwicks, NY	
Oct. 4, 1931	West New York, NJ	30,000
Oct. 13, 1931	Kansas City, MO	
	(cancelled; rain)	325,000
Oct. 14, 1931	Denver, CO	258,000
Oct. 18, 1931	Los Angeles, CA	580,000
Oct. 19, 1931	San Diego, CA	75,000
Oct. 20, 1931	LA Davies Clinic, CA	580,000
Oct. 21, 1931	Fresno, CA	46,000
Oct. 22, 1931	Oakland Stadium, CA	
	(cancelled; rain)	510,000
Oct. 23, 1931	Oakland, CA	220,000
Oct. 23, 1931	Seals' Stadium, CA	510,000
Oct. 24, 1931?	Sacramento, CA	70,000
Oct. 25, 1931	Oakland ball park, CA	
	(cancelled; rain)	220,000
Oct. 25, 1931	Seals' Stadium, CA	
	(cancelled; rain)	510,000
Oct. 26, 1931	Oakland ball park, CA	220,000
Oct. 27, 1931	Seals' Stadium, CA	510,000
Oct. 28, 1931	Seals' Stadium, CA	510,000
Oct. 29, 1931?	San Francisco, CA	510,000
Oct. 30, 1931	Ventura, CA (a.m.)	4,500
Oct. 31, 1931	Long Beach, CA (noon+)	56,000
Oct. 31, 1931	Los Angeles, CA (night)	580,000
Sept. 1, 1935	Minneapolis, MN	400,000
Sept. 29, 1935	Dyckman Oval, NY	
Oct. 13, 1935	Dexter Park, NY	
Oct. 21, 1935	Dexter Park, NY	

Chapter Notes

Preface

1. John Gross, "Books of the Times," *New York Times*, February 19, 1985.
2. Lisa Eisenberg, *The Story of Babe Ruth: Baseball's Greatest Star* (Milwaukee: Gareth Stevens, 1997), 34.
3. *Ibid.*, 91.

Introduction

1. John Thorn, *Baseball in the Garden of Eden* (New York: Simon & Schuster, 2011), xi.
2. "Babe Homered with Girls, Too," *Page Six*, April 27, 2007, http://pagesix.com/2007/08/12/babe-homered-with-girls-too/.
3. Blake Wilfong, Hooker Heroes." http://wondersmith.com/heroes/famous2.htm.
4. Plimpton, *The Norton Book of Sports* (New York: W.W. Norton, 1992), 382.
5. Mara Mather, et. al., "Amygdala Responses to Emotionally Valenced Stimuli in Older and Younger Adults," *Psychological Science* 15, no. 4 (April 2004): 259.
6. Jill Neimark, "The Diva of Disclosure, Memory Researcher Elizabeth Loftus," *Psychology Today* 29 (January 1996): 48–53.
7. Crepeau, *Baseball: America's Diamond Mind*, 94.

Chapter 1

1. Edward Woolley, "The Business of Baseball," *McClure's Magazine*, July 1912, 241.
2. Murray Schumach, "Babe Ruth, Baseball's Great Star and Idol of Children, Had a Career Both Dramatic and Bizarre," *New York Times*, August 17, 1948, 14.
3. Babe Ruth, *Babe Ruth's Own Book* (New York: A.L. Burt, 1928), 4.
4. Marshal Smelser, *The Life That Ruth Built: A Biography* (Lincoln: University of Nebraska Press, 1973), 5.
5. Babe Ruth, and Bob Considine, *The Babe Ruth Story* (New York: E.P. Dutton, 1948), 4.
6. Smelser, *Life That Ruth Built*, 26.
7. Allan Wood, *Babe Ruth and the 1918 Red Sox* (San Jose, CA: Writers Club Press, 2000), 57.
8. U.S. Commission on Industrial Relations, *Final Report and Testimony Submitted to Congress by the Commission on Industrial Relations*, 64th Congress, 1st Session, Senate Document No. 415, 1916, 771.
9. Stefan Szymanski and Andrew S. Zimbalis, *The National Pastime: How Americans Play Baseball and the Rest of the World Plays Soccer* (Washington, D.C.: Brookings Institution Press, 2005), 58.
10. Wood, *Babe Ruth and the 1918 Red Sox*, 67.
11. Schumach, "Babe Ruth, Baseball's Great Star and Idol of Children," 14.
12. "Baltimore Doesn't," *Baltimore Sun*, May 8, 1914.
13. Robert W. Creamer, "Ruth? He Is Still in the Spotlight, Still Going Strong," *Smithsonian*, February 1995, 68.
14. Creamer, *Babe: The Legend Comes to Life* (New York: Simon & Schuster, 1974), 91.
15. *Ibid.*, 98.
16. Roland Marchand, *Advertising the American Dream: Making Way for Modernity, 1920–1940* (Berkeley: University of California Press, 1985), 6.
17. National Collegiate Athletic Association, "Proceedings of the Annual Convention" (Chicago: 1913), 76.

Chapter 2

1. Creamer, *Babe*, 88.
2. Derks, 150.
3. *Bureau of Labor Statistics of the State of Missouri Annual Report*, Vol. 37.
4. K.S. Bartlett, "Johnny Igoe," *Daily Boston Globe*, April 17, 1935, B1.
5. *New London Day*, July 22, 1915.
6. *Pittsburgh Press*, October 07, 1915.

Chapter 3

1. Treasury Department United States Internal Revenue Statistics of Income, 31.
2. Wood, *Babe Ruth and the 1918 Red Sox*, 347.
3. Jonathan Frazier Light, *The Cultural Encyclopedia of Baseball* (Jefferson, NC: McFarland, 1997), 62.
4. *Fort Worth Star-Telegram*, October 9, 1916, 4.

Chapter 4

1. *St. Petersburg* (FL) *Evening Independent*, February 19, 1917.
2. Glenn Stout, *Fenway 1912: The Birth of a Ballpark, a Championship Season, and Fenway's Remarkable First Year* (Boston: Houghton Mifflin Harcourt, 2011), 339.
3. Harold Seymour and Dorothy Seymour Mills, *Baseball: The Golden Age* (New York: Oxford University Press, 1971), 188.
4. Stout, *Fenway*, 339.

Chapter 5

1. Robert F. Burk, *Never Just a Game: Players, Owners and American Baseball to 1920* (Chapel Hill: University of North Carolina Press, 1994), 83.
2. Seymour and Seymour Mills, *Baseball: The Golden Age*, 6.
3. *Ibid.*, 7.
4. Rod Dubey, *Indecent Acts in a Public Place: Sports, Insolence and Sedition* (Toronto: Charivari, 1990), 64.
5. David Wieneke, "The Boston Police Strike," Boston History and Architecture (website), http://www.iboston.org/mcp.php?pid=policeStrike.
6. Seymour and Seymour Mills, *Golden Age*, 169.
7. Gene Carney, *Burying the Black Sox: How Baseball's Cover-Up of the 1919 World Series Fix Almost Succeeded* (Washington, D.C.: Potomac, 2006), 150.
8. Ross Davies, "Along Comes the Players Association: The Roots and Rise of Organized Labor in Major League Baseball," *New York University Journal of Legislation and Public Policy* 16, no. 2 (2013): 334.
9. Seymour and Seymour Mills, *Baseball: The Golden Age*, 174.
10. Ross Davies, *Baseball Players*, entry for Summer 1923 (n.p.).
11. Robert F. Burk, *Much More Than a Game: Players, Owners and American Baseball Since 1921* (Chapel Hill: University of North Carolina Press, 2001), vii.

Chapter 6

1. Seymour and Seymour Mills, *Baseball: The Golden Age*, 253.
2. Burk, *Never Just a Game*, 244.
3. Wood, *Babe Ruth and the 1918 Red Sox*, 9.
4. *Ibid.*, 183.
5. *Ibid.*, 105.
6. *New York Times*, July 21, 1918, 24.
7. Wood, *Babe Ruth and the 1918 Red Sox*, 196.
8. Creamer, *Babe*, 52.
9. "Ruth Helps Red Sox to Drive Within One Victory of World's Baseball Title," *New York Times*, September 10, 1918, 10.
10. *Ibid.*
11. "1918 World Series," Worldseries.com, http://mlb.mlb.com/mlb/history/postseason/mlb_ws_recaps.jsp?feature=1918.

12. Associated Press, "World Series Ball Game Delayed by Strike of Players," *Cape Girardeau Southeast Missourian*, September 11, 1918, 6.
13. *New York Times*, September 25, 1918.
14. *Sporting News*, October 31, 1918, 4.
15. Bill Jenkinson, "The Great Debates," Personal Website of Bill Jenkins, http://billjenkinsonbaseball.webs.com/thegreatdebates.htm.
16. *Ibid.*
17. "Forging America: The History of Bethlehem Steel—Chapter 3," http://www.sun-sentinel.com/topic/all-bethsteel-c3p13,0,5559082.story.
18. Mike Drago, "Kelchner Honored as Baseball Pioneer," Reading Eagle, July 6, 2008, http://reading eagle.com/article.aspx?id=98039.
19. Charle DeMotte, *Bat, Ball and Bible: Baseball and Sunday Observance in New York* (Dulles, VA: Potomac, 2013), 219.
20. Creamer, *Babe*, 345.
21. Kal Wagenheim, *Babe Ruth; His Life and Legend* (New York: Praeger, 1974), 43.

Chapter 7

1. Smelser, *Life That Ruth Built*, 564.
2. Myron Lieberman, *Public Education: An Autopsy* (Cambridge, MA: Harvard University Press, 1993), 51.
3. Robert J. Taylor, and Susan Taylor, *The Aupha Manual of Health Services Management* (Gaithersburg, MD: Aspen, 1994), 213.
4. Associated Press, "The Red Sox Are Sold for Record $660 Million," December 21, 2015.
5. "The Commissionership: A Historical Perspective," Official Website of Major League Baseball, http://mlb.mlb.com/mlb/history/mlb_history_people.jsp?story=com.
6. Robert C. Berry, et al, *Labor Relations in Professional Sports* (Dover, MA: Auburn House, 1986), 38.
7. "Ban Johnson," Baseball-Reference.com Bullpen, http://www.baseball-reference.com/bullpen/Ban_Johnson.
8. Carney, *Burying the Black Sox*, 150.
9. Burk, *Much More Than a Game*, 24.
10. Robert Peyton Wiggins, *The Federal League of Base Ball Clubs: The History of an Outlaw Major League, 1914–1915*. Jefferson, N.C.: McFarland, 2009), 302.
11. Smelser, *Life That Ruth Built*, 60.
12. *Ibid.*
13. Edward J. Rielly, *Baseball: An Encyclopedia of Popular Culture* (Santa Barbara, CA: ABC-CLIO), 2000, 110.
14. Smelser, *Life That Ruth Built*, 60.
15. *Ibid.*, 124.
16. Lee Lowenfish, and Robert W. Creamer, *The Imperfect Diamond: A History of Baseball's Labor Wars* (New York: Simon & Schuster, 1974), 103.

Chapter 8

1. Wood, *Babe Ruth and the 1918 Red Sox*, 348.
2. "Sports Chatter," *Cedar Rapids Evening Gazette*, November 8, 1919, 16.
3. "The Business Side of Baseball," *Current Opinion* 53 (August 1912): 170.
4. Smelser, *Life That Ruth Built*, 109.
5. *Ibid.*, 349.
6. "A Super Umpire for Baseball," *The Outlook*, November 24, 1920, 535.
7. Scott Derks, *Working Americans, 1880–1999*, vol. 1, *The Working Class* (Lakeville, CT: Grey House, 2000), 155.
8. Richard Abel, *Encyclopedia of Early Cinema* (New York: Routledge, 2005), 328.
9. Glenn Stout, *Impossible Dreams: A Red Sox Collection* (Boston: Houghton Mifflin, 2003), 91.
10. Carney, *Burying the Black Sox*, 150.
11. *Baltimore Sun*, September 9, 1919.
12. *Sporting News*, October 19, 1919, 5.
13. "History of the Park," Official Site of the Sanford Mainers, http://sanfordmainers.pointstreaksites.com/view/sanfordmainers/history-of-the-park-1.
14. *Attleboro Sun*, September 2, 1919.
15. Kerry Keene et al., *The Babe in Red Stockings: An In-Depth Chronicle of Babe Ruth with the Boston Red Sox, 1914–1919* (Champaign, IL: Sagamore, 1997), 263.
16. Mark Flanagan, "When Baseball World's Eyes were on the Attleboros," *Attleboro Sun Chronicle*, October 25, 2007, http://www.thesunchronicle.com.
17. Bob Bennett, "Elmer Bowman," SABR Biography Project, http://sabr.org/bioproj/person/a436b1d7.
18. *Ibid.*
19. Wagenheim, *Babe Ruth*, 60.
20. Creamer, *Babe*, 74.
21. Bill Jenkinson, *The Year Babe Ruth Hit 104 Home Runs: Recrowning Baseball's Greatest Slugger* (New York: Carroll and Graf), 2007, 35.
22. *Desert News*, November 18, 1919.
23. Edward Mott Woolley, "The Business of Baseball," *McClure's Magazine* 39, no. 3 (July 1912).
24. *Oakland Tribune*, November 14, 1919, 16.
25. James Cruisenberry, *Fort Worth Star Telegram*, December 29, 1919.
26. *Bakersfield Californian*, December 18, 1919.
27. *Los Angeles Times*, December 22, 1919.
28. Jenkinson, *The Year Babe Ruth Hit 104 Home Runs*, 159.

Chapter 9

1. Kenneth T. Jackson, and David S. Dunbar, eds., *Empire City: New York Through the Centuries* (New York: Columbia University Press, 2002), 317.
2. Leo Braudy, *Frenzy of Renown* (New York: Oxford University Press, 1986), 593.
3. "Yankee Stadium History," Official Site of Major League Baseball, http://newyork.yankees.mlb.com/nyy/ballpark/stadium_history.jsp.

4. Michael Haupert, and Kenneth Winter, "Pay Ball: Estimating the Profitability of the New York Yankees, 1915–1937," *Essays in Economic and Business History* 21 (2012): 89–101.
5. Wood, "Babe Ruth," SABR Baseball Biography Project, http://sabr.org/bioproj/person/9dcdd01c.
6. Smelser, *Life That Ruth Built*, 59.
7. Bob Greene, "Fans Call Foul Ball on Baseball Strike," *Chicago Tribune*, July 31, 1985, http://articles.chicagotribune.com/1985-07-31/features/8502200028_1_baseball-fans-owners-side-baseball-strike.
8. Lawrence S. Ritter, and Mark Rucker, *The Babe: A Life in Pictures* (New York: Ticknor & Fields, 1988), 147.
9. Smelser, *Life That Ruth Built*, 263.
10. Ruth and Considine, *The Babe Ruth Story*, 116.
11. *Ibid.*, 6.
12. Wayne Stewart, *Babe Ruth: A Biography* (Westport, CT: Greenwood, 2006), 13.
13. Waite Hoyt, *Babe Ruth as I Knew Him* (New York: Dell, 1948), 15.

Chapter 10

1. *New York Times*, January 16, 1920.
2. Allan Wood, "Carl Mays," SABR Biography Project, http://sabr.org/bioproj/person/99ca7c89.
3. *Ibid.*
4. Eliot Asinof, *Eight Men Out: The Black Sox and the 1919 World Series* (New York: Henry Holt, 1987), 142.
5. Frank Graham, *The New York Yankees: An Informal History* (New York: G.P. Putnam's Sons, 1943), 47.
6. Harvey Frommer, *Remembering Yankee Stadium: An Oral and Narrative History of the House That Ruth Built* (New York: Stewart, Tabori & Chang, 2008), 67.
7. Harvey Frommer, and Frederic J. Frommer, *Red Sox vs. Yankees: The Great Rivalry* (Champaign, IL: Sports Publishing, 2005), 78.
8. Leigh Montville, *The Big Bam: The Life and Times of Babe Ruth* (New York: Doubleday, 2006), 97.
9. *Ibid.*, 97.
10. Robert Weintraub, *The House That Ruth Built: A New Stadium, the First Yankees Championship* (New York: Little, Brown, 2011), 47.
11. Ruth and Considine, *The Babe Ruth Story*, 28.
12. Frommer and Frommer, *Red Sox vs. Yankees*, 81.
13. Daniel R. Levitt, *Ed Barrow: The Bulldog Who Built the Yankees' First Dynasty* (Lincoln: University of Nebraska Press, 2008), 167.
14. Creamer, *Babe*, 74.
15. "Babe Ruth Accepts Terms of Yankees," *New York Times*, January 7, 1920, 22.
16. *New York Times*, January 16, 1920.
17. Michael Haupert, "The Sultan of Swag: Babe Ruth as a Financial Investment," *Baseball Research Journal* 44, no. 2 (fall 2015): 100–107.
18. John H. Mandigo, "Outdoor Sports," *The Chautauquan* 19, no. 4 (July 1894): 388.

19. *New York Times*, January 6, 1920.

20. *New York Times*, January 5, 1920.

21. Levitt, "Ed Barrow," SABR Biography Project.

22. Koppett, *The Man in the Dugout: Baseball's Top Managers and How They Got That Way* (Philadelphia: Temple University Press, 2000), 127.

23. Geoffrey Ward, and Ken Burns, *Baseball: An Illustrated History* (New York: A.A. Knopf, 1994), 434.

24. *New York Herald*, January 6, 1920.

25. *New York Times*, February 5, 1920.

26. Wagenheim, *Babe Ruth*, 58.

27. Bill James, *The New Bill James Historical Baseball Abstract* (New York: Free Press, 2001), 25.

28. *Baseball Digest*, July 1969, 98.

29. "Plutocratic Incomes of Modern Athletes," *Current Opinion* 68, no. 1 (January 1920): 846.

30. "The Profession of Medicine," Boston Medical and Surgical Journal, Vol. 173, Issue 2, December 23, 1915, 970.

31. Gettysburg *Star and Sentinel*, October 9, 1920.

32. Winter and Haupert, "Pay Ball: Estimating the Profitablility of the New York Yankees," *Essays in Economic and Business History* 21 (2012): 21.

33. James, *The New Bill James Historical Abstract*, 121.

34. Editors of Publications International, "1920 Baseball Season," http://entertainment.howstuffworks.com/1920-baseball-season.htm.

35. Year In Review : 1920 National League. http://www.baseball-almanac.com/yearly/yr1920n.shtml.

36. Seymour and Seymour Mills, *Baseball: The Golden Age*, 425.

37. "To Boost Yanks' Visit, Jacksonville Will Advertise Spring Trip Like Circus," January 8, 1920, 18.

38. Guy Emerson, *The New Frontier: A Study of the American Liberal Spirit, Its Frontier Spirit, and Its Application to Modern Problems* (New York: Henry Holt, 1920), 226.

39. Steven Gaines, *The Sky's the Limit: Passion and Property in Manhattan* (New York: Little, Brown, 2005), 174.

40. Stewart, *Babe Ruth*, 51.

41. Montville, *Big Bam*, 119.

42. Grantland Rice, *The Tumult and the Shouting: My Life in Sport* (New York: Barnes, 1954), 66.

43. *New York Times*, May 17, 1920.

44. Seymour and Seymour Mills, *Baseball: The Golden Age*, 344.

45. Wagenheim, *Babe Ruth*, 47.

46. https://www.baseball-fever.com/forum/general-baseball/history-of-the-game/566-babe-ruth-thread/page15

47. Jenkinson, *The Year Babe Ruth Hit 104 Home Runs*, 164.

48. "Huge Throng Sees Yankees Shut Out," August 1, 1920, 14.

49. Montville, 120.

50. Creamer, *Babe*, 102.

51. Harold Seymour, *Baseball: The Golden Age*, 428.

52. William B. Mead, and Paul Dickson, *Baseball: The Presidents' Game* (Washington, D.C.: Farragut, 1993), 68.

53. F.C. Lane, *Baseball Magazine*, quoted in "Ty and The Babe," 81.

54. "Comment on Current Events in Sports: Baseball," *New York Times*, October 3, 1920, 14.

55. Seymour and Seymour Mills, *Baseball: The Golden Age*, 247.

56. Ken Sobol, *Babe Ruth and the American Dream* (New York: Random House, 1974), 119.

57. *Ibid.*, 125.

58. "A New Hero of the Great American Game at Close Range," *Current Opinion,* 69 (October 1920): 478.

59. *Ibid.*

60. Sidney Reid, "Meet the American Idol," *The Independent*, August 14, 1920, 170.

61. "Cornelius J. Savage," *New York Times*, December 6, 1934, 23.

62. John Altavilla, "Negro League History," *Hartford Courant*, April 15, 1997, 15.

63. "Babe Ruth in Cuba," *Radio Rebilde* (website), http://www.radiorebelde.cu/48snb/

64. *Ibid.*

65. Levitt, *Ed Barrow*, 170.

66. Wagenheim, *Babe Ruth*, 77.

67. Montville, *Big Bam*, 191.

Chapter 11

1. Smelser, *Life That Ruth Built*, 273.

2. Montville, *Big Bam*, 271.

3. "Amtrak Ridership Rolls Up Best-Ever Records." JOC.com, http://www.joc.com/amtrak-ridership-rolls-best-ever-records_20111013.html.

4. Wikipedia Contributors, "20th Century Limited," https://en.wikipedia.org/wiki/20th_Century_Limited.

5. Joe Welsh, and Bill Howes, *Travel Pullman* (St. Paul, MN: MBI, 2004), 20.

6. *Ibid.*, 15.

7. George W. Hilton, and John F. Due, *The Electric Interurban Railways in America* (Stanford, CA: Stanford University Press, 1964), 47.

Chapter 12

1. W.J. Macbeth, "Ruth Features Great Season; Yanks Prosper," *New York Tribune*, December 26, 1920.

2. Seymour and Seymour Mills, *Baseball: The Golden Age*, 344.

3. Norman L. Macht, *Connie Mack and the Early Years of Baseball* (Lincoln: University of Nebraska Press, 2007), 466.

4. Hugh S. Fullerton, "Baseball—The Business and the Sport," *American Review of Reviews* (April 1921), p. 418.

5. Arthur Marx, *Goldwyn: A Biography of the Man Behind the Myth* (New York: W.W. Norton, 1976), 121.

6. Grantland Rice, "Ruth Is Stranger Than Fiction," *Vanity* Fair, April 1921, 65.

7. Joe Williams, Dennis Pernu and Grace Labatt, *Hollywood Myths: The Shocking Truths Behind Film's Most Incredible Secrets and Scandals* (Minneapolis: MBI and Voyageur Press, 2012), 18.

8. Rice, "Ruth Is Stranger Than Fiction," 65.

9. "Cardinal Asks Ruth Tribute Suggests K. of C. Help in St. Mary's Drive as Testimonial," *Baltimore American*, January 10, 1921, 14.

10. Pedersen, et al., 61.

11. Creamer, *Babe*, 272.

12. Smelser, *Life That Ruth Built*, 208.

13. Frank Presbrey, *The History and Development of Advertising* (Garden City, NY: Doubleday, 1929), 591.

14. Jonathan Goldman, *Modernism Is the Literature of Celebrity* (Austin: University of Texas Press, 2011), 175.

15. Hugh S. Fullerton, "Why Babe Ruth Is Greatest Home Run Hitter," *Popular Science Monthly* (October 1921): 21.

16. "And a Dealer Is Getting the Benefit of Novel Advertising," *Motor World Wholesale*, March 16, 1921, 35.

17. James, *The New Bill James Historical Abstract*, 121.

18. Carney, *Burying the Black Sox*, xv.

19. Henry L. Farrell, "Some Wonder as to What Will Take Place Now," *Beaver Daily Times*, October 22, 1924.

20. Smelser, *Life That Ruth Built,* 554.

21. Irvin S. Cobb, "Fans, Not Players, Quitters, Says Cobb," *New York Times*, October 14, 1921.

22. Asinof, *Eight Men Out*, 275.

23. *Ibid.*

24. Smelser, *Life That Ruth Built*, 81.

25. *Ibid.*, 263.

26. Jenkinson, *The Year Babe Ruth Hit 104 Home Runs,* 186.

27. Eddie Frierson, "Christy Mathewson," SABR Baseball Biography Project, http://sabr.org/bioproj/person/f13c56ed.

28. *New York Times*, October 6, 1921.

29. Seymour and Seymour Mills, *Baseball: The Golden Age*, 346.

30. "Babe Ruth Wearing Crown," *New York Times*, October 13, 1921.

31. *New York Times*, October 28, 1921, 24.

32. *New York Times*, October 14, 1921.

33. Smelser, *Life That Ruth Built*, 228.

34. Paul Votano, *Tony Lazzeri: A Baseball Biography* (Jefferson, NC: McFarland, 2005), 48.

35. *Washington Post*, November 2, 1921.

36. Seymour and Seymour Mills, *Baseball: The Early Game*, 191.

37. "The Babe and the Judge," *New Outlook*, October 26, 1921: 282.

38. Roger Bruns, *Negro Leagues Baseball* (Santa Barbara, CA: Greenwood, 2012), 26.

39. Eisen and Cahill, "Babe Ruth's Barnstorming Activities," 169.

40. *Buffalo Evening Times*, October 17, 1921, 17.

41. *The New York Times*, June 21, 1915.

42. *New York World*, November 14, 1921.

43. Smelser, *Life That Ruth Built*, 231.

44. Leverett T. Smith, Jr., *The American Dream and the National Game* (Bowling Green, OH: Bowling Green University Popular Press, 1975), 88.

45. Frank Litsky, "George Sauer, Jets Receiver and Rebel, Is Dead at 69," NY Times Online, http://www.nytimes.com/2013/05/11/sports/football/george-sauer-jets-receiver-and-rebel-is-dead-at-69.html?hpw&_r.

46. Creamer, *Babe*, 250.

47. Wagenheim, *Babe Ruth*, 99.

Chapter 13

1. Walsh, *Adios*, 14.

2. Alva Johnston, "Profiles: The Ghosting Business," *New Yorker*, November 23, 1935: 20.

3. Spatz and Steinberg, *1921*, 57.

4. Montville, *Big Bam*, 57.

5. *Advertising & Selling* 30, 22.

6. Alva Johnston, "Cash and Carry," *New Yorker*, December 8, 1928: 32.

7. Jules Tygiel, *Past Time: Baseball as History* (New York: Oxford University Press, 2000), 82.

8. Todd Georgelas, "And All That 'Ballyhoo': New Book Describes How Life Changed in the 1920s," *Mount Vernon Gazette*, November 20, 2009, 3.

9. Davies, *History*, 143.

10. Smelser, *Life That Ruth Built*, 209.

11. *Ibid.*

12. Tygiel, *Past Time*, 84.

13. Walter Lippmann, *Vanity Fair*, Vols. 28–29, 357.

14. Neal Gabler, *Winchell* (New York: Knopf, 1994), xii.

15. Donald G. Stein, *Buying in Or Selling Out? The Commercialization of the American Research University* (New Brunswick, NJ: Rutgers University Press, 2004), 21.

16. *Sport Collectors Digest*, March 5, 1999.

17. Smelser, *Life That Ruth Built*, 112.

Chapter 14

1. Glenn Stout and Matt Christopher, *Babe Ruth: Legends in Sports* (New York: Little, Brown, 2005), 24.

2. "Judge Landis Reversed and Censured." *Railway World,* 31 July 1908, 654.

3. Donald Gropman, *Say It Ain't So, Joe!: The True Story of Shoeless Joe Jackson* (New York, NY: Carol, 1992), 208.

4. Cited in Timothy Adams, *Still Not Forgiven* (Bloomington, IN: iUniverse, 2009), 129.

5. *Washington Post*, undated clipping.

6. Burk, *Much More,* 11.

7. "Commercial Value of Our Entertainers," *School Executive*, May/June 1922, 534.

8. Robert Grant and Joseph Katz, *The Great Trials of the Twenties: The Watershed Decade in America's Courtrooms* (Rockville Centre, NY: Sarpedon, 1998), 71.

9. White, 111.

10. David Pietrusza, *Rothstein: The Life, Times, and Murder of the Criminal Genius Who Fixed the 1919 World Series* (New York: Basic Books, 2011), 153.

11. Jeffrey L. Cruikshank and Arthur W. Schultz, *The Man Who Sold America: The Amazing but True! Story of Albert D. Lasker and the Creation of the Advertising Century* (Boston, MA: Harvard Business Review Press, 2010), 157.

12. Fred Stein, 147.

13. Wagenheim, Babe Ruth, 117.

14. Creamer, *Babe*, 254.

15. Seymour and Seymour Mills, *Baseball: The Golden Age*, 428.

16. Kenneth Winter and Michael J. Haupert, "Yankee Profits and Promise: The Purchase of Babe Ruth and the Building of Yankee Stadium," in *The Cooperstown Symposium on Baseball and American Culture. 2003–2004*, ed. William M. Simons (Jefferson, NC: McFarland, 2005), 211.

17. "Who's Who in the Best and Worst Paying Professions," *Current Opinion* 73 (November 1922), 659.

18. "Commercial Value of Our Entertainers," *The School Executive* 41 (May/June 1922), 534.

19. Keene Sumner, "Norma Talmadge: A Great Motion Picture Star." *American Magazine* (June 1922), 36.

20. "Candy's History Is Ruthless," *Lakeland Ledger*, April 7, 2002.

21. *NY Daily News*, September 26, 1921. http://therealbsmile.tumblr.com/page/9#sthash.lmjgvJ66.dpuf = http://sportsnetny.tumblr.com/search/babe+ruth.

22. Tim Delaney and Tim Madigan, *The Sociology of Sports: An Introduction* (Jefferson, NC: McFarland, 2009), 84.

23. Wiggins, *The Federal League of Base Ball Clubs*, 92.

24. George Castle, *Baseball and the Media: How Fans Lose in Today's Coverage of the Game* (Lincoln: University of Nebraska Press, 2006), 23.

25. John Shiffert, *Base Ball in Philadelphia: A History of the Early Game, 1831–1900* (Jefferson, NC: McFarland, 2006), 243.

26. J.A. Mangan and Andrew Ritchie, *Ethnicity, Sport, Identity: Struggles for Status* (London: Frank Cass, 2004), 59.

27. Richard J. Tofel, *Legend in the Making: The New York Yankees in 1939* (Chicago: Ivan R Dee, 2004), 10.

28. Paul Adomites and Saul Wisnia, *Babe Ruth: His Life and Times* (Lincolnwood, IL: Publications International, 1995), 67.

29. Smelser, *Life That Ruth Built,* 198.

30. Adomites and Wisnia, *Babe Ruth*, 70.

31. Montville, 149.

32. Montville, *Big Bam*, 136.

33. Wood, *Babe Ruth and the 1918 Red Sox,* 165.

34. Michael E. Parrish, *Anxious Decades: America in Prosperity and Depression, 1920–1941* (New York: W.W. Norton, 1992), 170.

35. Ken Sobol, *Babe Ruth and the American Dream* (New York: Random House, 1974), 158.

36. *New York Times*, October 5, 1922.

37. *New York Times*, October 10, 1922.

38. *Sleepy Eye Herald-Dispatch*, September 21, 1922.

39. *Sleepy Eye Herald-Dispatch*, October 12, 1922.

40. Wagenheim, *Babe Ruth*, 100.

41. Stew Thornley, *Baseball in Minnesota: The Definitive History* (St. Paul, MN: Minnesota Historical Society Press, 2006), 62.

42. "'Babe' Hits Two Homers in Game Here Monday," *Sleepy Eye Herald-Dispatch*, 19 October 1922, 1.

43. Jason Roe, "Kings of the City," Kansas City Public Library blog, 5 October 2015, http://www.kclibrary.org/blog/week-kansas-city-history/kings-city.

44. *Drumright* (OK) *Derrick*, October 23, 1922.

45. *New York Times*, November 10, 1922.

46. Creamer, *Babe*, 274.

47. Weintraub, *The House That Ruth Built*, 67.

48. Bob Allen and Bill Gilbert, *The 500 Home Run Club: Baseball's 16 Greatest Home Run Hitters from Babe Ruth to Mark McGwire* (Champaign, IL: Sports Pub., 2000), 220.

49. Montville, *Big Bam*, 159.

50. Smelser, *Life That Ruth Built*, 258–259.

Chapter 15

1. Terence J. Fitzgerald, *Celebrity Culture in the United States* (New York: H.W. Wilson, 2008), 9; and Leo Lowenthal, *Literature, Popular Culture, and Society* (Englewood Cliffs, NJ: Prentice-Hall, 1961), 110–14.

2. John Kieran, Sports of the Times, 14 October 1928, S2.

3. Lewis, *Smart Ball*, 55.

4. Robert F. Lewis, *Smart Ball: Marketing the Myth and Managing the Reality of Major League Baseball* (Jackson: University Press of Mississippi, 2010), 54.

5. Leo Braudy, *Frenzy of Renown* (New York: Oxford University Press, 1986), 593.

6. Bertolt Brecht, *Galileo* (New York: Grove Press, 1966), Scene 12, 115.

7. Jaques Ellul, *Propaganda: The Formation of Men's Attitudes* (New York: Knopf, 1965), 36.

8. Smelser, *Life That Ruth Built*, 145.

9. "The Kids Can't Take It If We Don't Give It," *Guideposts* (October 1948), http://www.catholiceducation.org/articles/catholic_stories/cs0431.htm.

10. Kieran, *Sports of the Times*, January 23, 1935.

11. *New York Times,* June 4, 1935.

12. Montville, *Big Bam,* 348.

13. Dave Blevins, *The Sports Hall of Fame Encyclopedia: Baseball, Basketball, Football, Hockey, Soccer* (Lanham, MD: Scarecrow Press, 2012), 847.

14. Stewart, *Babe Ruth*, 114.

15. Smelser, *Life That Ruth Built,* 529.

16. Murray Schumach, "Baseball's Great Star and Idol of Children," 14.

Chapter 16

1. Creamer, *Babe*, 262.

2. Burk, *Much More Than a Game*, 204.

3. Wood, *Babe Ruth and 1918 Red Sox*, 107.

4. Wagenheim, *Babe Ruth*, 62.

5. Smelser, *Life That Ruth Built*, 39.

6. *New York Times*, March 16, 1923.

7. Winter and Haupert, "Profits and Promise," 210.

8. Jim Prime with Bill Nowlin, *Tales from the Red Sox Dugout* (Champaign, IL: Sports Publishing, 2000), 95.

9. Montville, *Bib Bam*, 132.

10. Richard Goldstein, "Ray Kelly, 83, Babe Ruth's Little Pal, Dies," *New York Times,* 14 November 2001.

11. "Claire Ruth, Widow of Baseball Great; She Kept Yankee Star's Memory Alive in the Last 28 Years, Dies of Cancer at 76," *New York Times*, October 26, 1976.

12. Montville, *Big Bam*, 180.

13. Presbrey, *History and Development of Advertising*, 591.

14. Sobol, *Babe Ruth and the American Dream*, 170.

15. David E. Kyvig, *Daily Life in the United States, 1920–1940: How Americans Lived Through the Roaring Twenties and the Great Depression* (Chicago: Ivan R. Dee, 2004), 76.

16. Smelser, *Life That Ruth Built*, 258.

17. *Ibid.*, 290.

18. *Boston Daily Globe*, October 25, 1923.

Chapter 17

1. Warren Susman, *Culture As History: The Transformation of American Society in the Twentieth Century* (New York: Pantheon, 1984).

2. Lewis, *Smart Ball*, 54–55.

3. "Elite Chocolate Coated Baseball Co., El Paso, Tex," *Creamery and Milk Plant Monthly* 11, no. 11 (November 1922), 90.

4. *Media Law Reporter*, 1989, 19.

5. "Branding," Brandchannel (website), http://www.brandchannel.com/features_effect.asp?pf_id=183.

6. Crepeau, *Baseball: America's Diamond Mind*, 25.

7. Deron Boyles, *The Corporate Assault on Youth: Commercialism, Exploitation, and the End of Innocence* (New York: Peter Lang, 2008), 145.

8. Presbrey, *History and Development of Advertising,* 483.

9. Crepeau, *Baseball: America's Diamond Mind*, 87.

10. Kyvig, *Daily Life in the United States, 1920–1940*, 189.

11. Marchand, *Advertising the American Dream*, 6.

12. Katherine Morgan Drowne and Patrick Huber, *The 1920s* (Westport, CT: Greenwood, 2004), 66.

13. Eric Feigenbaum, "The 1920s: 'Sell Them Their Dreams' in Postwar America, Prosperity Drives *The New Aesthetic*," VMSD, 3 May 2001, http://vmsd.com/content/the-1920s-sell-them-their-dreams.

14. Sobol, *Babe Ruth and the American Dream*, 168.

15. Adomites, *Babe Ruth*, 11.

16. Paul Mark Pedersen et al., *Contemporary Sport Management*, 62.

17. *Printers' Ink* 113 (November 4, 1920), 100.

18. Ann Douglas, *Terrible Honesty*, 65.

19. C.L. Reely, "Capitalizing the Celebrity—and Making Him Responsible for the Product," *Advertising & Selling* 30 (August 28, 1920), 5.

Chapter 18

1. "Baseball as Big Business," *Youth's Companion* 98, no. 35 (August 28, 1924), 572.

2. Seymour and Seymour Mills, *Baseball: The Golden Age*, 428.

3. Tony Guadagnoli, "Harvard-Yale Rivalry a Tribute to the Student-Athlete," ESPN.com, 2 October 2008, http://espn.go.com/espn/thelife/news/story?id=3017562.

4. Eig, *Luckiest Man*, 115.

5. "Baseball as Big Business," 572.

6. Roland S. Hall and Richard M. Boren, *Advertising, Merchandise Display, Sales-planning, Salesmanship, Turnover and Profit-figuring in Modern Retailing, Including "Principles of Typography as Applied to Retail Advertising* (New York: McGraw-Hill, 1924), 127.

7. Christopher Lasch, "The Corruption of Sports," *New York Review of Books,* 28 April 1977, http://www.nybooks.com/articles/8525.

8. Arthur Robinson, "My Friend Babe Ruth," *Colliers* 74 (20 September 1924), 2, 7–8.

9. *Beaver* (PA) *Daily Times*, October 22, 1924.

10. Rice, *Tumult and the Shouting*, 27.

11. Zulal S. Denaux, David A. Denaux, and Yeliz Yalcin, "Factors Affecting Attendance of Major League Baseball: Revisited," *Atlantic Economic Journal* 39, no. 2 (2011): 117.

12. Sobol, *Babe Ruth and the American Dream*, 174.

13. Smelser, *Life That Ruth Built*, 306.

14. *Ibid.*, 258.

15. "Babe Ruth," Shanaman Sports Museum.com, http://tacomasportsmuseum.com.

16. Bart Ripp, "The Uncouth Ruth: The Bambino Ate Like a Hog and Cavorted with Babes of Ill Repute," *Tacoma News-Tribune*, 17 April 1992, F3.

17. Chris Dufresne, "Babe in Boomtown," *Los Angeles Times*, June 2, 2008, http://articles.latimes.com/2008/jun/02/sports/sp-breababe2.

18. Smelser, *Life That Ruth Built*, 300.

19. Burk, *Much More Than a Game*, 22.

20. Montville, *Big Bam*, 165.

Chapter 19

1. Seymour and Seymour Mills, *Baseball: The Golden Years*, 32.

2. Smelser, *Life That Ruth Built*, 145.

3. Hoyt, *Babe Ruth as I Knew Him*, 10.

4. Jenkinson, *The Year Babe Ruth Hit 104 Home Runs*, 184.

5. Smelser, *Life That Ruth Built*, 120.

6. Ruth and Considine, *Babe Ruth Story,* 116.

7. Montville, *Big Bam*, 170.

8. Smith, *The American Dream and the National Game,* 111.

9. Jenkinson, *Year Babe Ruth Hit 104 Home Runs*, 7.

10. Montville, *Big Bam*, 345.

11. Dennis Purdy, "Gopher Balls: The Bustin' Babes and the Laruppin' Lous," in *Kiss 'Em Goodbye: An ESPN Treasury of Failed, Forgotten, and Departed Teams* (New York: Ballantine Books/ESPN Books, 2010), 62.

12. Smith, *The American Dream and the National Game*, 77.

Chapter 20

1. Bob Luke, *Dean of Umpires: A Biography of Bill McGowan, 1896–1954* (Jefferson, NC: McFarland, 2005), 73.

2. *Milwaukee Sentinel*, December 8, 1925.

3. "Rudolph Valentino." IMDB. http://www.imdb.com/name/nm0884388/bio.

4. "Columbia, The Land of the Millionaires," 1920–1930.com, http://www.1920-30.com/business/millionaires.html. (First published, *Literary Digest*, April 16, 1927.)

5. Seymour and Seymour Mills, *Baseball: The Golden Age*, 431.

6. Smelser, *Life That Ruth Built*, 60.

7. Roger Kahn, *October Men: Reggie Jackson, George Steinbrenner, Billy Martin, and the Yankees' Miraculous Finish in 1978* (Orlando, FL: Harcourt, 2003), 49.

8. Hoyt, *Babe Ruth as I Knew Him*, 14.

9. Louis D. Rubin, Jr., "Babe Ruth's Ghost," in *Scoring from Second: Writers on Baseball*, ed. Philip F Deaver (Lincoln: University of Nebraska Press, 2007).

10. Creamer, *Babe*, 334.

11. *Ibid.*

12. Hoyt, *Babe Ruth as I Knew* Him, 15.

13. Creamer, *Babe*, 303.

14. *Jenkinson, The Year Babe Ruth Hit 104 Home Runs*, 84.

15. Robert M Coates, "Artie," *New Yorker*, May 22, 1937, 24–27.

16. Montville, *Big Bam*, 221.

17. Mrs. Babe Ruth with Bill Slocum, *The Babe and I* (Englewood Cliffs, NJ: Prentice-Hall, 1959), 138.

Chapter 21

1. U.S. Commission on Industrial Relations, *Final Report and Testimony Submitted to Congress by the Commission on Industrial Relations*, 64th Congress, 1st Session, Senate Document No. 415, 11 vols., 1916.

2. National Bureau of Economic Research, 1919, 48, 210.

3. Kyvig, *Daily Life in the United States*, 195.

4. Frederick Lewis Allen, *Only Yesterday: An Informal History of the Nineteen-Twenties* (New York: Perennial Library, 1964), 156.

5. *Ibid.*

6. Drowne and Huber, *The 1920s*, 331.

7. Gabler, *Winchell*, 76.

8. Steven A. Reiss, *Touching Base: Professional Baseball and American Culture in the Progressive Era* (Westport, CT: Greenwood, 1980), 15.

9. *Ibid.*, 39.

10. Wood, *Babe Ruth and the 1918 Red Sox*, 121.

11. Mike Farrell and Mary Carmen Cupito, *Newspapers: A Complete Guide to the Industry* (New York: Peter Lang, 2010), 14.

12. John D. Stevens, *Sensationalism and the New York Press* (New York: Columbia University Press, 1991), 117.

13. Emerson, *New Frontier*, 226.

14. Presbrey, *History and Development of Advertising*, 591.

15. *Fourth Estate*, December 4, 1920, 24.

16. David Q. Voigt, *American Baseball: From the Commissioners to Continental Expansion*: Volume 2 (Norman: University of Oklahoma Press, 1970), 130.

17. "Year in Review: 1914 National League," Baseball Almanac (website), http://www.baseball-almanac.com/yearly/yr1914n.shtml.

18. "Year in Review: 1915 National League," Baseball Almanac, http://www.baseball-almanac.com/yearly/yr1915n.shtml.

19. Wiggins, *Federal League*, 302.

20. Bill Ballew, "Sporting News Forever Linked to Baseball's Past," *Baseball America* (online), May 14, 2012, http://www.baseballamerica.com/today/majors/news/2012/2613392.html.

21. D.W. Grandon, letter to the editor, *Editor and Publisher*, April 16, 1921, 45.

Chapter 22

1. Wagenheim, *Babe Ruth*, 163.

2. *Ibid.*, 161.

3. Smelser, *Life That Ruth Built*, 327.

4. *Meriden Record*, March 31, 1926.

5. Hoyt, *Babe Ruth as I Knew Him*, 17.

6. Arthur Robinson, "The Babe," *New Yorker*, July 31, 1926, 15–17.

7. Crepeau, *Baseball: America's Diamond Mind*, 95.

8. Stats from Baseball-Reference.com; "1926 World Series," Baseball Almanac, Baseballalmanac.com.

9. Jan Finkel, "Pete Alexander," SABR Baseball Biography Project, http://sabr.org/bioproj/person/79e6a2a7.

10. Jenkinson quoted in Father Gabe Costa, "By the Numbers: Judging Babe Ruth's Attempted Steal in the 1926 World Series," CBS New York (website), July 29, 2011, http://newyork.cbslocal.com.

11. Bohn, *Heroes and Ballyoo*, 7.

12. "Movietone News," http://movietonews.com/the_fox_movietone_newsreel.html.

13. *St. Petersburg (FL) Evening Independent*, October 23, 1926.

14. *Baltimore Sun*, October 10, 1926.

15. Forker et al., *The Big Book of Baseball Brainteasers* (New York: Main Street, 2004), 224.

16. Eisen and Cahill, "Babe Ruth's Barnstorming Activities," 171.

17. *Chicago Defender*, October 23, 1926.

18. *Long Branch (NJ) Daily Record*, October 11, 1926.

19. Creamer, *Babe*, 330.

20. Mark Inabinett, *Grantland Rice and His Heroes: The Sportswriter as Mythmaker in the 1920s* (Knoxville: University of Tennessee Press, 1994), 47.

21. Jenkinson, *Year Babe Ruth Hit 104 Home Runs*, 145.

22. *Iron Mountain News*, http://www.wilkes.edu/pages/1636.

23. "Babe Ruth in Perth Amboy," Historic Perth Amboy Virtual Museum, October 4, 1926, http://historicperthamboy.blogspot.com/search/label/Babe%20Ruth.

24. "Broadway Limited."

Chapter 23

1. Murray Schumach, "Babe Ruth, Baseball's Great Star and Idol of Children," 14.

2. Dan Bern with Common Rotation, "Johnny Sylvester Comes Back to Visit the Babe," *Doubleheader*, released July 4, 2012, DBHQ, MP3 320Kbps.

3. Charles Poekel, "Babe Ruth vs. Baby Ruth: The Quest for a Candy Bar," in *The Cooperstown Symposium on Baseball and American Culture, 2009–2010*, ed. by William M. Simons (Jefferson, NC: McFarland, 2011), 225–228.

4. Keogh, Edward A., "A Brief History of the Air Mail Service of the U.S. Post Office Department (May 15, 1918–August 31, 1927)," Air Mail Pioneers (website), http://www.airmailpioneers.org/history/Sagahistory traffic.htm.

5. Eldon Ham, *Broadcasting Baseball: A History of the National Pastime on Radio* (Jefferson, NC: McFarland, 2011), 50.

6. Poekel, "Babe Ruth vs. Baby Ruth: The Quest for the Candy Bar."

7. Montville, *Big Bam*, 236.

8. Lieb, *Baseball as I Have Known It*, 103.

9. *Ibid.*, 103.

10. Crepeau, *Baseball: America's Diamond Mind*, 84.

11. Montville, *Big Bam*, 207.

Chapter 24

1. Wagenheim, *Babe Ruth*, 174.

2. Francis Wallace, "College Men in the Big Leagues," *Scribner's*, October 1927, 493.

3. Ruth with Slocum, *The Babe and I*, 139.

4. Harvey Frommer, *Five O'Clock Lightning: Babe Ruth, Lou Gehrig, and the Greatest Team in Baseball, the 1927 New York Yankees* (Hoboken, NJ: John Wiley & Sons, 2008), 12.

5. Burk, *Much More Than a Game*, 23.

6. *Washington Post*, October 9, 1927.

7. Hoyt, *Babe Ruth as I Knew Him*, 24.

8. Rick Cabral, "The Bustin' Babes and Larrupin' Lous: The Definitive History of the 1927 Barnstorming Tour Featuring Babe Ruth and Lou Gehrig," http://www.thepitchbook.com/Bustin%27-Babes-Lous-Barnstorming-1927.html.

9. *Border Cities Star* (Windsor, ONT), October 14, 1927.

10. Eig, *Luckiest Man*, 112.

11. Holway, *Smokey Joe and the Cannonball* (Washington, DC: Capital Press, 1983), 84.

12. Bill Jenkins, email to the author, May 5, 2006.

13. Eig, *Luckiest Man*, 100.

14. Bill Jenkinson, email to the author, May 5, 2006.

15. *Los Angeles Examiner*, October 17, 1927.

16. Frommer, *Five O'Clock Lightning*, 187.

17. Gregg Kaufman, *Symphony of Swat* (podcast), https://itunes.apple.com/us/itunes-u/symphony-of-swat/id401629321.

18. Stan Waldorf, *San Jose News*, October 24, 1927.

19. San Jose *Evening News*, October 24, 1927.

20. Associated Press, October 27, 1927.

21. "1927 World Series." http://www.angelfire.com/pa/1927/worldseries.html.

22. Wagenheim, *Babe Ruth*, 171.

23. Frommer, *Five O'Clock Lightning*, 189.

24. John Kiernan, *New York Times*, March 1, 1927.

25. Associated Press, November 10, 1927.

26. Alva Johnston, "Profiles: The Ghosting Business," *New Yorker*, November 23, 1935, 24.

27. Schumach, "Babe Ruth, Baseball's Great Star and Idol of Children," 14.

28. Ruth, *Babe Ruth's Own Book*, 46.

Chapter 25

1. "Hitting Lessons from Babe Ruth 1939 New York World's Fair," SNY on Tumbler, http://therealbsmile.tumblr.com/page/16#sthash.wizmYhu3.dpuf.

2. "Influence on Radio," Museum of Making Music, http://www.museumofmakingmusic.org/influence-on-radio.

3. Thomas H. White, "United States Early Radio History." http://earlyradiohistory.us/sec001.htm.

4. *Ibid.*

5. John Rodman, "The Media Support Industry," Higher Ed (website), http://highered.mcgrawhill.com/sites/dl/free/0073511951/671444/rodman3_sample_ch03.pdf.

6. Presbrey, *History and Development of Advertising*, 578.

7. Allen, *Only Yesterday*, 157.

8. Arthur A. Raney, and Jennings Bryan, eds., *Handbook of Sports and Media* (Mahwah, NJ: L. Erlbaum, 2006), 47.

9. *New York Times Guide to Essential Knowledge* (New York: St. Martin's Press, 2011), 843.

10. Jonathan Eig, "Ruth, Gehrig and the Birth of a Dynasty," in *The Yankees Baseball Reader: A Collection of Writings on the Game's Greatest Dynasty*, eds. Adam Brunner and Josh Leventhal (Minneapolis, MN: MVP Books, 2011), 81.

11. Scott, Carole E. "The History of the Radio Industry in the United States to 1940." http://eh.net/encyclopedia/article/scott.radio.industry.history.

12. *New York Times Guide to Essential Knowledge* (New York: St. Martins Press, 2011).

13. Mark Schubin, "Watching Remote Baseball Games Before TV," Schubin café (website), http://www.schubincafe.com/tag/baseball.

14. Hugh Mackay, and Tim O'Sullivan, *The Media Reader: Continuity and Transformation* (Thousand Oaks, CA: Sage, 1999), 60.

15. Schubin, "Watching Remote Baseball Games Before TV."

16. Michael J. Haupert, "Economic History of Major League Baseball," EH.net, http://eh.net/encyclopedia/article/haupert.mlb.

17. "Re-creating Our National Pastime," Connecticut History.Org (website), http://connecticuthistory.org/re-creating-our-national-pastime/.

18. Schubin, Mark, "Watching Remote Baseball Games Before TV." Schubin Cafe. http://www.schubincafe.com/tag/baseball.

19. *Fourth Estate,* August 30, 1919, 6.

20. Patrick K. Thornton, *Sports Law* (Sudbury, MA: Jones and Bartlett, 2011), 421.

21. Tygiel, *Past Time,* 67.

22. *Ibid.,* 79.

23. *The Mentor,* July 32, 1921.

24. Fred Stein, *A History of the Baseball Fan* (Jefferson, NC: McFarland, 2005), 159.

Chapter 26

1. Bill Nowlin, "Bill Cissell," *SABR Baseball Biography Project,* ttp://sabr.org/bioproj/person/8b4b3c55.

2. Charles Leonard Ponce de Leon, *Self Exposure: Human-interest Journalism and the Emergence of Celebrity in America, 1890–1940* (Chapel Hill: University of North Carolina Press, 2002), 83.

3. Montville, *Big Bam,* 253.

4. Associated Press, February 27, 1928.

5. James, *New Bill James Historical Baseball Abstract,* 592.

6. Arthur Mann, "The New Babe Ruth" *New York Evening World,* April 28,1928.

7. undated article, A. Bartlett Giamatti Research Center, National Baseball Hall of Fame and Museum, Cooperstown, New York.

8. Mann, "The New Babe Ruth."

9. Wagenheim, *Babe Ruth,* 227.

10. *Miami News,* October 17, 1928.

11. "Why Did the Number of American Newspapers Grow Rapidly?" Answers.com. http://www.answers.com/topic/north-american-newspaper-alliance.

12. Unsourced clipping, A. Bartlett Giamatti Research Center, National Baseball Hall of Fame and Museum, Cooperstown, New York.

13. *Spalding Baseball Guide,* 1929.

14. *Sporting News,* October 18, 1928, 2.

15. Smelser, *Life That Ruth Built,* 387.

16. *Battle Creek (MI) Enquirer* and the *Evening News,* October 27, 1928.

17. "Lee Keyser," BR Bullpen, www.baseball-reference.com.

18. Bob Feller, with Bill Gilbert, *Now Pitching, Bob Feller: A Baseball Memoir* (New York: Citadel Press, 1990), 21.

19. Purdy, "Gopher Balls," 62.

Chapter 27

1. Michael S. Kimmel, "Baseball and the Reconstitution of American Masculinity, 1880–1920," *Baseball History from Outside the Lines: A Reader,* ed. John E. Dreifort, 47–61 (Lincoln: University of Nebraska Press, 2001), 53.

2. Bret E. Carroll, *American Masculinities: A Historical Encyclopedia,* vol. 1 (Thousand Oaks, CA: Sage, 2003), 48.

3. Michigan Occasional Papers in Women's Studies, vols. 5–9 (Ann Arbor: University of Michigan Press, 1978).

4. Steven A. Reich, ed., "Demographic Patterns of the Great Black Migration," *The Great Black Migration A Historical Encyclopedia of the American Mosaic* (Santa Barbara, CA: Greenwood, 2014), 96.

5. John Mercurio, *Babe Ruth's Incredible Records and the 44 Players Who Broke Them* (New York: S.P.I. Books, 1993), 38.

6. Jerome Charyn, "Our National Exaggeration," FrugalFun.com. http://www.frugalfun.com/our-national-exaggeration.html.

7. Jim Parry et al., *Sport and Spirituality: An Introduction* (London; New York: Routledge, 2007), 86.

8. Crepeau, *Baseball: America's Diamond Mine,* 41.

9. Jason Kaufman, *For the Common Good?: American Civic Life and the Golden Age of Fraternity* (New York: Oxford University Press, 2002), 294.

10. Stephen C. Wood and J. David Pincus, eds., *Reel Baseball: Essays and Interviews on the National Pastime* (Jefferson, NC: McFarland, 2003), 121.

11. Kimmel, "Baseball and the Reconstruction of American Masculinity," 68.

Chapter 28

1. Montville, *Big Bam,* 284.

2. Smelser, *Life That Ruth Built,* 314.

3. Bohn, *Heroes & Ballyhoo,* 218.

4. Stewart, *Babe Ruth,* 88.

5. Jane Leavy, "Being Babe Ruth's Daughter," Grantland (website), 3 January 2012, http://grantland.com/features/being-babe-ruth-daughter.

6. Stewart, *Babe Ruth,* 88.

7. Hoyt, *Babe Ruth as I Knew Him,* 13.

8. *New York Times,* April 17, 1929.

9. Joseph J. Vecchione, *New York Times Book of Sports Legends* (New York: Times Books, 1991), 295.

10. Frank Parker Stockbridge, "Feeding 13,000,000 Radio Sets," *Popular Science Monthly,* October 1929, 40–41 and 153–155.

11. Presbrey, *History and Development of Advertising,* 55.

12. Smelser, *Life That Ruth Built,* 408.

13. Seymour and Seymour Mills, *Baseball: The Golden Age,* 346.

14. *Ibid.,* 347.

15. Nowlin, et al., *When Boston Still Had the Babe: The 1918 World Champion Red Sox* (Burlington, MA: Rounder Books, 2008), 109.

16. Crepeau, *Baseball: America's Diamond Mind,* 77.

17. Bohn, *Heroes & Ballyhoo,* 219.

18. Smelser, *Life That Ruth Built,* 404.

19. *New York Times,* February 27, 1927.

20. Fred Lieb, *Baseball as I Have Known It* (New York: Coward, McCann & Geoghegan, 1977), 154.

21. *New York Times,* October 18, 1929.

22. Associated Press, October 14, 1929.

23. Marcia Worth, "When Babe Ruth Played for South Orange," *South Orange Patch,* April 5, 2012, http://patch.com/new-jersey/southorange/murderers-row-on-deck-in-south-orange.

24. Jimmy Keenan, "Jack Dunn," SABR Baseball Biography Project, http://sabr.org/bioproj/person/e1addacb.

Chapter 29

1. Charles Poekel, "Babe Ruth: Boss of the Youth of America" (transcribed speech), BabeRuthCentral.com (website), http://www.baberuthcentral.com/thehumanitarian/baberuthbossoftheyouthofamerica.

2. Crepeau, *Baseball: America's Diamond Mind,* 84.

3. *Ibid.,* 39.

4. Tygiel, *Past Time,* 84.

5. Mann, "The New Babe Ruth."

6. *Ibid.*

7. Donald G. Stein, *Buying In or Selling Out? The Commercialization of the American Research University* (New Brunswick, NJ: Rutgers University Press, 2004), 21.

8. Tygiel, *Past Time,* 84.

9. *Advertising & Selling,* November 26, 1921, 10.

10. Lisa Jacobson, *Raising Consumers: Children and the American Mass Market in the Early Twentieth Century* (New York: Columbia University Press, 2004), 5.

11. S.C. Lambert, "Building a Business on Children's Good Will: A Firm That Makes Express Wagons Finds the Right Appeal in Selling Its Products to Boys," *Printers' Ink* 112 (July 29, 1920), 89.

12. Jacobson, *Raising Consumers,* 85.

13. "A Great Value" (ad for Reach baseball glove), *Boys' Life* 20, no. 5 (May 1930): 40.

14. Jacobson, *Raising Consumers,* 104.

15. E. Evelyn Grumbine, *Reaching Juvenile Markets: How to Advertise, Sell, and Merchandise through Boys and Girls* (McGraw-Hill, 1938), 161.

16. Lieb, *Baseball as I Have Known,* 162.

17. Dorothy Ruth Pirone, and Chris Martens, *My Dad, The Babe: Growing Up with an American Hero* (Boston: Quinlan Press, 1988), 124.

18. *Ibid.,* 159.

Chapter 30

1. *New York Times,* March 11, 1930.

2. Smelser, *Life That Ruth Built,* 413.

3. *Ibid.,* 409.

4. Wagenheim, *Babe Ruth,* 200.

5. *New York Times,* April 22, 1931: 27.

6. Nowlin, *When Boston Still Had the Babe,* 109.

7. Creamer, *Babe,* 255.

8. Hugh S. Fullerton, "Earnings in Baseball," *North American Review* 229 (June 1930), 743.

9. Vecchione, *New York Times Book of Sports Legends,* 294.

10. "When Lindenhurst Met Babe Ruth & Lou Gehrig," The Incorporated Village of Lindenhurst, http://www.villageoflindenhurst.com/when_lindenhurst_met_babe_ruth!.htm

11. "Babe Ruth Comes to Lindenhurst: When Lindenhurst Met Babe Ruth & Lou Gehrig," Website of the Village of Lindenhurst, New York, http://www.lihistory.com/specspor/chron.htm.

12. John McMurray, "Joe McCarthy," SABR Baseball Biography Project, http://sabr.org/bioproj/person/2c77f933.

13. *Ibid.*

Chapter 31

1. Crepeau, *Baseball: America's Diamond Mind,* 41.

2. Michael Mandelbaum, *The Meaning of Sports: Why Americans Watch Baseball, Football, And Basketball, and What They See When They Do* (New York: Public Affairs, 2004), 71.

3. Susman, *Culture as History,* 61.

4. *Baseball Magazine* 20 (June 1920).

5. Bohn, *Heroes & Ballyhoo,* 209.

6. G. Edward White, *Creating the National Pastime: Baseball Transforms Itself, 1903–1953.* Princeton University Press, 2014, 193.

7. Mark Starr, "Blood, Sweat and Cheers," *Newsweek,* October 25, 1999, 42.

8. Steven M. Chermak and Frankie Y. Bailey, *Crimes and Trials of the Century: From the Black Sox Scandal to the Attica Prison Riots* (Westport, CT: Greenwood Press, 2007), 12.

9. Shiffert, *Base Ball in Philadelphia,* 243.

10. White, *Creating the National Pastime,* 193

11. Jerome Holtzman, *No Cheering in the Press Box* (New York: Holt, Rinehart and Winston, 1974), viii.

12. Burton Alan Boxerman and Benita W. Boxerman, *Jews and Baseball: Entering the American Mainstream, 1871–1948* (Jefferson, NC: McFarland, 2007), 69.

13. Montville, *Big Bam,* 162.

14. Henry Paul Jeffers, *The 100 Greatest Heroes: Inspiring Profiles of One Hundred Men and Women Who Changed the World* (New York: Citadel Press, 2003), 226.

15. Boxerman, *Jews and Baseball,* 69.

16. Sobol, *Babe Ruth and the American Dream,* 124.

17. Tracy Brown Collins, *Babe Ruth* (New York: Chelsea House, 2008), 19.

Chapter 32

1. Morris Markey, "Sport and the Showoff," *New Yorker*, August 15, 1931, 31.
2. Colorado Department of Public Health website, https://www.colorado.gov/cdphe
3. "What is Babe Ruth Worth to the Yankees?" *Literary Digest*, March 29, 1930.
4. Sobol, *Babe Ruth and the American Dream*, 172.
5. Winter and Haupert, "Yankee Profits and Promise."
6. BaseballAlmanac.com.
7. *Los Angeles Times*, October 18, 1931.
8. Sobol, *Babe Ruth and the American Dream*, 174.
9. Wagenheim, *Babe Ruth*, 171.
10. Sobol, *Babe Ruth and the American Dream*, 234.
11. Smelser, *Life That Ruth Built*, 436.

Chapter 33

1. Montville, *Big Bam*, 307.
2. Michael Haupert, email to the author, May 26, 2012.
3. Paul Adomites and Saul Wisnia, "Babe Ruth's Managerial Ambitions," How Stuff Works (website), http://entertainment.howstuffworks.com/babe-ruth34.htm.
4. Carmichael, *My Greatest Day in Baseball*, 1.
5. Sobol, *Babe Ruth and the American Dream*, 39.
6. "Book Examines Baseball During the Depression Era," Ohio University Communications and Marketing, http://www.ohio.edu/news/01-02/386.html.
7. Crepeau, *Baseball: America's Diamond Mind*, 96.
8. Bill Nowlin, "Herb Hunter," SABR Baseball Biography Project, http://sabr.org/bioproj/person/06f2e2e9.
9. Montville, *Big Bam*, 323.
10. Frank Ardolino, "Babe's Banyan Tree Grows in Hawaii," *National Pastime* 18 (1998): 62.
11. *Ibid.*, 63.
12. Rob Neyer, *Rob Neyer's Big Book of Baseball Blunders: A Complete Guide to the Worst Decisions and Stupidest Moments in Baseball History* (New York: Simon & Schuster, 2006), 43.
13. Dennis Van Langen, email to the author, January 22, 2013.
14. Montville, *Big Bam*, 325.
15. Smelser, *Life That Ruth Built*, 467.
16. Paul Adomites and Saul Wisnia, "Babe Ruth's Bad News," How Stuff Works, http://entertainment.howstuffworks.com/babe-ruth37.htm.
17. David George Surdam, *Wins, Losses, and Empty Seats: How Baseball Outlasted the Great Depression* (Lincoln: University of Nebraska Press, 2011), 167.
18. *New York Times*, July 19, 1934.
19. Smelser, *Life That Ruth Built*, 471.
20. John Dunning, *On the Air: The Encyclopedia of Old-Time Radio* (New York: Oxford University Press, 1998), 53.

21. Adam Graham, "The Great Detectives of Old Time Radio: The Fictionalized Adventures of Babe Ruth," http://www.greatdetectives.net/detectives/fictionalized-adventures-babe-ruth/.
22. *Williamsport Gazette and Bulletin*, October 24, 1934.
23. Wagenheim, *Babe Ruth*, 252.
24. *New York Times*, February 2, 1935.
25. Bill Bryson, "Real Babe Ruth Story Decries Half Truths—But Paints New Ones," *Baseball Digest*, May 1959, 21.
26. Jonathan Eig, *Luckiest Man: The Life and Death of Lou Gehrig* (New York: Simon & Schuster, 2005), 195.
27. Smelser, *Life That Ruth Built*, 220.
28. James P. Dawson, "Ruth Is Undecided on Future Plans," *New York Times*, June 4, 1935, 27.
29. *New York Times*, February 27, 1935.
30. Montville, *Big Bam*, 339.
31. John Kieran, "Potpourri," Sports of the Times, *New York Times*, March 7, 1935, 28.
32. *St. Petersburg* (FL) *Evening Independent*, March 14, 1935.
33. Kieran, "Potpourri," 28.
34. Montville, *Big Bam*, 339.
35. Glenn M. Wong, *Essentials of Sports Law* (Santa Barbara, CA: Praeger, 2010), 808.
36. Pietrusza, *Rothstein*, 142.
37. David Pietrusza, *Judge and Jury: The Life and Times of Judge Kenesaw Mountain Landis*. South Bend, IN: Diamond Communications, 1998), 182.
38. *Creamer, Babe*, 231.
39. Surdam, *Losses and Empty Seats*, 291.
40. Daniel Okrent, *Baseball Anecdotes* (New York: Oxford University Press, 1989), 128.
41. *New York Times*, June 3, 1935.
42. Dawson, "Ruth Is Undecided on Future Plans," 27.
43. *New York Times*, September 2, 1935.
44. *New York Times*, September 5, 1935.
45. Thomas Holmes, "Babe Makes Farewell Speech After Playing Final Game of Career," *Brooklyn Daily Eagle*, October 21, 1935.
46. *Lewiston Daily Sun*, September 3, 1935.
47. Associated Press, September 5, 1935.

Chapter 34

1. Wagenheim, *Babe Ruth*, 266.
2. Henry Super, "MacPhail Goes to Bat to Protect Babe Ruth," *Lodi News-Sentinel*, 11 August 1938, 7.
3. Smelser, *Life That Ruth Built*, 18.
4. Richard J. Tofel, *Legend in the Making: The New York Yankees in 1939* (Chicago: Ivan R Dee, 2004), 85.
5. *New York Times*, January 14, 1939.
6. Ray Robinson, "Baseball; Ruth and Gehrig: Forced Smiles," *New York Times*, 2 June 1991, http://www.nytimes.com/1991/06/02/sports/baseball-ruth-and-gehrig-forced-smiles.html.
7. Stewart, *Babe Ruth*, 190.
8. Mark Hyman, "For 'Lucky' Daughter, Babe Was Gem of a Dad," *Baltimore Sun*, February 3, 1995.

9. *Milwaukee Journal*, January 18, 1935.

10. Robert S. Fogarty, *The Righteous Remnant: The House of David* (Kent, OH: Kent State University Press, 1981), 145.

11. Susman, *Culture as History*, 146.

12. Stewart, *Babe Ruth*, 114.

13. Milton, 466

14. *Creamer*, Babe, 405.

15. Mark Moran, "Bar Time: Drinking Up Jersey with Babe Ruth," *Aquarian Weekly*, http://www.the aquarian.com/2014/01/08/bar-time-drinking-up-jer sey-with-babe-ruth.

16. Gabriel Schechter, "The 1911 Season: The Cream Rises to the Top," *National Pastime Museum*, February 10, 2016, http://thenationalpastimemuseum.com/art icle/1911-season-cream-rises-top.

17. Smelser, *Life That Ruth Built*, 527.

18. Thomas F. Brandy, "Communique from the West Coast," *New York Times*, March 1, 1942, X3.

19. Jack Doyle, "The Babe Ruth Story: Book & Film, 1948," PopHistoryDigwww, August 28, 2015.

20. Wagenheim, *Babe Ruth*, 268.

21. "1948 Louisville Slugger Babe Ruth Bat Movie Advertising Sign," KeyMan Collectibles, http://key mancollectibles.com/advertising/1948ruthhbsign.htm.

22. Susman, *Culture as History*, 178.

23. Richard Sandomir, "Legacy of Earning Power: Babe Ruth: Dead 41 Years, He Lives on in Endorsements That Bring Heirs Hundreds of Thousands," *Los Angeles Times*, 22 December 1989.

24. Creamer, *Babe*, 334.

25. Richard Sandomire, "Yankees Have Yet to Honor Ruth in His House's Final Season," *New York Times*, September 5, 2008.

Chapter 35

1. *The Collector*, Issues 375–384, 154.

2. John Thorn, Pete Palmer and Michael Gershman, *Total Baseball*, CD-Rom (Portland, OR: Creative Multimedia, 1993), 768.

3. Mills, Dorothy Seymour, *Chasing Baseball: Our Obsession with Its History, Numbers, People and Places* (Jefferson, NC: McFarland, 2010), 40.

4. *Autograph Magazine*, "Babe-Ruth Autographs Sultan of Signing," January 2010, http://autograph magazine.com/2010/01/babe-ruth-autographs-sultan-of-signing.

5. Creamer, *Babe*, 330.

6. Richards Vidmer, "Babe Ruth, Baseball Superman, Excels, Too, in Minor Sports," *New York Times*, June 10, 1928, 78.

7. Sobol, *Babe Ruth and the American Dream*, 119.

8. Poekel, "Babe Ruth: Boss of the Youth of America."

9. Ad for Sinclair Oil Corporation, *Life Magazine*, May 3, 1937, 58.

10. Robert W. Creamer, "Hey Mister, Can We Have Your Autograph?" *Sports Illustrated*, April 12, 1982.

11. *Billboard*, August 5, 1950, 90.

12. Ruth and Considine, *The Babe Ruth Story*, 42.

13. Zev Chafets, *Cooperstown Confidential: Heroes, Rogues and the Inside Story of the Baseball Hall of Fame* (New York: Bloomsbury USA, 2009), 102.

14. Dave Jamieson, *Mint Condition: How Baseball Cards Became an American Obsession* (New York: Atlantic Monthly Press, 2010), 157.

15. The Becket Marketplace, https://marketplace.beckett.com.

16. *Baltimore Business Journal*, August 2010, 35.

17. Harry L. Rinker, *Rinker on Collectibles* (Radnor, PA: Wallace-Homestead, 1989), 12.

18. Harold Uhlman, "The Baseball Card—Down but Not Out," ThinkBlueLA.com, http://www.think bluela.com/index.php/2013/01/04/the-baseball-card-down-but-not-out.

Afterword

1. Thomas L. Altherr, "The Game in Sepia and Soft Focus: Nostalgia and American Baseball in Historical Context," in *The Cooperstown Symposium on Baseball and American Culture* 2000, ed. William Simons (Jefferson, NC: McFarland, 2001), 161.

2. Arthur Daley, "Goodbye to All That," *New York Times*, June 13, 1948.

3. Jana Rutherford and Eric H. Shaw, "What Was Old Is New Again: The History of Nostalgia as a Buying Motive in Consumption Behavior," in *Proceedings of the 15th Conference for Historical Analysis and Research in Marketing*, ed. Leighann C. Neilson. (New York: Association for Historical Research in Marketing, 2011).

4. Gerald Eskenazi, "Baseball Nostalgia Is Beyond Peanuts," *New York Times*, May 14, 1989.

5. *Ibid.*

6. *Ibid.*

7. Malcolm Moran, "Playing Baseball for Old Times' Sake," *New York Times*, June 22, 1988.

8. "Town Ball: The Rules of the Massachusetts Game," Baseball Almanac, http://www.baseball-alma nac.com/ruletown.shtml.

9. Russell Ormiston, "Attendance Effects of New Stadiums," *Journal of Sports Economics* 15, no. 4 (August 2014): 338–364.

10. Adam Zaretsky, "Should Cities Pay for Sports Facilities?" website of the Federal Reserve Bank of St. Louis, https://www.stlouisfed.org/Publications/Reg ional-Economist/April-2001/Should-Cities-Pay-for-Sports-Facilities.

11. Steve Kilar, "The Economics of Orioles Park," Baltimore Urban Affairs Report, Philip Merrill College of Journalism, University of Maryland, http://bmore.jschool.umd.edu/summer11/?p=65.

12. Kevin Mulroy, *Baseball as America* (National Geographic Society, 2005), 43.

13. S.L. Price, Heart of the Game: Life, Death, and Mercy in Minor League America (New York: HarperCollins, 2009), 98.

14. Charles Fruehling Springwood, *Cooperstown to Dyersville: A Geography of Baseball Nostalgia* (Boulder, CO: Westview Press, 1996), 98.

Bibliography

Abel, Richard. *Encyclopedia of Early Cinema*. New York: Routledge, 2005.

Adams, Charles J. *Baseball in Reading, PA: Images of Baseball*. Charleston, SC: Arcadia Pub., 2003.

Adams, Timothy. *Still Not Forgiven: The 1919 White/ Black Sox and the Fixing of a World Series*. Bloomington, IN: iUniverse, 2009.

Adomites, Paul, and Saul Wisnia. *Babe Ruth: His Life and Times*. Lincolnwood, IL: Publications International, 1995.

Allen, Bob, and Bill Gilbert. *The 500 Home Run Club: Baseball's 16 Greatest Home Run Hitters from Babe Ruth to Mark McGwire*. Champaign, IL: Sports Publishing, 2000.

Allen, Frederick Lewis. *Only Yesterday: An Informal History of the Nineteen-Twenties*. New York: Perennial Library, 1964.

Altavilla, John. "Negro League History." *Hartford Courant*, April 15, 1997, 15.

Altherr, Thomas L. "The Game in Sepia and Soft Focus: Nostalgia and American Baseball in Historical Context." *The Cooperstown Symposium on Baseball and American Culture* 2000. ed. William Simons, Jefferson, NC: McFarland, 2001.

American Cinematographer, March 1922, 9.

American League Base Ball Club of New York. Records, 1913–1950, A. Bartlett Giamatti Research Center, National Baseball Hall of Fame and Museum, Cooperstown, New York.

"Amtrak Ridership Rolls Up Best-Ever Records." JOC.com. http://www.joc.com/amtrak-ridership-rolls-best-ever-records_20111013.html.

"And a Dealer Is Getting the Benefit of Novel Advertising." *Motor World Wholesale*, March 16, 1921, 35.

Andrews, David L. "Dead and Alive?: Sports History in the Late Capitalist Moment." *Sporting Traditions*, November 1999, 73.

Andrews, David L., and Steven J. Jackson. *Sport Stars: The Cultural Politics of Sporting Celebrity*. London; New York: Routledge, 2001.

"Another Popular Idol Upset by the Public Who Made Him." *Attleboro Sun*, September 2 1919.

Asinof, Eliot. *Eight Men Out: The Black Sox and the 1919 World Series*. New York: Henry Holt, 1987.

Associated Press. "The Red Sox Are Sold for Record $660 Million," December 21, 2015.

_____. "World Series Ball Game Delayed by Strike of Players." *Cape Girardeau Southeast Missourian*, September 11, 1918.

Autograph Magazine. "Babe Ruth Autographs Sultan of Signing." January 2010. http://autograph magazine.com/2010/01/babe-ruth-autographs-sultan-of-signing.

"Babe Ruth." Shanaman Sports Museum.com. http://Tacomasportsmuseum.Com.

"The Babe and the Judge." *New Outlook*, October 26, 1921, 282.

"Babe Hits Two Homers in Game Here Monday." *Sleepy Eye Herald-Dispatch*, October 19, 1922, 1.

"Babe Ruth Accepts Terms of Yankees." *New York Times*, January 7, 1920, 22.

"Babe Ruth Arrives in Portland." *Oregonian*, December 14, 1926.

"Babe Ruth Gets Trio for Locals." *Seattle Star*, October 20, 1924, 12.

"Babe Ruth Honor Guest at Banquet." *Seattle Post-Intelligencer*, October 20, 1924, 2.

"Babe Ruth in Cuba." RadioRebelde.cu (website). http%3A%2F%2Fwww.radiorebelde.cu%2F48 snb%2Fhistoria%2Fhistoria-george-herman-rth-visita-bambino-cuba.html&lp=es_en&.intl=us& fr=yfp-t-701.

"Babe Ruth in Perth Amboy." Historic Perth Amboy Virtual Museum, from October 4, 1926. http://historicperthamboy.blogspot.com/search/label/Babe%20Ruth.

"Babe Ruth Is a Visitor." *Kansas City Star*, October 14, 1931.

"Babe Ruth Socks Two at Spokane." *Seattle Post-Intelligencer*, October 18, 1924, 1.

"Babe Ruth to Play in Portland Tuesday." *Seattle Star*, October 20, 1924, 12.

"Babe Ruth Tosses Balls from P.I. Roof as Farewell Act." *Seattle Post-Intelligencer*, October 21, 1924, 1.

"Babe Ruth Wants to Be Manager in Two Years." *Norwalk Hour*, October 14, 1931.

"Babe Ruth Wearing Crown." *New York Times*, October 13, 1921.

"Babes of Ill Repute." *Tacoma News-Tribune*, April 17, 1992, f3.

Badenhausen, Kurt. "The World's 50 Most Valuable Sports Teams." *Forbes*, July 15, 2013.

Ballew, Bill. "Sporting News Forever Linked to Baseball's Past." *Baseball America*, May 14, 2012. http://www.baseballamerica.com/today/majors/news/2012/2613392.html.

"Baltimore Doesn't." *Baltimore Sun*, May 8, 1914.

"Baltimore Says It Doesn't Care." *Meridien Ct Daily Journal*, July 1, 1914, 8.

"Ban Johnson." http://www.baseball-reference.com/bullpen/Ban_Johnson.

Barthel, Thomas. *Baseball Barnstorming and Exhibition Games 1901–1962*. Jefferson, NC: McFarland, 2007.

Bartlett, K. S. "Johnny Igoe." *Daily Boston Globe*, April 17, 1935, B1.

Barzun, Jacques. *God's Country and Mine*, New York: Little, Brown, 1954.

"Baseball as Big Business." *Youth's Companion* 98, no. 35 (August 28, 1924), 572.

"Baseball Fans Agog to See Mighty Ruth in Game Today." *Seattle Post-Intelligencer*, 19 October 1924, 1.

"Baseball Parade Draws a Crowd." Sioux Falls *Daily Argus Leader*, October 17, 1922.

"Baseball Primer Newsblog." http://www.baseball thinkfactory.org/newsstand/discussion/sun_sen tinel_berardino5.

Batchelor, Bob, and Danielle Sarver Coomb. *American History Through American Sports: From Colonial Lacrosse to Extreme Sports*. Santa Barbara, CA: Praeger, 2013.

Baumbach, Jim. "Memories of a Lucky Day for Lindy." *Newsday*, June 28, 2008.

Beatty, Jeffrey F., and Susan S. Samuelson. *Essentials of Business Law*. Mason, OH: Thomson/West, 2008.

Bennett, Bob. "Elmer Bowman." http://bioproj.sabr.org/bioproj.cfm?a=v&v=l&bid=2876&pid=9578.

Bern, Dan. "Johnny Sylvester Comes Back to Visit the Babe." *Doubleheader* (album), DBHQ (label), released July 4, 2012, MP3.

Berry, Robert C., William B. Gould, IV, and Paul D. Staudohar I. *Labor Relations in Professional Sports*. Dover, MA: Auburn House, 1986.

Blevins, Dave. *The Sports Hall of Fame Encyclopedia: Baseball, Basketball, Football, Hockey, Soccer*. Lanham, MD: Scarecrow, 2012.

Bohn, Michael K. *Heroes & Ballyhoo: How the Golden Age of the 1920s Transformed American Sports*. Washington, DC: Potomac, 2009.

"Book Examines Baseball During the Depression Era." Ohio University Communications and Marketing. http://www.ohio.edu/news/01-02/386.html.

Boorstin, Daniel J. *The Image; Or, What Happened to the American Dream*. New York: Atheneum, 1962.

Boston Medical and Surgical Journal 177 (July–December 1917): 283.

Boxerman, Burton Alan, and Benita W. Boxerman. *Jews and Baseball: Entering the American Mainstream, 1871–1948*. Jefferson, NC: McFarland, 2007–2010.

Boyd, William. "Lindbergh" *Bamboo: Essays and Criticism*. New York, NY: Bloomsbury, 2007.

Boyles, Deron. *The Corporate Assault on Youth: Commercialism, Exploitation, and the End of Innocence*. New York: Peter Lang, 2008.

"Branding Channel." http://www.brandchannel.com/features_effect.asp?pf_id=259#more

Brandy, Thomas F. "Communique from the West Coast." *New York Times*, March 1, 1942:X3.

Braudy, Leo. *Frenzy of Renown*. New York: Oxford University Press, 1986.

Brecht, Bertolt. *Galileo*. Translated by Charles Laughton. New York: Grove, 1966.

Briggs, Kenneth L. *Oldtyme Baseball News*, 1995 Issue 6, 21.

Briley, Ron. *Class at Bat, Gender on Deck and Race in the Hole: A Line-Up of Essays on Twentieth Century Culture and America's Game*. Jefferson, NC: McFarland, 2003.

_____. "Ruth and Cobb as Cultural Symbols: The Development of a Mass Consumer Ethic for Baseball in the 1920s." In *Baseball and the Sultan of Swat: Babe Ruth at 100*, ed. Robert N. Keane, New York: AMS, 2008.

Broderick, Robert C. *Catholic Encyclopedia*. Nashville: T. Nelson, 1976.

Brother Gilbert C.F.X. and Harry Rothgerber. *Young Babe Ruth: His Early Life and Baseball Career from the Memoirs of a Xaverian Brother*. Jefferson, NC: McFarland, 1999.

Brougham, Royal. "Bambino's Bat Breaks Tribe Park's Record." *Seattle Post-Intelligencer*, October 20, 1924, 6.

Broun, Heywood. "Bambino the Maestro." *Vanity Fair*, May 1922, 79.

Brown, N. E. *Duluth News Tribune*, November 9, 1919.

Bruns, Roger. *Negro Leagues Baseball*. Santa Barbara, CA: Greenwood, 2012.

Bryson, Bill. "Real Babe Ruth Story Decries Half Truths—But Paints New Ones." *Baseball Digest*, May 1959.

Bureau of National Affairs (Washington, DC) *Media Law Reporter*, Vol. 17, 1989:1473.

Burk, Robert F. *Much More than a Game: Players, Owners and American Baseball Since 1921*. Chapel Hill: University of North Carolina Press, 2001.

_____. *Never Just a Game: Players, Owners, and American Baseball to 1920*. Chapel Hill: University of North Carolina Press, 1994.

"The Business Side of Baseball." *Current Opinion*, Vol. 53, August 1912, 168–172.

Butterworth, Michael L. *Baseball and Rhetorics of Purity: The National Pastime and American Identity During the War on Terror*. Tuscaloosa: University of Alabama Press, 2010.

Cabral, Rick. "The Bustin' Babes and Larrupin' Lous: The Definitive History of the 1927 Barnstorming Tour Featuring Babe Ruth and Lou Gehrig." http://www.thepitchbook.com/Bustin%27-Babes-Lous-Barnstorming-1927.html.

"Candy's History Is Ruthless." *Lakeland Ledger*, April 7, 2002.

"Cardinal Asks Ruth Tribute Suggests K. of C. Help in St. Mary's Drive as Testimonial." The *Baltimore American,* January 10, 1921, 14.

Carmichael, John P. *My Greatest Day in Baseball*. New York: A.S. Barnes, 1945.

Carnes, Mark Christopher, and Clyde Griffen. *Meanings for Manhood: Constructions of Masculinity in Victorian America*. Chicago: University of Chicago Press, 1990.

Carney, Gene. *Burying the Black Sox: How Baseball's Cover-Up of the 1919 World Series Fix Almost Succeeded*. Washington, DC: Potomac, 2006.

Carroll, Bret E. *American Masculinities: A Historical Encyclopedia*. Vol. 1. Thousand Oaks, CA: Sage, 2003.

Castle, George. *Baseball and the Media: How Fans Lose in Today's Coverage of the Game*. Lincoln: University of Nebraska Press, 2006.

Chafets, Zev. *Cooperstown Confidential: Heroes, Rogues, and the Inside Story of the Baseball Hall of Fame*. New York: Bloomsbury USA, 2009.

Charyn, Jerome. *Gangsters and Gold Diggers: Old New York, the Jazz Age, and the Birth of Broadway*. New York: Four Walls Eight Windows, 2003.

_____. "Our National Exaggeration." Frugal Fun.com. http://www.frugalfun.com/our-national-exaggeration.html.

Cherlin, A. *Marriage, Divorce, Remarriage*. Rev. ed. Cambridge, MA: Harvard University Press, 1992.

Chermak, Steven M., and Frankie Y. Bailey. *Crimes and Trials of the Century: From the Black Sox Scandal to the Attica Prison Riots*. Westport, CT: Greenwood, 2007.

Chisholm, Hugh. *Encyclopædia Britannica, 1922*: New York: Encyclopædia Britannica, Inc.

"Claire Ruth, Widow of Baseball Great; She Kept Yankee Star's Memory Alive in the Last 28 Years Dies of Cancer at 76." *New York Times*, October 26, 1976.

Clapp, Christopher M., and Jahn K. Hake "How Long a Honeymoon? The Effect of New Stadiums on Attendance in Major League Baseball." *Journal of Sports Economics*. August 2005 vol. 6 no. 3 237–263.

Coates, Robert M. "Artie." *New Yorker,* 22 May 1937, 24–27.

Cobb, Irvin S. "Fans, Not Players, Quitters, Says Cobb." *New York Times*, October 14, 1921.

The Collector: A Monthly Magazine for Autograph and Historical Collectors. New York: W. R. Benjamin.

Collins, Tracy Brown. *Babe Ruth*. New York: Chelsea House, 2008.

Colorado Department of Public Health. http://www.colorado.gov/cs/Satellite?blobcol=urldata&blobheader=application%2Fpdf&blobkey=id&blobtable=MungoBlobs&blobwhere=122957072 1386&ssbinary=true.

"Commercial Value of Our Entertainers." *The School Executive* 41 (May/June 1922), 534.

"The Commissionership: A Historical Perspective." MLB.com. http://mlb.mlb.com/mlb/history/mlb _history_people.jsp?story=com.

Connecticut History. "Re-Creating Our National Pastime." http://Connecticuthistory.Org/Re-Creating-Our-National-Pastime/.

Costa, Gabe. "By the Numbers: Judging Babe Ruth's Attempted Steal in the 1926 World Series." CBS New York (website), 29 July 2011, http://Newyork.Cbslocal.Com.

Cottrell, Robert C. *Blackball, the Black Sox, and the Babe: Baseball's Crucial 1920 Season*. Jefferson, NC: McFarland, 2002.

Creamer, Robert W. *Babe: The Legend Comes to Life*. New York: Simon & Schuster, 1974.

_____. "Hey Mister, Can We Have Your Autograph?" *Sports Illustrated*, April 12, 1982.

_____. "Ruth? He Is Still in the Sportlight, Still, Going Strong." *Smithsonian*, February 1995, 68.

Crepeau, Richard C. *Baseball: America's Diamond Mind, 1919–1941*. Orlando: University Press of Florida, 1980.

Cruikshank, Jeffrey L., and Arthur W. Schultz. *The Man Who Sold America: The Amazing but True! Story of Albert D. Lasker and the Creation of the Advertising Century*. Boston, MA: Harvard Business Review, 2010.

Cruisenberry, James. *Fort Worth Star Telegram*, December 29, 1919.

Daley, Arthur. "Goodbye to All That." *The New York Times*, June 13, 1948.

Davenport, Frederick M. "Special Correspondence." *New Outlook*, 1922:704.

Davies, Richard O. *Sports in American Life: A*

History. Chichester, West Sussex; Malden, MA: Wiley-Blackwell, 2012.

Davies, Ross. "Along Comes the Players Association: The Roots and Rise of Organized Labor in Major League Baseball." *New York University Journal of Legislation and Public Policy* 16, no. 2 (2013): 321–349.

Davis, Fred. *Yearning for Yesterday: A Sociology of Nostalgia*. New York: Free Press, 1979.

Davis, Ralph. "Babe Ruth Hit His 29th Home Run." Pittsburgh *Post Gazette*, September 27, 1919.

Dawson, James P. "Ruth Is Undecided on Future Plans." *New York Times*, June 4, 1935, 27.

de Leon, Charles Leonard Ponce. *Self Exposure: Human-Interest Journalism and the Emergence of Celebrity in America, 1890–1940*. Chapel Hill: University of North Carolina Press, 2002.

Delaney, Tim, and Tim Madigan. *The Sociology of Sports: An Introduction*. Jefferson, NC: McFarland, 2009.

DeMarco, Tony. *The Sporting News Selects 50 Greatest Sluggers*. St. Louis: Sporting News, 2000.

DeMotte, Charles. *Bat, Ball and Bible: Baseball and Sunday Observance in New York*. Dulles, VA: Potomac, 2013.

_____. "How World War I Nearly Brought Down Professional Baseball." *The Cooperstown Symposium on Baseball and American Culture 2009–2010*, edited by William M. Simons, 219–221. Jefferson, NC: McFarland, 2011.

Denaux, Zulal S., David A. Denaux, and Yeliz Yalcin. "Factors Affecting Attendance of Major League Baseball: Revisited." *Atlantic Economic Journal*, 39.2 (2011): 117–27. Print.

Derks, Scott. *Working Americans, 1880–1999*. Vol. 1, *The Working Class*. Lakeville, CT: Grey House, 2000.

Desert News, November 18, 1919.

Dickson, Paul. *Baseball's Greatest Quotations: An Illustrated Treasury of Baseball Quotations and Historical Lore*. New York: Collins, 2008.

Dorothy Ruth Pirone, and Chris Martens, *My Dad, the Babe: Growing Up with an American Hero* Boston: Quinlan, 1988.

Douglas, Ann. *Terrible Honesty*. New York: Farrar, Straus & Giroux, 1995.

Doyle, Jack. "The Babe Ruth Story: Book & Film, 1948." PopHistoryDigwww, August 28, 2015.

Drago, Mike. *Reading Eagle*, July 6, 2008. http://readingeagle.com/article.aspx?id=98039.

Drowne, Kathleen Morgan, and Patrick Huber. *The 1920s*. Westport, CT: Greenwood, 2004.

Drucker, Susan J., and Robert S. Cathcart. *American Heroes in a Media Age*. Cresskill, NJ: Hampton, 1994.

Dubey, Rod. *Indecent Acts in a Public Place: Sports, Insolence and Sedition*. Toronto: Charivari, 1990.

Dufresne, Chris. "Babe in Boomtown." *Los Angeles Times*, June 2, 2008. http://articles.latimes.com/2008/jun/02/sports/sp-breababe2.

Dunn, James A. *Driving Forces: The Automobile, Its Enemies, and the Politics of Mobility*. Washington, DC: Brookings Institution, 1998.

Dunning, Eric, and Dominic Malcolm. *Sport: Approaches to the Study of Sport*. London: Taylor & Francis, 2003.

Dunning, John. *On the Air: The Encyclopedia of Old-Time Radio*. New York: Oxford University Press, 1998.

Echevarria, Roberto Gonzalez. *The Pride of Havana: A History of Cuban Baseball*. New York: Oxford University Press, 2001.

Editors of Publications International, Ltd. "1920 Baseball Season." http://entertainment.howstuffworks.com/1920-baseball-season.htm.

Eig, Jonathan. *Luckiest Man: The Life and Death of Lou Gehrig*. New York: Simon & Schuster, 2005.

_____. "Ruth, Gehrig and the Birth of a Dynasty," In *The Yankees Baseball Reader: A Collection of Writings on the Game's Greatest Dynasty*. Edited by Adam Brunner and Josh Leventhal. Minneapolis, MN: MVP Books, 2011.

Eisen, Robert F., and William Cahill. "Babe Ruth's Barnstorming Activities." In *Baseball and the Sultan of Swat: Babe Ruth at 100*. ed. Robert N. Keane. NY: AMS Press 2008.

"The Elected Aristocracy: 12 Is Enough." *Wall Street Journal*, November 6, 1990, A22.

Elfers, Jim. "Tour Info" email to Thomas Barthel, March 12, 2012.

Elias, Robert. *Baseball and the American Dream: Race, Class, Gender, and the National Pastime*. Armonk, NY: M.E. Sharpe, 2001.

"Elite Chocolate Coated Baseball Co., El Paso, Tex," *Creamery and Milk Plant Monthly* 11, no. 11 (November 1922), 90.

Ellul Jacques. *Propaganda: The Formation of Men's Attitudes*. New York: Knopf, 1965.

Emerson, Guy. *The New Frontier: A Study of the American Liberal Spirit, Its Frontier Spirit, and Its Application to Modern Problems*. New York: H. Holt, 1920.

Epting, Chris. "The Day the Babe Came to Brea." *Orange Coast Magazine*, March 2008.

Eskenazi, Gerald. "Baseball Nostalgia Is Beyond Peanuts." *New York Times*, May 14, 1989.

Evensen, Bruce J. *When Dempsey Fought Tunney: Heroes, Hokum, and Storytelling in the Jazz Age*. Knoxville: University of Tennessee Press, 1996.

Ewen, Stuart. *Captains of Consciousness: Advertising and the Social Roots of the Consumer Culture*. New York: McGraw-Hill, 1976.

Fang, Irving E. *A History of Mass Communication: Six Information Revolutions*. Boston: Focal, 1997.

Farrell, Henry L. "Some Wonder as to What Will Take Place Now." *Beaver Daily Times,* 22 October 1924.

Farrell, Mike, and Mary Carmen Cupito. *Newspapers: A Complete Guide to the Industry.* New York: Peter Lang, 2010.

Feigenbaum, Eric. "The 1920s: 'Sell Them Their Dreams' in Postwar America, Prosperity Drives the *New Aesthetic*." May 3, 2001. http://vmsd.com/content/the1920ssellthemtheirdreams.

Feller, Bob, with Bill Gilbert. *Now Pitching, Bob Feller: A Baseball Memoir.* New York: Citadel, 1990.

Figueredo, Jorge S. "November 4 1920: The Day Torriente Outclassed Ruth. " *Baseball Research Journal* 1982: 130–131.

Finkel, Jan. "Pete Alexander." SABR Baseball Biography Project. http://sabr.org/bioproj/person/79e6a2a7.

Fitts, Robert K. *Banzai Babe Ruth: Baseball, Espionage, and Assassination During the 1934 Tour of Japan.* Lincoln: University of Nebraska Press, 2012.

Fitzgerald, Terence J. *Celebrity Culture in the United States.* New York: H.W. Wilson, 2008.

Flanagan, Mark. "When Baseball World's Eyes Were on the Attleboros." *Attleboro (MA) Sun Chronicle,* 25 October 2007. http://www.thesunchronicle.com/opinion/columns/flanaganwhenbaseballworldseyeswereontheattleboros/article_d3c754fdfff85ad9b9ead053eba33f35.html.

Fleming, E. J. *Wallace Reid: The Life and Death of a Hollywood Idol.* Jefferson, NC: McFarland, 2007.

Fogarty, Robert S. *The Righteous Remnant: The House of David.* Kent, OH: Kent State University Press, 1981.

"Forging America: The History of Bethlehem Steel—Chapter 3." http://www.sun-sentinel.com/topic/all-bethsteel-c3p13,0,5559082.story.

Forker, Dom, Robert Obojski, and Wayne Stewart. *The Big Book of Baseball Brainteasers.* New York: Main Street, 2004.

Fowler, Barbara Hughes. *The Hellenistic Aesthetic.* Madison: University of Wisconsin Press, 1989.

Fox, Stephen. *Big Leagues: Professional Baseball, Football, and Basketball in National Memory.* New York: Morrow, 1994.

Frierson, Eddie. "Christy Mathewson." SABR Baseball Biography Project. http://sabr.org/bioproj/person/f13c56ed.

Frommer, Harvey. *Five O'Clock Lightning: Babe Ruth, Lou Gehrig, and the Greatest Team in Baseball, the 1927 New York Yankees.* Hoboken, NJ: John Wiley & Sons, 2008.

_____. *Remembering Yankee Stadium: An Oral and Narrative History of the House That Ruth Built.* New York: Stewart, Tabori & Chang, 2008.

_____, and Frederic J. Frommer. *Red Sox Vs. Yankees: The Great Rivalry.* Champaign, IL: Sports Publishing, 2005.

Fuller, Todd. *60 Feet, 6 Inches and Other Distances from Home: The Baseball Life of Mose Yellowhorse.* Duluth, MN: Holy Cow! Press, 2002.

Fullerton, Hugh S. "Baseball—The Business and the Sport." *Review of Reviews and World's Work* (April 1921), 417–420.

_____. "Earnings in Baseball." *North American Review* 229 (June 1930): 743–748.

_____. "The Ten Commandments of Sport, and of Everything Else." *American Magazine* August 1921, 78.

_____. "Why Babe Ruth Is Greatest Home Run Hitter." *Popular Science Monthly,* October 1921, 99.

Furnas, J. C. *Great Times: An Informal Social History of the United States, 1914–1929.* New York: Putnam, 1974.

Futterman, Matthew. "Has Baseball's Moment Passed?" *Wall Street Journal,* March 31, 2011.

Gabler, Neal. *Winchell.* New York: Knopf, 1994.

Gaines, Steven. *The Sky's the Limit: Passion and Property in Manhattan.* New York: Little, Brown, 2005.

Georgelas, Todd. "And All That 'Ballyhoo': New Book Describes How Life Changed in the 1920s." *U.S. News & World Report,* November 25, 2009.

Gilbert, Brother C.F.X., and Harry Rothgerber. *Young Babe Ruth: His Early Life and Baseball Career from the Memoirs of a Xaverian Brother.* Jefferson, NC: McFarland, 1999.

Goebel, Thomas. *The Children of Athena: Chicago Professionals and the Creation of a Credentialed Society, 1870–1920.* Münster, DE: Lit Verlag, 1996.

Goldman, Jonathan. *Modernism Is the Literature of Celebrity.* Austin: University of Texas Press, 2011.

Goldstein, Richard. "Ray Kelly, 83, Babe Ruth's Little Pal, Dies." *New York Times,* 14 November 2001. http://www.nytimes.com/2001/11/14/sports/ray-kelly-83-babe-ruth-s-little-pal-dies.html.

Golenbock, Peter. *Wrigleyville: A Magical History Tour of the Chicago Cubs.* New York: St. Martin's, 1986.

Graham, Adam. "The Great Detectives of Old Time Radio: The Fictionalized Adventures of Babe Ruth." http://www.greatdetectives.net/detectives/fictionalized-adventures-babe-ruth/.

Graham, Frank. *The New York Yankees: An Informal History.* New York: G.P. Putnam's Sons, 1943.

Grant, Robert, and Joseph Katz. *The Great Trials of the Twenties: The Watershed Decade in America's Courtrooms.* Rockville Centre, NY: Sarpedon, 1998.

Greene, Bob. "Fans Call Foul Ball on Baseball Strike." *Chicago Tribune,* July 31, 1985. http://articles.chicagotribune.com/1985-07-31/features/

8502200028_1_baseball-fans-owners-side-base ball-strike.

Gregory, Paul Michael. *The Baseball Player; an Economic Study*. Washington: Public Affairs Press, 1956.

Grella, George. "Baseball Moment in American Film." *Reel Baseball: Essays and Interviews on the National Pastime*, eds. Stephen C. Wood and J. David Pincus, 208–221. Jefferson, NC: McFarland, 2003.

Gropman, Donald. *Say It Ain't So, Joe! The True Story of Shoeless Joe Jackson*. New York, NY: Carol, 1992.

Gross, John. "Books of the Times." *New York Times*, February 19, 1985.

Grumbine, E. Evalyn. *Reaching Juvenile Markets: How to Advertise, Sell, and Merchandise Through Boys and Girls*. McGraw-Hill, 1938.

Guadagnoli, Tony. "Harvard-Yale Rivalry a Tribute to the Student-Athlete." ESPN.com, 2 October 2008. http://espn.go.com/espn/thelife/news/story?id=3017562.

Hall, S. Roland, and Richard M. Boren. *Advertising, Merchandise Display, Sales-Planning, Salesmanship, Turnover and Profit-Figuring in Modern Retailing, Including "Principles of Typography as Applied to Retail Advertising."* New York: McGraw-Hill, 1924.

Hallengren, Anders. "A Case of Identity: Ernest Hemingway." August 28, 2001. http://www.nobelprize.org/nobel_prizes/literature/laureates/1954/hemingwayarticle.html.

Ham, Eldon L. *Broadcasting Baseball: A History of the National Pastime on Radio*. Jefferson, NC: McFarland, 2011.

Hamilton, Joyce. "Review of *Loss of Eden*: A Biography of Charles and Anne Morrow." *Los Angeles Times*, February 7, 1993.

Hampton, Wilborn. *Babe Ruth: A Twentieth-Century Life*. New York, NY: Viking, 2009.

Harris, Paul F. *Babe Ruth: The Dark Side*. Glen Burnie, MD: Paul F. Harris, Sr., 1998.

Harrison, James R. "Yanks Rout Pirates." *New York Times*, October 8, 1927, 1.

Harrison, William. Henry. *Colored Girls and Boys Inspiring United States History, and a Heart to Heart Talk About White Folks*. Allentown, PA: Searle & Dressler Co., 1921.

Haupert, Michael J. "Bonus Payments." e-mail Thomas Barthel, May 26, 2012.

_____. "Economic History of Major League Baseball." http://eh.net/encyclopedia/article/haupert.mlb.

_____. "The Sultan of Swag: Babe Ruth as a Financial Investment." *Baseball Research Journal* 44, no. 2 (fall 2015): 100–107.

_____, and Kenneth Winter. "Pay Ball: Estimating the Profitability of the New York Yankees 1915–1937." *Essays in Economic & Business History*, 21 (2012): 89–101.

Helyar, John. 1994. *Lords of the Realm: The Real History of Baseball*. New York: Villard, 1994.

Hendsch, Daniel A. "A Photo, a Tour, a Life." *The National Pastime*, 1998: 82–84.

Hilton, George W., and John F. Due. *The Electric Interurban Railways in America*. Stanford, CA: Stanford University Press, 1964.

"History of the Park." Sanford Mainers. http://www.sanfordmainers.com/goodall.htm.

"Hitting Lessons from Babe Ruth 1939 New York World's Fair." SNY on Tumbler. http://therealbsmile.tumblr.com/page/16#sthash.wizmYhu3.dpuf.

Holmes, Thomas. "Babe Makes Farewell Speech After Playing Final Game of Career." *Brooklyn Daily Eagle*, October 21, 1935.

Holtzman, Jerome. *No Cheering in the Press Box*. New York: Holt, Rinehart & Winston, 1974.

Holway, John B. *Smokey Joe and the Cannonball*. Washington: Capital, 1983.

Horace, *Carmina*, IV. 9. 25, 65 BC, https://izquotes.com/quote/363120.

Hotchkiss, Douglass. "Babe Ruth Is a Business Man!" *Sandusky Ohio Register*, March 10, 1922.

"How One Japanese-American Runner Took on Babe Ruth." D.S. *Christian Science Monitor*, 6 May 1997. http://www.csmonitor.com/1997/0506/050697.feat.sports.2.html./(page)/2.

Hoyt, Waite. *Babe Ruth as I Knew Him*. New York: Dell, 1948.

Hyman, Mark. "For 'Lucky' Daughter, Babe Was Gem of a Dad." *Baltimore Sun*, February 3, 1995.

Inabinett, Mark. *Grantland Rice and His Heroes: The Sportswriter as Mythmaker in the 1920s*. Knoxville: University of Tennessee Press, 1994.

"Influence on Radio." Museum of Making Music. http://www.museumofmakingmusic.org/influence-on-radio.

Jackson, Kenneth T., and David S. Dunbar, editors. *Empire City: New York Through the Centuries*. New York: Columbia University Press, 2002.

Jacobson, Lisa. *Raising Consumers: Children and the American Mass Market in the Early Twentieth Century*. New York: Columbia University Press, 2004.

James, Bill. *The New Bill James Historical Baseball Abstract*. New York: Free Press, 2001.

Jamieson, Dave. *Mint Condition: How Baseball Cards Became an American Obsession*. New York: Atlantic Monthly, 2010.

Jeffers, Harry Paul. *The 100 Greatest Heroes: The 100 Greatest Heroes: Inspiring Profiles of One Hundred Men and Women Who Changed the World*. New York: Citadel, 2003.

Jenkinson, Bill. "The Great Debates." http://bill-jenkinsonbaseball.webs.com/thegreatdebates.htm.

_____. "By the Numbers: Judging Babe Ruth's Attempted Steal in the 1926 World Series." http://newyork.cbslocal.com/2011/07/29/by-the-numbers-judging-babe-ruth%E2%80%99s-attempted-steal-of-second-base-in-the-1926-world-series.

_____. *The Year Babe Ruth Hit 104 Home Runs: Recrowning Baseball's Greatest Slugger.* New York: Carroll & Graf, 2007.

"Job in Outfield Awaits Ruth When Pitching Days End." Fort Worth *Star-Telegram,* 9 October 1916, 4.

"Joe Mccarthy." http://www.cbssports.com/mcc/blogs/entry/18516000/19420310.

Johnson, Walter. "Ruthmania." *Literary Digest,* September 18, 1920, 291.

Johnston, Alva. "Cash and Carry" *New Yorker,* December 8, 1928, 31–34.

_____. "Profiles: The Ghosting Business." *New Yorker,* November 23, 1935, 20–24.

"Judge Landis Reversed and Censured." *Railway World,* Vol. 52, July 31, 1908, 654.

Kahn, Roger. *October Men: Reggie Jackson, George Steinbrenner, Billy Martin, and the Yankees' Miraculous Finish in 1978.* Orlando, FL: Harcourt, 2003.

Kashatus, William C. "Babe Ruth Made Home Run History in Wilkes-Barre." http://www.milb.com/news/article.jsp?ymd=20070702&content_id=269068&vkey=news_t531&fext=.jsp&sid=t531.

_____. *Diamonds in the Coalfields: Twenty-One Remarkable Baseball Players, Managers, and Umpires from Northeast Pennsylvania.* Jefferson, NC: McFarland, 2002.

_____. "It Was So Outta There: The Bambino's Home Run Legacy at Artillery Park Commemorated in New Historical Kiosk." http://citizensvoice.com/arts-living/it-was-so-outta-there-the-bambino-s-home-run-legacy-at-artillery-park-commemorated-in-new-historical-kiosk-1.1306288.

_____. *Lou Gehrig: A Biography.* Westport, CT: Greenwood, 2004.

Kaufman, Gregg. "Symphony of Swat." https://itunes.apple.com/us/itunes-u/symphony-of-swat/id401629321.

Kaufman, Jason. *For the Common Good?: American Civic Life and the Golden Age of Fraternity.* New York: Oxford University Press, 2002.

Keane, Robert M., ed. *Baseball and the "Sultan of Swat": Babe Ruth at 100.* New York: AMS, 2008.

Keenan, Jimmy. "Jack Dunn." SABR.org. http://sabr.org/bioproj/person/e1addacb.

Keene, Kerry, Raymond Sinibaldi, and David Hickey. *The Babe in Red Stockings: An In-Depth Chronicle of Babe Ruth with the Boston Red Sox, 1914–1919.* Champaign, IL: Sagamore, 1997.

Keller, J. W. "Journalism as a Career" *Forum,* 15 August 1893, 691.

Kellogg, Caroline. "Time Machine." *Tacoma News-Tribune,* October 6, 1974.

Keogh, Edward A. "A Brief History of the Air Mail Service of the U. S. Post Office Department (May 15, 1918–August 31, 1927)." http://www.airmailpioneers.org/history/Sagahistorytraffic.htm.

"Kids Will Have Big Day When Ruth Plays Ball Here Sunday." *Seattle Post-Intelligencer,* 18 October 1924, 2.

Kieran, John. "Mr. Ruth, the Manager." *New York Times,* October 22, 1933, S2.

_____. "Potpourri." Sports of the Times. *New York Times,* March 7, 1935, 28.

_____. "Sports of the Times." *New York Times,* March 1, 1927, 25.

_____. "Sports of the Times." *New York Times,* October 14, 1928, S2.

Kilar, Steve. "The Economics of Oriole Park." Baltimore Urban Affairs. Philip Merrill College of Journalism, University of Maryland. Http://Bmore.Jschool.Umd.Edu/Summer11/?P=65.

Kim, Ray. "When Troy Was a Major League City." Http://www.Empireone.Net/~Musicman/Troyball.Html.

Kimmel, Michael S. "Baseball and the Reconstitution of American Masculinity, 1880–1920." *Baseball History from Outside the Lines: A Reader,* Ed. John E. Dreifort, 47–61. Lincoln: University of Nebraska Press, 2001.

"The King of Swat Meets the King of the Cards." *Kansas City Star,* October 14, 1931.

Kleber, John E. the *Kentucky Encyclopedia.* Lexington: University Press of Kentucky, 1992.

Klimchuk, Marianne R., and Sandra A. Krasovec. *Packaging Design: Successful Product Branding from Concept to Shelf.* Hoboken, NJ: John Wiley & Sons, 2006.

Koppett, Leonard. the *Man in the Dugout: Baseball's Top Managers and How They Got That Way.* Philadelphia: Temple University Press, 2000.

Krabbendam, Hans. *The Model Man: A Life of Edward William Bok, 1863–1930.* Amsterdam; Atlanta, GA: Rodopi, 2001.

Kyle, Donald G., Robert Bruce Fairbanks, and Benjamin G. Rader. *Baseball in America and America in Baseball.* College Station: Texas A & M University Press, 2008.

Kyvig, David E. *Daily Life in the United States, 1920–1940: How Americans Lived Through the Roaring Twenties and the Great Depression.* Chicago: Ivan R. Dee, 2004.

Lambert, S.C. "Building a Business on Children's

Good Will: A Firm That Makes Express Wagons Finds the Right Appeal in Selling Its Products to Boys," *Printers' Ink* 112 (29 July 1920), 89–91.

Lamberty, Bill. "Sam Crawford." http://sabr.org/bioproj/person/11b83a0d.

Lanctot, Neil S. *Fair Dealing and Clean Playing: The Hilldale Club and the Development of Black Professional Baseball, 1910–1932*. Jefferson, NC: McFarland, 1994.

Lasch, Christopher. "The Corruption of Sports." *New York Review of Books*, April 28, 1977.

Leavy, Jane. "Being Babe Ruth's Daughter. His Last Surviving Child Remembers Growing Up Ruth." December 19, 2011. http://www.grantland.com/story/_/id/7367918/beingbaberuth.

_____. *The Last Boy: Mickey Mantle and the End of America's Childhood*. New York: Harper, 2010.

"Legacy of Earning Power: Babe Ruth: Dead 41 Years, He Lives on in Endorsements That Bring Heirs Hundreds of Thousands." *Los Angeles Times*, 22 December 1989.

Leighton, Paul. "Beverly Event to Mark Day Babe Ruth Was Here." Salem, MA *Evening Times*, October 20, 1999. http://www.salemnews.com/local/x1907085754/Event-to-mark-day-Babe-Ruth-was-here/print.

Leisman, Louis J. "Fats." *I Was with Babe Ruth at St. Mary's*. Aberdeen, MD: Leisman, 1956.

Leonard, Thomas C. *The Power of the Press: The Birth of American Political Reporting*. New York: Oxford University Press, 1986.

"Let the Player Get This Straight." *Sporting News*, 27 October 1921, 2.

Levitt, Daniel R. "Ed Barrow." SABR Biography Project, http://Sabr.Org/Bioproj/Person/C9fdbace. http://sabr.org/bioproj/person/c9fdbace.

_____. *Ed Barrow: The Bulldog Who Built the Yankees' First Dynasty*. Lincoln: University of Nebraska Press, 2008.

Levy, Alan Howard. *Joe McCarthy: Architect of the Yankee Dynasty*. Jefferson, NC: McFarland, 2005.

Lewis, Robert F. *Smart Ball: Marketing the Myth and Managing the Reality of Major League Baseball*. Jackson: University Press of Mississippi, 2010.

Lieb, Fred. *Baseball as I Have Known It*. New York: Coward, McCann & Geoghegan, 1977.

Lieberman, Myron. *Public Education: An Autopsy*. Cambridge, MA: Harvard University Press, 1993.

Light, Jonathan Frazier. *The Cultural Encyclopedia of Baseball*. Jefferson, NC: McFarland, 1997.

Lippmann, Walter. *Vanity Fair*, Vols. 28–29, 357.

Litsky, Frank. "George Sauer, Jets Receiver and Rebel, Is Dead at 69." http://www.nytimes.com/2013/05/11/sports/football/george-sauer-jets-receiver-and-rebel-is-dead-at-69.html?hpw&_r.

Londré, Felicia H., and Daniel J. Watermeier. *The History of North American Theater: The United States, Canada, and Mexico: From Pre-Columbian Times to the Present*. New York: Continuum, 1998.

Lovinger, Jay, and Hunter S. Thompson. *The Gospel According to ESPN: The Saints, Saviors, & Sinners of Sports*. New York: Hyperion, 2002.

Lowenfish, Lee, and Robert W. Creamer. *The Imperfect Diamond: A History of Baseball's Labor Wars*. New York: Simon & Schuster, 1974.

Lowenthal, Leo. *Literature, Popular Culture, and Society*. Englewood Cliffs, NJ: Prentice-Hall, 1961.

Luhrs, Victor. *The Great Baseball Mystery: The 1919 World Series*. South Brunswick [N.J.]: A.S. Barnes, 1966.

Luke, Bob. *Dean of Umpires: A Biography of Bill McGowan, 1896–1954*. Jefferson, NC: McFarland, 2005.

Lynch, Michael T. *Harry Frazee, Ban Johnson and the Feud That Nearly Destroyed the American League*. Jefferson, NC: McFarland, 2008.

Macbeth, W. J. "Ruth Features Great Season; Yanks Prosper." *New York Tribune*, December 26, 1920.

Macht, Norman L. *Connie Mack and the Early Years of Baseball*. Lincoln: University of Nebraska Press, 2007.

Mackay, Hugh, and Tim O'Sullivan. *The Media Reader: Continuity and Transformation*. Thousand Oaks, CA: Sage, 1999.

Maiken, Peter T. *Nights Trains: The Pullman System in the Golden Years of American Rail Travel*. Chicago: Lakme, 1989.

Malloy, Daniel P. "Second Dimension: Negativity and Critical Theory." PhD Dissertation, University of South Carolina, 2006.

Mandelbaum, Michael. *The Meaning of Sports: Why Americans Watch Baseball, Football, and Basketball, and What They See When They Do*. New York: Public Affairs, 2004.

Mandigo, John H. "Outdoor Sports." *Chautaukuan* 19, no. 4 (July 1894): 387–394.

Mangan, J. A., and Andrew Ritchie. *Ethnicity, Sport, Identity: Struggles for Status*. London: Frank Cass, 2004.

Mankiw, N. Gregory. *Principles of Macroeconomics*. Fort Worth, TX: Dryden, 1998.

Mann, Arthur. "The New Babe Ruth" *New York Evening World*, April 28 1928.

"Many Stars in Benefit Game." *Kansas City Journal*, 14 October 1924.

Marchand, Roland. *Advertising the American Dream: Making Way for Modernity, 1920–1940*. Berkeley: University of California Press, 1985.

Markey, Morris. "Sport and the Showoff." *New Yorker*, August 15, 1931, 29.

Márquez-Sterling, Manuel. "Babe Ruth's Impact on Latin American Baseball and Latin American Ballplayers: Cuba: A Case Study" *Baseball and* the Sultan of Swat: Babe Ruth at 100. ed. Robert N. Keane. NY: AMS Press, 2008.

Marx, Arthur. *Goldwyn: A Biography of the Man Behind the Myth.* New York: W.W. Norton, 1976.

Mather, Mara, et al. "Amygdala Responses to Emotionally Valenced Stimuli in Older and Younger Adults." *Psychological Science* 15, no. 4: 259–264.

McCullough, Bill. "Flatbush Fans Mourn Huston as One of Clan." *The Brooklyn Daily Eagle,* March 30, 1938, 18.

McDonald, David. "When the Babe Came to Town." *Ottawa Citizen,* October 10, 2009.

McGovern, Charles. *Sold American: Consumption and Citizenship, 1890–1945.* Chapel Hill: University of North Carolina Press, 2006.

McMurray, John. "Joe Mccarthy." SABR.org. http://sabr.org/bioproj/person/2c77f933.

McNaron, David L. "From Dollars to Iron: Currency in Clint Eastwood's Westerns." In *The Philosophy of the Western,* ed. Jennifer McMahon, 149–170. Lexington: University Press of Kentucky, 2010.

Mead, William B., and Paul Dickson. *Baseball: The Presidents' Game.* Washington, DC: Farragut, 1993.

Meany, Tom. *Babe Ruth; the Big Moments of the Big Fellow.* New York: Grosset & Dunlap, 1951.

"Meet the American Idol." *Current Opinion,* October 1920, 194.

Menand, Louis. "Glory Days What We Watch When We Watch the Olympics." *New Yorker,* 6 August 2012. http://www.newyorker.com/arts/critics/atlarge/2012/08/06/120806crat_atlarge_menand.

Mercer, Paul. *Babe Ruth.* New York: Barnes & Noble, 2003.

Mercurio, John A. *Babe Ruth's Incredible Records and the 44 Players Who Broke Them.* New York: S.P.I., 1993.

"Millionaires." 1920–1930.com. Http://www.1920-30.com/business/millionaires.htmlhttp://www.1920-30.com/business/millionaires.html.

Mills, Dorothy Seymour. *Chasing Baseball: Our Obsession with Its History, Numbers, People and Places.* Jefferson, NC: McFarland, 2010.

_____. *A Woman's Work: Writing Baseball History with Harold Seymour.* Jefferson, NC: McFarland, 2010.

Missouri Dept. of Labor and Industrial Inspection, Missouri. Bureau of Labor Statistics, Missouri. State Employment Service 1915.

Montville, Leigh. *The Big Bam: The Life and Times of Babe Ruth.* New York: Doubleday, 2006.

Moran, Malcolm. "Playing Baseball for Old Times' Sake." *New York Times,* June 22, 1988.

Moran, Mark. "Bar Time: Drinking Up Jersey with Babe Ruth." The Aquarian Weekly. http://www.theaquarian.com/2014/01/08/bar-time-drinking-up-jersey-with-babe-ruth.

Moran, Mary C. "Babe Ruth Hit Home Runs, but His Foundation Struck Out." *Trusts & Estates,* August 2009, 148.

Morning Call. *Forging America: The History of Bethlehem Steel.* Allentown: Morning Call, 2003.

Motor World Wholesale, March 16, 1921, 66.

Mott, Frank Luther. *A History of American Magazines, 1930–1968.* Cambridge: Harvard University Press, 1938–68.

"Movietone News." http://movietonews.com/the_fox_movietone_newsreel.html

Mulroy, Kevin. *Baseball as America.* National Geographic Society, 2005.

Nack, William. "The Colossus." *Sports Illustrated,* 8 August 1998, 88.

Nathan, Daniel A. *Saying It's So: A Cultural History of the Black Sox Scandal.* Urbana: University of Illinois Press, 2003.

National Bureau of Economic Research, 1919:48.

National College Athletics Association, Proceedings of Annual Convention, 1913 "Rudolph Valentino." IMDB. http://www.imdb.com/name/nm0884388/bio.

National Collegiate Athletic Association. "Proceedings of the Annual Convention." Chicago: 1913.

Neimark, J. "The Diva of Disclosure, Memory Researcher Elizabeth Loftus." *Psychology Today* 29, 48–53.

Nemec, David. *The Baseball Chronicle: Year-By-Year History of Major League Baseball.* Montreal: Tormont, 1992.

"A New Hero of the Great American Game at Close Range." *Current Opinion* 69, October 1920, 477–478.

New York Times Guide to Essential Knowledge. 3d ed. New York: St. Martin's, 2011.

New York Times Sultans of Swat: The Four Great Sluggers of the New York Yankees. New York: St. Martin's, 2006.

"New York Yankees." http://newyork.yankees.mlb.com/index.jsp?c_id=nyy.

Newman, Roberta. "The Pitchmen: Ty Cobb, Yogi Berra, and Cal Ripken, Jr." In *The Cooperstown Symposium on Baseball and American Culture, 2002,* edited by Alvin L. Hall and William M. Simons, 95–109. Jefferson, NC: McFarland, 2003.

Newsom, D. Earl. *Drumright! The Glory Days of a Boom Town.* Perkins, OK: Evans Publications, 1985.

Neyer, Rob. *Rob Neyer's Big Book of Baseball Blunders: A Complete Guide to the Worst Decisions and Stupidest Moments in Baseball History.* New York: Simon & Schuster, 2006.

Nichols, E. H. "Discussion of Summer Baseball." *American Physical Education Review,* Vol. 19, 292.

"1918 World Series." Worldseries.com. http://mlb.mlb.com/mlb/history/postseason/mlb_ws_recaps.jsp?feature=1918.

"1948 Louisville Slugger Babe Ruth Bat Movie Advertising Sign." KeyMan Collectibles. http://keymancollectibles.com/advertising/1948ruthhbsign.htm.

"1927 World Series." http://www.angelfire.com/pa/1927/worldseries.html.

Nowlin, Bill. "Bill Cissell." SABR Baseball Biography Project. ttp://sabr.org/bioproj/person/8b4b3c55.

_____. "Herb Hunter." SABR Baseball Biography Project. http://sabr.org/bioproj/person/06f2e2e9.

_____, et al. *When Boston Still Had the Babe: The 1918 World Champion Red Sox*. Burlington, MA: Rounder, 2008.

Okrent, Daniel. *Baseball Anecdotes*. New York: Oxford University Press, 1989.

112th Congress. Public Law, 112–152, August 3, 2012.

Ormiston, Russell. "Attendance Effects of New Stadiums." *Journal of Sports Economics* 15, no. 4 (August 2014): 338–364.

Overman, Steven J. *Protestant Ethic and the Spirit of Sport: How Calvinism and Capitalism Shaped America's Games*. Macon, GA: Mercer University Press, 2011.

PageSix.com Staff. "Babe Homered with Girls, Too." *Page Six*, April 27, 2007. http://pagesix.com/2007/08/12/babe-homered-with-girls-too/.

Parrish, Michael E. *Anxious Decades: America in Prosperity and Depression, 1920–1941*. New York: W.W. Norton, 1992.

Parry, Jim, et al. *Sport and Spirituality: An Introduction*. London; New York: Routledge, 2007.

Patton, Phil. "A 100 Year Old Dream: A Road Just for Cars." *New York Times*, October 9, 2008. http://www.nytimes.com/2008/10/12/automobiles/12LIMP.html.

Pedersen, Paul Mark, et al. *Contemporary Sport Management*. Champaign, IL: Human Kinetics, 2011.

Peters, Charles Clinton. *Objectives and Procedures in Civic Education: An Intensive Study*. New York: Longmans, Green, 193.

Photoplay Magazine, September 1923.

Pietrusza, David. *Judge and Jury: The Life and Times of Judge Kenesaw Mountain Landis*. South Bend, IN: Diamond, 1998.

_____. *Rothstein: The Life, Times, and Murder of the Criminal Genius Who Fixed the 1919 World Series*. New York: Basic Books, 2011.

Pisano, Dominick A., ed. *The Airplane in American Culture*. Ann Arbor: University of Michigan Press, 2003.

Plimpton, George. *The Norton Book of Sports*. New York: W.W. Norton, 1992.

"Plutocratic Incomes of Modern Athletes." *Current Opinion* 68, no. 1 (January 1920), 846–847.

Poekel, Charles. "Babe Ruth: Boss of the Youth of America." Transcribed speech. BabeRuthCentral.com. http://Www.Baberuthcentral.Com/Thehumanitarian/Baberuthbossoftheyouthofamerica.

_____. "Babe Ruth Vs. Baby Ruth: The Quest for a Candy Bar." In *The Cooperstown Symposium on Baseball and American Culture, 2009–2010*, edited by William M. Simons, 225–228. Jefferson, NC: McFarland, 2011.

"The Political Economy of Small-Town America: Babe Ruth and the Great Pacific Barnstorming." *Popular Science*, July 1933, 7.

Potts, R. F. "A Red Sox Outing. World's Champions Tour New England as Ed Maynard's Guests" *Baseball Magazine*, December 1916.

Povich, Shirley. *All Those Morning at the Post: The Twentieth Century in Sports from Famed Washington Post Writer Shirley Povich*. New York: Public Affairs, 2005.

Powers, Albert Theodore. *The Business of Baseball*. Jefferson, NC: McFarland, 2003.

Presbrey, Frank. *The History and Development of Advertising*. Garden City, NY: Doubleday, 1929.

Price, Joseph L. *From Season to Season: Sports as American Religion*. Macon, GA: Mercer University Press, 2001.

Price, S.L. *Heart of the Game: Life, Death, and Mercy in Minor League America*. New York: HarperCollins, 2009.

Prime, Jim, with Bill Nowlin. *Tales from the Red Sox Dugout*. Champaign, IL: Sports Publishing, 2000.

Prothero, Stephen R. *American Jesus: How the Son of God Became a National Icon*. New York: Farrar, Straus & Giroux, 2003.

Purdy, Dennis. "Gopher Balls: The Bustin' Babes and the Laruppin' Lous." In *Kiss 'Em Goodbye: An ESPN Treasury of Failed, Forgotten, and Departed Teams*. New York: Ballantine/ESPN, 2010.

Quoted in Brands: Interdisciplinary Perspectives. Edited by Jonathan E. Schroeder. Routledge 2015, 292.

Rader, Benjamin. *American Sports: From the Age of Folk Games to the Age of Televised Sports*. Englewood Cliffs, NJ: Prentice Hall, 1990.

"Rain Halts Baseball So Babe Ruth Plays Golf." *Kansas City Star*, 13 October 1931.

Raney, Arthur A., and Jennings Bryan, eds. *Handbook of Sports and Media*. Mahwah, NJ: L. Erlbaum, 2006.

Reely, C.L. "Capitalizing the Celebrity—And Making Him Responsible for the Product." *Advertising & Selling* 30 (28 August 1920), 5–6.

Reich, Steven A., ed. "Demographic Patterns of the Great Black Migration." *The Great Black Migration a Historical Encyclopedia of the American Mosaic*. Santa Barbara, CA: Greenwood, 2014.

Reid, Sidney. "Meet the American Idol." *Independent*, August 14, 1920, 170.

Reisler, Jim. *Babe Ruth: Launching the Legend*. New York: McGraw-Hill, 2004.

Report to the Senate on "Survey of Pulp Woods on the Public" from the Secretary of Agriculture.

Rhodes, Don. *Ty Cobb: Safe at Home*. Guilford, CT: Lyons Press, 2008.

Ribowsky, Mark. *The Complete History of the Home Run*. New York: Citadel, 2003.

Rice, Grantland. "Ruth Is Stranger Than Fiction." *Vanity Fair*, April 1921.

_____. *The Tumult and the Shouting: My Life in Sport*. New York: Barnes, 1954.

Rielly, Edward J. *Baseball: An Encyclopedia of Popular Culture*. Santa Barbara, CA: ABC-CLIO, 2000.

Riess, Steven A. *Touching Base: Professional Baseball and American Culture in the Progressive Era*. Westport, CT: Greenwood, 1980.

Riley, James A. *Biographical Encyclopedia of the Negro Leagues*. New York: Carroll & Graf, 1994.

Rinker, Harry L. *Rinker on Collectibles*. Radnor, PA: Wallace-Homestead, 1989.

Ripp, Bart. "The Uncouth Ruth: The Bambino Ate Like a Hog and Cavorted with Babes of Ill Repute." *Tacoma News-Tribune*, April 17, 1992, F3.

Ritter, Lawrence S., and Mark Ritter. *The Babe: A Life in Pictures*. New York: Ticknor & Fields, 1988.

Robbins, Mike, ed. *The Yankees Vs. Red Sox Reader*. New York: Carroll & Graf, 2005.

Robinson, Arthur. "The Babe." *New Yorker*, July 31, 1926, 15–17.

_____. "My Friend Babe Ruth." *Colliers* 74 (20 September 1924), 7–8, 2.

Robinson, Ray. "Baseball; Ruth and Gehrig: Forced Smiles." *New York Times*, June 2, 1991. http://Www.Nytimes.Com/1991/06/02/Sports/Baseball-Ruth-And-Gehrig-Forced-Smiles.Html.

Rodman, John. "The Media Support Industry." http://highered.mcgraw-hill.com/sites/dl/free/0073511951/671444/rodman3_sample_ch03.pdf.

Roe, Jason. "Kings of the City." Kansas City Public Library blog, October 5, 2015. http://www.kclibrary.org/blog/week-kansas-city-history/kings-city.

Rubin, Louis D., Jr. "Babe Ruth's Ghost." In *Scoring from Second: Writers on Baseball*. Ed. Philip F. Deaver. Lincoln: University of Nebraska Press, 2007.

Ruiz, Yuyo. *George Herman Ruth: Visita Del "Bambino" a Cuba*. N.p: self published, n.d.

Ruth, Babe. *Babe Ruth's Own Book*. New York: A.L. Burt, 1928.

_____. "The Kids Can't Take It If We Don't Give It!" *Guideposts*, October 1948. http://www.catholiceducation.org/articles/catholic_stories/cs0431.htm.

_____, as told to Bob Considine. *The Babe Ruth Story*. New York: E.P. Dutton, 1948.

Ruth, Mrs. Babe, with Bill Slocum. *The Babe and I*. Englewood Cliffs, NJ: Prentice-Hall, 1959.

"Ruth Case Viewed as Important Test of Owners' Rights." *St. Louis Post-Dispatch*, October 18, 1921.

"Ruth Helps Red Sox to Drive Within One Victory of World's Baseball Title." *New York Times*, September 10, 1918, 10.

"Ruth Leads His Team to Victory." *Kansas City Journal*, October 14, 1924.

"Ruth Must Forego Hot Springs Trip; Yanks Decide to Abandon Annual Pilgrimage of Veteran Stars." *New York Times*, December 18, 1925, 27.

"Ruth Received $1,300 for Pitching One Game." *Philadelphia Evening Public Ledger*, 20 September 1918, 17.

Rutherford, Jana, and Eric H. Shaw. "What Was Old Is New Again: The History of Nostalgia as a Buying Motive in Consumption Behavior." In *Proceedings of the 15th Conference for Historical Analysis and Research in Marketing*, ed. Leighann C. Neilson, 157–166. New York, NY: Association for Historical Research in Marketing, 2011.

Rutland Historical Society Quarterly 7, no. 3 2000.

Ruxin, Robert H., and Darren Heitner. *An Athlete's Guide to Agents*. Boston: Jones and Bartlett, 1993.

Sage, George Harvey. *Power and Ideology in American Sport: A Critical Perspective*. Champaign, IL: Human Kinetics, 1990.

St. Petersburg Evening Independent, October 2, 1915.

St. Petersburg (FL) *Evening Independent*, February 19, 1917.

Salsinger, H.G. "Spanking Baseball's Baby and Petting Its Paragon." *Literary Digest*, 19 September 1925.

Sandage, Charles Harold, and Paul G. Hoffman. *Promise of Advertising*. Homewood, IL: R.D. Irwin, 1961.

Sandomir, Richard. "Legacy of Earning Power: Babe Ruth: Dead 41 Years, He Lives on in Endorsements That Bring Heirs Hundreds of Thousands." *Los Angeles Times*, December 22, 1989.

_____. "Yankees Have Yet to Honor Ruth in His House's Final Season." *New York Times*, September 5, 2008.

Sanford Tribune, 3 October 1919.

Schechter, Gabriel. "The 1911 Season: The Cream Rises to the Top." Http://Thenationalpastimemuseum.Com/Article/1911-Season-Cream-Rises-Top.

Schell, Michael J. *Baseball's All-Time Best Sluggers: Adjusted Batting Performance*. Princeton, NJ: Princeton University Press, 2005.

Schubin, Mark. "Watching Remote Baseball Games Before TV." Http://www.Schubincafe.Com/2012/09/26/Watchingremotebaseballgamesbeforetv/.

_____. "Watching Remote Baseball Games Before TV." Schubin Cafe. Http://Www.Schubincafe.Com/Tag/Baseball.

Schuck, Ray. "When the Broadway Limited Stopped in Lima: An Ohio Town Embraces 'The Babe.'" *Allen County Reporter*, 1995 No. 1.

Schuck, Raymond I. "Babe's in Tourland: How Babe Ruth Was Well-Suited for Barnstorming." *Baseball and the Sultan of Swat: Babe Ruth at 100*. Ed. Robert N. Keane, NY: AMS, 2008.

Schudson, Michael. *Advertising, the Uneasy Persuasion: Its Dubious Impact on American Society*. New York: Basic Books, 1984.

Schumach, Murray. "Babe Ruth, Baseball's Great Star and Idol of Children, Had a Career Both Dramatic and Bizarre." *New York Times*, August 17, 1948. Http://Www.Nytimes.Com/Learning/General/Onthisday/Bday/0206.Html.

Scott, Carole E. "The History of the Radio Industry in the United States to 1940." Http://Eh.Net/Encyclopedia/Article/Scott.Radio.Industry.History.

Scott, Leroy. "Millions for Minutes" *American Illustrated Magazine*, February 1906, 363.

Segrave, Kerry. "Endorsements" *Advertising: A Social History*. Jefferson, NC: McFarland, 2005.

Seideman, David. "Dispatches." *Time*, June 24, 2001, 18.

_____, and Kathleen Adams. "The Bambino Meets the Eggheads." *Time*, June 6, 1995. Http://Content.Time.Com/Time/Magazine/Article/0,9171,983011,00.Html. Vol. 145 Issue 23.

Seymour, Harold, and Dorothy Seymour Mills. *Baseball: The Early Years*. New York: Oxford University Press, 1960.

_____. *Baseball: The Golden Age*. New York: Oxford University Press, 1971.

Sherman, Jacob R. "When the 'Babe' Came to Rutland, October 1919." *Rutland Historical Society Quarterly*, Vol. 30 # 3 2000, 8.

Shiffert, John. *Base Ball in Philadelphia: A History of the Early Game, 1831–1900*. Jefferson, NC: McFarland, 2006.

Shur, Renee, ed. *Good Sports: Anthology of Great Sports Writing*, Vol. 2. Waterville, ME: Thorndike, 1992.

Simons, William M., ed. *Cooperstown Symposium on Baseball and American Culture, 2009–2010*. Jefferson, NC: McFarland, 2011.

Smart, Barry. "The Sport Star: Modern Sport and the Culture Economy of Sporting" Rader, Benjamin. *American Sports: From the Age of Folk Games to the Age of Televised Sports*. Englewood Cliffs, NJ: Prentice Hall, 1990.

Smelser, Marshal. *The Life That Ruth Built: A Biography*. Lincoln: University of Nebraska Press, 1973.

Smith, Leverett T., Jr. *The American Dream and the National Game*. Bowling Green, OH: Bowling Green University Popular Press, 1975.

Smith, Robert. *Babe Ruth's America*. New York: Crowell [1974.]

Sobol, Ken. *Babe Ruth and the American Dream*. New York: Random House, 1974.

"South Central Business Association Establishes World Civic Club Record; Three World Champions at One Meeting." *Kansas City Star*, October 14, 1931.

Southern Exposure, Vols. 30–31. Institute for Southern Studies 2002.

Sparks, Jared, et al. "Earnings in Baseball" the *North American Review*, June 1930, 743–744.

Spatz, Lyle, and Steve Steinberg. *1921: The Yankees, the Giants and the Battle for Supremacy in New York*. Lincoln: University of Nebraska Press, 2010.

Sport Collectors Digest, March 5, 1999.

"Sports Chatter." *Cedar Rapids Evening Gazette*, November 8, 1919, 6.

Springwood, Charles Fruehling. *Cooperstown to Dyersville: A Geography of Baseball Nostalgia*. Boulder, CO: Westview, 1996.

Stanton, Tom. *Ty and the Babe: Baseball's Fiercest Rivals: A Surprising Friendship and the 1941 Has-Beens Golf Championship*. New York: St. Martin's, 2007.

Starr, Mark. "Blood, Sweat and Cheers." *Newsweek*, October 25, 1999, 42.

Steedman, William. "Young Fans Howl Praise of Bambino" *Seattle Post-Intelligencer*, October 20, 1924, 2.

Stein, Donald G. *Buying in or Selling Out? The Commercialization of the American Research University*. New Brunswick, NJ: Rutgers University Press, 2004.

Stein, Fred. *A History of the Baseball Fan*. Jefferson, NC: McFarland, 2005.

Sterling, Manuel Márquez. "Babe Ruth's Impact on Latin American Baseball and Latin American Baseball Players: Cuba—A Case Study." In *Baseball and the "Sultan of Swat": Babe Ruth at 100*, ed. Robert N. Keane, New York: AMS, 2008.

Stevens, John D. *Sensationalism and the New York Press*. New York: Columbia University Press, 1991.

Stewart, Wayne. *Babe Ruth: A Biography*. Westport, CT: Greenwood, 2006.

Stockbridge, Frank Parker. "Feeding 13,000,000 Radio Sets." *Popular Science Monthly*, October 1929, pages 40–41, 153–155.

Stout, Glenn. *Fenway 1912: The Birth of a Ballpark, a Championship Season, and Fenway's Remarkable First Year*. Boston: Houghton Mifflin Harcourt, 2011.

_____. *Impossible Dreams: A Red Sox Collection*. Boston: Houghton Mifflin, 2003.

_____, and Matt Christopher. *Babe Ruth: Legends in Sports*. New York: Little, Brown, 2005.

Strasser, Susan. *Satisfaction Guaranteed: The Making of the American Mass Market*. New York: Pantheon, 1989.

Stuart, Elliott. "The Media Business: Advertising; Retro Look Thrives at the Old Ball Game." 28 May 1992. http://www.nytimes.com/1992/05/28/business/the-media-business-advertising-retro-look-thrives-at-the-old-ball-game.html.

Sullivan, Dean A. *Middle Innings: A Documentary History of Baseball, 1900–1948*. Lincoln: University of Nebraska Press, 1998.

Sumner, Keene. "Norma Talmadge a Great Motion Picture Star." *American Magazine*, June 1922:37.

Super, Henry. "Macphail Goes to Bat to Protect Babe Ruth." *Lodi News-Sentinel*, August 11, 1938, 7.

"A Super Umpire for Baseball" *Outlook*. November 24, 1920, 535.

Surdam, David George. *Wins, Losses, and Empty Seats: How Baseball Outlasted the Great Depression*. Lincoln: University of Nebraska Press, 2011.

Susman, Warren. *Culture as History: The Transformation of American Society in the Twentieth Century*. New York: Pantheon, 1984.

Swank, Bill. "Before the Babe." *Baseball Research Journal*, 2000: 51.

_____. "Gavvy Cravath." http://sabr.org/bioproj/person/35282ccd.

Swedlund, Alan C. *Shadows in the Valley: A Cultural History of Illness, Death, and Loss in New England, 1840–1916*. Amherst: University of Massachusetts Press, 2010.

Szymanski, Stefan, and Andrew S. Zimbalis. *The National Pastime: How Americans Play Baseball and the Rest of the World Plays Soccer*. Washington, DC: Brookings Institution, 2005.

Taylor, Robert J., and Susan B. Taylor. *The Aupha Manual of Health Services Management*. Gaithersburg, MD: Aspen, 1994.

Thomas, Henry W. *Walter Johnson: Baseball's Big Train*. Washington, DC: Phenom, 1995.

Thorn, John. *Baseball in the Garden of Eden*. New York: Simon & Schuster, 2011.

Thorn, John, Pete Palmer and Michael Gershman. *Total Baseball. Cd-Rom*. Portland, OR: Creative Multimedia, 1993.

Thornley, Stew. *Baseball in Minnesota: The Definitive History*. St. Paul, MN: Minnesota Historical Society, 2006.

_____. "Nicollet Park." http://sabr.org/bioproj/park/2e1a3a55.

Thornton, Patrick K. *Sports Law*. Sudbury, MA: Jones & Bartlett, 2011.

Thurston, Herbert. "Relics." *The Catholic Encyclopedia*. http://www.newadvent.org/cathen/12734a.htm.

"Time for Doubt." *Time,* 26 November 1990, 30–34.

Tofel, Richard J. *Legend in the Making: The New York Yankees in 1939*. Chicago: Ivan R. Dee, 2004.

"Town Ball: The Rules of the Massachusetts Game." http://www.baseball-almanac.com/ruletown.shtml.

Trimble, Patrick. "Babe Ruth in the Movies." In *Reel Baseball: Essays and Interviews on the National Pastime, Hollywood, and American Culture*, eds. Stephen C. Wood, and J. David Pincus, 120–133. Jefferson, NC: McFarland, 2003.

_____. "The Political Economy of Small-Town America: Babe Ruth and the Great Pacific" by A Barnstorming Tour of 1924. *North American Society for Sport History. Proceedings and Newsletter*, 2003, 767.

_____. "Tour of 1924." *North American Society for Sport History. Proceedings and Newsletter*, 2003, 76–77.

Tunis, John R. *The American Way in Sport*. New York: Duell, Sloan and Pearce, 1958.

"20th Century Limited." Wikipedia http://en.wikipedia.org/wiki/20th_Century_Limited.

"Two Sluggers Brought Together in Direct Mail Advertising." *Printers' Ink* 113, November 4, 1920, 100.

Tygiel, Jules. *Past Time: Baseball as History*. New York: Oxford University Press, 2000.

Uhlman, Harold. "The Baseball Card—Down but Not Out." http://www.thinkbluela.com/index.php/2013/01/04/the-baseball-card-down-but-not-out.

United States Commission on Industrial Relations. Washington, DC: Gov. Print. Office, 1916.

United States Congress. Sixty-fourth Congress, first session, on H. R. 13568, to protect the public against dishonest advertising and false pretenses in merchandising. House. Committee on Interstate and Foreign Commerce, 1916.

University of Michigan. Women's Studies Program. Ann Arbor, MI, 1978.

U.S. Commission on Industrial Relations, *Final Report and Testimony Submitted to Congress by the Commission on Industrial Relations*. 64th Congress, 1st Session. Senate Document No. 415. 11 vols. 1916.

U.S. Wholesale Price of Newsprint Paper Rolls. http://www.research.stlouisfed.org/fred2/series/M0493BUSM267NNBR

Van Langen, Dennis L. "Quote Source." e-mail Thomas Barthel, January 22, 2013.

Vecchione, Joseph J. *New York Times Book of Sports Legends*. New York: Times, 1991.

Vidmer, Richards. "Babe Ruth, Baseball Superman, Excels, Too, in Minor Sports." *New York Times*, 10 June 1928, 78.

Vila, Joe. *Philadelphia Inquirer*, March 19, 1918.

_____. *Sporting News*, February 28, 1918.

Voigt, David. *America Through Baseball*. Chicago: Nelson-Hall, 1976.

_____. *American Baseball: From the Commissioners*

to Continental Expansion. Vol. 2. Norman: University of Oklahoma Press, 1970.

Votano, Paul. *Tony Lazzeri: A Baseball Biography*. Jefferson, NC: McFarland, 2005.

Wagenheim, Kal. *Babe Ruth: His Life and Legend*. New York: Praeger, 1974.

Wallace, Francis. "College Men in the Big Leagues." *Scribner's*, October 1927, 493.

Walsh, Christy. *Adios to Ghosts!* New York, 1937.

_____. Babe Ruth scrapbooks: [microform] scrapbook, 1921–1935. Archive Material. National Baseball Hall of Fame and Museum.

Waples, Douglas. *Research Memorandum on Social Aspects of Reading in the Depression*. New York: Arno, 1972.

Ward, Geoffrey, and Ken Burns. *Baseball: An Illustrated History*. New York: A.A. Knopf, 1994.

Warren Evening Times 22 October 1918, 7. http://www.nathan.allegany.com/warrenhistory.

Watson, Nick J., Stuart Weir, and Stephen Friend. "The Development of Muscular Christianity in Victorian Britain and Beyond." matrix.msu.edu/muscular.pd.

"Weekly Review; Devoted to the Consideration of Politics, of Social and Economic Tendencies, of History, Literature, and the Arts." *National Weekly*, June 16, 1920, 624.

Weintraub, Robert. *The House That Ruth Built: A New Stadium, the First Yankees Championship*. New York: Little, Brown, 2011.

Weldon, Martin. *Babe Ruth*. New York: T. Y. Crowell Co., 1948.

Welsh, Joe, and Bill Howes. *Travel Pullman*. St. Paul, MN: MBI, 2004.

Whalen, Thomas. *When the Red Sox Ruled: Baseball's First Dynasty, 1912–1918*. Chicago: Ivan R. Dee, 2011.

Whannel, Garry. *Media Sport Stars: Masculinities and Moralities*. London; New York: Routledge, 2002.

"What Is Babe Ruth Worth to the Yankees?" *Literary Digest*, March 29, 1930, 384.

"When Lindenhurst Met Babe Ruth & Lou Gehrig." Incorporated Village of Lindenhurst. http://Www.Villageoflindenhurst.Com/When_Lindenhurst_Met_Babe_Ruth!.Htm.

White, G. Edward. *Creating the National Pastime: Baseball Transforms Itself, 1903–1953*. Princeton University Press, 2014.

White, Thomas H. "United States Early Radio History." http://earlyradiohistory.us/sec001.htm.

Whitty, Stephen. "A Huge Talent and a Mess of a Man John Barrymore at Last Gets His Due." *Star Ledger Staff*, May 29, 2009. http://www.nj.com/entertainment/tv/index.ssf/2009/05/_huge_talent_and_a_mess_of_a.html.

"Why Did the Number of American Newspapers Grow Rapidly?" Answers.com. http://Www.Answers.Com/Topic/North-American-Newspaper-Alliance.

Wieneke, David. "The Boston Police Strike." Boston History and Architecture (website). http://www.iboston.org/mcp.php?pid=policeStrike.

Wiggins, Robert Peyton. *The Federal League of Base Ball Clubs: The History of an Outlaw Major League, 1914–1915*. Jefferson, NC: McFarland, 2009.

Wilfong, Blake Linton. "Hooker Heroes." http://wondersmith.com/heroes/famous2.htm.

Wilkes-Barre Times, September 26, 1919.

Williams, Emelda L., and Donald W. Hendon. *American Advertising: A Reference Guide*. New York: Garland, 1988.

Williams, Joe, Dennis Pernu, and Grace Labatt. *Hollywood Myths: The Shocking Truths Behind Film's Most Incredible Secrets and Scandals*. Minneapolis: MBI and Voyageur Press, 2012, 18.

Williams, Ted, and John Underwood. *The Science of Hitting*. New York: Simon & Schuster, 1986.

Wills, Garry. *Values Americans Live By*. New York: New York Times. 1974.

Winkworth, Joe. "I Have Been a Babe and a Boob." *Colliers*, October 31, 1925, 28.

Winter, Kenneth, and Michael J. Haupert. "Yankee Profits and Promise: The Purchase of Babe Ruth and the Building of Yankee Stadium." *The Cooperstown Symposium on Baseball and American Culture, 2003–2004*. Jefferson, NC: McFarland, 2005.

Wong, Glenn M. *Essentials of Sports Law*. Santa Barbara, CA: Praeger, 2010.

Wood, Allan. "Babe Ruth." SABR Baseball Biography Project. http://sabr.org/bioproj/person/9dcdd01c.

_____. *Babe Ruth and the 1918 Red Sox*. San Jose, CA: Writers Club, 2000.

Woolley, Edward Mott. "The Business of Baseball." *McClure's Magazine*, 39, no. 2 (July 1912), 241–256.

Woonsocket Call, October 4, 1919.

"World Series Players Strike." *Reading Eagle*, September 10, 1918.

Worth, Marcia. "When Babe Ruth Played for South Orange." South Orange Patch. http://patch.com/new-jersey/southorange/murderers-row-on-deck-in-south-orange.

Wright, Ed. *Left-Handed History of the World*. London: Murdoch, 2007.

"Yankee Stadium History." MLB.com. http://newyork.yankees.mlb.com/nyy/ballpark/stadium_history.jsp.

"Year in Review: 1914 National League." http://www.baseball-almanac.com/yearly/yr1914n.shtml.

"Year in Review: 1915 National League." http://www.baseball-almanac.com/yearly/yr1915n.shtml.

Zaretsky, Adam. "Should Cities Pay for Sports Facilities?" Website of the Federal Reserve Bank of St. Louis, https://www.stlouisfed.org/Publications/Regional-Economist/April-2001/Should-Cities-Pay-for-Sports-Facilities.

Zimbalist, Andrew S. *in the Best Interests of Baseball?: The Revolutionary Reign of Bud Selig.* Hoboken, NJ: Wiley, 2006.

Newspapers and Magazines

Of the dozens of periodicals consulted for this book, many included no titles or bylines. Those sources are listed below. Fuller details—including publication dates, Vol. numbers, and page numbers, where available—may be found in the notes.

Allen County Reporter
American Cinematographer
Bakersfield Californian
Baltimore Business Journal
Baseball Digest
Beaver Daily Times
Boston Globe
Boys' Life
Brooklyn Daily Eagle

Bureau of Labor Statistics of the State of Missouri Annual Report
Current Opinion
Dubuque Telegraph Herald
Editor & Publisher
Fort Worth Star-Telegram
Fourth Estate
Insurance Press
Iron Mountain News
Los Angeles Examiner
Mentor
National Pastime: A Review of Baseball History
New London Day
New York Daily News
New York Times
Pittsburgh Press
Railway World
Rutland Historical Society Quarterly
St. Petersburg Independent
Saturday Evening Post
School Executive
Spectator
Sporting News
Youth's Companion

Index